Dessi Nikoltchev

THE HOLIDAY HUNTER

Modern Festivals and Folklore Rituals of TODAY

The World is as colorful as it gets!

"I spent a great deal of pleasurable time immersed in it and making one discovery after another. There was great humanity in the overall tone, underpinned with all the elements that ought to make us so grateful and happy to be among all the diverse and quirky human beings on the great ride that is our time on planet Earth."
— Deborah Hofmann
David Black Literary Agency
Former Editor of the New York Times Best Seller Lists

"This is an amazing body of research bringing together so many cultures in a month. I enjoyed reading about the specificity and background of each holiday. "
— Roberta Levine
Allegheny College

"A GREAT read! "
— Jaishree Dodia
Enterpreneur "Flowers by J.London"

This book aims to remind that Life has to be experienced!
Hope you'll enjoy reading it as much as I enjoyed writing it!

D.N.

Before planning a trip, verify the festival dates on the festival's website or with a local tourist information office (as dates may vary).

The Holiday Hunter © 2018 by Dessi Nikoltchev. All Rights Reserved.

All rights reserved. No part of this book may be reproduced in any form or by any electronic or mechanical means including information storage and retrieval systems, without permission in writing from the author. The only exception is by a reviewer, who may quote short excerpts in a review.

Cover designed by Cover Creator
Cover photo courtesy of: Ina Chervenova

Printed in the United States of America

First Printing: Sept 2018

ISBN-978-1-72-387355-3

CONTENTS

... January 1
... February 26
... March 50
... April 76
... May 96
... June 118
... July 139
... August 160
... September 183
... October 210
... November 238
... December 263
References: 290

... JANUARY

Replacing the Julian Calendar: The reason for substitution of the Julian with the Gregorian calendar was the formula it used to calculate leap years. The latter was introduced by Pope Gregory XIII in 1582, however its official adoption throughout the globe took two centuries (some countries refused to use the revised calendar and still use the Julian). However, in step with a not very highly regarded however fascinating theory, the aim of the new calendar (and allegedly the Catholic Church) was to eliminate ancient pagan rituals and practices once and for all. But as it turned out, this didn't stop the folks from keeping the pagan customs and even incorporating them into trendy celebrations.

01 January: Cursing Festival (Japan)

A weird custom celebrated on New Year's Eve, referred to as "Rowdiness Festival" and "Festival of the Abusive Language". Locals take a forty-minute hike up to a temple whereas shouting insults from the highest of their lungs! They aim their curses to the dark sky above as they would never use such language to a fellow – the Japanese are world-known with their politeness and pristine manners. The folks curse comcerning politics, the stock market, long operating hours, daily life, schools etc. This is the sole night when it is acceptable for ladies to curse as well.

The cursing crowd is led by thirteen monks dressed as legendary demons, accompanied by "horagai" music – an oversized shell used as a trumpet in Japan for hundreds of years to keep at bay evil spirits. Several of the hikers carry paper lanterns and a few wear hats with a picture of the God of Fortune. As the procession reaches the temple at midnight sharp, bells are rung and wishes for a Happy New Year exchanged. Afterwards, a priest pours sake over the heads of the cursing devotees to bring good fortune. The liquid drips down their foreheads into a bowl from which they drink. This ceremony is meant to ensure happiness for the whole year.

Dessi Nikoltchev:

The festival was created over two centuries ago and is amongst the few cursing festivals which take place in December and January acting as a tribute to the overworked folks (men and women, often employed as kimono makers).

Travel to: Japan (Ashikaga). The festival is held in the Saishōji Temple. The most common curse is... "You idiot!" (bakayaro).

Other holidays on this date: Peace Day (Iroquois, Navajo, Cherokee tribes), World Hangover Day, Celebrate those whose last names begin with Z Day (USA), Junkanoo Jump Up (Turks and Caicos Islands), Survakane (Bulgaria), Moving the Pole (Antarctica)

02 January: Merfest Festival (USA)

An annual celebration of "all things Mer"!

Thousands of Mermaids and Mermen from round the world gather to find out the ways of mermaiding for entertainment, performances, photography, attend workshops and talks, purchase new tails from the poolside vendors and more.

All participants dress in mermaid costumes, often wearing glow-in-the-dark colorful tails, shell bras, shiny bracelets, stunning jewelry and hairpieces.

They all participate in underwater modeling session, so this spectacular event takes you deep beneath the water surface into the magical kingdom of The Little Mermaid. This unconventional convention was initiated by a bunch of mer-fans who frequently swum along as merfolks.

Travel to: USA (North Carolina). The venue is the Triangle Aquatic Centre in Cary.

Other holidays on this date: Run Up the Flagpole and See if Anyone Salutes Day (USA), Maldon Mud Race (England), Carnival (Saint Kitts and Nevis)

03 January: Turtle Dance – USA (Native American)

One of several stunning celebrations to the Native Americans. This pattern dance is performed a few times a year (coinciding with the change of seasons) and celebrates Life and therefore Creation once Father Sky embraced Mother Earth and Life was conceived.

The Turtle dance ritual is usually held on the same day every year, though the tribe's Elders and War chiefs have the last word when to be performed.

For Native Americans, the dance is a sacred ritual, a prayer. It tells a story and to know the way to communicate that story, one ought to learn for several years.

The ceremonial Turtle dance begins at sunrise with a slow buzzing chant in the native language accompanied by the beat of a buffalo drum. The boys start to dance with slow and soft steps as if attempting no to disturb the air surrounding them.

They represent the turtle – an animal that moves so slowly, as if it carries the troubles of the world on its back.

The movements are in excellent harmony with turtle shell rattles and bell anklets tied to the feet of the performers. The dancers hold small white gourds adorned with ribbons.

The costumes consist of leggings and kilts. Majestic headpieces richly adorned with colourful feathers swing with the rhythm of the dance. The dancers have their bare chests painted in red paint.

The Elders, the ladies of the tribe as well as all guests sit afar, closing the dancers in a circle. They watch in silence, caught within the magic of the ceremony. The smell of wood smoke and therefore image of old buildings within the ancient village offer mesmeric background – the natives have thickly settled the sacred area for over 1,000 years and have unbroken it pristine and frozen in time.

As the Turtle Dance is a sacred ritual – all use of phones, cameras or other recording devices is strictly taboo. After all, the people of the Pueblo tribe open doors to public, wishing to share their distinctive rituals and wonderful cultural heritage, and which ought to be respected.

Travel to: USA (New Mexico). The traditional Turtle Dance is performed by the Pueblo and Navajo tribes. The dance takes place at the Taos Pueblo Church in the ancient village of Taos Pueblo – homeplace to the Pueblo people.

Other holidays on this date: Festival of Sleep Day, Humiliation Day (USA), Last Lap (Saint Kitts and Nevis)

04 January: Incwala Celebration (Swaziland)

This is the native New year and a ceremony highlighting the absolute power and supremacy of the King of Swaziland.

The Swazis celebrate New Year within the last week of December and also the first week of January. The festivities that last for six days show an ancient ritual controlled by the priests (the alleged "people of the water"). The precise date of the celebrations is proclaimed near to the time because it derives from ancestral astrology. All locals are expected to attend, however not all Royal relatives are invited, in worry of overshadowing the majestic figure of the King. Guests are permitted to attend most of the festivities however ought to ask for a special permission to take photos because the ritual is considered sacred for the native folks.

The celebration starts with young, unmarried boys marching deep into the woods to chop the branches of a sacred shrub. The wood is used to build a sacred enclosure for the main event. However, the boys should cut solely throughout a night on a full moon.

Once they do that, they have to catch a raging bull and take it to the newly-built enclosure where the King performs a sacred ritual to get the animals' strength.

The Main Day is marked with dances and songs, performed by men wearing traditional warrior attire (leopard skin, cloaks of cattle-tails and white feathers). An important ritual is the throwing of a sacred gourd (by the King) that must be caught on the spikes of a warrior's shield.

The last day is known as a day of abstinence – folks aren't allowed to take a seat, greet or shake hands, scratch, wear decorations, sing or dance and this is controlled by patrolling warriors (any disobedience is punished).

The festival ends with an enormous bonfire (with logs gathered by young unmarried boys) in which the folks burn symbols of the past year - this way welcoming the new with hope for a better one.

The last service for the boys to perform before going home is weeding of the Queen's Maze and also the King's Gardens.

Travel to: Swaziland (Ludzidzini Royal Kraal, Lobamba). The sacred shrub is cut in the Egundvwini Royal kraal near the Bulunga Mountains.
Other holidays on this date: National Spaghetti Day, Trivia Day (USA)

05 January: La Befana (Italy)

An alternative to Santa Claus, The Witch of Christmas or Befana is a kind old witch flying round the world on a broomstick, coming into homes through the chimney each year on January 5th.

The good witch delivers presents to the well-behaved children and fills their socks with candy. She also puts onions and garlic in the socks of the naughty ones.

This custom is related to the story of the Three Wise Men (the Magi) who visited Befana and asked her to join them in welcoming the baby Jesus. The witch refused, as she was too busy cleaning up the house and then, the Magi were gone. It's believed that ever since, she wanders round the world and carries gifts to the kids, hoping to seek out the baby Jesus.

As per tradition – on the night of Befana, parents should leave out a plate piled up with local food delicacies and since this is Italy - a glass of wine for Befana.

Another custom in some parts of Northern Italy is to burn an effigy of a witch (called Giubiana) at New Years. The tradition goes back to Celtic times – the witch, an old lady symbolizing the past year, is burned to make room for the new one.

Travel to: Italy (Tuscany). Barga claims to be the home town of the good witch, although according to the legend, Befana originated from Rome. If you are up to a massive festivity – then visit Festa Nazionalle della Befana in Urbania. The festival lasts for 4 days (2-6th January) and offers great fun, lots of Befanas walking around and hanging from rooftops, street food, music, dances and of course...wine! Another option is the Befana Race in the Grand Canal in Venice held on January 6th.

Other holidays on this date: National Bird Day (USA), Haxey Hood Game (England)

06 January: Epiphany and Voditsi Ritual (Bulgaria)

The native legend has it that the night before St. Jordan's Day (Epiphany) is the last night of the year for bogeymen and demons to be seen roaming the planet. On this very night, the sky cracks open and God answers to the prayers of those who look up.

Epiphany in Bulgaria is widely celebrated with a festive liturgy in churches followed by an ancient tradition involving a dip in ice-cold water.

The festivities begin early in the morning after the liturgy. Orthodox clergymen, followed by many folks, lead a procession to the closest river or lake. Once they reach it, a priest throws a blessed silver or wood cross into the water. Then many enthusiastic young and old men (often inspired by a glass or two of homemade plum brandy, or wine and a band of bagpipers) jump in the freezing waters and try to fetch the cross. The one who retrieves it will be healthy and freed froom evil spirits all year round. In some villages, it is a tradition to dance "horo" (traditional Bulgarian line dance) in the bitterly cold waters.

Epiphany coincides with another ancient ritual - Voditsi. The celebration has its roots back within the B.C. era. The legend has it that the night of January 6th is a magical night. A night when the water will "hear" and "remember". A century-old custom is to pour a glass of fresh water (or even better – fetch the water from a lake or river), leave it out in the open to allow time for it to "breathe and cleanse". First, one ought to say his name aloud to introduce himself to the water. Then, to share his deepest wishes aloud finishing with the words "Let it be". The water is left outside overnight. On the next morning, he ought to wash his eyes and drink from it throughout the whole day. No other person ought to touch it or drink it.

It is believed that the water makes the wishes come true (if they come from the heart). The ritual is performed in solitude and deep concentration because it is very intimate.

Travel to: Bulgaria (Kalofer). Tundzha River is a good spot for cross diving and dancing "horo" accompanied by drummers and bagpipers.

Other holidays on this date: World Cuddle Up Day, Bean Day (USA), Witches Downhill Race (Switzerland), Nalajuk Night (Canada)

07 January: Straw Bear Day (England)

An ancient English ritual declined at the end of the XIX C., revived within the 1980s.

This traditional festival, held over three days in January, marks the start of the English agricultural season.

The celebrations begin with a concert on the first day and continue with street parade on the second, that is the main event day. The procession involves a randomly chosen boy, dressed up in straw costume, carrying a straw headpiece and a chain round the armpits. He dances in front of houses in exchange for treats – tipically including beer, food or cash. Refreshments along the way are quite vital as the poor boy carries generally up to 30kg of straw on top of his own weight.

The procession, led by the Straw Bear (boy) and his keeper is followed by musicians, Morris dancers (pagan dancers carrying bells and wielding swords, sticks or handkerchiefs), masqueraded performers, mummers and embelished plow pulled by workers. The parade is very much anticipated by the locals, who are highly entertained by the clumsy movements of the bear. The appearance of the Straw Bear is on a Saturday. The Sunday that follows is the last day of the festival, when a huge effigy of The Straw Bear, symbolizing the past year is burned, to make room for a new bear/a new year.

Travel to: England (Cambridgeshire). The three-day festival is held in the small town of Whittlesey. Make sure to buy a festival programme once you arrive as there are several processions taking place at the same time. Also, don't miss to taste the Straw Bear Ale, which is specially brewed for the occasion.

Other holidays on this date: Old Rock Day (USA)

08 January: Coming of Age Festival (Japan)

This is an annual holiday (in fact a rite of passage), observed on the second Monday in January, to celebrate all youngsters who have turned 20 between April 1st of the previous year and April 2nd of the current one. It is to honor their entry into "adulthood" which in Japan is considered the age of 20. This is a huge turning point, coming with new responsibilities and liberties.

Coming of Age Day has been an official holiday in Japan since 1948 though it may be derived back to the 700 A.D. to an event when a prince wore new gown and haircut on his transition to adulthood to celebrate the end of his teen years.

All municipal authorities within the country host special congratulatory ceremonies with speeches held by officials and small gifts given to the participants.

The women wear traditional "furisome" – glorious kimono with extra-long sleeves, worn solely by single ladies. One can easily cost about $10,000. As dressing in a kimono needs the assistance of few folks (so does the hairstyle) – some girls book a year beforehand session with stylists.

Some men wear "hakama" – male kimono, however most of them prefer trendy western suits.

After a visit to local shrine, day-long celebrations and tiresome photo shoots, the families have lunch to mark reaching of the legal drinking age. Later, the "new adults", or those who survive the lunch – meet up with friends and party overnight.

As the day is an official holiday – the streets are flooded with food-on-a-stick stands, musicians, and street performers.

Travel to: Japan (Tokyo). A huge ceremony is held at the Shibuya ward office.
Other holidays on this date: Bubble Bath Day, Male Watcher`s Day, Navajo Night Chant (USA)

09 January: Festival-au-Désert (Mali)

The Festival in the Desert is known as "the most remote music festival in the world". Created in 2001, its main purpose is to showcase the culture of the Tuareg people - indigenous nomadic "blue people" of the Sahara Desert. They are named "blue people" as a result of their bright blue robes and dark turbans protecting them from the scorching sun.

The festival changed sites a few times due to security concerns however always took place in the Northern part of Mali. The gathering, originally strictly for Tuaregs, was held when the nomadic people would gather for deciding and to reconnect with one another, recite poetry and sing songs. With time it turned to an occurence celebrating the local culture and Tuareg heritage.

Traditional Tuareg music and dances combine with international artists (including Bono, Robert Plant, Manu Chao) who perform on the main stage, enclosed by sand dunes. The festival is peaceful throughout the day however comes alive at nighttime with fashionable Malian music, DJ sets and dances under the stars.

There also are camel races, artifacts exhibitions, varied competitions, souvenir and native food stalls.

Since 2012, the festival, which is additionally a message of tolerance and celebration of peace for the Malian people, has been in exile, due to the uncertainty within the region and therefore militants ban any kind of music or performance.

The organizers supposed to re-open in 2017 when peace talks were held, however in the last minute, Malian officials decided to cancel due to security threats. Festival au Désert is presently postponed till further notice, however the organizers hope to revive it as soon as possible.

Travel to: Timbuktu (venue and dates are to be announced)
Other holidays on this date: Play God Day (USA), Toku Ebisu Festival (Japan)

10 January: Voodoo Festival (Benin)

A week of Voodoo and... gin! Lots of it, because it is used in several of the rituals performed by native priests.

Voodoo was formally recognized as a religion in 1996 and is more than the fundamental perception of black magic and rag dolls. It is a spiritual bridge between life and death; a philosophy and a medicine at the same time.

The Beninese Voodoo is the oldest one and a principal source for the Haitian Vodou, Puerto Rican Vodú, Cuban Vodú, Dominican Vudú, Brazilian Vodum and Louisiana Voodoo.

People practicing Voodoo (60% of the population in Benin) believe that Gods and spirits govern the forces of nature and human society and that everything on Earth possesses a spirit – humans, trees, lakes etc. They worship the spirits of the ancestors and believe that the dead still live among us.

Thousands of devotees roll up in a small town to be blessed by the Voodoo leader (the Roi) and to participate in a procession to a Sacred Forest, to pray and honor the ancestors. Locals carry Voodoo symbols, wearing traditional animal skin costumes as well as skulls and bones as decoration, representing Voodoo idols. A number of them cover their bodies in palm oil and powder.

The start of the festival is marked with slaughtering a goat by the Supreme Voodoo priest, to honor the Gods and also the spirits of the ancestors. The tradition is followed by chanting, dances, bamboo pole acrobatics and animal sacrifices at local shrines.

Highlight is, of course, a plethora of pierced voodoo dolls hanging outside tents and dwellings, adorned with flags that represent numerous Voodoo sects.

For many individuals, believers or not, this is often not simply another weird festival but a route to search out their own soul and path within the world, quite a spiritual journey.

Travel to: Benin (Ouidah). Visit the Kpasse Zoun Sacred Forest – the birthplace of Voodoo, where the First King of Ouidah died and turned into a tree. Voodoo symbols and shrines are spread all around the forest. Worth visit is the Python Temple just outside Ouidah. The main festivities are held on the beach near the Point Of No Return Monument.

Other holidays on this date: National Bittersweet Chocolate Day, National Save the Eagles Day, National Cut Your Energy Costs Day, Houseplant Appreciation Day (USA)

11 January: Burning of The Clavie (Scotland)

An ancient pagan ritual annually celebrated on January 11th – the New Year per the Old Style calendar.

The UK adopted the revised Gregorian Calendar in the 1750s and dropped 11 days from the month of September. This moved the New year celebration from January 11th to January 1st.

But locals weren't terribly keen on giving up their custom and chose to celebrate New year twice – on January 1st and on January 11th.

As most pagan rituals, Burning of the Clavie is a fire ceremony. The "Clavie" is a wooden barrel cut in half, full of tar and wood shavings, mounted on a carrying pole. In the past, herring barrels were used instead, however these days – iron-hooped whisky barrels do the job just as good! The barrel is carried in a procession through the streets to an ancient stone altar within an old fort. The pole carriers (should be local fishermen, usually a group of 10), go in clockwise direction and take turns.

Once the procession reaches the fort, the Clavie is positioned and ignited at the stone altar. Flammable liquid is added till the forthill becomes a large beacon of fire.

When the barrel burns completely, the official New Year celebration starts.

Cheering people bring smoldering embers to their homes. They use them to light a New Year fire and bring luck and happiness to the household. Pieces of the burned Clavie (small coals) are even sent to relatives abroad.

The roots of Burning of The Clavie can't be traced because of the various disputes regarding its origin – Roman, Celtic or Pictish. The aim of the ritual is also unknown, nevertheless it is another excuse for the Scots to celebrate!

Travel to: Scotland (Burghead). The procession starts from Brander Street and the Clavie is burned to the ground on Doorie Hill.

Other holidays on this date: National Milk Day, National Human Trafficking Awareness Day, Step in a Puddle and Splash your Friends Day (USA)

12 January: Kanchu Misogi Festival (Japan)

One of the most bizarre festivals in Japan.

It is an old Shinto mid-winter ritual for soul purification, still practiced all over Japan. The ritual is supposed to bring good fortune to the upcoming year.

The word "Shinto" interprets to "way of the spirits" - it isn't religion, but a way of life. Devotees believe that no matter what beliefs they have, the spirits wish them to be happy and prosperous. Shinto permits people to practice alternative religions and teaches ethical principles – how to be good (to others and to yourself) and how to avoid committing sins – moral and physical. Kanchu Misogi is a ritual of cleansing and pleasing the "spirits of power".

Men holding large blocks of ice, wearing loincloths and headbands take a dip into ice-cold pool to pray. The ritual is linked to the New Year, as purifying ceremonies are performed to give the people a fresh start of the year.

The ritual is carried out in local temples and shrines. It may include a dip in a pool of freezing water (temperatures being just around -6C), a pour with buckets of cold water or snow. There is always a warm-up rowing exercise with group chants. The complete ritual lasts about 30 minutes and is a great experience for body and soul. Both men and women can participate.

Travel to: Japan (Tokyo). A huge event takes place at the Teppozu Inari Shinto Shrine including an icy-cold pool for the participants to dip in.

Other holidays on this date: International Kiss a Ginger Day, Feast of Fabulous Wild Men Day, National Pharmacist Day (USA), Duruthu Full Moon Poya Day (Sri Lanka)

13 January: The Carnival of Vevchani (Macedonia)

A 1400-year custom based on ancient pagan rituals.

Carnival of Vevchani is celebrated annually on the eve of the Feast of Saint Vasilij (January 12th - 14th). The festival is one of the oldest cultural celebrations in the country.

Its main purpose is to replicate on current events in a humorous or sarcastic manner. A highlight to the event is a huge street procession of performers wearing richly embelished costumes, disguised with scary or funny masks. Some imitate individuals or events from the past year (political, religious etc.) whereas others represent pagan idols, devils, mummers, zombies or mythical figures. The colourful procession features musicians playing zurla (traditional woodwind instrument), drums, bells and even pots and pans. This festival brings together the entire town, turning it into a theatre stage. Numerous teams of masqueraded merrymakers perform on the streets and in front of randomly chosen houses. Of the various characters, the most important one is August the Stupid who communicates with the audience by screaming and gesturing. Other distinct characters are a bride and a groom symbolizing fertility, and also the Devil representing all things evil.

Travel to: Macedonia (Vevchani). The small village became part of the World Federation of Carnival Cities in 1993.

Other holidays on this date: Rubber Ducky Day, International Sceptics Day, Make Your Dream Come True Day (USA), Appenzell Silvester Claus (Switzerland), The Return of the Sun (Greenland)

14 January: International Kite Festival (India)

A colorful two-day festival, locally known as Uttarayan, celebrated every January 14th since its creation in 1989. This is one of the biggest festivals in the world gathering around 8-10 million visitors from around the world. In the past, kite flying has been a privilege and entertainment exclusively reserved for the Royals to express their power and strength, however over time it reached the masses and became popular.

The kites symbolize the spirits of the gods, awaken from their deep winter sleep. Many locals begin manufacturing kites months in advance, preparing to meet the high demand throughout the festival days. A number of them even open in-house pop-up shops.

The festival attracts many participants to represent their countries, each of them bringing something new in terms of kite shape, color and message, enhancing the standard Uttarayan kite that is rhomb-shaped, made of light paper and bamboo sticks.

The event is exceptionally stunning at nighttime once the dark sky is lit by thousands of illuminated kites and candle lanterns.

Local pop stars and celebrities participate in the accompanying events, even politicians hold opening speeches. Lots of stalls with delicious local food and merchandise lure the guests. The event features all kinds of kite competitions, as well as a kite battle with fighter kites (Patang kites) – small and unstable kite with thin cutting line attached to it (to cut through and destroy other kites).

Kites had been known to mankind since forever, however the first official lead points to the Han Dynasty in China when General Huein Tsang flew a kite at night to overawe the army of Liu Pang.

Travel to: India (Gujarat province). The event takes place in the capital city of Ahmedabad. Sabarmati riverfront provides the best view. Worth a visit is also Patang Bazaar – a huge all-things-kite market open 24/7 during the festival week.

Other holidays on this date: Dress Up Your Pet Day (USA), Pongal Festival (India), Maghe Sankranti (Nepal), Bango Vasil (the Gypsy New Year in Bulgaria)

15 January: Dondo Yaki (Japan)

A Japanese "happiness" custom observed across the country in the beginning of the new year (usually on January 15th).

It is a ritual of burning old good luck charms and amulets at Shinto shrines – particularly objects related to the Japanese Zodiac symbol/animal of the preceding year. This is a cleansing celebration, when one breaks with the past and starts the new year with a clean sheet.

Buying talismans from shrines is a centurial tradition in Japan. Their purpose is to bring good fortune throughout the year, and later – simply to be discarded. However, to throw an amulet in the garbage is simply not acceptable and brings very bad luck.

That is why the Japanese have Dondo Yaki - to "get rid" of the old lucky charms.

The ritual is held either in shrines where all unwanted objects are thrown in a huge bonfire without bringing bad luck to their owner or out in the open in pyres of bamboo sticks, that are set alight.

Some people make the most of the occasion and roast rice cakes and citrus fruits over the smoldering ambers.

There are, of course, the legends – if one attends a lucky charm bonfire – his handwriting can improve, or have luck in love, or grow wiser etc.

Dondo Yaki is also the time to burn all New year decorations like garlands, wreaths, paper figurines and so on. According to the Japanese philosophy, the aim of the annual winter decoration is to invite and please the gods, so it would be quite disrespectful to use the same decoration twice!

Travel to: Japan (Tokyo). Huge bonfires are lit on the banks of the Tamagawa River and in Oyama Dairi Park in Tokyo, but the biggest one in the country is at Mima City – Tokushima Prefecture.

Other holidays on this date: National Hat Day (USA)

16 January: Iroquois Mid-Winter Festival (USA – Native American)

A century-old tradition to the Iroquois people and one of the most important ceremonies, marking the beginning of Spring.

The history of the celebration goes way back, in times of excruciating cold during the winter months. The Iroquois tribe members lived in so-called longhouses. They lit fires to stay warm, but since their only ventilation was a small hole above the fireplace - the entire premise filled with smoke, making the inhabitants cough and stinging their eyes. Unfortunately, they couldn't open a door or go outside because it was too cold and dangerous. That is why, with the first rays of the Spring sun –all of them gathered outside – happy to celebrate the fresh air and reviving nature. As all traditions of the Iroquois, this one is no different – prayers and chants are said to thank the gods and secure luck and well-being in the year to come.

The ceremony is held in the second week of January for nine days. The exact date is set according to the Dipper Constellation and five days after a new moon. It is also referred to as the New Year ceremony, as a new year of rituals begins.

Tribal messengers formally announce the start of the ceremony and invite everybody inside the longhouse. Then all children born in the previous year are given their Indian names.

After the formalities – a Bear Dance (ritual performed to cure misfortunes of the past year) and Feather Dance (sacred ritual performed to give thanks and honor The Creator; people sit and sing face-to-face) are performed. The celebrations continue with dream sharing and tobacco leaf smoking. An interesting fact is that the Iroquois believe dreams contain a cure for mental and physical diseases. That is why they believe that once somebody shares a dream and receives opinion by others – he can find a way to cope with his problem. The Iroquois have adopted the "Dreamcatcher" (created by the Chippewa tribe) as their own idol and believe that the little beads tied to the hanging feathers show the way to the good dreams, while the nightmares will be lost in the web and perish with the morning sun.

Another interesting fact is that tobacco smoking is an integral part of their culture – the Iroquois are known as "the tobacco people" (the word "ierokwa" translates to "they who use tobacco"). They believe that the smoke from burning tobacco carries their prayers and reaches the Great Spirit (The Creator).

A popular game is played during the festival – the Peach Stone game. It is not just for fun but also used to predict the weather and the harvest in the new year. Six peach stones are blackened on one side (using fireplace or stove), thrown into a bowl and shaken. Then the white and black ends showing are counted to predict the fortune in the upcoming year.

Travel to: USA (Great Lakes, New York, Oklahoma), Canada (Ontario) are the places where the people of the Six Nations live today (The Iroquois people, known as the Six Nations, include the tribes: Mohawk, Oneida, Onondaga, Cayuga, Seneca, and Tuscarora). There are many museums, gathering places and administrative services that offer information on when and where different ceremonies will be held.

Other holidays on this date: Appreciate a Dragon Day, National Religious Freedom Day, National Without a Scalpel Day (USA)

17 January: Wassailing the Apple Trees (England)

This is yet another custom that has its roots in the old pagan rituals. It is celebrated annually on the old Twelfth Night (17th January). The ceremony is observed across the cider-making regions of England and protects the orchards from evil spirits. The custom of wassailing was created back in the days (some believe it was around XVI C), when the workers were paid in apple cider. This, of course, meant that it was of foremost importance to the orchard owners, to ensure a good harvest and attract the best workers. The "Wassail" is the main ingredient used in the ritual – it is, in fact, a type of hot sweet cider. The wassailing ceremony slightly differs according to the region it is being observed in, however always includes a King and Queen who lead a procession and visit each orchard garden in the area. They gather round the biggest apple tree in the orchard and sing songs for fruitful year and good harvest. This way, they chase away evil spirits and appeal to the Apple gods. In the meantime, all participants drink hot cider from a ritualistic wassail bowl, that is handed over from one person to another. The ceremony continues with the Queen climbing up an apple tree to stick toasted bread soaked in cider onto a branch. The others follow suit and by the time they get to the next orchard - the apple tree turns into a Christmas tree with toast garlands. Before the assembled crowd moves on - they sing and shout, bang on pots and pans, shoot with guns and make an awful lot of noise while dancing around the tree.

The ceremony takes place in the evening and is spectacular to see because the participants often wear flower wreaths on their heads and some carry lit torches.

Travel to: England (Somerset). The best place to be is Carhampton and Dunster where the ceremony is highly cherished. Added value to the holiday will give you a visit to Clevedon in North Somerset, where along with the ritual, you`ll see Morris Men (Morris folk dances are performed by men dressed in traditional costumes wielding handkerchiefs, swords or sticks).

Other holidays on this date: National Hot Buttered Rum Day, National Bootlegger`s Day (USA)

18 January: Sinulog Festival (Philippines)

An annual 9-day festival held on the third Sunday in January to celebrate the acceptance of Catholicism by the locals and its prevalence over other religions and pagan beliefs.

In the XVIth C, members of the Royal family, along side locals, were baptised and this changed the entire course of religious development on the island country, setting it apart from the other Asian countries.

The Sinulog Festival is one amongst the grandest and most colourful events in the Philippines featuring a spectacular parade lasting for up to 12 hours. The attendance can reach up to 4 million people!

Beautifully adorned wooden platforms make their way through the town streets in the beat of music. Ritualistic prayer dances, performed on the floats, remind of ocean waves – the very name "Sinulog" derives from the word "sulog" which can be translated as "the motion of water".

The festival pays tribute to baby Jesus – Santo Niño. A statue of Santo Niño was given to the town by Fernando Magellan in 1521. The legend has it that the wave-like dance was invented some years later when the local ruler`s consultant fell sick. He was isolated in a hut that housed the statue at that point. A couple of days later he was found laughing and dancing – apparently fully recovered. The consultant later explained that a child woke him up from a deep sleep – pinching, tickling and making fun of him. The kid made strange and complex moves and therefore the man started to dance with it, imitating the little boy`s steps that reminded very much of ocean waves.

The highlight of the festivities is a Grand Parade featuring numerous floats adorned with flowers, candles and festive spirit.

Thousands of people, arriving from every part of the country, take part in the street parade – dancers, musicians, and different performers sway in the rhythm of trumpets, drums, and the native gongs. The performing groups represent various styles – from modern and street to more formal or even historical dances. Their state-of-the-art outfits had taken months to make.

Accompanying the Grand Parade also are open-air concerts, huge street market offering low-cost items, pyro-musical show, a parade of the Filipino celebrities and plenty of fireworks.

At dawn, a breath-taking sailing procession takes place with a centerpiece – the adorned with colourful flowers and lit candles statue of Santo Niño. The procession ends with re-enactment of the Christianization of the Islanders.

During the festival, the streets are flooded with small kiosks, selling hand-woven bags and baskets, local souvenirs, tasty food and the famous traditional dried mangoes.

Travel to: Philippines (Cebu City). A huge dance contest is held at the Cebu City Sports Complex. The Sinulog Festival is of such importance that it even has a coat of arms – a two-headed eagle incorporated to a native warrior's shield.

Other holidays on this date: National Peking Duck Day, National Winnie the Pooh Day (USA)

19 January: Timkat (Ethiopia)

Timkat is the Ethiopian Epiphany, that celebrates every year on January 19th (the 10th day of Terr according to the Ethiopian calendar) the divine ritual of the Baptism of Jesus Christ in the Jordan River. It is for sure the most colourful celebration and a much-anticipated holiday for the Orthodox Christians in the country. The night preceding the festival, replicas of the Ten Commandments (Tabots) are carried out in a procession and placed next to rivers and lakes where the celebrations take place. The Tabots, wrapped in red silk mantels are carried by priests, shaded by colourful ceremonial umbrellas. The procession is accompanied by drum beats, bells, trumpets, chants and a special dance performed by the priests. Throughout the entire night, the priests remain on the river bank and pray until dawn. On the day of the celebration, they bless the water, extinguish a candle in it and sprinkle the crowd to mark the Baptism of Christ. Many people dive into the water for purification and to chase away the evil spirits.

The end of the ceremony is marked by a procession back to the church – once more accompanied by the beat of traditional drums, songs, and dances.

Travel to: Ethiopia (Addis Ababa). Many people spend the night under the stars together with the praying priests at Jan Meda Grounds (there are tents available too)

- close to the Kebena River where the ceremony takes place in the morning. Some bring oil lamps and picnic on the grounds. Gondar is another option for the celebrations – they are held on the banks of the Lesser Angereb River.

Other holidays on this date: National Tin Can Day, Get to Know Your Customers Day, Popcorn Day (USA), Jarramplas Festival (Spain)

20 January: Thorrablot (Iceland)

A very, very ancient holiday - believed to have its roots in the Viking Age and named after Thor - the God of Thunder. Thorrablot was a sacrificial midwinter festival in pagan Iceland– abolished and reinstated in the XIXth C. Also referred to as the Ugly Food Festival nowadays, the event according to the historical Icelandic calendar falls on a date in late January/early February. Locals gather in the evening to recite poems and sing songs honoring Thor, and feast on unusual choice of local food delicacies. The dinner could be very intimate with just the family attending or can be an indoor event with performances, music, and dances. Some of the typical dishes served are rotten shark's meat, poached sheep's head, blood pudding, liver sausage, pickled ram's testicles, wind-dried fish, sheep head jam and more. The traditional drink to accompany the menu is named Black Death and is made of potatoes and caraway.

Travel to: Iceland (Reykjavik). Many restaurants offer themed buffets on Thorrablot, or one could buy the ingredients and Thorrablot sets from most shops. If you are in for a real Viking dinner/party treat, visit the Fjörukráin Viking Village which is just 20min by bus from Reykjavik (Strandgata 55, 220 Hafnarfirði in the town of Hafnarfjörður).

Other holidays on this date: National Cheese Lover Day, National Buttercrunch Day, National DJ Day (USA)

21 January: Mari Lwyd (Wales)

A local custom to South Wales, performed in the past during the Christmas festivities - nowadays, taking place in January. The custom dates to the 1800s and has various theories on why it was created in the first place. Some believe it was an ancient fertility ritual, others – that it has a far darker background. The characters involved in the performance are: a resurrected horse (Mari Lwyd), a Leader, Mr. Punch and Judy (popular characters from a rather violent puppet show) and the Merry Men. For the Mari Lwyd personage, a horse's skull is decorated with colourful ribbons and mounted onto a pole. The carrier of the pole is fully covered with large white sheet attached to the horse's skull, therefore the assembly resembles a white horse. The Leader walks ahead of Mary Lwyd, usually carrying a stick or a whip pretending to try taming it. The ritual is performed in the evening and tipically lasts till very late at night. After roaming the streets, once all personages gather in one place, they start visiting random residents in the area, knock on their doors and sing songs. The hosts do not let them in and sing a song back – the lyrics from both parties are meant to be insulting, containing riddles and challenges, and in rhyme! The rhyme battle repeats till the hosts ran out of ideas why they shouldn't let the merry procession inside their house. Once they allow them in, they have to treat them with a pint of Ale and food. During the feast, Mari Lwyd (the horse) runs round the house with the Leader trying to chase away the animal, that purposely creats great deal of chaos. After entertaining the hosts, the group sings a farewell song and moves on to the next house.

Travel to: Wales (Llangynwyd). The ancient ritual is still performed in the small village where the Mari Lwyd group visits pubs and interacts with people. Another option to see Mari Lwyd is to attend the festivities in Chepstow, where the so-called grey mare is celebrated together with mummers and other pagan characters.

Other holidays on this date: International Balloon Festival (Switzerland), National Granola Bar Day, Squirrel Appreciation Day (USA)

22 January: Winter Wahoo Rodeo (Turks and Caicos Islands)

The Wahoo fish is a real crown jewel to the sports fishermen because it is one amongst the quickest – swimming up to 90km/h! A Wahoo can easily weigh up to 80kg, grow up to 2.5m and is a local delicacy to the Caribbean countries. Having such impressive characteristics, it is understandable why the Turks and Caicos Islands created a contest to honor the ocean beast. The Winter Wahoo Rodeo, formerly known as Who Cares Wahoo Tournament, is held annually at the local marina, attracting experienced and novice fishermen from around the world. The event features various categories – the Largest Wahoo being the most important one, but also the largest tuna, barracuda, mahi mahi fish and others. The contest is called Wahoo Rodeo, thanks to the massive fight the Wahoo fish puts up before being caught. The participants win different awards and cash prizes. In the evening, the marina bay turns into a mouth-watering feast with delicious meals and drinks. And lots of fish, of course.

Travel to: Turks and Caicos Islands. The contest is held at the Turtle Cove Marina.

Other holidays on this date: Unity Day (Ukraine)

23 January: Carnival of Venice (Italy)

This Baroque celebration is one of the best-known carnivals in the world well preserving the glamour and magnificence of the distinctive Venetian culture. In the past, masks were used to hide the identity and status of the people wearing them. Carnival was the sole time of the year for one to have no boundaries, and freedom to do things desired all year without feeling any guilt. The Venice Carnival was banned in 1797 under the rule of the King of Austria and after a long absence returned in 1979. Today, it takes place in the days before Lent until Shrove Tuesday (January/February) and attracts over 3 million people. Street musicians, jugglers and entertainers can be seen everywhere. The beautiful Venetian water canals are full of colorfully decorated gondolas. Nighttime lures visitors to lavish parties and masquerade balls. It gives a feeling as if fairy tales have come alive!

The traditional masks, created by the mascherari, are hand-painted and embelished with gems and feathers. They are extremely expensive; however, authentic copies can be purchased much cheaper. There are several distinctive mask personages:

1. The Bauta – a simple mask, tipically painted in white, with square jaw and lacking a mouth, covers the whole face. Worn with a black cape and black tricorn hat, it was obligatory for the government officials to wear it during decision-making events in the XVIII C.

2. The Pantalone – a half-mask representing the old and greedy Venetian merchant who deals with those who want to take away his gold.

3. The Colombina – half-mask, worn by ladies, painted in bright colours, with innumerable ornaments, ribbons, and gems. It is believed that the mask was created for the Commedia dell'Arte actresses who didn't wish to completely cover their beautiful faces. This mask represents the independent, brilliant and spicy woman.

4. The Zanni – half-mask made of leather with a very low forehead and extremely long nose. Zanni represents ignorance and stupidity although at the same time manages to outsmart everybody else. And is always hungry!

5. The Arlecchino – one of the most significant in Commedia dell'Arte, the mask of Arlecchino has evolved through the centuries from poor and stupid to a noble and humurous character. There is a theory that Michelangelo himself would have created it. This is a half-mask made of leather with big and furry eyebrows giving it a questioning look.

6. The Medico della Peste – the Plague Doctor, one of the most bizarre masks. A French doctor invented the mask in the XVIIth C while treating patients with plague. The mask was never designed for a carnival character. It is usually white with huge round eyeholes and a very long hollow beak. During the plague, doctors used to put flowers and herbs in the hollow beak to keep away the foul odors. The mask is worn with a black cloak, white gloves, black brim hat, and overcoat.

7. The Volto – covering the whole face, this mask represents a person who wants to make a mysterious entrance and a quiet exit. Usually, with fewer ornaments, the highlighted features are the lips or the eyes.

Along with the festivities, private masquerade events, street performances and contests, this is the only time of the year when all bakeries sell the famous carnival sweets – Frittelle (fried sweet dumplings by an original ancient Roman recipe) and Galani (sweet fried thin pastry strips sprinkled with icing sugar – once more an ancient Roman recipe).

Travel to: Italy (Venice). The best festivities take place at Piazza San Marco. If you are looking for a costume – make sure to check what Horst Raack has to offer – the famous costume designer has won "The Most Beautiful Mask" category the impressive 4 times since 2009!

Other holidays on this date: National Pie Day, National Handwriting Day, Measure Your Feet Day (USA)

24 January: Goat Throwing Festival (Spain)

The annual Goat Toss in northwestern Spain is dedicated to the town's patron - St. Vincent and is celebrated on the fourth Sunday in January. In line with the legend, a priest owned a magical goat which could feed all poor people with its milk. One Sunday, the goat climbed up the church bell tower and fell over frightened by the tolling bells. Luckily, it was caught by townsfolks in a blanket and survived. Until 2002, the locals used to throw a live goat from the 15-meter church bell tower and catch it with a blanket. Then the animal was carried in a large street procession around the village streets. Over the years of this tradition, several animals didn't survive the "throw", making activists very eager to ban the weird custom. After a long battle (legal and with the locals), they won and live goat throwing was banned in 2002. The celebration still goes on today - with lots of dancing, singing, drinking... and the throwing of a plush goat to honor the tradition.

Travel to: Spain. The festival is held in the village of Manganeses de la Polvorosa.
Other holidays on this date: Beer Can Appreciation Day, Compliment Day (USA)

25 January: Tunarama (Australia)

The 4-day festival is held in the weekend nearest to the Australia Day holiday in January. Originally meant to promote the continent's tuna industry, this festival (now in its 50+ year celebration) is today known for its centerpiece event...the tuna toss. In 1979, locals decided that the festival needed something unique to be identified with. Many came up with different ideas, but none was spectacular and fun. However, two friends suggested "Tuna Toss". They came up with the idea while watching local men toss fish from overflowing fishing boats into loading trucks! And that is how the Tuna Toss competition was created! The long weekend celebrations feature cheering on the boat builders, a dinner show with cook-offs with some of the world`s best known chefs, a movie festival, Steakarama, performances from local and international artists and bands, circus, a street procession with floats (including a contest for best costume and best float) representing the local businesses and culture, Rockarama Dinner and Dance with live music, watermelon eating competition and magnificent fireworks display to mark the end.

The crown jewel of the festival – the Tuna Toss, takes place at the Tuna Toss Arena where participants try to throw a 10kg tuna fish as far as they can. The best of the best win cash prizes and a special trophy. People from all over the world come to try their luck and compete in the contest, so places fill out quickly.

Last, however not least – there are countless street food stalls offering the freshest seafood throughout the festival days!

Travel to: Australia (Port Lincoln). The Grand Opening takes place at the Eyre Square overlooking the magnificent Boston Bay.

Other holidays on this date: Opposite Day (USA), Burns Night (Scotland)

26 January: Sancheoneo Ice Fishing Festival (South Korea)

This is a winter ice fishing festival and is great fun! Created in 2003, it lasts for nearly a month, and attracts a lot of people every year. Locals and visitors gather to try and catch a mountain trout (sancheoneo) in three different ways: by carving out holes in the 30cm thick ice cap of the frozen stream; by barehand in the nearby stream pool specially designed for the purpose (people need to jump in the icy-cold water) or by lure fishing. The participants in the so-called "fish pool" who attempt to catch fish with their bare hands are all given a T-shirt and shorts to change into before they jump in the water on a given signal. The catch in all categories can be kept and the participants are welcome to take the fish into one of the many food centers, where for a small fee, they can have it filleted and deep-fried. For international visitors – there is a special "novice" zone created on the frozen stream where they would have more luck to catch a fish or two!

In addition, the festival features ice sledding with traditional Korean sleds – a wood plank to sit down and two wooden sticks to hold in each hand for steering, bobsleigh and ice soccer. The entire city is beautifully lit with salmon-shaped paper lanterns and ice sculptures in various shapes and colours. Visitors can enjoy traditional Korean games and of course magnificent local cuisine – sweet and savory dishes, dumplings, rice cakes and plenty of fish!

Travel to: South Korea. The event is held close to Hwacheon city - at the Hwacheoncheon stream. Hwacheon Train Pension B&B is close to the festival site and a suitable place to stay.

Other holidays on this date: National Green Juice Day, National Peanut Brittle Day (USA), Tet Holiday (Vietnam), Yabun Festival (Australia)

27 January: Tapati Rapa Nui (Easter Island)

This annual festival is celebrated since 1969 at the end of January/beginning of February and lasts for two weeks. It started as a small gathering to the locals with singing, dancing, and a small parade, however quickly turned into a much-anticipated event attracting many visitors to the most remote island in the world. Today, the celebrations consist of numerous dancing and singing competitions, religious chanting, swimming, canoeing, horse racing and crowning of a Queen of the Island that takes place by moonlight at the Tahai complex. Without any doubt, the highlight of the event is the Haka Pei – a banana trunk slide at very high speed from the top of a volcano. The participants wear nothing but a loin cloth (hami) and body paint. They mount two banana tree trunks lashed together with twine and slide down a steep hill with unimaginable speed (up to 80km/h).

The whole idea behind the many competitions is to choose the Queen of the Island – a title that lasts for a year. So, the folks of Hanga Roa city divide into two teams, representing the indigenous tribes of the island, and compete against each other for days and nights (with two rival candidates for a Queen who compete with their teams as well) – the team to score more points gets the right to crown its candidate as Queen of the Island. Tricky in the above-mentioned competitions is that they are not traditional: the swimming competition features a reed float and participants in body paint and traditional costumes; the body-paint competition uses only natural pigments so the contestants should know how to mix them and to explain the story behind every drawn symbol; the chanting should be without any mistakes or repeating lyrics; the running marathon involves two banana clusters tied to a stick carried by the participants etc.

The rumor has it that in the beginning, the festival was pretty much a local thing with simple but creative costumes, made of bed sheets or cardboard. That, however, changed after Kevin Costner's film had scenes shot on the island. Many locals involved in the production managed to learn a thing or two about staging, costume-making, and dramatic lighting effects and carried these new skills and concepts into their annual festival to make it more appealing and grander.

Travel to: Chili (Easter Island). The Easter Island famous for its 887 stone head statues called moai, is recognized by UNESCO as a World Heritage Site. The event takes place in the capital city – Hanga Roa.

Other holidays on this date: Chocolate Cake Day, National Punch the Clock Day (USA)

Dessi Nikoltchev:

28 January: Surva and the Mummers Games (Bulgaria)

This pre-spring ritual with deep pagan roots is held annually in the last weekend of January and is one of the most colorful and large events on the Balkans. The aim is to scare away evil spirits and bring good fortune into the coming year. The Mummer's Games (Kukeri) is a tradition of Thracian origins in honor of god Dionysus. The festival (called Surva), created in 1966 lasts for three days (Friday-Sunday), during which more than 6 000 people (mostly men) dressed in hand-made scary costumes and wearing ornate masks, dance, and parade on the city streets. They are divided in groups, representing every ethnographic region of the country, and are judged by their costumes, masks, and overall performance. The group with best and most scary costumes receives "The Golden Mask" as a prize. The men perform a magical dance – each Mummer has a belt adorned with huge copper bells to enhance the protective power of the costume. The men clap, jump and perform to chase away the evil and bring luck as well as land fertility and good harvest. A Mummer's costume can weigh up to 25-30kg depending on the decoration and is tipically made of goat or sheep fur. The masks are decorated with threads, ribbons, sometimes with horns or antlers, and represent different animals like goat, bull and ram. Masks can even be double-faced and represent good and evil that co-exist in everything. The distinct colors of the outfits have different meanings – red symbolizes reviving nature and land fertility; black is the Mother Earth and white color represents water and light.

The festival features many workshops on costumes and mask making, bazaars, food markets and local wine and brandy.

As of 2015, the festival is part of the UNESCO List of Intangible Cultural Heritage.

Travel to: Bulgaria (Pernik). The event is held in the city center, which as from 2009 is officially named a European Capital of Sourvakar and Mummer Traditions. An alternative for accommodation is Sofia which is just 20km from Pernik.

Other holidays on this date: Data Privacy Day, National Blueberry Pancake Day, National Seed Swap Day (USA), Cirque de Demain (France)

29 January: Wakakusa Yamayaki (Japan)

This is a truly fiery festival held annually on the fourth Saturday in January.
"Yamayaki" literally translates to: "the mountain roast"!

During the celebration, a whole mountain is burned down to provide a breath-stopping show to the visitors.

There are two main theories on how the odd ritual was initiated:

The first one is, that in the 1760s there was a great religious dispute between two Buddhist temples and a Shinto shrine concerning a piece of land and its ownership status. Meetings and talks were held, however none of them led to a peaceful resolution. Because of that, the land that happened to be the Wakakusa Mountain was torched and burned to ashes.

The second theory is that the locals were fed up with the attacking wild boars and burned down the whole mountain to chase them away.

The first theory is more likely to be true. More than that – nowadays, the mountain is set ablaze annually to celebrate mutual respect and harmony.

Before noon, the locals and hundreds of thousands of visitors gather at the foot of the mountain and toss rice crackers in the air – announcing the stunning fireworks display to follow.

In the late afternoon, a huge procession led by monks and priests dressed in traditional costumes and holding paper lanterns winds its way to a bridge in the foot of the mountain, symbolizing the unity of faith and peaceful co-existing.

Then, a selected group of people light torches from a sacred fire, visit a few temples to get blessings and then... set the mountain alight. This is accompanied by lots of colourful fireworks. The fantastic and nonetheless terrifying blaze show goes on for a good hour before the eyes of the smitten spectators.

Of course, a whole fire department is stationed nearby to make sure that there are no casualties and that the fire burns within the alloted perimeter only.

The festival ends with a traditional Taiko drum concert and festive cheer.

This beautiful and green part of Japan, known for its serenity and harmony, where deer (the messengers of the gods) roam freely, celebrates a true pyromaniac's dream each year... What are the odds?! On top of that, the foot of the hill is a sacred forest (Kasugayama), forbidden for people to enter (for more than 1,000 years), however that forest never burns despite the annual festival.

Travel to: Japan (Nara). The event takes place in Mount Wakakusa.
Other holidays on this date: National Cornchip Day (USA), World Puzzle Day

30 January: Lantern Festival (Greece)

The Lantern Festival, or Fanarakia as it is locally known, was created in 1823. It is celebrated every year on January 30th. The legend has it that a nun who lived on the island had visions of Virgin Mary in her dreams for several months. Virgin Mary commanded her to find a holy icon, buried on the island many years ago. So, she started a search for the lost treasure along side the elders, as she was commanded. It took several months, until the night of January 30th when the precious artefact was discovered during excavations on the island. As the news spread across, locals gathered to witness the sacred find of the miraculous icon of Virgin Mary. As the evening fell, they lit lanterns to illuminate their way back to town in the dark night, which created a feeling of magic. Since that day in 1823, the villagers meet in the courtyard of the Church of Annunciation to honor the find and worship the icon.

Everyone carries a hand-made lantern made of wood and gelatine mounted on top of a tall pole, so it can be seen from afar. The lanterns are cut and carved in different shapes representing island history, biblical scenes, items and objects related to the locals such as boats and seashells. The celebration is marked by a huge street procession starting from the church and ending at the harbor. As this is an evening procession, hundreds of colorful lanterns and candles light the way and add a mysterious and deeply spiritual ambiance to the parade completed by the chanting of the people as they walk toward the shore. Lots of beautiful fireworks mark the end of the festivity.

Travel to: Greece (Tinos Island). The celebration is held in Chora City where The Church of Virgin Mary was built to house the miraculous icon. The icon, called Panagia Evangelistria, or Our Lady of Good Tidings – is allegedly made by the Apostle Saint Luke himself. There are many documented miracles that have taken place at the church – a Turk who was cured built a marble fountain in the yard of the holly place and an American Greek donated a silver orange tree which can be found at the right candle counter in the church (he was blind and promised to offer the first thing he sees – he was cured and the first thing he saw was an orange tree.)

Other holidays on this date: National Inane Answering Message Day, National Croissant Day (USA)

31 January: Up Helly Aa (Scotland)

The largest and craziest "fire" festival takes place on the last Tuesday in January and represents a tradition created in the 1880s to mark the end of the Yule season. For the whole history of its existence, the festival has been canceled just three times because of the death of Queen Victoria, the First and the Second World Wars. Up Helly Aa grew out of an old tar-barreling tradition when locals would set alight barrels full of tar and roll them down the streets. This ritual took place over the Christmas and New Year holidays in the past, but it was banned around the 1880s giving way to torch processions instead.

Up Helly Aa involves thousands of pseudo-Vikings and a replica of a Viking war vessel set on fire and burned to the ground.

Preparations for the festival begin months in advance and several thousand people take part in creating the costumes and building the warship. However, it is in strictest secrecy – particularly who the Jarl will be and what would he wear. Guizer Jarl, dressed to represent a character from the Nordic mythology (different character every year), is the main character and leader of the Viking squads. To be considered as a candidate for Jarl, one should be a member of the Up Helly Aa committee for 12 years.

At 7:30 pm sharp all torches are lit and a signal rocket marks the beginning of the celebration. The squads drag the Viking warship to a burning site - Guizer Jarl proudly standing at the helm of the doomed ship. Once the vessel is positioned at the "altar", the squads encircle it in slow motion. After another signal rocket is fired, Guizer Jarl abandons the ship and the Viking squads hurl their torches into it. While the galley burns, locals sing "The Norseman's Home" – a really sad Viking requiem. Once the warship is burned to the ground – it's time to party! Huge celebrations are organized in every big hall, barn and house and each squad group should visit every one of them during the night to perform a dance, act or a joke. Also, each Viking should dance with at least one lady (only men are allowed to take part in Up Helly Aa). The night ends around 8:30 am, and fortunately for the participants – the following day is an official holiday and the town looks completely abandoned with no people to be seen. However, in the evening – the party starts once again, this time everyone celebrating the "Guizer's Hop" – the second night of Up Helly Aa.

Travel to: Scotland (Shetland Islands). The event is held in the town of Lerwick – the main port of the Shetland Islands. During the summer months, there is a Up Helly Aa exhibition in the Galley Shed on St Sunniva Street in Lerwick which can be visited. In Autumn, the Shed is used by the carpenters to build a new warship.

Other holidays on this date: National Backward Day, Inspire Your Heart with Art Day (USA), Darkie Day (England)

... FEBRUARY

Carnival: It is possible that carnival derives from the Latin words carne and vale, that translate to "farewell to meat", in regard to the approaching fast. That could be the explanation why all festivities categorised as "carnival" take place before Lent, in the months of January, February, March and early April (depending on the Easter date).

01 February: International Hair Freezing Day (Canada)

The event, created in 2011, is held annually in February. The exact date is not fixed as the competition depends very much on weather conditions and is usually celebrated on the coldest day of the month. The unusual contest sees people dipping their hair in hot springs (with temperature around 42C) and freezing it in fantastic and peculiar shapes with the help of the ice-cold Canadian air. For ideal hairdo's the outside temperature should not exceed -20C and the contestants should have lots of patience to get the proper look. Participants with long hair usually lay it down on the sides of the pool to freeze in single, long strand and stick straight up. All wet hair easily freezes, so be ready to have a snow-queen look in a jiff, with eyelashes, brows, and beard all covered with snow crystals. Once the desired hairdo is achieved, the contestants take photos and send them to an official committee which decides who the winner is (the prize is cash + free SPA treatments). After the photo shoot, another quick dip in the hot water restores the hair to its original glory. Fun fact is that the competition was created by a former manager of the hot springs who didn't have a lot of hair himself!

The Hair Freezing competition is part of a 7-days Yukon Sourdough Rendezvous Festival, running for over 50 years and aims to promote the local culture and the winter tourism in the region. The festival features frozen turkey bowling, snowshoe Can-Can dancing, axe throwing, dog sledding, flour packing as well as pub crawls, tea socials, Queen of the Festival contest and many more. But, of course, the highlight is the Hair Freezing competition which is gaining more and more publicity. Started with just 10 participants in 2011, the event now attracts international interest and is viral on the social media websites.

Travel to: Canada (Whitehorse). The event takes place at the Takhini Hot Springs.

Other holidays on this date: National Freedom Day, Hula in The Coola Day (USA), Tilling Festival (Taiwan – Thao tribe))

02 February: Feast of Candelaria (Bolivia)

This is a three-day mixture of Christian and pagan celebrations honoring the Patron Saint of Bolivia – The Lady of Copacabana, also known as The Dark Virgin of the Lake. Festivities take place annually on February 2nd and turn the quiet fishermen village into a street fiesta. In line with the legend, in 1576 Inca fishermen got caught in a horrific storm in the lake. The Virgin Mary answered their prayers and saved them from drowning. To thank her and show their enormous gratitude, the men built a shrine to honor and praise the miracle that they had witnessed. They asked a local sculptor who had a vision of the Virgin Mary himself, to carve a sculpture of the saint. The vision was so vivid, that the artist decided to learn to carve stone (he wasn`t a sculptor at the time). Ever since that day, there have been many encounters of miracles related to the sculpture. As per historical facts, the crops of people who doubted the power and abilities of the statue dried out and died. The sculpture was never moved or taken outside, ever since it had been carved and placed inside the shrine. The locals believe that if they move it – another storm can hit them, so for any celebrations – they bring out a replica.

A highlight of the festival is the traditional "blessing of new vehicles" or the cha`lla ritual. Folks from around the country drive to the shrine in Copacabana, where a priest sprinkles holy water over the vehicles and the drivers and says prayers for a safe Christian drive. Then the drivers shower their cars with flower petals and then… comes the beer. Shaken vigorously, it is squirted all over the vehicles and the drivers. In a totally different part of the town, the indigenous Aymara people bring a toy car covered with brightly colored paper banners to be blessed by the local priest. If the gods approve – the people are going to be fortunate enough to purchase their dream car and drive it to the holy shrine to be blessed just as everybody else.

The festival features lots of parade-goers wearing traditional costumes, performing traditional music and dances, stalls with local food delicacies, free-flowing brew, as well as a traditional 'running of the bulls'. Exceptional to witness and experience are the dances of the Aymara people (archeologists say that they have occupied the Andes between 800 to 5 000 years, descending from the Incas). This is one of the most anticipated and sacred local celebrations.

Dessi Nikoltchev:

Travel to: Bolivia (the town of Copacabana on Lake Titikaka). Visit Basilica de Virgen de la Candelaria to see the miraculous statue. The bulls run along Yampupata Road. The festival is also celebrated in Peru, Venezuela, Chile and Uruguay.

Other holidays on this date: Candlemas, National Heavenly Hash Day (USA), Groundhog Day (world)

03 February: Bean Throwing Day (Japan)

Setsubun or Bean-Throwing Day is part of a Spring Festival celebrated every year on the first day of Spring in accordance with the lunar calendar (February 2nd, 3rd or 4th). It has its roots in the VIIIth C. "ritual to exorcise evil spirits on the last day of winter". Setsubun, which means "seasonal division", involves throwing beans around homes, shrines, and temples to frighten off evil spirits and bring in good luck. The ritual is known as Mamemaki and tipically uses soybeans. This is a word-game, because the Japanese word for "beans" resembles the word for "demon eyes", so throwing beans is much like destroying demons. The person to perform the ritual is the male who is born in the corresponding animal year, as an alternative – the head of the household. Some members of the family wear scary masks resembling evil spirits, so beans are thrown at them too, accompanied by the chant "Demons Out! Fortune In". For those who are really into the spirit of celebration – a certain number of beans, corresponding to the age +1 should be eaten for good luck.

At Buddhist temples and Shinto shrines, the Mamemaki ritual attracts many visitors and local celebrities. The beans used, are wrapped in foil. The priests use sweets and money as well. There are many public and sports events on that day throughout Japan, open-air Setsubun rituals are performed throughout the country. The celebration is much loved by children especially, as they can throw beans at random people.

Travel to: Japan (Kansai Region). Visit Osaka or Kyoto for best experience. Typical for the celebrations is the eho-maki sushi which is rolled in "lucky" direction. The uncut eho-maki roll is typical only for this province, but thanks to a vast marketing campaign – one can surely find it in Tokyo too and one of the biggest Setsubun rituals in Tokyo takes place at the Zojoji Temple.

Other holidays on this date: The Day the Music Died, Feed The Birds Day, National Carrot Cake Day, National Wear Red Day (USA), Mantoro Lantern Festival (Japan), Feast of St Blaise (Croatia)

04 February: Festival on the River (Mali)

The festival, created in 2014, is celebrated over four days in the beginning of February. The setting is on the banks of the attractive Niger River. Held in a small farming town, known as the first stop en route to Timbuktu, the festival has a major impact on the regional economy and attracts tens of thousands of people every year. A day of the festival is dedicated to cleaning the debris in the river and educating young people on the importance to keep the riverbanks clean.

On the several stages within the festival grounds, traditional acts mix with world music – local artists and music bands play their native instruments adding a modern twist to the sound – jazz with acoustic Malian instrumentalists, blues reggae etc. The event features pirogue boat races, dance concerts with costumed choreography, antelope-horn-playing, ancient Malian hunting rituals, art shows, contemporary performances and visual art exhibitions. Traditional local troupes of puppeteers engaged only on special occasions and rites of passage perform too, so this is part of the very heart of the Malian cultural heritage.

The featuring Quai des Arts is an annual fair for Arts and Crafts, and a marketplace for ethnic jewelry, Malian hand-woven scarves, wooden figurines, paintings and more.

The event aims to show the rich cultural heritage of the torn by rebels and extremists country and highlight the importance of tolerance and peace between all nations. There are many workshops and discussions on the Malian Empire history, culture, customs, literature and more, so anyone interested in ethnology can benefit from a free lesson from a local.

There is one act worth encountering – The Koredugaw – a typical Malian cult. People, dressed in colorful costumes, adorned with bird's beaks, plastic bottles, feathers, shells, rosary bead necklaces and regal headpieces, dance in a circle around the festival grounds and often on river banks. They carry wood-carved masks symbolizing different animals and various rituals for initiation.

The first evening is dedicated to a peace concert from the Culture Caravan for Peace – artists from festivals in exile (mainly due to security concerns) from around West Africa gather to perform for solidarity.

This event has a strong message for peace in Mali (especially in North Mali) and is one of the most exciting celebrations of tribal tradition and culture.

Travel to: Mali (Segou). While enjoying the festival program – try visiting some of the art and heritage symposiums organized in the mornings. Worth visiting is the National Museum of Mali in the capital Bamako, which is 2.5 hours drive from the festival site.

Other holidays on this date: Eat Ice cream for Breakfast Day, Thank a Mailman Day, National Homemade Soup Day, Two Rivers Renaissance Fair (USA), Day of the Armed Struggle (Angola)

05 February: Man`s World (Switzerland)

An annual event celebrating "all things men". It runs for three days in the beginning of February, with Man`s World hot-spots throughout the whole hosting city. The festival features motorbike shows, sport`s car test drive, cigar and whiskey lounges and tastings, flight simulators, displays of watches and weapons, mobility and technology gadgets and much more. There are lifestyle sessions and workshops, tailored suits and jewelry, Italian barbers and custom bikes, poker and blackjack... and in general – the show is a huge playground for men.

However, women are not forgotten - there are special lounges where they can get a free manicure and a fizzy drink!

Travel to: Switzerland (Zurich). The event is held in Zurich City, however usually in the Autumn Man`s World visits other cities in Switzerland and Germany.

Other holidays on this date: National Shower with a Friend Day, World Nutella Day (USA), Coffee Harvest Festival (Guatemala)

06 February: Barranquilla Carnival (Colombia)

Dating back to the XIX C., Barranquilla is one of the biggest carnivals in Colombia and the world, recognized by UNESCO as one of the Masterpieces of the Oral and Intangible Heritage of Humanity. The festivities start on the Saturday before Ash Wednesday and last four days. Initiated as a holiday for the slaves, nowadays the carnival is a celebration of the region and aims to show the local cultural diversity. It is a mix between the heritage and traditions of Colombia's ancient inhabitants, European colonialists, and African slaves – all of them played a great part in forming the Colombian people of today.

The festival starts with Battle of the Flowers – a six-hour long street procession with decorated floats parading along a colorful carpet of flowers. The procession itself is divided into themed sections representing the different ethnical groups along with their typical folklore music, dances, and costumes. A pre-elected Carnival Queen stands on the best-decorated float and throws flowers into the cheering crowd. She is an important character in the festivities as the Mayor of Baranquilla formally hands her the keys to the city for as long as the carnival lasts. Participating in the Carnival is a knowledge and tradition passed from generation to generation – it reminds the young of their roots and the culture of their ancestors.

The following days of the carnival are marked by a Great Parade during which the whole city turns into a dance floor. Orchestras, Caribbean and Latin bands play non-stop while the public enjoys Children`s Carnival (with small-size floats), Orchestra Festival (musicians compete in various genres), Gay Parade (officially introduced in the program in 2002), Great Fantasy Parade (a beautiful parade of costumed dancers who mix traditional dances such as cumbia and porro with international rhythms such as salsa, samba and reggaetón).

The 4th and last day of the carnival is marked by the formal "burial" of Joselito Carnaval – he is the "joy figure" which resuscitates on the first and dies on the last day of the festivities drunk, but content and ready to be revived the following year!

Barranquilla's Carnival slogan is: Those who live it are those who enjoy it (Quien lo vive, es quien lo goza).

Travel to: Colombia (Baranquilla). The opening event – The Battle of the Flowers, takes place on Via 40. Worth visiting is the Museo Romántico – the home of artifacts from past festivals.

Other holidays on this date: National Frozen Yogurt Day, Lame Duck Day (USA), Waitangi Day (New Zealand)

07 February: Carnival de Granville (France)

One of the oldest in the French History, this carnival has been celebrated for more than 140 years now. It takes place on the Friday preceding Shrove Tuesday and lasts four days. It was created back in the days when the main food supply in town was a cod fishery. As fishing boats sailed away, locals would throw a huge farewell feast with dances and music, that would last for few days.

The Carnival is included in the UNESCO List of World Heritage sites and in the Inventory of the Intangible Cultural Heritage of France.

The celebration starts with the Mayor formally handing out the keys to the city to a papier-mache figure – the Carnival King. Then a huge parade with decorated floats and marching bands takes place. The floats take a humorous look on current events, politics and celebrities and involve the work of thousands of 'carnivalists' who spend about six months to design and build the massive platforms. As the Carnival has a charity aspect, there is a special float - the Charity Chariot, that collects funds and goods to help the homeless and poor. On the festival days, social balls for different age groups are held round the city – Children's Ball, Teen Ball, Ball of the Always Young, Dad's Ball, Candy Ball and Mother's Ball. The last day of the carnival is marked by a huge

confetti battle on the main square (7 tons of confetti!!). One more thing takes place on that last day – the "Night of Intrigues". Participants (intriguers), completely disguised in costumes and wearingmasks, start rumours and tell jokes to friends or loved ones, or settle scores with impunity. The Carnival ends with formal sentencing and burning of the Carnival King.

Travel to: France (Granville). Make sure to visit Cours Jonville – the main square in the city where the big confetti battle takes place.

Dessi Nikoltchev:

Other holidays on this date: National Fettuccine Alfredo Day, National Periodic Table Day, National Send a Card to a Friend Day (USA)

08 February: Sapporo Snow Festival (Japan)

This is one of the largest and coolest (literally) winter events in the land of the rising sun. The festival which runs for 7 days in February, was created in 1950 when six local high school students carved six snow statues which attracted many admirers. Members of the City Council were very impressed and decided to initiate an annual snow-carving festival (lasting 1 day only). Over time, the military got involved in bringing trucks with ice and snow from surrounding regions and the event gained more and more popularity. The Winter Olympic Games in 1972 helped for its international recognition too. Now the world-known festival (attracting more than two million visitors every year) showcases ice and snow creations, making the area a winter wonderland. A different theme is set each year (usually referring to an event or a person of interest from the past year) which makes the event even more spectacular and exciting. Accompanying concerts and bands usually use the snow sculptures as a stage. Visitors also enjoy ice-maze, fairground, snow rafting, ice slides and many stalls with local merchandise, draught beer from the local brewery, open-air barbecues and typical fresh food of the Hokkaido region. There is also a beauty contest and crowning of the Ice Queen.

All state-of-the-art snow sculptures representing castles, cartoon characters, sci-fi objects and fairy tale animals are beautifully lit until 22:00h-23:00h every day. Some of them measure the impressive 25m in width and 15m in height.

Important note from the organizers is that flying drones over the festival grounds is strictly prohibited!

Travel to: Japan (Hokkaido Island). The event takes place in at Odori Park, Sapporo City, Susukino (the red-light district) and the Sapporo Community Dome. For a great eagle-view of the ice sculptures – go up the top of the Sapporo TV Tower located in Odori Park (there is a fee).

Other holidays on this date: Boy Scout Day, Kite Flying Day (USA), Castrovillari Carnival (Italy)

09 February: Sausage Tossing (Switzerland)

The bizarre festival, locally known as Eis-Zwei-Geissebei, combines a century-old tradition with the need of Swiss people to enjoy themselves and just have a good time. This "ceremony" is observed annually on Shrove Tuesday exactly at 3:15 pm. Kids and adults gather in front of the City Hall of a small town near Lake Zürich. The Mayor would open the windows and ask: "Are all my boys here?". The kids would answer "One, Two, Goat leg!" and then he would start tossing out sausages, bread and pastries. The festivals origin goes back to the siege and destruction of the city in 1350 by Rudolf Brun, the first independent mayor of the city of Zürich (famous for a few things: 1/. Reserving the title of Mayor for himself for life; 2/. Defeating his political opponents who had retreated to the city of Rapperswil and destroying the city; 3/. Leading the Zürich Guild`s Revolution and changing the constitution which led to appointing an equal number of Guild leaders to the number of Knight members in the City Council). During his "reign", compassionate citizens would serve food to poor and hungry children through the windows of their houses.

Travel to: Switzerland (Canton of St Gallen). The event is held in the city of Rapperswil.
Other holidays on this date: Thaipoosam Cavadee (Mauritius), National Bagel Day, National Pizza Day (USA), Sauti za Busara (Zanzibar)

10 February: Thaipusam (Malaysia)

Thaipusam is a Hindu festival, celebrated on a full moon in the tenth month of the Hindu calendar (January/February). Many countries with Hindu population celebrate it and in some of them, it is a national holiday. The festival can stretch to 3-4 days of celebrations depending on the region. The origin goes back to the battle between "demons" and "divine beings". When the latter were defeated several times, they asked Shiva to give them a true leader who could lead them to win the battle once and for all. Shiva rewarded them with a brave warrior – Lord Murugan, under whose leadership they defeated the demons. Thaipusam was created in his honor. Today the festival, brought to Malaysia in the 1800s, attracts more than a million devotees and hundreds of thousands of visitors.

The celebrations begin with a chariot parade – a silver plated chariot carrying the statue of Lord Murugan makes its way along the city streets to sacred caves where a ritual takes place. People approach the chariot with offerings, asking for blessings and throwing flowers.

People express their devotion in diverse ways – some just attend the parade, others hold jars of milk over their head, but the most devoted subject themselves to masochistic experiences in order to show their absolute and strong faith. Although intended to celebrate the life and heroism of Lord Murugan, this is an excruciating festival to watch.

Preceded by hypnotic dance and drum beats some people insert spears through their tongue and/or cheeks, walk in shoes full of nails, carry frameworks attached to their bare backs with giant hooks etc. The skin piercing represents a few things: a spear through the tongue means that the person prefers to focus on the prayer than talk; the hooks through the back represent that the god/goddess will not allow this person to suffer any pain and in general, everything represents the transience of the body. Once the devotees reach the sacred caves, they take off the hooks and spears and pray to the gods.

Crucial part of this ritual is the preparation – strict vegetarian diet and prayer so that one can get into trance-like state of mind and not feel pain.

Travel to: Malaysia (Kuala Lumpur). There is a holy shrine in the Batu Caves just outside of Kuala Lumpur. A huge effigy of Lord Murugan is carried and kept in the caves for the duration of the Thaipusam. The festival is celebrated in India, Singapore, Fiji, Sri Lanka, Mauritius, Myanmar, Trinidad and Tobago, Guyana, Suriname, Jamaica and parts of the Caribbean.

Other holidays on this date: National Cream Cheese Brownie Day, National Home Warranty Day (USA), Royal Hobart Regatta (Australia, Tasmania)

11 February: Lantern Festival - Yuan Xiao (China)

This is a beautiful ancient festival which can be traced 2,000 years back. At that point, in the Eastern Han Dynasty, the Emperor discovered that monks lit lanterns in the temples to show respect to Buddha. He decided to do the same, that actually started the tradition.

The festival falls on a full moon which marks the return of Spring and symbolizes family reunion. It is celebrated annually on the 15th day of the first Chinese lunar month (usually falls in February). This is a very important event as it ends the New Year celebrations – hence after the Lantern Festival, all decorations are taken off and Chinese New Year taboos are no longer to be observed. The Chinese believe that everything one does in the beginning of the year affects the rest of it and that is why the taboos are important part of the celebration. Some of them are: no sweeping, no crying, no unlucky words, no black and white clothes, no hospital visits, no baby crying (it is believed to bring bad luck to the household, so the parents do everything possible to prevent that from happening) and more.

As the very name of the festival suggests – the main activity is lighting lanterns of various shapes and sizes but they should all represent objects from the Chinese culture – traditional images such as fruits, flowers, birds, buildings. Most of them are painted in red because it symbolizes good fortune. The lanterns are everywhere – in households, shops, parks, on the streets. It is common for kids to carry small lanterns and walk the streets. Guessing (solving) lantern riddles is one of the most popular activities during the Festival. Lantern owners write riddles on paper notes and pin them to the colorful lanterns. Folks try and guess the riddles – and if they do, they get a little gift as a prize.

Another traditional feature of the festivities is the Dragon Dance. The dragon is a symbol of China and very important character to the locals. The dance can be traced back to the Han Dynasty (206BC-220AD) when it was performed as a worship dance to the ancestors and a prayer for rain. It was centuries later when it was popularised as a ceremonial dance.

The Lion Dance (traditional folk dance symbolizing strength and chasing away all things evil), fireworks, appreciating the full moon, walking on stilts and eating tangyuan (traditional sweet stuffed dumplings) are also typical features of the festival. As China is a vast country, the celebrations vary in the different regions.

Lighting lanterns for the locals is a way to express best wishes to their families and pray for a good year ahead.

Travel to: China. The biggest Lantern Festival is Qinhuai at Confucius Temple in Nanjing. Other worth visiting lantern festivals take place in Beijing, Shanghai (at Datuan Peach Garden) and Xiamen in Xiamen City (at the Yuanboyuan Garden). Great place to visit is the city of Chengdu in the Sichuan Province as a huge lantern fair takes place at the Culture Park.

The festival is also celebrated in Malaysia, Hong Kong and Taiwan where it is the equivalent to St Valentine's Day (in the past, people were matched for marriage during the festival and the tradition is still kept in some regions)

Other holidays on this date: National Don't Cry Over Spilled Milk Day, National Inventor's Day, National Make a Friend Day, National White Shirt Day (USA), Bloco de Latinha (Brazil)

12 February: Rajasthan Desert Festival (India)

Krishna predicted that a descendant of the Yadav clan will build a kingdom on the golden sand hills of Jaisalmer. In 1196, the prophecy came true. It was a time of grand celebrations.

This is one of the most anticipated events, held in the heart of the desert over three days in the end of January/beginning of February.

The spectacular music party set within the magnificent yellow sandstone architecture which serves as a stage for the performers attracts visitors from around the world. In addition to the exotic surrounding – there are turban tying contests, camel races, camel polo, local nomad performances, puppeteers, jugglers, traditional artists and the famous best mustache contest. The festival aims to show the cultural heritage of the Rajasthani people.

The start of the festival is marked by a procession from Jaisalmer Fort to Shahid Poonam Singh Stadium. All participants wear native costumes, representing the rich culture of the region, and sing traditional songs. The parade is led by Gair dancers dressed in long pleated tunic-skirts, usually carrying swords or sticks. This traditional dance is performed by the indigenous Rajasthani people of the Bhil community. Another traditional feature is the Fire Dance – it ends with the dancers stepping and dancing on smoldering embers.

In the final days of the festival, numerous bands perform on each of the four stages (open-air and in marquees), there is open-air movie screening (in the midst of the gorgeous sand dunes), nomad market, various art installations, dances under the moonlit sky, music jams by campfires and stalls with typical Rajasthani cuisine. The official transport within the festival grounds is camel riding and camel carts. For a truly unique experience – the organizers set up a nomad camp with tents available for accommodation.

Travel to: Northern India (Rajasthan). The venue is by the Sam Sand dunes around the city of Jaisalmer - a former medieval trading center in the heart of the Thar Desert. *Other holidays on this date:* Abraham Lincolns` Birthday (USA), International Darwin Day, Carnival (Trinidad and Tobago)

13 February: Mardy Gras (USA)

Mardi Gras, "Fat Tuesday", or "Shrove Tuesday" is the last day of the Carnival season and always falls on the day before Ash Wednesday, the first day of Lent. New Orleans is considered the hometown of the festival since in 1699, the French explorer Jean Baptiste Le Moyne set up a camp about 60km from what today is the city of New Orleans. He named it Pointe du Mardi Gras as he realized the date was the Tuesday of Mardi Gras. In the following years, European settlers brought their colorful masquerade costumes and began organizing private balls. The holiday gained lots of publicity and kicked off the first street parades in the late 1830s. By the mid-1840s, the party had gone so wild, that some relatively sober locals demanded from the authorities to ban all public celebrations of Mardi Gras. This, however, never happened. Instead, a Mardi Gras secret society was initiated. For many years, it organized secret high-society balls sending only 3 000 invitations, turning it into the event of the year. Because of the success of the newly-formed secret organization, many more followed suit – each one of them staging its own street parades, masquerade balls, public celebrations etc. These social clubs still exist and are known as "krewes".

Mardi Gras, like Christmas, is a whole season - not just one day – it starts on Epiphany (Jan 6th) and is celebrated until Ash Wednesday (in many countries this time of the year is Carnival season).

Preparations for Mardi Gras include serious stocking up on bead necklaces!

This is a holiday of colours, costumes, music, dances, street parades, and beads! Party-goers who dance on parading floats throw beads into the crowd as they pass by. This is the most exciting part as one could end up with dozens of bead necklaces to take home. The traditional bead colors are purple (symbolizing justice), green (symbolizing faith) and gold (representing power). In fact, these are the Romanoff family colors – the Grand Duke of Russia happened to arrive in New Orleans on Mardi Gras in 1872. A parade named "Rex" (Latin for King), held in his honor, adopted the three colors as official colors for the celebration.

Throws can include also cups, homemade trinkets, toys and more!

During Mardi Gras only, a special sweet brioche-dough cake is sold – every King Cake contains a bean or a small plastic baby figure – whoever finds the baby has to buy the next round of drinks or host a party!

Fun fact is that in the late 1800s the Parisian papier-mache' artist Georges Soulie' was commissioned to create all of the Carnival's floats and outfits for 40 years!

In 1875, the Mayor of Louisiana signed the Mardi Gras Act, making the holiday official.

Travel to: USA (Louisiana). The best celebrations are in New Orleans. All "krewes" have different parade routes, however most of them are focused in the French Quarter and Uptown New Orleans.

Other holidays on this date: Get a Different Name Day, Clean out Your Computer Day, National Tortellini Day (USA), Nice Carnival (France), La Sartiglia Carnival (Italy)

14 February: World Sacred Spirit Festival (India)

This is a fairly new festival, created in the late 1990s and celebrated for three days (formerly known as the World Sufi Festival). It gives stage to performers from Asia and Africa who take the audience on a spiritual and musical journey. The extraordinary sacred and historical event is aimed towards the conservation of the Sufi culture and traditions (Sufi regards to "the one who wears wool", in relation to the typical clothing of the devotees). The core of the Sufism, that is usually described as Islam Mysticism, is the transmission of divine light from the teacher's heart to the heart of the student in any aspect. And it is believed that this bond lasts forever. Sufis deny the material world and welcome the genuine thirst for spiritual knowledge and solemn worship, they embrace the divine presence into life.

The festival started as a celebration marking the UNESCO World Heritage Award for conservation, which was held at in Nagaur – a IVth C. fort of historical importance, named "the Fort of the Hooded Cobra". This is the ultimate setting for such festival with its majestic presence and serene atmosphere being used as a center stage. Mesmerizing palace houses, numerous fountains and pristine gardens surround the performing artists. Lit by flickering oil lamps and thousands of sparkling candles, this magical travel-through-time experience carries one to the roots of a century-old tradition linked to the ancient travels of the spirit who brought a sense of inspiration and meaning to the people of the old world.

The Festival features music and recitals, mystical poetry, dervish whirling dances (a form of physically active meditation) and spiritual stories. This is an event uniting people of different beliefs and cultural background, to be better human beings and to celebrate the power and beauty of the Sufi spirit.

Travel to: Northern India (Rajasthan). The venue is split between the Ahhichatragarh Fort in the city of Nagaur and Mehrangarh fort in the neighboring city of Jodhpur.

Other holidays on this date: National Organ Donor Day, St Valentine's, Safer Internet Day (USA), Ferris Wheel Day (world), Sardinia Carnevale (Italy)

15 February: The Igloo Festival (Japan)

The two-day festival takes place in February, in a region known for its harsh winters and snow piling up to 2 meters. According to one of the many legends, the 400-year-old festival was created to get the attention of the god of water at times when the city suffered from lack of drinking water.

Hundreds of full-sized and miniature igloos (called "Kamakura") are carved out of ice blocks – all of them lit by candle lights, producing a peaceful, beautiful spectacle against the darkness of the night sky. Inside them, an altar is set up to honor the god of water. Sake and rice cakes are given as offerings to the deities. A century-old tradition for the local kids is to invite passers-by inside the igloos offering them to take a seat on fluffy cushions for a chat and rice cake treat (they grill the rice cakes over a snow-built BBQ in the igloos). It is left to the kids' judgment who gets a shot of sake or amazake (the local rice drink) together with the rice cake. To keep warm, the hosts wear traditional straw cape, called "mino" and traditional winter coat with thick cotton padding. In return for the pleasant time spent in the igloo, visitors give offerings to the god of water in each Kamakura.

Travel to: Japan (Yokote City). Everyone can have a hands-on experience in building kamakuras at Komyoji Park during the open building sessions. The festival spreads from Yokote Station to Yokote Castle along the frozen riverbank. The Castle is open from 10:00h to 22:00h throughout the festival days and offers a stunning observation deck. The Kamakurakan Hall in town preserves a couple of igloos all year round in a small -10-degree Celsius room.

Other holidays on this date: National Gumdrop Day, Singles Awareness Day (USA), Islander Day (Canada, Prince Edward Island), Green Monday (Cyprus), Carnival Satriano (Italy)

16 February: Golden Mask Festival (Russia)

Established in 1994, this is the biggest festival for Performing Arts in Russia, presenting the most significant acts and plays from around the country. Held over two months in Spring, it turns Moscow into a fascinating art stage! All genres of the theatre art are included in the program - from drama to modern dance and puppet theatre. Two jury panels (one for drama and one for musical theatre) judge hundreds of contesting acts in more than 30 categories, to choose the winners. The event is supported by the Moscow Government and the Ministry of Culture of the Russian Federation and is considered one of the most important in cultural aspect. The festival receives the widest possible media coverage and headlines in newspapers, on TV and radio programs. The Golden Mask is accompanied by series of other art events, like: New Drama Festival of Contemporary Plays, Russian Case program (addressed to the international experts and visitors, providing information about modern Russian theatre), Performing arts market, art workshops, tours of Bolshoi, Mariinsky, Alexandrinsky and Mali Drama theatres, street performances and more. This is a fantastic opportunity for young people trying to make it in the performing arts, because many international producers show up to scout for new talents.

Travel to: Russia (Moscow). The venue is Stanislavsky and Nemirovich-Danchenko Musical theatres in Moscow, however there are performances in locations all over the city.

Other holidays on this date: National Almond Day (USA), Birthday of Kim-Jong II (North Korea), Carnival (Bolivia)

17 February: Seollal (South Korea)

Seollal is the Korean New Year. It corresponds to 12 animals – the legend has it that Buddha invited animals from around the world, but only 12 showed up, so he named the 12 consecutive years in their honor and in the order, they had arrived. The holiday starts on the first day of the Korean lunar calendar and lasts for three days. Seollal is a widely-celebrated and much-loved holiday. It is a time to re-connect with family members and honor the spirits of the ancestors. This is one of the few times in the year when families get together to catch up. It is important and considered polite for all members to join the celebration. Most people travel a lot to reunite with their loved ones – tickets sell out months before and prices for travel go up.

Locals start to prepare for the holiday a week in advance – they cook and buy small gifts for their relatives – usually gift cards, cash, cosmetics and dried fruit or seafood.

Dessi Nikoltchev:

The New Year day begins with the Charye ancestral rite – the whole family, dressed in festive "hanbok" clothing, gathers around a table piled with traditional food, to pay respect to the ancestors. Koreans believe that if the food isn't appealing – the spirits of the ancestors will get upset, that is why everything is prepared with care. Typical on Seollal is tteokguk – soup made with sliced rice cakes, beef, egg, vegetables and jeon – a savory pancake. After the festive meal, kids bow to the elders to pay respect receiving in return words of wisdom, blessings for a happy year and money. The rest of the day is spent in playing traditional games, flying kites, telling stories or playing yutnori – board game with wooden sticks. In some parts of the country, people burn a "moon house" made of wood, to chase away the evil spirits.

This is a great time to see the locals out and about in the many parks and palaces, wearing their spectacular bell-shaped hanboks and to catch a glimpse of various Korean traditions.

Travel to: South Korea (Seoul). Some places worth visiting are Jongmyo Shrine, Amsa-Dong Prehistoric Settlement Site and Dongdaemun Design Plaza. The tourist spots offer different activities to celebrate the occasion, such as performing sebae (traditional New Year bow), eating tteokguk (rice cake soup) and playing traditional folk games.

Other holidays on this date: National Cabbage Day, National Caregivers Day (USA), Menton Lemon Festival (France)

18 February: The Naked Man Festival (Japan)

Hadaka Matsuri has been celebrated during one of the coldest nights of the year for more than 500 years. It is considered "one of the most eccentric festivals in the country" involving naked men who run round in a temple and chase lucky sticks called shingi. The origin of the celebration dates back in times when worshippers competed to receive lucky paper talismans from the priests. Hadaka Matsuri is annually celebrated on the third Saturday in February.

Thousands of participants strip down to wearing just a loincloth and test their manhood and bravery to secure luck in the upcoming year.

First, they perform a purifying ritual. They immense in the nearest river or lake (or just get buckets of icy-cold water), then run in circles and try to catch the sacred lucky sticks thrown by the priests (the lights go out when the sticks are thrown). The one to catch a stick is promised a year of happiness. There is, however, one large stick filled with incense – whoever catches it is the big winner. Catching a stick is a risky business, because the participants smash into each other, and also – one has to make his way out through the front gates without having his stick stolen which can be tricky just as much. Usually, the winners are members of … judo clubs!

During the festival, a street market with numerous food stalls offers local food, drinks, and merchandise.

Travel to: Japan (Okayama). The festival is held at the 1,200-year old Saidaiji Temple.
Other holidays on this date: World Religious Day, National Battery Day, National Drink Wine Day (USA), Verona Carnival (Italy)

19 February: Iroquois Maple Ceremony (USA – Native American)

The Maple Ceremony is a century-old tradition, observed nowadays mainly by the Seneca people (part of the Iroquois League, also known as Six Nations).

As Native Americans live in harmony with the nature, they divide the seasons in accordance with the harvest of fruit, trees and roots. The beginning of the Spring is associated with the Maple Tree harvest – hence the Maple Tree ceremony. This is a ritual praising the Maple tree and its sugary syrup. In the past, natives used funnels to extract the syrup from Maple trees and boil it into sugar syrup used for cooking (usually to flavor soups), for candy canes and mostly – for medicine.

As in all traditions native to the Iroquois, this one is no different – prayers and chants are said to thank the gods and secure luck and well-being. The ceremony is held in mid to late February or the beginning of March "after the first thunder which awakes the trees and lasts for one day". The Seneca people gather around Maple trees, set a small fire and throw tobacco leaves in it chanting prayers to The Creator to keep them safe while they harvest the trees. Tobacco leaves are an integral part of the Iroquois culture and are involved in every ritual. They believe that the smoke from burning tobacco carries their prayers and reaches the Great Spirit (The Creator). During the ritual, they perform The Feather Dance - a sacred ritual to thank and honor The Creator.

When the harvest is over, the Seneca gather again to drink maple sap (syrup) - a medicine to prevent diseases and to bring good fortune.

Travel to: USA (Great Lakes, New York, Oklahoma), Canada (Ontario) are the places where the people of the Six Nations live today. There are many museums, gathering places and administrative buildings that offer information on where the different ceremonies are held. The Iroquois Confederation (Haudenosaunee) is based in Ontario, Canada.
Other holidays on this date: National Lash Day (USA)

20 February: Desert Festival (India)

An old celebration turned into a three-day festival in February (the Hindu month of Magh, three days prior to the full moon).

The beginning of the celebration is marked by a morning procession with locals singing and dancing, all dressed in traditional bright costumes. Their songs tell the stories about the tragedies and accomplishments of the desert.

The festive program continues with breathtaking fire dances, acrobatic acts performed by nomads, folk music, recitals, magnetic snake charmers, puppeteers, parachuting, turban-tying, camel tattoo, Mr. Desert competition. Delicious traditional food and lots of stalls selling local merchandise complement the desert safari and available overnight camping.

Travel to: Northern India (Rajasthan – known as "the Land of Kings"). The event takes place in the sand dunes near the city of Jaisalmer.

Other holidays on this date: Cherry Pie Day, Love Your Pet Day (USA), Rorosmartnan (Norway)

21 February: Carnival (Greece)

The small hosting island which is a major place of Orthodox worship in Greece turns into a magical place during the Carnival – the days offer a plethora of parades while the cool nights plenty of entertainment, music, dances and wine. The 3-day Apokries Carnival takes place annually, 40 days before Lent.

Each village has its own theme for the carnival, but celebrations are held everywhere. There is a common parade, however: A lucky (or not that much) winner is chosen amongst the crowd to be mounted up on a ladder and disguised with greens and ribbons so nobody would recognize him. He is carried around the village, followed by a crowd that sings mocking songs and holds canes decorated with artichoke leaves and ribbons. The four men carrying the "Karnavas" (that is the poor man on the ladder) visit random houses and knock on doors. They are invited inside for a drink with the hosts, however without revealing who the "Karnavas" is. The carnival goes on for three days, during which participants visit each house and entertain everybody. The famous Raki (drink) is produced in the village of Falatados, so during the carnival, it flows abundantly. There is also free food and local musicians never stop playing on their violins and guitars. In the village of Agapi, locals celebrate the custom of "Makaronas" – that is carrying a straw effigy throughout the village streets only to burn it in the end. Then they all gather in the local church to eat... spaghetti!

Travel to: Greece (Tinos Island). Have a coffee at the local café in Triantaros, where traditional musicians sing songs known as "The Alphabet of Love" (usually funny lyrics).

Other holidays on this date: National Sticky Bun Day (USA)

22 February: Magha Puja (Thailand)

The holiday is observed on a full moon in the third lunar month (February/March). This is a 2500-year-old sacred Buddhist celebration that became an official holiday in Thailand in 1957. It commemorates the day when 1,250 monks had gathered to be ordained by Buddha who was staying in a monastery in Northern India. He taught the monks three principles (the main teachings of Buddhism): to cease from all evil, to do what is good and to cleanse one's mind. On Magha Puja, no sins should be committed, and everyone should be at peace and do only honorable deeds. This holiday is a spiritual observation and the Thai gather at temples to join the Buddhist monks in a candlelight procession that goes around the temple three times, holding flowers and incense sticks. The gathering is called "wian thian", which translates to "circling around with a candle". This is a day for meditation and spirit purification. The people give offerings of food, clothes, money and different services to honor the monks, practice meditation and stay in a temple for a number of days wearing white robes. However, the food for the offerings should be home-cooked and given only to the monks. During the celebration, the locals observe the Five Precepts: not to harm living things, not to steal, not to lie, to abstain from sexual immorality and to abstain from all intoxicants. True devotees would also abstain from eating after midday, using a high bed and soft chair, wearing perfume and accessories.

On that day, the King invites thirty monks for breakfast. They read aloud and together the Buddha`s sermon from 2,500 years ago. Then he lights 1,250 candles – equal to the number of monks who attended Buddha`s sermon all those years ago. The whole ritual is aired on TV.

Travel to: Thailand (Bangkok). The Golden Mount and the Marble Temple are great places to observe the celebration. Worth visiting is the Wat Phra Dhammakaya temple in Pathum Thani province as it is regarded as Thailand's richest Buddhist temple. One can also be part of the night prayers of the monks in front of lit candles.

Other holidays on this date: Be Humble Day, Walking the Dog Day, Margarita Day (USA) International World Thinking Day

23 February: Naked Festival (Japan)

The 2-day Naked Festival or Kokusekiji Sominsai is held in February for more than 1000 years. It has its roots in an ancient celebration for health and good fortune.

In the coldest of the months, amidst heaps of snow, men strip down to wearing just a thin loincloth (fundoshi), push, shove and wrestle with each other to get to a sachet bag with the word "Sominsai" on it. The one to get it will have good fortune in the year ahead. There is a strict diet for those who consider participating in the ritual – meat, fish, eggs or garlic are not allowed for a week before the festival. The challenge tests men against series of daring rituals. It starts around midnight and lasts until past dawn.

Just before the battle for the sachet, all men bathe in ice-cold water – they dunk in a river, pool, or are being poured over with freezing water buckets. Afterwards, they climb up a wooden platform built for the occasion (3-4 meters high), with a bonfire burning steadily beneath it. This is the time for chanting and prayers to the gods for health and luck. They hold lit lanterns and try not to slip down the piled logs whilst yelling from the top of their lungs to scare off the evil. The event takes place outside the temple and the only light comes from the swinging lanterns. To show how strong their faith is, the participants continue chanting even when they choke on the smoke of the burning fire. After a few hours spent on the platform, they run inside the temple, just to climb up on another platform and remain there for another few hours, repeating the chants and yelling to chase away the evil spirits. After this, the remaining ones try to catch the lucky bag – the tricky part being that whoever gets to it first, needs to take it and go out of the temple to a designated spot without being tripped over, or having the sachet "stolen" by another participant.

All this takes place in temperatures of around -7C and stinging wind. The festival deserves to be in the top three most bizarre festivals of Japan!

Travel to: Japan (Oshu). The event is held at the Kokusekiji Temple. It was built in 729 and is the first Shugendo Temple in Japan. Shugendo is a Buddhist sect that blends mountain worship, mysticism, shamanistic beliefs and the Chinese Yin-Yang mysticism in the hope of achieving magical powers.

Other holidays on this date: Tennis Day, Banana Bread Day, National Toast Day, National Chili Day (USA)

24 February: International Eelpout Festival (USA)

The 3-day Festival, created in 1980, is organized every year in February. This fishing contest draws tens of thousands of people in pursuit of the ugliest bottom-dwelling fish ever - the eelpout. The event is listed as one of the top "15 Weird Midwestern Festivals You Never Knew Existed". An interesting bit is that most of the main sponsors are… liquor producing companies! There are certain rules that should be observed by all participants:

1. All fish should come from Leech Lake and participants should agree if a DNA sample from the fish is requested for a test.
2. All fish should be caught by hook and line.
3. All fish should be weighed-in by the judges dead or alive. Any frozen fish is disqualified.

Participants are responsible to dig their own ice-fishing holes and build a fishing shelter above it (there is an award for most impressive shelter too!).

Featuring events are the frigid Polar Plunge, a black-tie dinner, an eelpout beer pong tournament and races, and family-friendly activities and games. One can even kiss an eelpout for good luck! In the evening – live music and dances are organized in two marquees.

Travel to: USA (Minnesota). The event is held in the small town of Walker with population of just over 1,000 people, however attracting thousands during the festival days.

Other holidays on this date: Tortilla Chip Day (USA), Dragobete (Romania)

25 February: Battle of the Oranges (Italy)

The mother of food fights in Italy! There are many theories on how the festival started, however most likely it was in the XIIth C that an evil Marquis - the city's tyrant (allegedly from the Ranieri Family) tried to rape a young woman just before her wedding (the so-called "lord's right"), but she killed him in self defense. When the rumor of the tyrant's intentions spread out, locals burnt the palace down. A festival was created to commemorate the brave girl and is celebrated every year over three days in February. People split into nine squads and recreate the revolt against the tyrant with a fruity twist – instead of using weapons, they throw oranges at each other. A young girl is chosen to play the part of Violetta and her role is to throw yellow flowers and candies to her admirers. Some of the teams represent the local people of the XIIth C. and others - the tyrant's soldiers (they ride in carts/chariots and are dressed as knights). The oranges represent the stones and weapons which were used in the past.

The festival ends with a silent march and a funeral. Traditionally, the "General" shouts: "I'll see you again on Thursday at one o'clock" – referring to the Thursday of the following year when the next Carnival will take place.

It is quite a mystery why exactly oranges are being used, since they don't even grow in the area, but need to be imported from Sicily!!! More than 200 tons of them are used in the battle!

The event is open to viewers but is not a free-for-all to take part. The rule is that one should be a member of a mercenary group to represent the ruler's soldiers for example. The unofficial rule is that – it is such a mess that no one would notice if you throw a couple of oranges at someone.

There also is a Thanksgiving parade in honor of Violetta and her bravery and awards for best performing teams. Local food and mulled wine accompany the celebrations at all times.

Travel to: Italy (Ivrea). There are special spots for visitors who don't want to get involved in the orange battle – there are also safety nets around many buildings. To be on the safe side- one can purchase one of the special red hats that signifies support to the revolutionaries (nobody aims at them).

Other holidays on this date: National Clam Chowder Day, National Chocolate Covered Nut Day, Open That Bottle Night, Pistol Patent Day (USA), Casanova Grand Ball (Italy), Tschäggättä Carnival (Switzerland)

26 February: Drinking Live Fish (Belgium)

Ok – this is a weird festival as it involves the consumption of fish that is very much alive! And soaked in red wine. This event is part of the KRAKELINGEN festival (on the last Sunday of February), which commemorates an unsuccessful siege of the city. The festival-goers consume small grey fish (Grondeling) and throw bread rolls at each other. Activists have tried, and tried, to ban the ritual or at least to substitute the fish with marzipan, but with no success whatsoever. The best they have done so far is to limit the people permitted to eat the fish to two dozen.

There is a theory that the history of the festival goes centuries back and is related to the ancient belief that swallowing live things was a revitalizing spring custom.

And the bread rolls represent the medieval siege when people had been throwing food at the town walls to show that they had unlimited supplies and wouldn't surrender.

Travel to: Belgium (Geraardsbergen). Worth visiting is another main attraction in the city – a fountain called "Mannekin Pis" – apparently this is the oldest fountain in Belgium of a naked peeing boy...

Other holidays on this date: Carnival Day, National Pistachio Day, Oscar Night, Tell a Fairy Tale Day (USA), Carnival de Oruro (Bolivia), Carnival (Denmark)

27 February: Rio Carnival (Brazil)

Not much to add about this one as it is THE best-known festival in the world. It was established in 1723 when Portugal immigrants from the nearby islands introduced the "carnival" to Brazil (at that time the festivities were smaller, quieter and focused on the accompanying food and drinks). However, in the 1800s, when the Brazilian Emperor decided to join in with his aristocrats – the festival really picked up. For years later, the event was a platform to expressing the ironic public opinion on military censorship. It was years later when the carnival started to shape up as the grand event it is today.

The word "carnival" usually pops an association with Rio. Local Samba Schools - nearby rivals, parade on the streets dancing on floats, as throngs of folks line the route, singing, dancing, drinking, cheering, and generally having the time of their lives. The event welcomes millions of visitors every year and all other carnivals are inevitably compared to the lush exotic of the Rio Carnival.

The 5-day event of non-stop dancing is held 40 days before Lent. The celebration is very important to the locals, because it shows their rich cultural heritage and rhythm of life. Months of preparation and thousands of people and dance schools are involved. The Carnival starts with crowning of King Momo who is presented with the keys to the city – a silver and a gold one – from the Mayor of Rio himself. And the fun begins! People sing and dance on the streets, day and night, until the culmination of the festival, that is marked by the Samba Parade – a dance-off involving the local samba schools which represent different favelas (neighbourhoods) of the city. Samba is a traditional Rio dance, invented in the past by the poor Afro-Brazilians (the word samba derives from the Angolan "semba" – a ritual music played to invoke the sacred spirits of the ancestors). Each samba school has to compose the music, write the lyrics, make the colorful costumes adorned with gems and feather headpieces, and design its own float for the dancers to perform on. The float procession is divided into 4 or 5 parts – first to go are dancers who represent the samba school (they "dance a short story" to get the people in the right mood), then the theme is set by the second float of dancers. The last float is the school's brass orchestra. The Samba Schools represent the different favelas or neighborhoods.

Every street band and independent brass orchestra have an allocated area to perform - for the most well-known bands, the streets are usually closed for traffic. For instance, the Carmelitas – allegedly created by nuns, now parade in the hills of Santa Teresa.

Drag queen parade and children's parade are also on the Carnival program. The end is marked by a grand ceremony awarding the best Samba schools.

Travel to: Brazil (Rio de Janeiro). The Samba Parade is held at the Sambadrome Marques de Sapucai (purposely built for the parade in 1984) while fancy balls are organized in the Copacabana Palace and on the beach. There are numerous street festivals throughout the city over the carnival days (the biggest are on Cinelandia Square).

Other holidays on this date: The Oscar's, National Kahlua Day, National Polar Bear Day, National Strawberry Day, No Brainer Day (USA), Carnival (Panama)

28 February: Entroida Festival (Spain)

Another fiery festival. Having deep pagan roots, Entroida is the Galician reply to European Carnivals and, of course, is held every year before Lent (on the three Fridays before Lent). But unlike carnivals, as we know them, this one features angry fire ants, vinegar, and mud, along with festival costumes, food, drinks and joyous atmosphere. Its aim is soul purification.

Each part of the program has a specific routine and rituals. On the three Fridays, locals run along the village streets carrying hay torches. Those who decide to choose the safety of their home – just throw from the balcony heaps of dust, dirt and mud on the runners below, trying to hit as many as possible. This apparently is for purification! The Saturday is very calm – people dance on the streets and enjoy festive meals like pig's head, grilled goat, and sweets. The actual Entroida is on Sunday. Local men disguise in carnival costumes and masks (including quite funny lingerie-looking shorts and huge headpieces with images of different animals on them) and carry many and noisy cowbells tied to their outfits. These men represent mischievous Peliqueros, that randomly whip innocent people on the streets. When they get hungry or thirsty from all the whipping, they enter random houses unannounced and eat and drink before the astonished hosts who aren't allowed to chase them away or even touch them. However, as naughty as they are, Peliqueros should be respected because they are the sacred spirits which are very much involved in the purification process (another theory is that the Peliqueros represent the XVIth C tax-collectors who were ready to whip anyone who hasn't paid his dues).

The afternoon is time for the Farrapada – a weird and quite painful part of the Entroida Festival. It takes place on the town's square – entry is free for all. It reminds a lot of a water battle, however includes muddy rags and sometimes flour fight along with the water. Some folks (who happen to be too deep in the purification aspect of the carnival) soak rags in vinegar and cover them with fire ants, who get very angry when thrown around. A whip with a rag like this and one can scratch all over for a week at least. All participants dress up in costumes, some wear masks – usually, resembling hilarious characters of the past year. It is common to see a street band disguised as pink bunnies, a mad priest wondering the streets or just ordinary people trying to get home from work in their work clothes, but covered in flour head-to-toe.

The late afternoon gets a bit calmer again as it is time for the Moreno (a masked guy holding a cow's head on a stick). The Moreno lifts the skirts of unsuspected women with the cow's horns and makes insulting gestures. This "playful" creature roams the streets just before the big parade with decorated floats.

The end of the Entroida is on Tuesday and is marked by a weird ritual (as by the way is the whole carnival...). It is time for Testament do Burro (testament of the donkey). So... different donkey body parts are distributed to relatives, friends, and neighbors in hope to bring them good fortune for the year ahead and dispose of all bad and evil that had taken place in the previous year. And, yes, the locals also meet for a night of sarcasm and torch a huge effigy of a sardine! This one goes on the bucket list!

Travel to: Spain (Galicia). The festival is held in the small town of Laza.

Other holidays on this date: National Chocolate Soufflé Day, National Floral Design Day, National Public Sleeping Day, National Tooth Fairy Day, Rare Disease day, Spay Day (USA), Carnival (Canada), Carnival (Haiti), Carnival (Liechtenstein), Carnival (Lithuania)

29 February: Habano Cigar Festival (Cuba)

The Habano is considered the best Cigar due to its triple bonus of best soils, weather conditions and producers' know-how. This is the biggest party for cigar aficionados in the world and celebrates the world's finest tobacco! Held annually in the end of February till the first week in March, the festival offers workshops and discussions, trade fairs, new cigar brand launches, cigar tastings, visit to many plantations and factories, cigar rolling masterclasses. The celebration ends with a Gala dinner with an auction of rare humidors to raise money for the Cuban Public Health System (the amount raised is millions of dollars). One of the recently auctioned humidors had a 24-carat gold tobacco leaf and its price went up to a few hundred thousand dollars. International artists perform during the closing event. The highlight of the evening is "Premio Habano del Año" – annual award given to cigar manufacturers (and users) in the categories of business, production, and communication. In 2005, the British actor Jeremy Irons was awarded a prize for a Cigar Ambassador!

Fact: US travelers to Cuba are allowed to bring back up to $100 in cigars and alcohol combined.

Travel to: Cuba (Havana). Palacio de Convenciones is the home of the event and where most of the workshops as well as the welcome drinks take place. There is a Welcome evening at the Club Havana on the beach, unfortunately it is invitation only. Worth a visit are the plantations in Vuelta Abajo – considered the region of the world's best tobacco, it is the home of the crop for Cohiba cigars. Interesting fact is that the old tradition of reading the daily news aloud as workers roll the cigars is still kept!

Other holidays on this date: International Leap Day

... MARCH

Masquerade: An interesting theory is that the noblemen and in general the high-class society in the past used costumes and masks to disguise and mingle with the lower class as a way to meet ladies and drink large amounts of alcohol without being recognized. This may well be the reason why masquerade balls were so popular in the old times.

01 March: National Beer Day (Iceland)

This celebration is held annually on March 1st. It was initiated when the country's 75-year ban on beer was lifted in 1989. After a referendum in 1908, local officials banned all alcoholic drinks in Iceland starting from the year 1915. The ban was partially lifted six years later because of Spain – the Spanish refused to buy any fish from Iceland unless the Icelanders bought Spanish wine in return (the ban was lifted only for imported red Spanish wines)! Years later, in 1985 the government banned adding spirits to non-alcoholic beer to make it stronger (this faux beer was an invention of the local pubs called BJÓRLÍKI and their own way to deal with the situation) – this led to less support on the prohibition and hence, the referendum of 1989 when the ban was completely lifted. Ever since, Icelander's preferred drink has been beer.

National Beer Day is a real nationwide "pub-crawl" drinking party. Although most businesses are open with regular working hours, all pubs stay open longer than usual, sometimes until the early hours of the morning. Locals really take the celebrations seriously and enjoy a night of beer-drinking-marathon, trying to taste as many different brews as possible. Some of the popular brews on the island are Viking Dimmur, Thule and Litli-Jón. Ölvisholt, a brewery on the south coast, is considered the pioneer of Icelandic beer. Fun fact is that two days before the grand opening of the brewery there was a massive earthquake in Iceland... and their first beer was named... Skjálfti (Earthquake).

Travel to: Iceland (Reykjavik). For a taste of over 100 different brews – visit the trendy Micro-Bar downtown.

Other holidays on this date: Bell Dorado (Switzerland), Baba Marta Day (Bulgaria), National That's Good Day, National Fruit Compote Day, National Horse Protection Day, National Pig Day (USA), Carnival (Germany), Martisor (Moldova)

02 March: Blue Dragon Festival (China)

This is a traditional festival welcoming the first signs of Spring and is celebrated in the rural parts of China. The dragon that controls the rain (as well as all other creatures), awakens after the long winter and the folks celebrate in hope to have plenty of rain for a good harvest. The festival is known as Longtaitou - "a dragon raising its head". It is held annually on the second day of the 2nd Lunar month (between February 21st and March 21st).

For it is an agricultural celebration, there are no public events in big cities – to get a taste of the festival, one should head towards remote rural villages.

As the holiday falls on a day after the Chinese New Year, the locals clean their houses in the morning and get a haircut. This is because the New Year taboos are no longer enforced (they include: no sweeping as it sweeps away the wealth, no haircuts as it brings bad luck and more). The Chinese eat *dragon food* - dumplings (called the dragon's ears), spring pancakes (dragon's scales) and noodles (dragon's beard).

In the past, people believed that this was the time to kill all insects arising from hibernation, so they used to burn herbs inside their homes, that had insect repellent effect.

People should also abstain from using needles – it is believed they can hurt the dragon's eyes when he rears his head towards the Earth.

Travel to: China. As the festival is ancient and no longer widely celebrated, it's best to head to the Huobali Village in Chandong Province.

Other holidays on this date: National Banana cream Pie Day, National Read Across America Day (USA), Seedling Festival (Taiwan – Thao tribe)

03 March: Food and Fun Festival (Iceland)

This is a five-day fiesta for food and fun aficionados! The idea to create such a festival was born in 2002 during a competition between local and international culinary professionals. The event was originally held to boost the economy as February and March are traditionally low season months for tourism. The cook-off became so popular that it turned into an annual event – a real Taste of Iceland, served in local restaurants for a week.

The rules: Local chefs and chefs from around the world join forces to prepare the ultimate Icelandic feast. They create gourmet menus at affordable prices.

Competition stages: There are two main stages:

1. All chefs are assigned to different restaurants in which they cook their 4-course masterpieces. Judges nominate the 3 best chefs to compete in a final public cook-off.

2. Two chefs compete for the title Chef You Wish to Drag To Your Kitchen – meaning each one of them will try to please your taste buds as much as he can.

The catch: They should use Icelandic ingredients only!

And in case you are wondering what a typical Icelandic ingredient is... well: Brennivín or Black Death (kind of a schnapps), cod tongues, sheep's head, whale and shark meat, dried fish, sour ram's testicles, hot spring rye bread (can be prepared by putting the dough in the ground close to a hot spring and wait 1 night), blood pudding, blubber, fish stomach and more.

They also are allowed to use other ingredients that are available and grown in Iceland like lamb, fresh vegetables, and organic dairy products.

Icelanders also benefit from discovering new recipes – for example, the typical Icelandic "skyr" which is a low-fat dairy product with rich creamy texture was used by an international chef in various sauces – an idea that had never occurred to the locals before! A true culinary adventure for the locals and visitors alike. And to top it all off – the legendary nightlife of Iceland is more vivid than ever during the festival days.

Travel to: Iceland (Reykjavík). Some of the participating restaurants in the festival are: Apotek, Bazaar Oddsson, Bryggjan Brugghus, Grillid, Haust, Matarkjallarinn, Kolabrautin and Mathus Gardarbaejar.

Other holidays on this date: National Mulled Wine Day, National Day of Unplugging, National Employee Appreciation Day, National Salesperson Day (USA), Dolls Festival (Japan), Yap Day (Micronesia), Peasants Day (Myanmar), Doll Floating Festival (Japan)

04 March: Carnival of the Country (Argentina)

The tradition of celebrating Carnival was brought to the New World by European settlers in the seventeenth century – in Argentina they were Spanish. The word carnival derives from the Medieval Latin word carnelevarium - "remove the flesh", which refers to the religious prohibition to eat meat during the forty days of fast during Lent. Therefore, usually, Carnivals are held in the months preceding Easter, although nowadays the religious meaning is lost to some extent. However, as the celebration derives from the old pagan ritual of honoring Bacchus – the God of Wine, the tradition still keeps the spirits high, offering a plethora of unforgettable experiences for soul and body alike.

The annual festival takes place every Saturday, from January 14th to February 26th and has been celebrated for more than 30 years. This is the biggest and most spectacular carnival in Argentina and considered to be one of the best in the world together with the ones in Rio de Janeiro and Venice. Numerous processions with richly decorated floats, performers wearing colorful costumes and masks parade and dance in front of crowds of visitors, the local carnival dance clubs ("comparsas") engage in Samba competitions (the winning club dancers are crowned Kings of the Carnival). The impressive costumes are made of more than 70 000 feathers and 1 000 000 sequins and pearls.

Five dance troupes compete to be crowned the winners – it is an epic dance battle with investments of around 5-6 million pesos for each troupe and its impressive number of 280 dancers! The judges take into consideration choreography, costumes and the number of floats/carriages.

As tens of thousands of people gather to experience one of the greatest carnivals on Earth, early accommodation booking is essential as places sell out quickly (the town is quite small and has around 90 000 residents in total).

Travel to: Argentina (Gualeguaychú). Carnival celebrations are held in the Corsódromo, a former railway station converted in 1997. If one opts for a stay out of the buzzing city should look for accommodation round the natural hot springs about one mile outside the city or consider staying at an *estancia*—Argentina's quintessential, ranch-style Bed&Breakfast.

Other holidays on this date: Holy Experiment Day, National Grammar Day, National Pound Cake Day, March Forth and Do Something Day (USA), Todorovden (Bulgaria)

05 March: Custom Chief's Day (Vanuatu Islands)

The islands of Vanuatu claimed by the British and the French, proclaimed their independence only in the 1980s (during the Coconut War).

They have been home to the people of Melanesia for more than 2,500 years. That is why most of the locals keep a traditional way of life – they believe in magic and are ruled by village chiefs who are the brightest among them.

Custom Chief's Day was created in the late 1970s, as a reminder that the tribal Chiefs (locally called "Jifs") have the power and the ultimate knowledge about politics, economy and more, and to honor their purpose of preserving the rituals and cultural heritage of the Vanuatu life. Ever since 1977 when the Chiefs Council was established, the islands have celebrated Custom Chief's Day on March 5th. The

Council doesn't really have any legislative power, but since the Jifs are the most important people in the tribe – they are well listened to!

The public holiday is marked in each village with lavish feasts, sports activities, cultural shows, and carnivals. This is the best way to take a glimpse of the colorful and rich culture of the different tribes. The locals sing, dance and play on their typical musical instruments (giant tree logs set on tripods and huge seashells are just some of them) all dressed in traditional outfits – the interesting part is the costumes are mainly made of grass, plants, and leaves (looking almost as some sort of exotic feathers due to the bright colors of the leaves). They are all adorned with bracelets and necklaces made of beads and small seashells.

This a wonderful opportunity to learn more about the local customs and to see some of the most important men of the islands - the Jifs.

Travel to: Vanuatu Islands (Port Villa). The event takes place at the Chiefs Nakamal at Saralana Park. The Republic of Vanuatu consists of 13 larger islands and about 70 smaller ones and they all celebrate Custom Chief's Day.

Other holidays on this date: National Absinthe Day, National Cheese Doodle Day (USA)

06 March: Tincunaco Ceremony (Argentina)

The Tincunaco Ceremony is part of the Carnival season in Argentina and is celebrated on the Thursday before Ash Wednesday (it always takes place on Thursday, however in some cities, the carnival is celebrated every weekend from January till the end of March). Although the tradition of "carnival" was brought to Argentina by the Spanish settlers, it is heavily influenced by the African rituals and traditions. Preparations for the festive season in Argentina include spring cleaning of the houses, charango music (played on a small string instrument, similar to the ukulele) and two drinks in large amounts – aloja de chaucha (a fermented drink made of carob tree, aka pea shrub) and chichi (similar to pina colada).

The Tincunaco Ceremony is a sacred ritual between a mother and grandmother and honors the special bond between the two. The women split into two teams, mothers on one side and grandmothers on the other and "meet" under an arch made of willow branches decorated with sweets, fruit, cheese, blossoms, and lanterns. They touch each other's forehead with a special doll - it is made of candy and symbolizes the bond that can never be broken.

The carnival celebrations are marked with a beautiful dance by the local women, who wear wide ruffled skirts, ponchos and big white hats. Their faces are covered with starch and they ride on horseback and sing folk songs honoring Pukllay – a rag doll, representing the Spirit of the Carnival. After the so-called "death dance", the doll is "buried" in a grave covered with sweets and flowers, to mark the end of the Carnival days.

Travel to: Northern parts of Argentina (Jujuy province). The Carnival is celebrated throughout the country, but only parts of it perform the Tincunaco Ceremony.
Other holidays on this date: Dentist`s Day (USA)

07 March: Maslenitsa (Russia)

This is one of the biggest festivals in Russia and the Eastern European answer to Fat Tuesday, so – lots of pancake eating involved. Celebrated annually during the last week before Lent, there is evidence that Maslenitsa can be the oldest surviving Slavic holiday (2nd century A.D.). The festival has deep pagan roots and derives from an ancient Slavic sun-festival honoring Volos (the god of earth, waters, forests, cattle, fertility, magic and the underworld).

During Lent, all meat and festivities are forbidden, so the week before it is the last chance to go wild and enjoy the food that is still allowed to consume – milk, eggs, and butter. Maslenitsa celebrations include eating tons of pancakes (bliny) with the traditional fillings - caviar, sauerkraut, mushrooms or jam. The pancake is a very important part of the ritual – its round shape symbolizes the Sun, pancakes were given to women in labor and on funerals as they represent the circle of life. In general, the round shape is sacred, and people believe it chases away evil. Many festivals feature parades with decorated cartwheels carried on poles, walking around churches in a circle and more.

The beginning of the festivities is on Monday. It is marked by building a huge straw effigy of Lady Maslenitsa and fixing it onto a pole. Then locals carry it on sleigh around town and offer pancakes to the poor. Tuesday is "game day" - wherever you go, you'll meet skomorokhi (clowns) with the gusli (harp), Petrushka (traditional puppet), and other favorite characters of Russian fairy tales, sleigh riding, folk festivals and street vendors with trays full of Russian souvenirs. On Wednesday, husbands visit their mothers-in-law and eat pancakes. Thursday is for outdoor family activities and this is when the real fun begins because people are not allowed to work. On this day, notorious bare-knuckle street fights take place – men box each other as a sign of respect and friendship...and to commemorate the Russian military history when soldiers allegedly fought each other in hand-to-hand combat! On Friday, husbands invite their mothers-in-law for dinner – this is a tricky part because the son-in-law has to send the invitation the night before and then organize a "group of ambassadors" to pick her up – the bigger the group, the greater the honor for the mother-in-law. On Saturday, wives meet with their sisters-in-law (the Russian word for sister-in-law is "zolovka" which derives from the word for "evil", and the word for their brother`s wife is "nevestka" which means "outsider"). The Sunday is a very important day, not only because it is the last day of the festivities, but also because it is "Forgiveness Sunday" and all people ask for forgiveness from their family, relatives and friends. The celebrations end with burning Lady Maslenitsa and spreading her ashes in the snow to fertilize the crops (in Pre-Christian times a real person was sacrificed).

Along with the traditional part, Maslenitsa is about having fun in the snow and enjoying the first rays of the Spring Sun. Children ice skate and slide downhill, while relatives and friends join the families for a long night of delicious festive dinner.

Travel to: Russia (Moscow, Suzdal, Vladimir, Rostov and Veliky Novgorod). The festival was officially recognized in Moscow in 2002 and some of the biggest celebrations taking place in the Russian capital are on Vasilyevsky Spusk square.

Other holidays on this date: National Crown Roast of Pork Day, National Be Heard Day, National Pancake Day, National Cereal Day (USA), Asa Baako Festival (Ghana)

08 March: International Women`s Day (North Korea)

The celebration began in the late 1800's and early 1900s and grew from women's socialist movements and trade union groups. The focus is upon women workers and women's rights in all aspects of life.

An interesting fact is that North Korea is one of the few countries in the world to have announced the day as a National holiday. Various formal and informal events are held throughout the country and especially in Pyongyang, where the leader Kim Jong-Un delivers a speech (usually highlighting that his father and predecessor had a scientific theory on the role of women in the advancing of revolution and construction). The Leader doesn`t meet with any of the extinguished women of North Korea, but his Seniors pass on food and cosmetic gifts on his behalf. Women who work hard to glorify the State are considered a role model in North Korea and given the highest honors.

The celebrations on this day include a Women`s Union march and laying flowers at the statues of the founders of the State.

Travel to: North Korea (Pyongyang). International Women's Day is an official holiday also in Armenia, Azerbaijan, Belarus, Bulgaria, Kazakhstan, Kyrgyzstan, Macedonia, Moldova, Mongolia, Russia, Tajikstan, Ukraine, Uzbekistan, and Vietnam. In addition, events are held all over the world.

Other holidays on this date: Be Nasty Day, National Peanut Cluster Day, National Proofreading Day (USA), Decoration Day (Liberia), Nari Diwas (Nepal)

09 March: Nyepi (Bali)

This is the Balinese New Year celebrated over 6 days in accordance with the Balinese calendar.

Also known as The Day of Silence – a time of self-reflection and meditation. The island's businesses are closed, except for hospital emergency wards. There is an ancient myth that after the first two days of festivities and parades, locals wanted to hide the island from the eyes of evil spirits and witches, so they would think it is deserted, hence they created The Day of Silence.

Since this day is meant for purification, there are many restrictions – no people walking on the streets (incl. tourists!), no vehicles (incl. bikes), no work, no parties (songs, dances etc.), no fires or candles (and lights should be kept low), no traveling, the hotel windows should be covered and for the real devotees – no talking or eating at all. The beaches are deserted, there are no people on the streets and the island reminds of a ghost town as everybody stays home. More than that - there are no scheduled inbound/outbound flights. To ensure that the traditions are strictly observed, local policemen patrol the island all day and night.

The preparations for the festival start a few days before and include various purification ceremonies and colorful processions from the Balinese temples and on the streets. Locals build huge and demonic bamboo effigies representing the evil, parade them around the streets and then burn them. They symbolically scare off evil forces by hitting (as loud as one can) pots and pans and other instruments while holding fiery bamboo torches. Each household performs a blessing ritual at the family shrine representing its will to reconnect with God, Mankind, and Nature. The people sacrifice different animals – chicken, ducks, even bulls and make offerings of different plants to the deities. Most rituals take place in temples close to the sea.

The following day is time for Omed-Omedan, known as "The Kissing Ceremony" which has been celebrated for more than 100 years. Single men and women gather on the main street and pray together. Afterward, they divide into two groups – men and women facing each other. After a signal given by the Hindu leader, the men approach the women and kiss them while the locals pour buckets of water over them.

The week of celebration ends with reading of sacred ancient manuscripts.

Travel to: Bali (Denpasar). "The Kissing Ceremony" is performed in Denpasar. Each village has its own parade with Ogoh-Ogoh effigy, however the best places to experience the colorful parades are the beaches of Kuta, Seminyak, Nusa Dua and Sanur.

Other holidays on this date: Panic Day, National Barbie Day, National Crabmeat Day, National Get Over It Day, National Meatball Day (USA)

Dessi Nikoltchev:

10 March: International Sand Sculpture Festival (Portugal)
Created in 2003, this is the largest sand sculpture event in the world. It covers an area of 15,000sq.m. in the so-called Sand City and showcases more than 60 magnificent works of art, made of 35,000 tons of sand. The gigantic sculptures resemble of people, places, buildings, even famous paintings. The festival has a different theme set each year, so the participants sculpt their masterpieces accordingly.

The event is a real sensorial experience, dragging the visitors into a wonder-world with magical kingdoms, centuries of history presented by huge visual projections and dramatic ambient lighting at nighttime. The festive atmosphere is complemented by a fish SPA, icicle SPA, 360˚ sand stage, snack bars, shop, workshops on sand sculpting.

The best bit – one can plan a suitable visit as the festival is held from March till October (weather permitting as this is an outside enclosure).

Travel to: Portugal (Algarve). The event is held in Areias de Pêra (on E524, between Pêra and Algoz). Worth visiting in the area are: Praia dos Salgados (3km), Praia Gale (5km), Praia Sao Rafael (7km).

Other holidays on this date: National Mario Day, National Pack Your Lunch Day, Middle Name Pride Day (USA)

11 March: Frozen Dead Guy Days (USA)
This is one of the quirkiest festivals in the world that celebrates... a frozen dead person! The three-day event was created in 2001 and takes place in March every year. The story behind it is a rather weird one, but then – so is the festival itself! In 1989 Trygve Bauge brought the corpse of his grandfather, Bredo Morstøl, from Norway to the USA because he wanted to store it at a cryonics facility. And so he did. The body was stored in liquid nitrogen in California until 1993 when it was transported to the small town in Colorado, where Trygve and his mother had built their own cryonic facility (apparently the residents didn't have a clue of their plan nor the corpse at that point). However, Trygve had the misfortune to be deported back to Norway and his mother took over the care for Grandpa Bredo. Unfortunately, due to unforeseen circumstances, she was evicted, but not before sharing her long-kept secret with a local reporter. The result – a sensational story and a ban from the local government outlawing any keeping of people who are not alive in domestic environment. However, because of the publicity, the body of Grandpa Bredo was considered an exception (the so-called "Grandfather clause"), so it stayed in the cryonic shed. It is still there and the city celebrates its unusual resident every year.

The so-called by the organizers "Frost Fest" celebrates all things frozen and features coffin racing, corpse parade, Ice Queen and Grandpa Bredo look-alike contest, cryogenics workshop, survival skills workshop, ice turkey bowling, frozen salmon toss, Newly Dead game for couples, Brain Freeze contest (with slushies), ice carving, costumed polar plunging, frozen t-shirt contests and more. You will also find Ice Bars, Beer tents, gift shops, heated tents with live music, food and drinks by simply following the signs "Re-Animate Yourself".

Isn't that cool?!

Travel to: USA (Colorado). The event takes place in the town of Nederland and Grandpa Bredo is stored in the Tuff Shed.

Other holidays on this date: National Proposal Day, National Oatmeal Nut Waffles Day (USA), Omizutori Festival (Japan)

12 March: Holi - Festival of Colors (India & world)

The most fun, artistic and beautiful festival marking the end of Winter and beginning of Spring, as well as the victory of good over evil. People forgive each other for all things past and gather to have a good time. The festival is celebrated annually on a full moon between the end of February and the beginning of March and lasts for one night and one day. Having its origins from an ancient Hindu religious tradition (dating back to the IVth C), the colorful event is now celebrated in many countries as a holiday of love. According to one legend, the baby Krishna was poisoned from the breast milk of a demoness, which turned his skin blue. While he was young, he was afraid that his beloved fair-skinned Radha would never like him because of his color. Tired of Krishna's desperation, his mother asked him to paint Radha's face in any color he wants. So - he did, and they became a divine couple.

The evening before the festival is time for self-purification – people gather around bonfires and pray to cleanse themselves from internal evil. In line with another legend evil demoness - Holika, tricked King Prahalad into the fire. The cloak she wore to protect herself from the flames flew and enclosed Prahalad, so she burnt. That is why the pyre signifies the victory of good over evil.

The next morning is when the fun begins – people throw colorful powder over each other, smear their body and face, hug and wish "Happy Holi". Traditionally the colors are derived from washable natural plants –yellow from turmeric, purple – beetroot, brown from tea leaves, blue from berries or indigo plant etc. By the end of the day all streets, temples, and houses are smeared in the colours of the rainbow. This is an open event so anyone can participate (as long as they throw color powder over people). No one is safe – kids, elders, women, everyone ends up color-covered head-to-toe. Water guns and water balloons filled with dissolved color powder are also used. A handy tip is to cover the body with coconut oil before attending Holi as this prevents the color from absorbing into the skin. There are singers, dancers and street musicians playing on giant drums all the time. "Bhang" (a paste made from cannabis plant) is traditionally consumed during the celebrations in the form of a drink. Typical food delicacies during the festival are puran poli (sweet flat bread), dahi vada (lentil dumplings in a creamy yoghurt sauce with sweet spices) and gujia (sweet dumpling filled with aromatic nuts mixture).

In the evening, locals usually visit friends and family.

Travel to: India (Delhi, Mumbai, Barsana, Mathura, Vrindavan, Shantiniketan, Purulia, Udaipur, Jaipur, Hampi). The Holi Festival, it is believed, has its origins in the State of Gujarat. In Ahmedabad locals perform another ritual - young boys make human pyramids to try and catch a pot of buttermilk hung over a street (Krishna is also called "makhan chor" which means butter thief).

Other holidays on this date: National Girl Scout Day, National Plant a Flower Day (USA), Sumo Spring Basho (Japan)

13 March: The Elephant Festival (India)

The Elephant Festival takes place every year on the day of Holi (The Festival of Colors) and usually falls in March. It was created to honor the magnificence of the elephant, which is a sacred animal in the state of Rajasthan – once a royal playground for the Indian aristocrats. According to one theory, gods and demons stirred the ocean in hope to become immortal. Nine precious stones surfaced – one of them was in the shape of an elephant. Not only that, but according to the mythology –elephant-headed God Ganesha is the remover of obstacles and is one of the most worshipped in India. The elephants have always been an important part of the ceremonies – marriages, funerals, religious events, battles etc.

The festival has been canceled twice – in 2012 and 2014 due to protests from Animal Welfare groups who had concerns about the chemicals used for the festive paintings which adorn the skin of the animals.

The event begins with a huge parade of regally dressed elephants, camels, and horses, accompanied by traditional Indian dancers. The elephants, being the main focus, are covered with jewels and velvet rugs embroidered with gems, head-pieces, anklets and rings, their tusks wrapped in glittering gold and their bodies painted in bright colors. Many of them stride gracefully hidden under the shade of decorated parasols. Their caretakers/riders, called Mahouts, wear bright clothes covered with gems and gold, and royal turbans. In addition, in the procession, there are chariots, lancers on horses and palanquins.

There is a competition for most beautifully adorned elephant, as well as an award for best Elephant dance. Featuring events are Elephant Polo, Elephant race, tug-of-war between elephants and people, Elephants splashing colored water onto the cheering crowd and many more. All elephants participating in the festival have to be female.

During the parade, there are musical bands and traditional singers and dancers.

Travel to: India (Rajasthan). The event is held at the Jaipur Polo ground in Jaipur.

Other holidays on this date: National Coconut Torte Day, National Earmuff Day, National Good Samaritan Day, National Jewel Day, National Open an Umbrella Indoors Day, National Napping Day (USA), Eight Hours Day (Australia, Tasmania)

14 March: Dita e Verës Day (Albania)

The first day of Spring in Albania is called Summer's Day – go figure?! This is an annual spring celebration which honors the rebirth of nature and rejuvenation of spirits awaken from the long and cold wintertime. According to the legend, the Goddess of hunting, forests, and nature would come out of her temple (which was built near Elbasan and maybe that is the reason this holiday is best celebrated there) only on March 14th to mark the beginning of Spring. The legend has it that it never rains on that day. This pagan-rooted holiday is celebrated as a national holiday since 2004.

Streets and houses are adorned with garlands of spring flowers (yellow mimosas, which bloom all over Albania in the Spring) and greenery and there is a spirit of festivity everywhere. Local merchants sell traditional food, drinks (incl. thick Turkish coffee), beautiful hand-made souvenirs and spring flowers. Young unmarried folks wear a traditional red and white bracelet, which they tie on a tree branch at the end of the day for good luck. It is a tradition for all families to have festive dinner the night before Summer's Day and invite their closest friends – the menu is turkey legs, figs, nuts, dried fruit and boiled eggs. In the morning, elders are the first to wake up - they leave the front door open and put a pitcher of fresh water outside to welcome any guests. Then they fetch soil and fresh grass and bring it inside the house to celebrate the rebirth of nature. The grass and turf fetching comes from an Albanian community which moved to Italy in the XVth C – they still bring turf and grass into their houses to commemorate the anniversary of their emigration from Albania.

The street festivities start with children's parade and continue with carnivals and numerous concerts during the afternoon. People have picnics in the parks, the cafés are full of locals enjoying a glass of Raki, street merchants sell balloons, ice cream, candied apples, sunflower seeds and popcorn. Traditional treat sold everywhere on this day is a type of handmade cornbread cookie, called Ballakume (each family has a different recipe, and this is considered a family heirloom). Kulace (special bread with raisins) is also common.

This is a day to spend outside and have fun!

Travel to: Albania (Elbasan – home of the festival). Concerts are held on the grounds of the Elbasan Castle – a XV C fortress. Closest to the venue are Hotel Guri and Real Scampis Hotel, although Hotel Le Olive which is on the other side of the river is a real treat!

The holiday is celebrated throughout Albania, so if one can`t make it to Elbasan – Tirana is a great option.

Other holidays on this date: National Children`s Craft Day, National Learn About Butterflies Day, National Pi Day (USA)

15 March: Pujllay Festival (Bolivia)

The festival is held every year on the third Sunday in March. Created to commemorate the March 12th, 1816 Battle of Cumbate, liberating the town from the Spanish, the celebration also honors the Andean Goddess Pachamama (Mother Earth). The festival coincides with a weekly Sunday open-air market which is a unique and colorful display of local produce and culture of the indigenous Yampara people. The festival starts with a Quechua Mass (Quechua people are direct descendants of the Incas) and continues with a huge street procession. Tens of diverse groups representing different areas of Bolivia parade the streets of the rural town. They are all dressed in traditional costumes for their region. Some of them wear colorful hand-loomed ponchos, skirts and headdresses, while others or the "tarabuqueños" – helmets and wide-leg trousers – much resembling the outfit of the Spanish Conquistadors (they conquered the Incan Empire in 1533, when the natives were suffering the consequences of new diseases brought by the Europeans to their lands and ongoing wars between two ruling Incan brothers – both of which had weakened the empire). The beautiful parade ends around a huge wooden tower, known as the "pukara". The pukara is adorned with all sorts of agricultural treats – corn, meat, fruit and bread products, and rosquetas (various baked sweets). What is the meaning of the tower? This is the way for locals to pay tribute to Mother Earth (Pachamama) and ask for a good harvest. They all dance, sing, play on drums and traditional panpipes. A ritual dance - Ayarichi, celebrating new life and rain, accompanied by flutes and hornpipes is performed around the pukara. At the end of the festival, food offerings from the tower are shared among the people. During the celebration, many locals put out stalls with handmade merchandise, Andean dresses, musical instruments, drinks and typical Bolivian food – a variety of meat chunks garnished with corn, potatoes or rice flatbread.

As from 2014, the Pujllay is on the UNESCO Representative List of the Intangible Cultural Heritage of Humanity.

Travel to: Bolivia (Chuquisaca). The festival is held 65km east of Sucre in the town of Tarabuco. It is best to book accommodation in Sucre though, as Tarabuco is quite small and fills up quickly. There is public transport to the festival site (2hrs).

Other holidays on this date: National Shoe the World Day, National Kick Butts Day, Dumbstruck Day, Everything You Think Is Wrong Day (USA)

16 March: Argungu Fishing Festival (Nigeria)

The four-day festival was created to entertain Sultan Hassan Dan-Mua'zu during his visit to the village in 1931. He was the first Sultan of Sokoto (the Fulani tribe) to sleep in a Kabawa people village, so the festival played the role of a peace pact between the two nations. The Emir of the Kabawa people put a lot of thought on how to entertain the Sultan since he already had in-depth knowledge of boxing and wrestling. A fishing festival in his honor was the obvious and best choice. With the growing popularity of the event, eventually the Nigerian government took over the organization. Many facilities were built to make the event more convenient for visitors – Grand Hotel, game village, pavilions and others.

The first three days are dedicated to ordinary fishing –people enjoy the beautiful scenery, the cool breeze around the river banks, local food and drinks. Other featured events are boxing, wrestling, songs and dances by the locals, beauty pageant, animal races, car and bike races, hunting, agricultural show, wild duck catching, archery, and canoe racing.

The main event takes place on the fourth day and is the culmination of the festival. Thousands of fishermen line up like an ancient army, carrying only traditional fishing tools, including dried and hollowed pumpkins and nets (they are also allowed to try and catch a fish barehanded). At the sound of a gunshot, all of them simultaneously jump in the river. They have just one hour to catch the largest fish. The prize for the winner is about 7,500 US dollars plus a minibus! In 2004 the winner was an 80kg catfish!

Travel to: Nigeria (Kebbi State in the North-western part). The festival is held in the city of Argungu in the Malan Fada River.

Other holidays on this date: National Artichoke Hearts Day, National Freedom of Information Day, National Everything You Do Is Right Day, Incredible Kid Day (USA)

17 March: St Patrick (Ireland)

The Feast of St Patrick, the patron saint of Ireland, is celebrated annually on March 17th not only in its homeland but all over the world. This is one of the most internationally recognized holidays. Since the early XVIIth C, most Catholic, Anglican, Eastern Orthodox and Lutheran churches celebrate the day. This a cultural and religious holiday, commemorating the arrival of Christianity in Ireland and the

Irish heritage. According to the legend, Patrick who was born in the IVth C was kidnapped and sent to Gaelic Ireland, where he worked as a shepherd for six years. During this time, he found God, who told him about a ship waiting on the coast to take him home. Indeed, there it was and Patrick returned to his home where later became a priest and converted thousands of Pagan Irishmen into Christians. He died on March 17th.

Celebrations generally include church services, street parades (often masquerades where locals paint their faces in green or draw clovers on their cheeks, wear green wigs and green top hats), Irish dances and songs, festivals and wearing of green attire complemented by lots of shamrocks. The "shamrock" which is a young clover, symbolizes the Holy Trinity and is a national symbol of Ireland. Many buildings, in Ireland and around the world, of cultural importance, are lit up in green color to honor the Irish.

Fact 1: the Lenten restrictions on eating and drinking alcohol are lifted for the day, which has encouraged the holiday's tradition of large alcohol consumption (and to top it all – there is a special green-colored beer for the occasion);

Fact 2: St Patrick is not Irish! He was born in what is now England, Scotland or Wales (the exact location varies according to different sources);

Fact 3: The first St Patrick's parade took place in New York in 1762, when Irish soldiers marched through the town. The parades in Ireland started years later;

Fact 4: Since 1961, St Patrick is recognized as a patron saint of Nigeria as well.

The motto of the festivities: If you're not wearing green - you ought to get pinched!

Travel to: Republic of Ireland (Dublin). By 2006 the festival had grown into a 5-day event with many festivals, concerts and cultural events, visited by more than a million people every year. The celebrations coincide with the Irish language week. Outside big cities, the small village of Downpatrick (it is believed that St Patrick is buried there) has a very special celebration as well.

Other holidays on this date: Submarine Day, National Corned Beef and Cabbage Day (USA)

18 March: Cherry Blossom Festivals (Japan)

This is a month-long festival to cherish the world-known cherry blossoms of Japan. What better way to celebrate Spring than to admire its beautiful colors? This is one of the most-loved and cherished rituals in the country. Locally known as "Hanami" - "viewing flowers", the celebration dates back a thousand years, to a time when the Japanese aristocrats admired blooming cherry trees and wrote poems inspired by the beautiful pink colors. For ordinary folks, the cherry blossom just announced the rice-planting season.

Everything turns pink in Japan from March until June (depending on the region, as the cherry trees blossom at different times) and locals host parties under the trees - a tradition that has taken place for centuries. In the past, the Japanese thought that the cherry trees were spirits, so they made offerings of rice wine and sweets to honor them. Nowadays, they make barbecues, hold tea ceremonies, bring out home-made food (grilled fish, rice and steamed vegetables, herb dumplings and fish cakes), or just buy snacks and drinks from the shop (especially sake). Parks and gardens are crowded, with locals and visitors enjoying the breath-taking beauty of the trees at their fullest. The shops are full of cherry-flavored products and souvenirs – even cherry beer and cherry coffee are sold. Delicate fragrance spreads all over and the fallen petals form a soft and colorful natural carpet to walk on. During the day, many events are held and performed under the shade of the trees – parades, beauty pageants, folk songs singing. The atmosphere gets truly magical in the evening with different light-up events including ambient light from many torches and colored paper lanterns.

The cherry blossom is very important to the Japanese and features in folklore songs, films, as a kimono pattern, in paintings, poems, religious ceremonies etc. Its beauty and volatility are often associated with mortality. A symbol of cherry blossom was even worn by the first Kamikaze's (as it showed the ultimate devotion to the Emperor), there was also a subunit called Yamazakura (Wild Cherry Blossom). Cherry blossoms were painted on the sides of military planes as well, to show Japanese affiliation.

Unfortunately, the magnificent blossoms last only a few days, they fall off the trees blown by the wind or are washed away by rain – this reminds of the fragile nature of life itself as per the Buddhist main concept - Japanese believe one should appreciate the beauty in all things, while it lasts.

Travel to: Japan (Mount Yoshino, Shinjuku Gyoen, Himeji Castle, Mount Fuji, Philosopher's Path in Kyoto, Kenrokuen Garden Kanazawa, Miharu Takizakura, Hirosaki Castle). The cherry trees in Tokyo and Kyoto usually bloom in March and April.

Other holidays on this date: National Sloppy Joe Day, National Quilting Day, National Supreme Sacrifice Day (USA), World Awkward Moments Day

19 March: Donkey Race Tradition (Italy)

The Donkey Race was created in 1966 to celebrate a woodworking tradition in the Medieval town and has been held ever since - every year on the Sunday after March 19th. The date is not chosen at random – this is the day of St Joseph, the patron saint of the woodworkers.

Preparations for the significant event start months before the weeklong celebrations. The actual donkey race is preceded by 6 days of open-air concerts, crafts markets, art exhibitions, Medieval street performances, fairs, food and wine tastings at the local trattorias.

Local townsmen dress in embroidered Medieval costumes to greet and entertain visitors. Many merchants set up stalls along the narrow-cobbled alleys of the
setting and the small shops are flooded with food delicacies and the traditional for Tuscany full-bodied red wine.

Beautifully dressed young men re-enact an ancient ritual of flag throwing before the race, showing their mastery in the craft to the public.

The race starts with a magnificent street parade including the flag bearers as well as knights, archers, priests, jesters, jugglers and Medieval gentry accompanied by drummers and trumpeters.

Each donkey wears a vest with a number, matching the one on its jockey. The animals are kind of trained for the race, however, some of them tend to suddenly stop in the middle of the route or even walk in the opposite direction bedazzling the respective rider. This is a rather comical tradition which leaves the crowds bursting with laughter.

The number of the teams is 8 – one for each of the village districts. Each jockey holds a colored flag with a coat of arm representing his neighborhood.

The donkey to cross the finish line first is the winner. The winning neighborhood treats everyone to a lavish buffet, lots of dances and good cheer.

Travel to: Italy (Tuscany). The race takes place in the small town of Torrita di Siena at the Piazzale Gioco del Pallone.

Other holidays on this date: National Chocolate Caramel Day, National Let's Laugh Day, National Corn Dog Day (USA)

20 March: Charnshambe Suri – Prelude to the Persian New Year (Iran)

A custom created around the 1700s B.C. of the Zoroastrian Era and celebrated in the beginning as a ritual to honor the spirits of the dead. People believed that the week before New Year the spirits of the ancestors visited the living to reunite with them and be entertained. Over the centuries, the celebration grew into a Fire Festival, which is now held annually on the Wednesday before the Iranian New Year. The name of the festival – Charnshambe Suri, literally means "Red Wednesday" - associated with the red color symbolizing good health as per Persian belief.

In the evening, locals make bonfires on the streets and jump over them reciting the words "take my sickly yellow paleness, give me your fiery red" –an ancient purification ritual. The wording means that the fire will take away the sickness and give in return energy and good health. The fire was very important for the Persians and they believed it had healing and cleansing powers. The idea of the lighting bonfires is not to let the sun set, but keep it shining all night until dawn.

Iranians practice the custom of spoon tapping as well – a lot like trick-or-treating, children covered with shrouds (representing the spirits) go from door to door. They knock on plates with a spoon, leave a hat on the threshold and hide. In return, they receive sweets and berries. It is believed that wishes come true this night.

The day is celebrated with huge fairs, fireworks, modern Iranian music, and dancing. The typical family dinner in Iran must include 7 dishes starting with the letter "S" (in the Perso-Arabic alphabet): green vegetables; samanu (sweet wheat pudding); dried fruit; garlic; apples; berries; vinegar.

Travel to: Iran (Tehran). The countries that celebrate the Persian New Year - Nowruz as a public holiday and have celebrations are: Afghanistan, Albania, Azerbaijan, Georgia, Iraq, Kazakhstan, Kosovo, Kyrgyzstan, Tajikistan, Turkmenistan and Uzbekistan and the Kurd population in Turkey and Syria.

Other holidays on this date: World Storytelling Day, National Proposal Day, Alien Abductions Day (USA), Eiffel Tower Day (France), Tower Hill Druid Ceremony (England)

21 March: Drowning of Marzanna (Poland)

Marzanna often called the Winter Witch, is the old Slavic Goddess associated with the death of the frosty winter and the rebirth of nature (Spring). In modern history, this is a day to celebrate the beginning of Spring and the longer days. The festival, dating back to about 1000 years, usually falls on the days of the Spring Equinox – around March 21st.

A Marzanna effigy is put together – a doll, usually made of straw. It is then wrapped in linen sheets or old clothes and adorned with ribbons and beads. Once beautified, the effigy is paraded through the streets and carried to a river or a lake. The decorated doll is then set ablaze and tossed into the water, symbolizing the end of winter's wrath and the spring rebirth. The burning of the effigy is an ancient pagan ritual – in the past the people believed that burning Marzanna will also remove all obstacles she is associated to - chilly weather, dark and short days, starvation, disease and all things evil, and they will have a good harvest season.

After the ritual, the procession of people holding green twigs and branches decorated with eggshells, handmade ornaments, and ribbons, returns to the village and the festivities begin with lots of music and dances. Competitions for the most beautiful or the biggest effigy are held in the big towns.

Travel to: Poland (Warsaw). In the Silesia region, there is a male equivalent to the Marzanna effigy and it is called Marzaniok.

Other holidays on this date: Common Courtesy Day, Harmony Day (Australia), Fragrance Day, Credit Card Reduction Day (USA)

22 March: Explosion of the Cart Folk Tradition (Italy)

This is one of the most important quasi-pagan traditions associated with Easter and the good harvest in Tuscany. The event is held annually on Easter Sunday and involves a 9-meter-high cart covered in fireworks. The actual cart that is used was built at the beginning of the XVIIth C. The tradition itself has been celebrated since the XVth C.

The wooden cart is pulled by two oxen adorned with spring flowers and colorful garlands and paraded through the streets of the town all the way to the central plaza – in front of the Duomo.

The custom was started during the First Crusade to the Holy Land when the young Pazzino (member of a local noble family), known as the first one to climb the walls of the Holy City and raise a Christian flag, returned from Jerusalem with three sacred rocks as a proof of his courage. These relics are preserved in the local church.

The celebration starts with a priest who rubs the rocks together until they spark and ignite the Easter candle. Then some coals are lighted and put in the wooden wagon to deliver the Holy fire to the Archbishop in the Duomo.

The procession is led by the oxen pulling the cart, followed by men dressed in Medieval costumes, flag bearers, and drummers.

The moment the official parade reaches the square in front of the Duomo – series of events take place very fast: the Archbishop uses the Holy Fire to light up a dove-shaped rocket symbolizing the Holy Spirit which is set inside the Duomo, just in front of the altar. The rocket slithers its way and collides with the cart out-front thus igniting it. This leads to a major explosion of the loaded with fireworks wagon.

The crackling fireworks, gunpowder smoke and spectacular display of colors are cheered for, because as the legend has it: a good and smooth explosion will bring good fortune and plentiful harvest to the city!

But! The legend also has it that this will happen only if the dove-shaped rocket returns safely to the Duomo (it runs on a wire). There had been a time when it didn`t make its way back and the city was hit with a disaster.

Travel to: Italy (Florence). The big bang takes place at the city square in front of the Duomo and the three stones are kept in the Church of Santi Apostoli. The ancient cart has a name – it is called "Brindellone".

Other holidays on this date: World Water Day, As Young as You Feel Day, Cherokee First Full Moon of Spring Festival (USA), Cavalcade of Herve (Belgium)

23 March: Day of the Sea (Bolivia)

This is a rather strange celebration considering Bolivia is a land-locked country. The day commemorates the loss of Port of Calama – Bolivia's last ocean-front property, to Chilean forces during the War of the Pacific. The country though maintains its Naval Force in hope of regaining its coastal territory. Ever since that unfortunate Bolivia battle, the two countries haven't been the best of neighbors and don't have diplomatic relations. Ever since the day of the battle – March 23rd, 1879, when many Bolivians gave their lives to save the coast from invasion, El Día del Mar has been celebrated.

The essence of the conflict is also a rather strange one – the war began over a new tax imposed by the Bolivian government. At that point, a Chilean company had been mining saltpeter (a type of nitrate used to make gunpowder) on the Bolivian coastline. The Chileans didn't agree with the new tax and sent armed forces to occupy the shore on Valentine's Day. Maybe the Bolivians were too distracted in the celebrations because they underestimated the power of the Chilean forces and lost the sea territory... For more than 120 years Bolivia insists on revising the treaty and Chile refuses to do so. Funny fact is that Bolivia has vessels sailing under Bolivian flag and has a Naval Force – the only thing missing is a coastline.

It is a sad celebration – at noon-time, thousands of people gather out on the streets in silence and listen to recordings of the sound of the sea and the seagulls played over loudspeakers. The day is marked by solemn ceremonies and a parade of the Naval Force. Many people put flowers at the Eduardo Abaroa monument – the national hero who died defending the coastal town of Calama. He is most famous for his last words before being killed in the battle – when asked to surrender, he simply replied: "Tell your grandmother to surrender" – and he was shot dead.

Travel to: Bolivia (La Paz). A huge parade featuring the Naval Force, locals and children groups takes place in the capital. Many of them carry pictures of the sea and model ships.

Other holidays on this date: National Chip And Dip Day, National Near Miss Day (USA)

24 March: Laetare of Stavelot (Belgium)

This three-day festival was created against all odds and is held annually starting on the fourth Sunday of Lent!

At the end of the XVth C, the ruler of the city - a Prince-abbot, trying to tighten the religious discipline, forbid all his clerics to take part in any of the city festivities – including carnivals.

The locals, however, thought the ban was ridiculous and decided to make fun of it by dressing up as monks for the masquerades (this was because the townsfolk really liked the monks and missed them joining in the celebrations). The Prince-abbot forbid that too.

A few years later, the locals came up with another idea – a new costume. A white robe with a hood, yet again subtly referring to the monk's attire. Surprisingly, the ruler accepted this version of the costume, but the residents decided to take things even further adding a hideous long red nose prop. Being already accepted, the costumes were named Blancs Moussis and became part of the local folklore and culture.

The Blanc Moussis have a specific act – when parading, they throw colorful confetti and ribbons to the crowds, and randomly hit people with... inflated pig bladders! If that isn't enough – they dangle dried fish in the people's faces too! They remind them of Jesters as they make fun and imitate other people, dance, and grunt, and put posters on windows and doors often ridiculing a fellow resident.

Being celebrated for five centuries, the Blancs Moussis are so popular now, that they are invited to take part in international festivals, representing the Stavelotian cultural heritage.

The festival features performers dressed as animals on decorated floats, locals pushing homemade carts with fruits and bakery goods which they throw to the public, marching bands, folklore groups, concerts, grand ball in the Abbey, food stalls and cannons disguised as cartoon characters which fire 5 tons of confetti!

Travel to: Belgium (Stavelot). A traditional line dance, led by the Blancs Moussis is held on the St Remacle Square.

Other holidays on this date: National Chocolate Covered Raisins Day (USA)

25 March: Cimburijada (Bosnia)

Cimburijada, or the Festival of Scrambled Eggs, is the celebration marking the first day of Spring. It is held in a small Bosnian town every year. It is believed that the first festival took place at the end of World War II, but there is no trace of who and why organized it.

Locals share food with friends and visitors to mark the first day of Spring. They gather early in the morning on the river bank and eat breakfast – scrambled eggs and egg sandwiches. Everything is cooked in giant pots over an open fire (usually) so anyone can have a bite for free. As the day proceeds and more people join in, the celebration turns into a huge picnic. There is music, dances, rafting on the river and some participants even bring tents for a true camping experience.

Travel to: Bosnia (Zenica). Lots of eggs are scrambled in a park on the banks of Bosnia River.

Other holidays on this date: National Medal of Honour Day, Waffle Day, Pecan Day (USA)

26 March: Prince Jonah Kuhio Kalanianaole Day (USA)

This day commemorates Prince Jonah Kuhio Kalanianaole, known as The Prince of Hawaii, and is celebrated annually on March 26th since 1949. Prince Kuhio was a legitimate heir to the throne of The Kingdom of Hawaii. Never an active monarch, he was one of the most distinguished statesmen of the State of Hawaii – he passed many bills in the US Congress in favor of the Hawaiian cultural heritage and is one of the most respected citizens ever lived on the Hawaiian Islands. Dedicating his life to the future interests of the islands, he was also a Royal Ambassador to the European heads of states and to Japan.

The celebrations are held on his birthday – March 26th, or the day after – depending if the day falls on a weekend or not. It is a state holiday so government offices, schools, and many businesses are closed. Parades, craft fairs, coconut carving, live music and dancing events, canoe races, cultural demonstrations and traditional Hawaiian Luaus are held during the festival. "Luau" is the traditional way to celebrate a variety of occasions and includes ukulele music, traditional Hula dance, games, and food. Typical food on this day would be Kahlua Pig – a shredded pork cooked in an underground oven for hours. Locals begin to set the "imu" (underground oven) in the early hours of the day – they dig up a giant hole in the ground and put firewood and stones on top. They cover the stones with green vegetation suitable for cooking and place the pig over it. Hours later and you have the most delicious and tender pork meat cooked in an underground stone oven!

Travel to: USA (Hawaii). There is a big celebration in Honolulu, although for a true experience – head to the island of Oahu, which is the final resting place of the Prince. Traditional Hawaiian celebrations take place at the Royal Mausoleum in Maunaala.

Other holidays on this date: National "Joe" Day, National Spanish Paella Day (USA)

27 March: Reindeer Herder`s Festival (Russia)

This is an annual festival of the indigenous nomadic people of the Yamal Peninsula in Russia. It is held in the last Saturday of March since 1995.

The Nenets – one of the most isolated people on earth, have kept their ancient way of life for centuries (which includes eating of raw meat, drinking warm reindeer blood and sacrificing animals to the gods of their ancient religion).

They are known to have the biggest reindeer herds and to travel the longest nomadic routes in the world. They migrate up to 1,000km per year, taking along their herds of deer and all their belongings. The Nenets transport their tents called "chums" (conical teepees made of reindeer fur) and possessions using handmade wooden sleds. They dress in hand-sewn deer fur clothes and keep a simple way of life, but are one of few to still preserve their religious beliefs, culture, and language. The Nenets are the world's best reindeer herders and the last to still practice this unique way of herding in one of the world's harshest environments. Just 15,000 Nenets guard about 600,000 reindeer!

The folks arrive in the small Arctic city only for the Reindeer Herders Festival. This is a major event as it is the only time of the year when the families are not that busy with their animals (each family owns between 1,000 and 2,000 reindeer to look after every day, which makes the communication between the family members... kind of not there at all).

So... What is the festival all about?

They gather to compete in games of strength and dexterity, and to meet with friends and relatives and have a bit of fun after the long and exhausting migration.

The women put on their best clothes and the men decorate their sleds and reindeer.

Traditional games that take place during the event are reindeer sled races, nomad wrestling, jumping through sleighs, axe throwing, traditional clothes competition and reindeer lassoing. The grand prize is a snowmobile!

The Nenets also use the opportunity to stock up on provisions such as medicines, or to find a wife or a husband and get married there and then (as they all leave after the festival only to be back the next year, which unfortunately leaves no time for dating).

The festival is accompanied by an open-air nomadic market, with local merchants selling handmade crafts, reindeer meat, and sausages, cloudberry jam, beads, and lace.

To imagine the whole experience, one should imagine being transported hundreds of years back... The word "Yamal" - the region where the Nenets live, means "the end of the world" in their own language.

Travel to: Russia. The festival is celebrated along the banks of the frozen Ob River in Salekhard in the Yamal-Nenets region.

Other holidays on this date: National Nougat Day, National Spinach Day (USA)

28 March: Chaitra Sukhladi (India)

This is the first day of the Hindu New Year and is celebrated in the month of Chaitra – the first month of the year according to the religious lunar calendar (the day falls on a new moon in March or April). The holiday is also a harvest festival and marks the beginning of Spring. Unique for the celebration is that it falls on a different day depending on the region it is being celebrated, as India is a vast country.

In some areas, celebrations begin with oil bath and visit to a temple. Locals clean their houses, often decorate them with colorful patterns and buy new clothes for the occasion. This is followed by a feast of a certain dish including all six tastes - happiness, sadness, anger, fear, disgust and surprise – and this is to reflect life itself as being a mixture of different experiences. Afterwards, they gather to make predictions about the year ahead. In some parts, they exchange small gifts and sweets. All business owners start the day with a small ceremony and invite the customers to settle their dues. In return, they offer them free refreshments.

In all parts of India, there are fairs, games, traditional music, festivals, and cultural activities.

Travel to: India – depending on the area, the New Year celebrations are as follows: March (Kashmir, Karnataka and Andhra Pradesh, Maharashtra); April (Bengal, Punjab, Assam, Kerala)

Other holidays on this date: National Black Forest Cake Day, National Something on a Stick Day, National Weed Appreciation Day (USA)

29 March: Splashy Fen Festival (South Africa)

Some of the ground rules are: "Check for snakes before sitting down on rocks" and "Don't use shampoo in the river".

The iconic festival runs annually for four days in the end of March since 1990.

An idea born around a dinner table and a bottle of wine evolved into one of the premier music fests in the country and also the longest running ones. The setting – a charming country farm cuddled along a river bank against a backdrop of marvelous mountain peaks!

The event showing off the best of South African music (including mbaqanga and isicathamiya), started as friends' gathering under the stars, with guitars, around a bonfire. Today, it attracts more than 100 000 people from around the world.

The event, named "South Africa's friendliest festival" features music bands, art performances and is for all music, fun, life and laughter aficionados.

The farm grounds are filled with small stalls selling handmade arts and crafts, food-on-a-stick, drinks, dedicated coffee village, and several workshop stands. Some of the activities available to the visitors are horseback riding, hiking, hot air ballooning, paragliding, golf, storytelling, puppet shows and movies.

Four stages with non-stop music performances from local and international performers and a natural amphitheater with great acoustics take care of the festival spirit along the duration of the fest. The vast farm fields offer perfect conditions for camping and the nearby river is a great spot to cool off!

Travel to: South Africa (KwaZulu-Natal province). The event takes place in the Splashy Fen farm in the small town of Underberg.
Other holidays on this date: National Mom and Pop Business Owners Day, National Little Red Wagon Day (USA)

30 March: Mebuug Buugan Ritual (Indonesia)

This is an ancient Hindu ceremony, observed annually on the day after Nyepi – the Balinese New Year. The exclusive to Bali ritual aims to wash away the bad energy, chase away bad spirits and all misfortunes. This is a traditional "mud bath", usually taking place in the rural areas of the island. An interesting fact is that in the past, the ceremony was banned for 60 years due to the requirement for completely nude participants. Nowadays the rules have changed and the locals strip down to wearing pants or a traditional Balinese cloth. After a prayer, they cover their whole body with mud (incl. face and hair) and then run to the beach to wash it away. It is a tradition in which only men can participate (due to the partial nudity).

Travel to: Indonesia (Bali Island). A true mud bath ritual is held in the home town of Mebuug Buugan – the Kedonganan village near Denpasar.
Other holidays on this date: National Doctors Day, National I Am in Control Day (USA)

31 March: Goat Races and Crab Races (Trinidad and Tobago)

This is one of the best ways to finish off the Easter weekend festivities! The unofficial but hilarious holiday takes place annually on the Tuesday following Easter.

An entertainer from the lower classes came up with the idea in 1925 and ever since, the event has been celebrated, turning to one of the most anticipated on the island.

It is like horse racing, but racing with goats instead. And yes, there are jockeys who run along the 150m track, encouraging and guiding the animals to cross the finish line as fast as possible. The goat and its jockey are a team and train together for a few months before the festival. It is important that they run in pristine harmony, because if a goat outruns its jockey – they both get disqualified.

The jockeys are dressed in crisp white shorts and colored vests. Each one holds the respective goat on a long rope.

It may sound odd of an event, but goat race aficionados bet lots of money on their favorite goat!

In the end – the winners in all three categories collect their awards: Champ of Champs, Champion Jockey and Most Outstanding Goat.

In the afternoon, a similar race event is held – but this time, instead of goats... the contestants are blue crabs.

Attached by a string to their "jockey" and poked with a bamboo stick, the mer animals are urged to cross a finish line. It is a bit awkward of a race, having in mind that they run sideways... Not to mention that the losers get cooked after the race!

The whole seafront village where both races take place turns into a festival town – there are dancers performing between the different races, musical bands playing Caribbean music and keeping the festive atmosphere with their traditional drums, and of course, the streets are flooded with street vendors selling the best of the Caribbean food (including the traditional crab & dumplings) and exotic drinks.

A huge party is thrown right after the races and the dances continue all night long.

Travel to: Trinidad and Tobago (Buccoo). The small village is the home of the races.

Other holidays on this date: National Bunsen Burner Day, National Clams on The Half Shell Day, National Crayon Day (USA)

... APRIL

Paganism: Ancient belief and practices before the doctrinal religion came around. Pagan is a Latin word referring to many "old" beliefs like Wicca and ancient Hinduism. Paganism honors either several deities or only one appearing in different forms and images – usually in the form of an animal. The pagan celebrations are focused around the change of the seasons - Winter Solstice and Spring Equinox, and worship nature. Devotees pursue the divinity as a personal experience. It is amazing how many of the current traditional holidays (such as Christmas and Easter) derive from Paganism.

01 April: April Fool`s Day (World)
A day for pranks! This well-known and much-loved holiday has been celebrated in many countries for centuries. Only a few know that it was created by mistake and originates in France. In 1582 Charles IX switched the calendar from Julian to Gregorian. This changed the New Year`s week from March 25th – April 1st to January 1st. Since there were no e-mails or cell phones at that time and news traveled fairly slow – it took a few years for some folks to acknowledge the new dates. These people were labeled "Poissons d`Avril" (April fish) and the general populace started pulling pranks on them, like inviting them to non-existent New Year parties on April 1st etc.

In the XVIIIth C, the tradition became so popular that it spread from France to England and Scotland, and from there – to America.

Today, in England, the "April fools" are called "noodles". It is considered bad luck to play a joke on someone after noon time.

In Portugal, some people throw flour at their "victims".

Travel to: USA (California). Visit the Museum of Hoaxes in San Diego (or sneak a peek online at www.hoaxes.org). Established in 1997 and dedicated to the exploration of hoaxes, mischief, and misinformation throughout history. There is a special gallery dedicated to April Fool's Hoaxes.

Other holidays on this date: National One Cent Day, National Love Our Children Day (USA), International Have Fun at Work Day

02 April: A Drop of Water Is A Grain of Gold (Turkmenistan)

A National holiday in Turkmenistan observed on the first Sunday in April, since 1995. The day is dedicated to those employed in the water management sector. Since most of the country's territory is covered by the Karakum Desert (about 70%), water is the biggest treasure. Development of the water infrastructure is crucial for the country, that is why 15 water reservoirs, irrigation canals, and even rivers had been built. Water supply and effective water management are national priorities.

The entire country celebrates this day - concerts, theatre performances, sport competitions, street festivals, speeches and fairs are held across the territory. Traditional food to complement the festivities are freshly baked bread, chorek (typical sweet bread) and different pastries. People sing traditional songs praising the Turkmen people and the water. The day is also a professional holiday for all employed in water management.

Travel to: Turkmenistan (Ashgabat). The main event takes place on the banks of the Karakum River in the northern part of the city. The river is a main source of drinking water and people often gather to pray and picnic there.

Other holidays on this date: National Ferret Day, National Peanut Butter and Jelly Day, Children's Book Day, Tweed Day (USA)

03 April: Miyako Odori – Geisha Festival (Japan)

This is one of the wonders of the world – the magnificent Geisha dance performance - a high-skilled and elite entertainer with in-depth knowledge of grace, beauty, conversation, calligraphy, traditional music instruments, theatre, traditional games, politics, current affairs and, of course, tea ceremony.

The Geisha performance is a living example of a thousand-year-old historical tradition deeply rooted in the Japanese aesthetics.

A typical day of a Geisha and a Maiko (aspiring Geisha, literally meaning "dancing child") includes the following activities: complex make-up and hairstyle, dressing up in kimono (which takes hours and needs a few people to be involved in the process), networking with business and political leaders, theatre, singing and dancing performance practice, participating in local festivals and entertaining guests in tea houses (Ochaya).

Miyako Odori is a Geisha Festival held annually in Kyoto in the month of April, attracting visitors from around the world. The event was initiated in 1873. A few years earlier the capital city was switched from Kyoto to Tokyo. By Miyako Odori, which translates to "The Dance of the Capital", the Kyoto folks showed their disapproval and unacceptance of the new capital.

The beautiful dance of Geisha evolves around cherry blossom theme (Sakura dance). Guests in the audience sit on tatami (traditional Japanese soft mat flooring) and admire the colors and magnificence of the dancers. Each performance is choreographed to absolute perfection. The steps are slow and graceful, in absolute harmony with the music played by the orchestra on traditional Japanese instruments. The dance has eight stages which include songs and drama acts. The theme is stylized around the four seasons, the nature, shrines, and aesthetics in everyday life.

Before the start of the dance, guests are invited to a traditional tea ceremony.

The hot drink is prepared, brewed and served by a Geisha. Although it may sound quite simple – this is a ceremony which can never be perfected, because it should leave one with the feeling of wanting more. Certain rules have to be followed followed at all times by the Geisha during the tea ceremony performance:

- "Wabi-Sabi" – imperfection is unique (an asymmetric cup, or a distinctive feature of the Geisha while pouring the tea)
- "Yugen" – the mystery (unknown ingredients when preparing the tea, or a subtle gesture)
- "Shibui" – simplicity (a simple painting, or a flower in a vase that just fits right in)
- "Miyabi" – elegance in every move
- "Iki" – uniqueness
- "Geido" – discipline and following ceremonial rules
- "Jo-Ha-Kyu" – not rushing through the ceremony but establishing the right rhythm

The dance performances take place in the whole month of April – 4 performances per day, each about 4 hours long.

Miyako Odori is often referred to as "The Cherry Blossom dances", as April is the month when the cherry trees blossom in beautiful pink colors.

Travel to: Japan (Kyoto). The performance is held at the Kyoto Art Theater Shinjuza.

Other holidays on this date: National Chocolate Mousse Day, National Find a Rainbow Day, Don`t Go To Work Unless Is Fun Day (USA), Inuyama Festival (Japan)

04 April: Rama Navami (Nepal)

This is a Hindu festival, held to honor the birthday of God Rama (the seventh avatar of Vishnu). It is observed annually in the month of Chaitra (March or April). Although not recognized as a major religious holiday, big celebrations are held especially in cities featured in the book of Ramayana – the life and story of God Rama.

The day is marked with visits to temples, or praying at home shrines, devotional worshipping, fasting and reading passages about Rama's life.

The Nepalese visit temples and make offerings of flowers. The much-anticipated day is celebrated with processions of elephants and flower decorated floats, colorfully dressed people who dance and sing, praising the life of Rama. Among thousands of pilgrims, the celebrations attract many "sadhus" – wandering Hindu monks.

Travel to: Nepal (Kathmandu). Any of the following temples are worth visiting: Ram Mandir (Battisputali), Changu Narayan (Bhaktapur), Ichangu Narayan and Bichangu Narayan in Kathmandu, Ram Janaki Temple in Janakpur.

Other holidays on this date: Tell A Lie Day, National Chicken Cordon Bleu Day, National Hug a Newsperson Day (USA), World Rat Day, The Passion of Coldrerio (Switzerland)

05 April: Tomb Sweeping Day (China)

Tomb sweeping, or Qingming, is a centuries-old ritual, showing respect to the ancestors, and is celebrated annually on the fifteenth day after the Spring equinox (either April 4th or 5th). It is a public holiday in China and the only traditional Chinese holiday celebrated in accordance with the solar calendar.

A theory has it that this festival derived from the Cold Food Festival (created around the 600 B.C.) by a Chinese Prince in honour of his servant Jie who provided for him during his years of exile – he even cut part of his thigh to make soup for his master. Jie retired in the forest when the Prince became a King. After an unsuccessful attempt to find him, the King ordered his men to burn down the forest. Jie was killed and in his grief, his former master ordered an annual three-day memorial without fire, which meant that only cold food could be eaten.

As this is also a Spring holiday, everyone is encouraged to go out, families make picnic and fly kites in the parks. The celebration includes sweeping the ancestors' graves from any dirt, pulling any weeds and overgrown shrubs, making offerings of food, tea, chopsticks and wine.

Nowadays, the "no fire" restriction is no longer in effect. Burning of joss paper is very common because Chinese believe that the deceased still need their material belongings. The so-called ghost cash is made of bamboo or rice paper, cut and shaped as cars, houses, clothing and even servants. These "gifts" of paper are burned as offerings in return for advice and guidance from the ancestors. After this ritual, the whole family gathers around the grave or at a nearby park and has a picnic. Typical food consumed on this day is the qingtuan – green dumplings made of rice and barley grass.

Recently many entrepreneurs have developed unique services, such as: hire a professional mourner for Tomb Sweeping Day (it gets more expensive if he is required to cry on the grave); send an online card to your ancestors, joss paper packages including iPhone replicas and more...

Travel to: China. This is a National holiday lasting for three days and is celebrated across the country.

Other holidays on this date: National Deep-Dish Pizza Day, National Read a Road Map Day, National Walking Day (USA)

06 April: Lazarovden (Bulgaria)

The ancient Spring Festival of St Lazarus originally celebrated to honour the miracle of Lazarus rising from the dead, is observed annually a week before the Orthodox Easter (on a Saturday). Lazarovden is also known as "zadushnitsa" (All Soul's day) and falls on the day before "Tsvetnitsa" - the day when the souls of the ancestors come out of their graves to reunite with family and friends.

People visit cemeteries and bring ritualistic bread, boiled wheat sprinkled with icing sugar and wine. They share the food with friends and family and leave some of it on the graves of their deceased relatives.

The other aspect of the celebration is a custom dedicated to youth and fertility known as Lazaruvane, which is mainly practised in the rural areas. It is a ritual performed by young unmarried girls (10-16 years old). They dress in traditional for the region costumes, wear flower wreaths and hold woven baskets decorated with flowers and willow branches. The girls stroll down the village streets going from house to house, dance a traditional line dance called "horo" and sing songs for happy marriage, harmony and fertility, bringing joy to their hosts. In return, they receive boiled eggs (dyed in bright colours for Easter), money and small gifts. After they visit every home, the maidens run to the nearest river/lake to throw their wreaths in the water. The wreath that outsails the others, belongs to the girl who will marry first.

Travel to: Bulgaria (Veliko Tarnovo). For best experience pop by the open-air ethnographic complex "Etara" - make sure to visit the Sweet House and taste the walnut cookies. Worth visiting is also the Café (Kafene) for its exquisite "white jam" served in glass of water and the traditional thick coffee prepared on hot sand.

Other holidays on this date: National Teflon Day, National Caramel Popcorn Day (USA), National Tartan Day (Canada)

07 April: Tsvetnitsa (Bulgaria)

A holiday with many names!

Tsvetnitsa (Flower Day, Flower Sunday), The Feast of the Willow Branches (in pagan Bulgaria, people believed that the willow had magical powers and used it as protection from black magic and nature disasters), or Palm Sunday is one of the most joyous Orthodox Spring holidays in the country. It is the day that marks the arrival of Jesus Christ in Jerusalem (people laid blossoming twigs on the ground and waved palm leaves to welcome him – hence Palm Sunday). Held on the Sunday preceding Easter, it is also celebrated as a "name day" – folks named after a flower or plant celebrate by hosting a family lunch or giving chocolates to friends and colleagues, in return receives flowers or small gifts. It is a Bulgarian custom for any guest to show up uninvited to the celebrating person's home and expect to be treated to a snack or drink.

The day also coincides with the most beautiful time of the year – it is warm and a scent of freshly picked flowers fills the streets. In the past, this day was also a holiday of the forest, fields and meadows.

Street stalls offer variety of spring flowers and wreaths made of weeping willow. It's a custom to light a candle in a church for good health. People are given a blessed reef of weeping willow from the priest on their way in, to put on their front door. Even when it dries – it is never thrown away but kept in the house until the following year (to keep evil away). In some rural areas, people adorn animals with willow branches and sing songs about flowers.

Typically celebrated outside, however families often host a festive lunch and invite relatives and friends to join in. Traditional food on this day is fish.

In some parts of the country, young girls gather by a river, place breadcrumbs on "willow boats" and throw them into the water. The girl whose boat sails farthest invites the rest to her house and offers traditional bread and dried corn mash (kachamak).

Travel to: Bulgaria. Tsvetnitsa is celebrated everywhere – from the smallest village to the largest city. For best experience, visit Sofia, Plovdiv, Veliko Tarnovo, Varna or Burgas.

Other holidays on this date: National Beer Day, National Coffee Cake Day, National Walk to Work Day (USA)

08 April: Ugaadhi (India)

Dessi Nikoltchev:

A holiday celebrated on the first day of Chaitra in accordance with the Hindu calendar and the New Year day in three Indian states (the date usually falls in March or April). "Ugaadhi" derives from the Sanskrit words "yug" meaning "era" and "aadi" - "the beginning". It is associated with Lord Brahma, the Creator of the Universe and is a fun and happy occasion to celebrate.

For locals, the day begins with Sesame oil body massage and visit to a temple for purification. All houses are cleaned up and tidied, front doors and entrances are often decorated with green mango leaves and beautiful flower leaf patterns. The locals buy new clothes and give charity to those in need. In some parts of India, people make garlands of sweetly scented Jasmine blossoms and bring them to the temples. After purification rituals and prayers, the whole family gathers and dines delicious dishes prepared for the occasion. Typical meal is a mango sweet and sour chutney consumed as a side dish or on its own – it combines the flavours of life (sweet, salty, tangy, spicy) - Hindus believe that one should be ready for any experience during the new year – sweet or sour.

Travel to: India (Karnataka, Telangana, Andhra Pradesh)
Other holidays on this date: All Is Ours Day, National Zoo Lovers Day, Take Your Parents to The Playground Day, Draw A Picture of a Bird Day (USA), International Roma Day

09 April: Smelling the Breeze (Egypt)

Sham El-Nessim (Smelling the breeze) is an ancient Spring Festival, annually celebrated in Egypt. It always falls on the Monday following the Orthodox Easter. The holiday is one of a few celebrated by Christians and Muslims alike. The tradition goes back 4500 years to the time of the pharaohs when the custom was called "Shamo", or "renewal of life", referring to the start of the new agricultural season. Ancient Egyptians used to define the exact date by measuring the angle of sunlight over the Giza pyramids.

People decorate boiled eggs and write wishes and questions on them - dyed eggs from Pharaonic times are a direct predecessor of the Easter eggs today. Locals often hang them on trees and wait for the gods to answer their questions and prayers. Another tradition survived from ancient times is eating salted fish with spring onions (fiseekh – fermented grey mullet which is caught, salted and left to pickle for a few months). Onions are believed to keep evil spirits away, and the fish is a symbol of fertility and welfare. And since the meal has a very distinct smell – it gives a true meaning to the phrase "smelling the breeze". It is a custom for all families to gather and picnic in the park, or just meet outside to enjoy the warm weather and festive atmosphere. There are also folklore concerts, military music parades and dances.

Travel to: Egypt (Cairo). In Alexandria, the Montazah Palace opens doors to its gardens of 20 000 different types of plants to the public. Half a million people usually visit the Qanater Gardens north of Cairo.

Other holidays on this date: National Cherish an Antique Day, National Winston Churchill Day (USA)

10 April: Semana Santa (Guatemala)

One of the most sacred celebrations in Guatemala - Semana Santa, or Holy Week, combines Catholicism and ancient Mayan rituals. In the past, Mayans adopted and incorporated certain Catholic observances. For example – for them, the Sun represented God, Ix Chel -a jaguar-Goddess of midwifery and medicine was associated with Virgin Mary.

Semana Santa commemorates the Passion, Crucifixion and Resurrection of Christ. Festivities start on Palm Sunday and continue until Good Friday before Easter (the dates are between March 22nd and April 23rd). The week is filled with street processions, starting from different churches, gem embelished floating platforms called "andas", representing religious scenes. Huge statues of Jesus Christ are mounted on floats and carried by hundreds of purple-robed men called "cucuruchos" (some of them wear pointy purple hats with two small eyeholes). The platforms with Virgin Mary are surrounded by women dressed in black. Funeral marching bands and people holding thick incense sticks create a ghost-like fog to the end of the procession.

A very distinctive feature of the Guatemalan celebrations is the "alfombras de Acerrin" - flower carpets – beautiful masterpieces of Colonial and Mayan art, biblical symbols and scenes from nature can be seen everywhere on the streets. Colourful patterns made of flower petals, rainbow-coloured sawdust, fruit and even vegetables cover every inch. Made for the parading people with floats to pass through and eventually destroy them, they are meant only to adorn the processional route. Locals make flower patterns of the Sun as one of the most important Mayan deities, a symbol of life and afterlife.

Some people - flower carpet makers for decades, have several generations worth of knowledge.

To sum it all up – rainbow-coloured streets, scent of spring flowers in the air and licking-fingers good local food!

Travel to: Guatemala. The cities with most distinctive processions are Antigua Guatemala, Guatemala City and Quetzaltenango. The procession of La Merced in Antigua Guatemala on Good Friday starts in the evening and ends early in the morning – it goes all night and is also the one that walks over the longest flower carpet.

Other holidays on this date: National Encourage a Young Writer Day, National Farm Animals Day (USA)

11 April: Ceremony of Pleureuses (Switzerland)

The ceremony dates in the XVth C. and takes place on Good Friday. This beautiful and solemn ritual, commemorating the Passion and Crucifixion of Jesus Christ, starts with readings from the Bible of the Passion of Christ and continues with a mourning procession through the cobblestone streets of a Medievall town. Mourners (weepers), all dressed and veiled in black, walk slowly behind a young girl representing Virgin Mary. She walks behind a black-hooded penitent who carries large wooden cross. Each mourner holds a red velvet cushion with a symbol of the Passion – crown of thorns, whip, nails, hammer, tongs and St veronica's shroud. During the procession, the whole town turns into a very spiritual place, embraced by chants and prayers.

Travel to: Switzerland (Canton of Fribourg, Romont). The procession starts from the Church of Romont.

Other holidays on this date: National Cheese Fondue Day, National Barbershop Quartet Day (USA)

12 April: Punta Gorda Festival (Honduras)

A festival held annually on April 12th, celebrating the culture of the indigenous inhabitants - the people of Garifuna. Visitors from around the country travel to an island to commemorate the day in which the first Garifuna people (about 4,000 of them) arrived in Central America from the Caribbean island of St Vincent in 1797. The day is full of festivities – dances under drum rhythm, local art troupes performing scenes of the natives' arrival and music bands playing traditional songs in the Garifuna language, which is included in the UNESCO List of Intangible Heritage of Humanity.

Locals wear black, white and yellow colours – they sing and dance all day long. There are numerous food stalls selling traditional food - "machuca" (mashed plantain or plantain soup), coconut bread and "guifity" (a local alcoholic brew with Rum, herbs and roots).

Travel to: Honduras (Roatan). The festivities are held in Punta Gorda.

Other holidays on this date: National Grilled Cheese Sandwich Day, Russian Cosmonaut Day (USA)

13 April: Water Gun Festival (Thailand)

The Water Gun festival is part of a Buddhist festival celebrating the Thai New Year (April 13th -15th). This holiday is observed by Thai and Malaysian Siamese and marks the end of the dry season.

People dress in traditional festive Thai dress and visit temples, where they make offerings to the monks and pray for a better year ahead. Water is a main feature of the celebrations and that is the reason the Water Gun Festival was created. Part of a specific purification ceremony is to pour water over the heads of family and relatives (usually kids pour water buckets over the elders, or wash their hands), but mainly, this is the largest water gun fight in the world! Anybody can spray water over anybody – there are no rules and no one is safe. Many streets are closed for traffic due to street parties with loud music and tons of water-soaked people dancing and having fun, often dressed in swimsuits. Some people go even further – they throw white chalk powder or even use elephants to spray as many people as possible (ouch!). Tourists are a tempting target for the locals, who splash them with icy-cold water, shouting it is for good luck!

There are some rules on this day: work as little as possible, don't kill animals and don't lie!

Travel to: Thailand (Bangkok). The festivities in Bangkok last for three days, but in the northern city of Chiang Mai, they last for a whole week!

Other holidays on this date: Scrabble Day, National Make Lunch Count Day (USA), Khmer New Year (Cambodia)

14 April: Aluth Avurudda (Sri Lanka)

This is the Sinhalese Buddhists and Tamil Hindus New Year and is celebrated annually on April 13th or 14th during a night of a full moon. The holiday marks the end of harvest season and coincides with one of two instances when the sun is directly above Sri Lanka. Locals start preparing weeks in advance – they clean houses, throw out unwanted items, buy new clothes, light oil lamps and prepare sweet meat dishes. They visit temples where priests anoint them with oils as part of a purification ritual. It is a very "friendly" holiday - people open doors to encourage friends, relatives and even strangers to pop in for a chat and a snack. Typical food delicacies are tiny oil cakes and tropical plantain dishes.

Traditional ritual is the lighting of the hearth – it is performed by the lady of the house. She puts a pot of Kiribath (traditional New Year dish – rice pudding as rice is a symbol of prosperity) over the fire after worshipping it three times. The festive menu also includes bananas and local sweets. Another tradition is children showing respect to elders by making small offerings and receiving money in return. Neighbours exchange plates full of sweets and wish each other good fortune through the new year. Usually, after the visit to a temple and the festive lunch, everyone spends the day celebrating on the streets.

Travel to: Sri Lanka (Anuradhapura).
Other holidays on this date: National Ex-Spouse Day, National Reach as High as You Can Day, Look Up at The Sky Day (USA), Bengali New Year (Bangladesh)

15 April: Rocket War (Greece)

Unique celebration held at midnight just before Easter every year. The custom allegedly appeared in the Ottoman era when the Turkish rulers wouldn't let the Christian folks, inhabiting the island, to celebrate Easter the way they wanted. So, locals decided to fake a war and started firing rockets from two churches standing on opposite hills. As long as rockets were fired, the Turkish kept distant from the churches, where the Christians had their Easter service exactly the way they wanted.

Two hills, two churches built 400m away from each other and two rivaling parishes. The idea of the festival: to hit the bell tower of the church opposite with a handmade wooden

rocket! The locals light thousands of rockets (about 60 000) from purpose-built platforms and fire them in the direction of the opposite hill, waiting to hear the church bell ring. The rockets are loaded with gunpowder. All of this takes place while there is active service in both churches. At the end of the fierce battle - both churches declare themselves winners and agree to disagree actually who had won. Instead, they decide to settle the score in the next year.

The locals start preparing months in advance – they cover the two churches and all nearby houses with metal boards to avoid fires, and handcraft the rockets (which turns out to be slightly illegal, but the police apparently turns a blind eye on this one).

Travel to: Greece (Chios Island). The wars are held in the town of Vrontados and the two rival churches are Agios Markos and Panaghia Ereithiani.
Other holidays on this date: Rubber Eraser Day, National Take A Wild Guess Day, Titanic Remembrance Day (USA)

16 April: Lao New Year (Laos)

Pimai Lao is a three-day colourful party which is also a time for people to reconnect with their families and relatives and to think about how to do better in the year to come. It is observed annually in the middle of April and is one of the liveliest festivals in Laos.

On the first day, which is the last day of the passing year, locals visit temples to pour scented water with flower petals over Buddha images (the water is then collected and taken home as it is considered blessed). Many pour buckets of scented water over themselves or friends, thus performing a purification ceremony but also to cool off as April is one of the hottest months too.

The second day is a "day of no day" because it falls between the old and the new year. Locals clean their houses, sweep temples and the young pour water over the palms of the elders - a way to chase the evil from the past year away.

The last day is a time to ask for forgiveness – from the elders, from the monks and the Buddha statues and images. People exchange small gifts and wish prosperity and good fortune in the year ahead. The temples are full of devotees listening to the chanting monks. The end of the celebrations is marked by candlelight processions around temples.

The festivities also feature sand sculptures built along the coast of the Mekong River and in front of the temples – they aim to stop evil spirits from entering in the new year and are decorated with colourful ribbons, flags, flowers and splashed with scented water. Flower scent spreads on the streets as monks gather fresh flowers and adorn the Buddha statues with them.

There are also: water fight with scented water, lantern parades, street processions with Buddha images carried in golden palanquins and a Miss New Year float procession.

Typical food for the festival is sticky rice with padaek (fermented fish sauce) and roasted mushrooms.

Travel to: Laos (Luang Prabang). The Prabang monk's procession starts from the former Royal Palace. Luang Prabang is the city with most ancient traditions in the celebrations and keeps the party going for almost a week.

Other holidays on this date: National Eggs Benedict Day, National Stress Awareness Day (USA), Water Festival (Myanmar)

17 April: Blue Egg Swim (Switzerland)

Blaueierschwimmen takes place annually on Easter Monday and is... a different way to welcome Spring. Brave men dive into the still icy waters of a lake to fetch a hidden blue egg. After the refreshing challenge, they warm up with egg liqueur, egg consommé and hot tea. The event is organized every year at 14:00h sharp!

Travel to: Switzerland (Canton of Zurich). The swim takes place in the district of Uster in the Greifensee Lake.

Other holidays on this date: National Haiku Poetry Day, National Poem in Your Pocket Day, Blah Blah Blah Day (USA)

18 April: Dajia Mazu Holy Pilgrimage (Taiwan)

Dessi Nikoltchev:

This pilgrimage dates in the XIXth C. It is the largest religious festival in the country and one of the greatest religious festivals in the world. Celebrated annually over nine days, it is also included in the UNESCO List of World Intangible Heritage. The exact start date varies but usually falls in April (a special ceremony is held in the Jenn Lann temple, asking the gods for the date to hold a pilgrimage).

This is a 330km procession route involving about 12-hour walking and hiking per day.

Devotees parade through the village streets and carry a chair with a statue of the Mazu Goddess. Mazu is one of the most cherished deities and a Goddess of the Sea. During the eight nights of the procession, the statue stays overnight in a different temple and is taken out in the crack of dawn to continue along the route. Locals believe that the deity meets other Mazu statues residing in the temples - they exchange energy and bring good luck to the villagers. The participants in the parade are forced to look for accommodation along the way, but all locals open their homes, yards and garages to offer a shelter. Many public buildings such as train and bus stations, post offices are also converted to accommodate people. Free food and drinks are provided as well. Each stopover is accompanied by fireworks and local performances while the procession itself features lion dances and drum players walking behind the Mazu statue.

Each devotee holds a holy flag with his/her name written on it – on each temple visit, the flag is stamped with a seal and pinned with charms (the people take it home for good luck).

Travel to: Taiwan (Taichung City). The procession route goes through 21 cities and 80 temples and involves around 5 000 000 participants every year. The pilgrimage starts and ends at the Jenn Lann Temple.

Other holidays on this date: National Animal Crackers Day (USA), International Jugglers` Day

19 April: Bloemencorso Bollenstreek (The Netherlands)

The Bulb Flower Parade - one of the oldest and most anticipated Spring festivals in the southern part of the Netherlands. As this part of the country is well known for its abundance of flowers – the Flower Festival is a wonderful way to show the beauty of nature! Started in the 1940s after the war, the event is celebrated annually in April (always on a Saturday).

The festival starts with a beautiful evening light show. It features tens of breathtaking floats called "praalwagens", built especially for the procession – all of them richly decorated with millions of colourful locally grown flowers – tulips, hyacinths, daffodils and others, and all in different shapes, representing a specific theme. They parade along a 40km route accompanied by musicians and local bands. The parade attracts many local and international visitors.

Travel to: The Netherlands - the parade starts in Noordwijk and ends in Haarlem. Visitors can observe the float making process in Klinkenberghal.

Other holidays on this date: National Amaretto Day (USA)

20 April: Dragon Boat Festival (Philippines)

A festival created in China to honour the Dragon God. The event is celebrated in the Philippines since 2007 and falls in a different month every year.

Surrounded by white sand beaches, turquoise water, magnificent sunsets and great nightlife, the festival is also known as "The Paradise Boat Race". Dragon Boating was introduced only in 2001 and represents an ancient way of transportation and trade, using long boats with fierce dragon heads, rowing under the beat of a hollow drum. The men and women in the boats (around 20 people in each boat) look like ancient warriors, however, this is a race of skill, not a battle.

The event is accompanied by beauty pageants, street fests, sand sculpture competitions, surfing contests and tons of dumplings – the local delicacy for the occasion.

Travel to: Philippines (Boracay Island). Other countries which celebrate the festival are Singapore, Malaysia, Riau Islands and Greater China (on different dates).

Other holidays on this date: National High Five Day, National Cheddar Fries Day, National Look Alike Day (USA), First Day of Summer (Iceland)

21 April: 20-Rappen Coin Throwing Custom (Switzerland)

Locally known as "Zwänzgerle", the XVIIIth C. custom takes place on the morning of Easter Monday and is celebrated annually. Crowds of people gather on a cobbled square in the Old Town and carry brightly coloured hard-boiled eggs and small coins. They divide into two teams – adults (holding the coins) and children (holding the eggs). The adults aim and toss a 20-Rappen coin in an attempt to break the eggshell. If they succeed – they get to keep the coin and the egg. But, since this is an almost impossible task – the children keep the egg and all coins for themselves. It is like a kids payday!

Vendors and locals selling drinks and food bites take care of the festive atmosphere on the square.

Travel to: Switzerland (Zurich). The celebration takes place on Rüdenplatz, in the heart of the Old Town. The custom is local and is observed only in Zurich.

Other holidays on this date: National Yellow Bat Day, National Chocolate Covered Cashews Day (USA), World Tuna Rights Day

22 April: Crying Sumo Festival (Japan)

A 400-year-old tradition observed to give good fortune and health to babies. Japanese believe the ritual scares away demons and chases away evil from the newborns. As locals say: "crying babies grow fastest".

The ritual itself involves pairs of Sumo wrestlers holding babies, dressed in tiny Sumo belts and colourful aprons, doing everything possible to make them cry (that including scary faces, different noises etc). The winner is the wrestler who's baby cries first. If two babies start crying at the same time – the louder one wins. And when a baby starts crying, the Sumo wrestler lifts it as high as he can to increase the strength of the blessing. If the baby doesn't cry... a referee puts on a scary mask to speed things up! There have been instances when babies just end up laughing...

The ceremony takes place at the peak of Spring and usually coincides with the Day of the Children in Japan. It is held in temples and shrines all over the country.

Travel to: Japan (Tokyo). The biggest ritual with around 100 participating babies takes place at the Sensoji Temple.

Other holidays on this date: Jelly Bean Day, National Earth Day, National Girl Scout Leaders` Day (USA)

23 April: National Beer Day (Germany)

Celebrated annually on April 23rd, National Beer Day honours a German Beer Purity Law which came into force in 1516 in Bavaria. The law specifies that the only ingredients to be used in beer production should be water, hops, yeast, and barley. On this day breweries, beer gardens and beer museums open doors for the public to experience the art of brewing as well as its long history. There are many beer festivals, workshops, beer-tasting events and discussions held all over the country, and everyone celebrates all things beer. The holiday has been observed since 1994.

An interesting fact is that German beers are often labelled "Gebraut nach dem Bayerischen Reinheitsgebot von 1516" – meaning they are brewed as per the regulations of the Beer Law from 1516.

Another fact is that there is an actual phobia of having an empty beer glass – it is called Cenosillicaphobia!

Travel to: Germany. Take a brewery tour in the North-Rhine Westphalia breweries. In Munich: about 1,000 liters of beer are flowing from a specially designed fountain - free of charge!

Other holidays on this date: National Picnic Day, National Talk Like Shakespeare Day, Sikh Day Parade (USA), Racing Horse Festival (Turkmenistan), St Jordi (Spain, Catalunya)

24 April: The 6 o'clock Bell Toll - Sächsilüüte (Switzerland)

This Spring Festival dating back to Medieval times is one of the two biggest holidays in the Canton of Zurich famous for its guilds and ancient traditions. It is celebrated annually, usually on the third Monday in April following the Spring Equinox.

Guilds and workers celebrated the first Summer working hours. In the past, a working day lasted as long as there was daylight leaving the workers with no free time during the bright hours of the day. With the coming of Spring (and a law from 1525), the working day was set to end with the church bell at 6 o'clock, which meant that locals would have some free time in the daylight hours.

The day is celebrated with a huge parade of the Guilds accompanied by music bands. A half-day long procession features every single guild in the city (25 in total and represented only by men - Merchants, Painters, Carpenters, Winemakers, Clockmakers, Bakers, Shoemakers, Butchers, Fishermen etc.) – all wearing traditional clothing of the Guild they represent. Most of them parade on horseback, or on beautifully decorated floats and carriages.

After the parade, a traditional burning of the Böögg takes place. It is a giant snowman effigy representing Winter, with his head packed with explosives and perched atop a huge bonfire. The effigy serves as a weather oracle – locals believe that the time between lighting the pyre and the actual explosion of Böögg's head predicts the forthcoming Summer – if the snowman explodes quickly, the Summer will be very hot.

All spectators are armed with branches and skewers because the burnt remains of the effigy are used as coals for what becomes the largest open-air BBQ in the country!

Travel to: Switzerland (Zurich). The route of the parade is around the Limmat River and the burning of the *Böögg* takes place at 6 o'clock in front of the Opera House. The BBQ is there too!

Other holidays on this date: Pig in A Blanket Day, Poem In Your Pocket Day (USA)

25 April: La Festa di San Marco (Italy)

La Festa di San Marco, also known as the rosebud festival, commemorating the patron saint of the city - San Marco, is held annually on April 25th.

The legend has it that in the VIIIth C, a man from the lower class fell madly in love with a noblewoman from Venice (the Doge's daughter). He went to war seeking fame and glory to win the Doge's approval in marrying his daughter but was badly wounded. However, before the poor man died, he picked a beautiful rose from a nearby rosebush and entrusted a friend to bring it to his loved one. A day after receiving this gift, the Doge's daughter was found dead with the blood-stained flower on her chest.

A beautiful and heart-breaking story celebrated in one of the most romantic cities in the world.

On this day, men give to the one they love a single red rose, to show their affection and commemorate the love story.

There is another legend, as interesting as the first one. When St Mark reached the shore of the Venetian lagoon, an angel told him "Your remains will rest here". However, he was buried in Alexandria, but this story gave food for thought to two Venetian merchants. They went to Alexandria, stole the remains, put them in their boat and covered them with pork meat knowing that the Muslims (who would check the cargo) are not allowed to touch pork. That is how the remains got to Venice where they rest ever since. There is a beautiful mosaic on the floor of St Mark's Basilica depicting two merchants covering the remains with pork meat.

The official celebration includes a gondola race in Grand Canal – Regata di Traghetti". Also, there are music, dance performances, concerts, fresh food markets and feasts throughout the day. Beautiful view to observe are people dressed in green and red who form a single red rose on Piazza San Marco.

Travel to: Italy (Venice). The Regata starts from the island of Sant'Elena.

Other holidays on this date: National DNA Day, National Hug a Plumber Day, National Telephone Day (USA)

26 April: Nenana Ice Classic (USA)

This celebration is in fact ... a lottery! It was created in 1906 with only six participants and a prize - a round of drinks at a local bar. After some time of inactivity, the lottery was revived during a long and cold winter back in 1917 when railroad engineers bet on when the ice cap on the river would crack. Ever since the event is held annually and the tickets are on sale from January until April. The ice can break anytime from late April to late May.

Players in the "draw" should guess the exact time and day the Winter ice on the Tenana River will crack and make way to Springtime (the ice is about 100cm thick). And since the event is held in Alaska – that is indeed the very question.

Locals build a giant wooden "tripod", set it on the ice-covered river and tie it to a clock on the shore. When the ice melts, it sinks the "tripod" which pulls the rope tied to the clock. This stops the clock at the exact time of the melt and a winner is declared. The largest reward given in 2014 amounted to $363,627 (so far over 10 million USD have been given away in rewards).

The lottery is used as a climate indicator with its data collected over a period of 100 years.

Travel to: USA (Alaska). As the name suggests, the event is organized in the city of Nenana, but tickets for the lottery are sold worldwide.
Other holidays on this date: National Pretzel Day, Hug An Australian Day

27 April: AfrikaBurn (South Africa)
The festival created in 2007 is celebrated for seven days annually, in April or May. The event is a replica of a Burning Man festival, held annually in August/September in the Black Rock Desert in Nevada, US (a temporary built city – Black Rock City, hosts the event). The Burning Man was started as "radical self-expression platform" by a few friends in San Francisco in 1986.

AfrikaBurn is held in a semi-desert setting and showcases various artworks that are eventually burned in the end. There is a theme with which participants should go and it changes every year.

The main sculpture – San Clan, representing a group of people symbolizes the idea of unity and shared effort which is the essence of the festival.

The event observes "Leave No Trace" principles of outdoor ethics, which include: dispose of all waste, leave what you find, respect wildlife and the other visitors etc. It is a gathering of art aficionados from all walks of life – free spirits and wanderers alike.

What is unique is that participants contribute to the organization of the campsite too. They build different theme camps to enhance the visitors' experience – be it food tents, drink kiosks or workshop sites. People wear costumes, drive handmade cars (mutant cars) and parties pop up everywhere, all the time. There is no electricity, no main stage, so every piece of the desert in the campsite can become one. In Tankwa Town (the temporary campsite) money is not an issue – nothing is for sale, instead - people trade or simply ask for the thing they want. The idea of the whole festival is to let go of the material world and enjoy the individual talents and gifts of nature, so don`t expect any shops or bars nearby.

Travel to: South Africa. The event is held at the Stonehenge Farm in Tankwa Karoo National Park.
Other holidays on this date: National Prime Rib Day, National Take Your Son/Daughter to Work (USA)

28 April: Miracle Sea Road Festival (South Korea)
This so-called "Moses miracle" gained international exposure in 1975 when a French Ambassador to South Korea wrote about it in a French newspaper.

For about 90 minutes every year in April, the Yellow Sea magically recedes giving way to a sand path linking the small islands of Jindo and Modo. The legend has it that Jindo villagers fled the island chased away by hungry tigers, but one member of the family – Grandma Bbong – was left behind. The woman prayed to the Dragon King of the Sea to reunite her with her family. A magical rainbow appeared easing her to escape safely to the neighbouring island and re-join with her relatives (unfortunately she died of exhaustion before reaching the shore). The festival features shamanic rituals and traditional performances such as a Circle Dance, to honour the Sea God, as well as fresh whale meat, clams and crabs feast. The main attraction, of course, is a walk along the 3km long and 40-60m wide sea path where people gather clams, crabs and other sea delicacies which can be later cooked in any of the coastal restaurants. The procession is led by a local band making their pilgrimage to Modo island and the statue of the waiting family. Many locals consider this a magical event and come to pray to the gods.

Travel to: South Korea (Jindo Island). For authentic experience – rent a room in a minbak (private home) and don't forget a pair of rubber boots.

Other holidays on this date: National Hairball Awareness Day, Great Poetry Reading Day (USA), Trujillo Cheese Festival (Spain)

29 April: Wyld Fire Beltane Hunt (USA)

This is a four-day event combining pagan rituals, camping and great entertainment, held annually in April/May. Beltane is a transition between Spring and Summer when the energy of the Earth is strongest. The ritual celebrates life, love, fertility and new beginning. The celebration begins at dawn with people dividing into two teams – predators and prey. A designated maiden Queen is placed among the prey. Both groups (dressed in hunting clothes and blessed by a priest) run to the forest, the prey group hiding from the predators. Then the chase begins – the goal of the predators is to find the maiden Queen while being slowed down by riddles from the prey group. The predator who gets to outsmart the prey is crowned Oak King. He then "marries" the maiden Queen in a sacred ritual.

The festival is accompanied by energy sessions, yoga classes and pagan ritual workshops.

The opening ceremony is the burning of the Wickerman (a straw effigy), marking the end of Winter.

On the last night, there is a huge party around a Jacuzzi, with fire and belly dances, lots of food and fun. The festival ends with a ritualistic Maypole dance.

Travel to: USA (Louisiana). The ritual is held at Gryphon's Nest Campground in Springfield.

Other holidays on this date: National Shrimp Scampi Day, National Zipper Day, Texas Sandfest (USA), International Yacht Sailing Regatta (Antigua)

30 April: Feria de Abril de Sevilla (Spain)

One of the most cherished celebrations of the Spanish culture dating back to 1847. It is celebrated two weeks after Easter and lasts for six days.

Each morning a parade of carriages and horseback riders (representatives of the high society and prominent families) make their way to a bullring where bullfighters and breeders meet (before becoming a festival, the event was purely a cattle fair). Women dress in traditional "faralaes" – flamenco style dress, accompanied by hair jewels and a matching flower. Men nowadays wear trendy suits, replacing the tight trousers and short jackets of the old times. During the day, visitors are entertained with bullfights and later enjoy dancing and eating tapas, drinking Sherry and the famous rebujito (a mix of sherry and soft drink).

For the duration of the festival, the whole fairground is covered with colourful marquees called "casetas" (around 1,000 total), belonging to wealthy businesses, organizations, or just friends and prominent families. They are equipped with small kitchen, bar and sound system which plays traditional local Sevillanas (the folklore music of the region which has its own dance too). Unfortunately, only the communal marquees are open to public, the private ones require an invitation.

A typical meal on the first day of the festival is fried fish, but there are also kiosks selling cured ham, seafood and churros (fried-dough sweet pastry).

Travel to: Spain (Seville). The event is held at the Real de la Feria (in Los Remedios). The entrance to the fair is through a huge gate, specially built for the occasion months in advance and beautifully lit during the celebrations. The bullfights are held at the Real Maestranza bullring.

Other holidays on this date: Eeyore's Birthday Party, National Honesty Day (USA), Walpurgis Night (Germany, Sweden, Czech Republic), Beltaine Fire Festival (Scotland)

... MAY

Festival: Celebration uniting a typical custom, or tradition of the locals. Usually festivals are created around a harvest start/end or change of the seasons. A festival can be religious, folkloric or agricultural.

01 May: International Festival of Worm Charming (England)
On a night in 1983, two friends had one too many Ales in a local pub. On their way home, one of them needed urgently to "relieve" himself and did so in the nearby field. However, much to his surprise, worms started to surface from the ground! This is exactly how this strange festival was created. It is celebrated every year in May on a Bank holiday.

A church bell marks the start of a worm charming competition. Teams start charming on their designated 1 square meter grassland. The participants do everything possible to make the worms surface without touching, digging or forking the ground. It is quite comical to watch people sing, dance and tap the ground to collect a single worm.

The festival program features Morris dancers, live music, dog show, fancy dress competition, football, donkey rides, scones, hog roast, bacon butties and lots of beer and cider.

Travel to: England (Devon). The event takes place in the village of Blackawton.
Other holidays on this date: May Day, Loyalty Day, Law Day, Save The Rhino Day (USA)

02 May: National Truffle Day (France)
This day is all about.... The Chocolate truffle! Thanks to its inventor Mr Dufour of Chambéry, who came across it in 1895, the entire world can now enjoy it. The treat is traditionally made with a chocolate ganache centre coated in chocolate, icing, cocoa

powder, chopped nuts or coconut. A truffle may be filled with other fillings such as cream, melted chocolate, caramel, nuts, fruit, nougat, fudge, toffee, mint, marshmallow or liqueur. The recipe for the best-known truffle - "Napoleon III" made in 1902 ...remains a secret.

National Truffle Day is celebrated on May 2nd every year.

Travel to: France (Paris). A weekend getaway to Paris or London where the tiny treats are most cherished! A must do is a visit to the Prestat Chocolate shop – opened by a relative of Mr Dufour in 1902 and still selling the Napoleon III truffle by original recipe!

Other holidays on this date: National Life Insura nce Day, Baby Day, Brothers and Sisters Day (USA)

03 May: Ear-shooting Ceremony of the Bunun Tribe (Taiwan)

This is a 1,000-year-old rite of passage marking the coming of age of the Bunun tribe boys. It is celebrated annually in late April or May and represents a tribal ceremony - archery competition to sharpen the hunting skills of young boys. In the past, after hunting, Bunun men hung carcasses for the young boys to practice shooting with bows and arrows. Shooting the prey's ears from a distance was considered the toughest feature in the contest.

This is the only hunting celebration left from the past to the Bunun people. Members of other tribes and many internationals visit as guests of honour. The festival starts with blessings from the Shaman and includes pig hunting, ear-shooting (on animal-shaped cardboard targets), archery, wrestling, pig roasting, witch inductions and other. Some activities are reserved for women only – such as planting, weeding and turning millet to flour using only mortar and pestle. This is a festival showcasing survival skills.

The tribal women wear a traditional dress in vibrant blue, accompanied by colourful beaded headbands. The men wear traditional hunting attire.

Typical food for the occasion is smoked deer meat and, of course, the tribal speciality – millet wine. There is also a traditional slaughter of pigs for the festive dinner.

Travel to: Taiwan (the festival rotates each year among the nine villages of the Bunun tribes). Visit the village of Yongkang in Taitung County for best experience of the festivities as it brings together Bunun tribe families from the whole district.

Kaohsiung and Taitung counties are also inhabited with Bunun people and have their own annual ear-shooting festival.

Other holidays on this date: National Garden Meditation Day, National Two Different Color Shoes Day, National Specialty-Abled Pets Day (USA)

04 May: Spirit of Speyside Whisky Festival (Scotland)
Created in 1999, this festival celebrates Scotland's national drink and is one of the biggest of its kind in the world. Observed annually at the end of April/beginning of May, it brings together thousands of whisky aficionados.

The festival itself has over 500 different whisky events taking place over the five days it is being held, such as new and rare whisky tastings and workshops, old and new distillery visits, discussions, whisky bars, visits of historic castles, educational movies and talks (with main topic – whisky, of course), whisky markets, open-air stages with live music, vintage halls with music and dances, whisky and chocolate and whisky and cheese pairing workshops, whisky aroma academy, distillery production sessions, whisky masterclasses, Single Malt journey on the Steam Train and more.

Numerous shops and street stalls sell everything from scotch to Scottish souvenirs and clothes. The pubs offer traditional delicacies and cold pints!

Travel to: Scotland (the area between Aberdeen and Inverness). The event takes place in Speyside – the biggest whisky-producing region in Scotland and the spiritual home of the world famous Scottish Malt.

Other holidays on this date: National Orange Juice Day, National Day of Reason (USA), Weeding Festival (Taiwan – Thao tribe)

05 May: Cinco de Mayo (Mexico)
This annual celebration commemorates the victory of an outnumbered Mexican army over the Great French Army at the battle of Puebla on May 5th, 1862 (at that point the French had not been defeated for 50 years). The holiday is greatly celebrated in Mexico and in the USA, although the latter celebrates Mexican culture in general, rather than a historic victory.

A huge parade with decorated floats, dancers dressed in traditional Mexican attire and mariachi music take place in the historic city of Puebla where the battle was won. People dress up like Mexican and French soldiers and recreate the war scene. Many food stalls offer traditional treats including the famous poblano – a sauce made with chilli peppers and chocolate, and Margaritas. There is fun for the kids too - they beat with a stick piñatas, filled with candy and treats made especially for the occasion.

Travel to: Mexico (Puebla State). Although other parts of Mexico held celebrations too, it is Puebla State that has announced the day as a public holiday and hosts the best celebrations.

Other holidays on this date: World Password Day, National Totally Chipotle Day, International Tuba Day (USA), Arrival Day (Guyana)

06 May: Gergyovden (Bulgaria)

Celebrated annually on May 6th as the day of St George and the Bulgarian Armed Forces Day, this is one of the most anticipated holidays of the year. It is also a "name day" in Bulgaria – everyone named George (or similar) celebrates by usually hosting a festive dinner (or buying a round of drinks).

This is an ancient Spring holiday, allegedly with roots in a Slavic pagan feast with sacrificial traditions (related to the annual breeding and farming cycle). St George is a patron saint of all shepherds and flocks, so the ritual of sheep slaying on this day is very common (the meat is slowly cooked over an open fire). St George is also a patron saint of the Army – he is displayed on all holly icons as the Dragon Slayer.

Some people in rural areas, still observe the tradition of collecting morning dew on meadows - they believe it is blessed by St George himself. They wash their faces, hands and feet for good fortune. Young unmarried girls gather flowers and herbs to make three wreaths: one for the goat that will be milked first, second for the sacrificial lamb and third for the pot of milk. Landowners take the first red coloured egg (coloured at Easter) and bury it in the fields praying for a good harvest to come. Locals dance "horo" – a traditional Bulgarian line dance with asymmetrical rhythm – they dance around houses, barns and sheds. Then a lamb is sacrificed (usually the first male born), however not before being ritually fed and adorned with a mulberry branch wreath. On this day all evil spells are broken.

In cities, people visit churches to light candles and pray for happiness and good luck for the whole family. They buy spring flowers and flower wreaths to bring home. The day ends with festive dinner with roast lamb, rice, fresh green leaf salad, ritual bread, fresh garlic, yoghurt and boiled eggs.

It is very common for small towns to take the feast outside (in front of the church or on the main square) and the whole town celebrates as one big family.

Travel to: Bulgaria. Everyone everywhere celebrates Gergyovden – small town villages and big cities. A huge military parade takes place in Sofia (in front of the St Alexander Nevsky Cathedral), honoring the saint and celebrating the Bulgarian Armed Forces Day.

Other holidays on this date: National Beverage Day, National Nurses Day, National Bombshell's Day (USA)

07 May: Lotus Lantern Festival (South Korea)

Dessi Nikoltchev:

This is a 1200-year-old tradition of celebrating Buddha's birthday held over three days in early May. Hundreds of thousands of people throw a huge party to honour the anniversary. All streets are adorned with colourful lanterns creating a magical ambience.

The festivities start with a beautiful lantern exhibition in a temple, each lantern symbolizing part of the life and mission of Buddha. The lanterns are of different shapes and sizes, all made of silk and paper.

The next day is marked by a grand opening ceremony with lots of dances and traditional performances.

A huge parade is held on the last day – all participants, dressed in traditional hanbok clothes, parade through the city streets carrying lit lanterns in the shape of animals, fruit, religious symbols and flowers. The lanterns represent wishes for happiness and luck - according to the Buddhism belief, by lighting a lantern one commits to do good. The festival ends with a massive circle dance amidst a carpet of scattered flower petals and the releasing of lanterns into the starry sky (before releasing them, people burn their wishes written on small pieces of paper).

Along with the celebrations, everyone can take part in tea ceremony demonstration, taste a traditional temple dish, talk with a Buddhist monk, Zen meditation or make their own lantern.

Travel to: South Korea (Seoul). The celebration starts with a traditional lantern exhibition in the Bongeunsa Temple. The lantern parade starts at Dongdaemun History and Culture Park.

Other holidays on this date: National Homebrew Day, Free Comic Book Day (USA)

08 May: Santabary Festival (Madagascar)

Pagan in its origin, the 3-week Santabary Festival takes place annually in late April/early May and celebrates the rice harvest. Events are held around the country.

The celebrations vary depending on the region, but they all include indigenous dances, traditional music and songs performed by the Malagasy people.

Locals dress up in brightly coloured celebratory clothes, paint their faces and adorn their headpiece with flowers, leaves and tribal symbols. Dance groups perform beautiful ritualistic dances under monotonous drum beat. Specific steps and moves honour the gods and represent the people's gratitude for a rich harvest and their prayers for an even better one in the year ahead.

This is a very important festival for the locals because it celebrates rice - and rice is the main crop on the island.

Local delicacies enjoyed during the fest are boiled rice, steamed and fried vegetables, meat, maize porridge, rice cakes and meals cooked in coconut water. The typical drink is rice water.

Travel to: Madagascar (Antananarivo). All 18 Malagasy ethnic groups are represented in the capital and largest city on the island.
Other holidays on this date: National Have a Coke Day (USA), World Red Cross Day

09 May: Procession of the Holy Blood (Belgium)

This tradition dates back to the XIIIth C when allegedly, a small container, a sacred relic holding a piece of cloth with the blood of Jesus was brought into a Belgium town. The Procession of the Holy Blood is celebrated annually exactly 40 days after the Easter holidays.

People believe that on the 40th day after Easter, a miracle occurs - the sacred blood becomes wet once again and that is why this day is observed.

The celebrations start with a huge street parade with locals, dressed up as crusaders on horsebacks, pilgrims, peasants, beasts, donkeys and even Adam and Eve.

Among them are representatives of the Brotherhood of the Holy Blood – the very ones who look after the precious artefact. Devotees re-enact the moment when the relic was brought to town and different art groups perform scenes from the history of the town.

The parade is accompanied by live music bands, choirs and floats representing different biblical scenes. However, the air stands still when the relic with the Holy Blood passes.

The celebration culminates with a prayer in different languages.

The day is known as "The Most Beautiful Day in Bruges" and is visited by many pilgrims, priests and nuns from around the world. The town is also known as "The Venice of the North" due to its numerous water canals.

This tradition is on the UNESCO List of Intangible Cultural Heritage of Humanity.

Travel to: Belgium (Bruges). The street procession lasts for around 3.5 hours. The relic is kept inside the Basilica of the Holy Blood.
Other holidays on this date: National Teacher Appreciation Day, National Butterscotch Brownie Day, Lost Sock Memorial Day (USA)

10 May: Buddha Purnima (Bangladesh)

This is the largest Buddhist festival in Bangladesh, commemorating three important events in Buddha's life – his birth, his enlightenment and death. An agreement to celebrate all three life phases was made at the World Fellowship of Buddhists conference in 1950. Every year the date falls on a different day in May, but always on a night of a full moon. It is a time of festivity - all Buddhist temples are decorated with flowers and National and Buddhist flags are put atop. Locals visit temples to sing songs and bring offerings of candles and flowers. Many devotees dress in a simple white dress and spend the whole day at the temple. Everyone becomes vegetarian for a day, as slaughterhouses are closed during the festival because killing livestock is prohibited. No drinking is allowed as well. There are group meditations, recitals praising the life of Buddha, seminars and discussions marking the religious harmony between people of different faiths and colourful street processions in major cities. As Buddha preached a message of peace, the festival is a time for charity – people are encouraged to help the poor, sick and hungry by paying for medical expenditures and distributing food and clothes to the disadvantaged. In some areas, folks release birds and other animals, living in captivity, as a symbol of goodwill. By displaying peace, love and kindness, followers honour Buddha and his teachings.

Unique about this holiday is that people from all religions in Bangladesh celebrate the day, bringing religious harmony between the faiths.

Travel to: Bangladesh (Dhaka). Colorful processions are organized in Chittagong as well.

Other holidays on this date: National Bike to School Day, National Third Shift Workers Day, National Receptionists Day (USA)

11 May: Bun Festival (Hong Kong)

The annual festival is held in early May and usually coincides with the celebrations of Buddha`s birthday. Created in the XVIIIth C. as a ceremony to chase away evil spirits and the plague from the island, the ritual is now a fun day attended by thousands of people.

Locals make food offerings and pray in temples – or in any of the temporary altars set up on the streets. Colourful celebrations accompany the festival – there are traditional lion and dragon dances, a street parade with decorated floats and people dressed in costumes resembling different deities, music and drum beating, martial arts demonstrations and locals selling souvenirs and worship items. Children, dressed as legendary warriors or mythological creatures float on ropes above the street procession and perform different acts and air-dances (they are secured within purposely-built frames).

However, highlights during the festival are three bun towers – 18m bamboo scaffolds covered with buns. In the past, people would climb up the towers and try to snatch the bun from the top – the highest the bun, the better the luck. But, due to safety precautions (as a tower once collapsed injuring many participants), nowadays the construction is made of steel instead of bamboo and only trained athletes can climb up to collect replica buns (the original ones can become slippery in bad weather).

The event has even an official bun supplier – Kwok Kam Kee delivers more than 60,000 sweet buns steamed in bamboo baskets for the festival every year and they are sold everywhere. They are all branded with the Chinese symbol for peace.

The festival ends at midnight with a burning of the King of the Ghosts effigy and distributing the sweet buns to the crowd.

The festival is listed in the UNESCO List of Intangible World Heritage.

Note: only vegetarian food is allowed during the festival days.

Travel to: Hong Kong (Cheung Chau Island). The bun towers are built in front of the Pak Tai Temple – Pak Tai is the Taoist God of the Sea.

Other holidays on this date: National Foam Rolling Day, National Twilight Zone Day, Eat What You Want Day (USA)

12 May: Czech Beer Festival (Czech Republic)

The festival is held annually over 17 days in early May. Known as the biggest beer event in the country, showcasing more than 150 different brands of beer (local and imported). With around 10 000 seats available to visitors and lovely staff wearing traditional Czech costumes, this is the perfect getaway on a sunny day. Each of the festival tents set along the street offers a different kind of entertainment, music and dances.

Local chefs, butchers and bakers offer a variety of food delicacies to match with the choice of beer. There are also gastronomic workshops, beer tastings, music performances, DJ sets, weekend afterparty and a Beer Diversity Tent with foreign beers.

Travel to: Czech Republic (Prague). The address of the venue is Letenská 120/7.

Other holidays on this date: International Nurses Day, Child Care Provider Day (USA)

13 May: A Festival Called Panama (Tasmania)

This is a two-day, three-night exclusive and ultra-boutique event, held in the Tasmanian forest since 2012.

The event takes place annually in a secluded cider brewery.

All visitors have the rare opportunity to witness great international music acts, as well as late-night cabaret, morning yoga sessions in the field, pop up open-air markets with delicious local food and drinks, DJ parties, storytelling workshops and more.

Huge canvas tents, natural amphitheatre made of logs and small and cosy candlelit bars can take one on a journey through the world of wild jazz, classic burlesque and nostalgic acoustic jams.

There is a tradition on the last day of the festival – the Panama clothes swap – everyone should leave and take a piece a piece of clothing!

Travel to: Australia (Tasmania). The event is nestled in the breath-taking Lone Star Valley in the Panama Forest of Tasmania.

Other holidays on this date: National Apple Pie Day, National Frog Jump Day, International Migratory Bird Day (USA), International Blame Someone Else Day

14 May: Beltaine In the Forest Festival (USA)

The iconic Pagan celebration of Beltaine (or Beltane), also known as the Celtic May Day is celebrated annually on May 1st in many parts of the world. The rituals slightly differ, but they always celebrate fertility and revival of nature after the heavy rains in Spring. It is believed that in this time of the year, the earth powers are strongest. Celebrations include lit torches and bonfires as this is a fire festival. The name Beltaine comes from the Celtic God "Bel", which means "the bright one" and the Gaelic word "teine" meaning "fire". People jump over bonfires for purification and good luck in the coming year.

This particular festival was created in 2008.

A truly magical experience that travels through time. Fire dancers illuminate the fairground while half-naked people covered with mud and body paint wind as they dance in an ancient drum rhythm, chased by mystical creatures with horns. The costumes include feathers, headpieces and scary masks, flower wreaths and long cloaks.

The culmination is the burning of the Wicker Man – a giant effigy built of wood and straw. This is a sacrificial ritual and in the past, living people used to be caged inside a Wicker Man construction and offered to the gods (the offerings included animals, food and flowers too). Nowadays, of course, no people are being sacrificed or harmed, but the Wicker Man is still set ablaze.

Beltaine is also a time for an ancient marriage ceremony called "handfasting" – couples say their vows and have their hands ritually tied together as a symbol of partnership and devotion. After the ritual, they jump together over a broom – again symbolizing that they have crossed together a threshold. Their marriage is bound to last for 1 year and 1 day – after which they could choose to stay together or go their separate ways.

Traditional Maypole dance takes place at the end of the festival. The Maypole, usually made of birch, symbolizes the potency of God and the flower wreath at the top of the pole symbolizes the fertility of Goddess. As people dance in circle around the Maypole holding the ends of colourful ribbons tied to the top of the pole, they represent the spiral of life itself, the union between Earth and Sky as it was in Pagan times.

The festival features also healing, massage and energy workshops, artisan shops with stone jewellery and magical oils, Tarot card readers, stalls with witch-crafted runs, charms and potions.

Travel to: USA (West Virginia). The festival is organized at Coonskin Park in Charleston.

Other holidays on this date: Mother's Day, Dance Like a Chicken Day (USA), Cat Parade (Belgium)

15 May: Russefeiring or Russ (Norway)
Many people call it: "Incomparable insanity".

Russefeiring, or simply Russ is a rite of passage into adulthood - 3-week non-stop party for high school leavers. The celebration, created in 1905, starts in the end of April and lasts until May 17th - the Norwegian National Day. This is a party madness as it also coincides with the age when young people can buy alcohol and obtain a driving license (most school leavers have just turned 18 which is the legal age to consume alcohol).

Those who take part wear matching clothes and drive a matching car – the colours are often bright red or blue and this is linked to the colour of the graduation ceremony hats. Red is for everyone seeking higher education, Blue is for business graduates, white – for medical science and green for agricultural studies. Some students group and buy or rent a pimped-up party bus in which they spend every night during the festivities. Many of them create Russ group party meetups – where several schools party together.

Students divide into teams of classmates and prepare a list of mischiefs (known as Russ Knots – every achieved task brings a knot which is tied to the hat). Each teammate should complete the full list (each completed "knot" brings points). The list may include running naked in the middle of a crossroad; getting a tattoo that says "Russ"; order at a drive-through riding in a shopping cart; act drunk in a library; wear clothes inside out; sleep up on a tree; kiss a police officer; spend the day crawling on all fours; bark like a dog in the park; put a "for sale" sign on a police car etc. In addition, each student makes and prints out his own Russ card – it looks like a business card and is exchanged with "new acquaintances" during the Russefeiring.

The celebration ends on May 17th – Norway's Constitution Day, when the Russ follow the official city parade through the streets.

Dessi Nikoltchev:

Where to celebrate: Norway (Oslo). The capital city has the best public parade for the celebration of the National Day on May 17th, so why not get the best of both celebrations and attend Russ and the National Day exactly there!

Other holidays on this date: National Chocolate Chip Day, Police Officer's Memorial Day, National Nylon Stocking Day (USA), Aoi Matsuri (Japan)

16 May: Tumbuna Sing-Sing (Papua New Guinea)

This is an annual celebration of the ancestors' way of life and traditions and takes place in May. More than 300 indigenous people from 15 different tribes gather to honour their cultural heritage in a massive festival with lots of tribal dances and traditional music. All participants wear bilas (traditional festive costume), decorated with plant leaves, feathers, seashell necklaces and headpieces. Their faces are painted in bright colours.

In the spirit of the happy occasion, a huge "mumu" is prepared for lunch. It is roasted in an underground oven, sometimes called earth-oven – a very basic cooking pit in the ground.

Travel to: Papua New Guinea (Paiyagona Valley)
Other holidays on this date: Wear Purple for Peace Day

17 May: Crossbow of Grifalco Medieval Tradition (Italy)

A real Medieval tradition held annually after mid-May (on a Sunday around May 20th which is St Bernardino Day – the patron saint of the city).

A magnificent crossbow tournament held in a majestic Renaissance town, the residents of which are known for their mastery of the crossbow ever since the Middle Ages.

In the XVth C, local authorities created a tournament to provide training to the folks to keep their skills sharp and restrain them from hunting instead.

Years later – in the 1960s, the Crossbow of Girifalco was officially initiated.

The entire village is decorated with flags of each neighbourhood and welcomes the visitors in a festive manner.

Preparations for the competition continue the entire year – archers dust off their skills and flag bearers practice their unique technique – the latter mark the start of the games with a dance while throwing their flags up in the air.

On competition day, there is an official Medieval ceremony and parade in which locals dressed in velvet costumes take part.

Each city district is represented by eight archers who only have one shot to hit the centre of a target using exact replicas of an XVth C. wooden crossbows.

Locals show support to their champions by wearing a scarf with the distinct colours of their neighbourhood.

The event takes place in front of a Cathedral where the crowd welcomes the "heroes" with chants and songs. Drummers and brass bands add vibe to the festive atmosphere.

The archers take place behind the enormous wooden crossbows and aim. After each shot – a designated referee announces the result.

Whoever hits the centre of the target is declared a winner, and his neighbourhood – the winning neighbourhood, which is a grand honour.

Then, the champion is lifted high into the air and carried by cheering representatives of his neighbourhood.

The prize – a golden arrow trophy!

After tears of joy and pride – the town folks dine together and celebrate within the district-winner till morning hours.

This event is held twice a year – the second date is August 14th.

Travel to: Italy (Tuscany). The tournament is held in the small town of Massa Maritima.

Other holidays on this date: National Walnut Day (USA), National Day (Norway)

18 May: Festival des Jardins (France)

Created in 1992, this event is the crown jewel of all garden festivals. Held annually over a few months between April and November, the lovely flower celebration takes place in a beautiful chateau along the Loire Valley.

The festival features magnificent display of around 30 themed gardens designed by landscape architects and florists.

The arrangement of blooming flowers, trees, plants and randomly placed everyday objects is unique to each design and shows the beautiful colours and shapes of nature.

The breath-taking masterpieces are illuminated, which gives a chance to visitors to adore them at nighttime.

And not just the beautiful backdrop of the Medieval chateau, but also 2000 candles are lit at dusk to enhance the experience.

The festival is a true fairyland – giant mushrooms peek behind a centurial oak tree; golden fish swim in an illuminated lake; a bridge leading to a giant hive made of willow winds its way over a river with huge water lilies. The theme is different every year and so are the titles of the gardens. A recent example were names, such as: "A table!" - showing a selection of cannibal plants, "Can a Rarity Be Eaten" – displaying rare spices, "Dyer`s Garden" – presenting natural colours obtained by plants etc.

During the summer months – private candlelit tours are available to book.

Travel to: France. The event takes place at Chateau Chaumont sur-Loire – a fortress built around the year 1000 and owned by Catherine de Medici at some point.

Other holidays on this date: National No Dirty Dishes Day (USA), International Museum Day

19 May: Festival Medieval de Sedan (France)

The festival, inaugurated in 1996, is held annually over a weekend in the end of May.

The celebration takes place in a Renaissance castle (in the past – the greatest castle in Europe) and features concerts, Medieval parades and re-enactments of historical scenes, art performances and open-air markets.

The entertainment includes medieval banquets, flag throwing and jousting competitions, horse races, chivalry tournaments, music plays performed on medieval musical instruments and much more.

During the festival, the entire city turns into a medieval stage – visitors can spot peasants washing their laundry out on the streets in ancient wooden barrels; men roasting meat; knights having a drink in a local pub; town criers announcing the news accompanied by monotonous drumming; jugglers; wrestling and sword duels; fire-eaters; ancient medicine and potion workshops; Middle Ages fair and more.

The Medieval Festival lasts for two days and ends with a truly spectacular display of fireworks in the courtyard.

Travel to: France (Sedan). The event takes place in Chateau Fort de Sedan.

Other holidays on this date: National Endangered Species Day, Boy`s Club Day (USA)

20 May: Weighing the Mayor (England)

This weird custom goes back to Medieval times as a mean to measure corruption but is still observed every year in May (3rd Saturday), in a small town in England. This is the only place in the world where the Mayor is weighed annually, in front of a cheering crowd. The ritual has two parts – "tolling out" the former Mayor at the end of his service and "weighing in" the new one (a new Mayor is elected every year) – both using a special scale from the 1700s (a brass tripod with a hanging seat). The ceremony was introduced in the XVIIth C, when the Mayor was believed to have been drunk and acting strangely (indeed he was both).

So, right after the election, the new Mayor is publicly weighed in by men in period dress, tricorn hats and white gloves which makes the ritual quite spectacular. His/her weight is recorded to be compared later on to the weight at the end of the service (in 1-year time). At the "tolling out", if the Mayor has gained weight, it is considered to be at the expense of the taxpayers (aka – he/she has done a poor job).

In Medieval times, people would throw rotten fruits and tomatoes, but this part is abandoned now. Instead, the residents just "Boo" the Mayor and his officials - it is the shame that is taken into account nowadays.

However, if the Mayor has lost weight – the crowd cheers as apparently, he/she had worked hard during the past year.

The "tolling out" result is publicly announced in a loud voice by an appointed town crier – if the Mayor has gained weight, the town crier calls out "And some more" and if the Mayor has lost weight, the town crier announces, "And no more".

Travel to: England (Buckinghamshire). The weighing takes place in the town of High Wycombe. The ceremony begins at the Guildhall.

Other holidays on this date: Be A Millionaire Day, National Learn to Swim Day, Armed Forces Day, Pick Strawberries Day, Cherokee Heritage Gospel Sing (USA), World Whisky Day (Scotland), Mifune Matsuri (Japan)

21 May: Anastenaria Fire Walking Ritual (Bulgaria, Greece)

This unique celebratory fire-dance is observed annually in villages in Southern Bulgaria and Northern Greece during two festival periods – in January (January 18th on St Athanasius Day) and in May. The 3-day festival in May which starts on the 21st and ends on the 23rd, Anastenaria (Nestinarstvo in Bulgarian) is a ritual cycle associated with St Constantine and St Helena (May 21st is the day when the two saints are commemorated). The legend behind it goes back to the Middle Ages (XIIIth C) when the Church of St Constantine accidentally caught fire engulfing in flames the icons of St Constantine and his mother St Helena. The locals heard the cries of the holy icons and ran to try and save them. The brave men went inside the burning church and came out unharmed by the fire, holding the sacred idols in their hands. They believed that the two saints protected them from the flames.

Another theory is that the celebration derived from an ancient cult to God Dionysus.

The ceremony has its roots in Pagan times and originated in the Thrace region (now part of Turkey). The reason it is celebrated in parts of Bulgaria and Greece are the many refugees after the Balkan Wars who relocated and kept the tradition.

The festivities include lots of traditional dances, music, street processions and animal sacrifices. It all ends with barefoot fire-dancing over red-hot coals.

The fire dancers are blessed with holy water before the ritual. The fire walking takes place at night, after a huge fire lit by the oldest participant is left to die down until the scorching hot coals are the only thing to remain. The participants, known as spiritual leaders of the ritual, dance in a circle around the smouldering embers, carrying icons of St Constantine and St Helena, which during the year are kept in a sacred place (shrine), wrapped in red cloths. The celebratory dance under the rhythm of a Thracian lyre and drum beat takes the dancers to a state of trance, a moment when they believe they are "seized" by St Constantine. At this very moment, they step on the blistering hot coals (over 500 degrees Celsius) spread on the ground before them and begin the ritual dance holding the holy icons high up above their heads.

The "fire walkers" claim to not feel the flames under their feet. The right to perform the ritual is hereditary.

This ancient ritual is included in the UNESCO Representative List of Intangible Cultural Heritage of Humanity.

Travel to: Southern Bulgaria and Northern Greece (Strandzha Mountain). A legend has it that the Church of St Constantine which caught fire and the very home of the saint, was in the village of Kosti in Bulgaria.

Other holidays on this date: National Memo Day, National Waitstaff Day (USA)

22 May: La Doudou (Belgium)

The annual festival takes place 57 days after Easter.

It originated in the Middle Ages – in the mid-1300s when a city was hit by plague.

At that time, locals decided to hold a street procession carrying a holy image of Waltrude – the city patron saint, praying she would help them fight the terrible disease.

They paraded down the city streets, praying for a blessing – and a miracle happened! The outbreak of the sweeping plague stopped. The grateful residents began celebrating the day every year.

The observation is divided into two main parts: a procession with Waltrude`s icon and a re-enactment of St George`s battle and a Dragon (the latter was added later in the celebration).

The procession starts in the evening before the grand celebrations. The holy icon is taken out of the church where it is being kept, only for the duration of the festivities, and given to the authorities. The locals hold lit torches while parading in the streets of the city.

On the next morning, a lush parade starts, with the icon placed on top of the Car d`Or (golden wagon pulled by horses). The relic is accompanied by representatives of each of the city guilds – wearing medieval costumes.

Later in the afternoon, the re-enactment of the epic combat between St George and the Dragon begins. The fight represents the historical victory of good over evil.

St George is represented by a local man. In his fight against evil, his helpers are folks disguised as dogs.

The wicker dragon which is about 10 meters long is carried by the so-called white men. His "helpers" are little devils holding balloons which they use as a weapon to hit the dogs and random people from the audience.

The Dragon attacks St George with his tail which is guarded by other important characters in the play – the Leaf Men, covered in real ivy leaves.

St George attacks the Dragon, but his spear breaks every time. The battle ends when St George pulls out a pistol and shoots the ferocious beast! The victory is marked by the sound of a carillon.

In line with the legend, if one manages to grab a handful of the wicker dragon's tail – it can bring him good fortune through the year.

La Doudou is included in the UNESCO List of the Oral and Intangible Heritage of Humanity.

During the festivities, there are also concerts, massive street clearance sale, art performances and more.

Travel to: Belgium (Mons). Food and drink stalls line up along the procession route which starts from the Collegiate Church of St Waltrude. The epic battle takes place on the main square in the city.

Other holidays on this date: Buy A Musical Instrument Day, National Maritime Day (USA), World Goth Day

23 May: Sacred Mayan Journey (Mexico)

This ancient journey, going back thousands of years (to around 1250s AD), recreates one of the oldest Mayan traditions – a pilgrimage to the island of Cozumel to receive a message from the Goddess Ix`Chel and correspond it to the villages (Ix`Chel is the Moon Goddess and the jaguar deity of midwifery and medicine in the ancient Mayan culture celebrated by shamans). Every year, Mayan descendants on the Yucatan peninsula paddle in wooden canoes from the mainland to an island, to bring offerings, ask for health and fertility and receive a divine message from their goddess over two days in May. According to mythology, the turquoise waters were a source of food, but also a door to the underworld –Mayans believed that the ocean was an entrance to Xibalba, a place of fear ruled by the gods of death. This belief made the journey a real test of faith, devotion, strength and willpower. This ancient ritual had been forgotten for centuries, but thanks to ethnologists it was brought back and nowadays attracts massive international interest. The once "purely religious" journey is now a huge showcase of the Mayan cultural heritage.

Every year 300 men prepare for six months to take the journey which starts from the beautiful Riviera Maya. The area south of Cancun was once an important port city of the Mayan Empire and also a starting point of this massive pilgrimage.

Dessi Nikoltchev:

On the night before the sacred journey, the magnificent coastal streets open shops for a traditional Mayan market (Kíi'wik where goods from all regions of the Mayan world are sold) – merchants all dressed in pre-colonial clothes sell artisan products and local food, while visitors exchange their cash for cocoa seeds – the traditional Mayan currency. There is also a performance telling the story of the ancestors and their pilgrimage through songs and dances.

On the following morning, before taking off with the canoes, paddlers representing ancient Mayan warriors participate in an opening ceremony with ritual Mayan dances under a monotonous drum beat. They are covered with red body paint and blue handprints as they had been "touched" by the Goddess who summoned them on this journey. An "appointed" devotee representing Ix'Chel makes her way to the beach and the statue of the young goddess through a pathway lit by torches carried in a palanquin by her "subjects" all dressed in white robes. The air is filled with a fruity scent of incense sticks while the rising sun creates a magical ambience. At dawn, a priest gives his blessings to the participants and they paddle off into the turquoise waters.

Their return the next day is celebrated with a grand reception ritual including a priest, bongo's music, dances, variety of churros (traditional sticks of sweet fried dough) and different meats.

Travel to: Mexico (Quintana Roo). The sacred journey begins at Xcaret Park on Playa del Carmen and visits the Ix'Chel shrine on the island of Cozumel before returning the next day (from 6 to 9-hour paddling each way depending on the weather). It is believed that the ancient temple of the Goddess had been in San Gervasio.

Note: Anyone in the world can apply to take part in the Sacred Mayan Journey, but should live in Playa del Carmen during the training period.

Other holidays on this date: National Taffy Day (USA)

24 May: Bermuda Day (Bermuda Islands)

A holiday created because of a civil unrest in the 1960s. After a thorough research conducted by local authorities, folks came up with an idea that a public celebration would bring people together. And that's exactly what happened in 1979 when the first Bermuda Day Heritage Parade took place. However, locals didn't agree that one day of festivities is enough to show their rich culture and turned the day into a Heritage Week. But the week wasn't enough too... So, now the Bermudians celebrate a whole Heritage Month, with a highlight – Bermuda Day!

Celebrated annually on May 24th, this day is important because of the following three life-changing events:

1. This is the (un)official start of the Summer on the island;

2. The locals take their first dip in the ocean and release their boats on the water for the first time in the year;
3. Bermuda shorts are officially considered acceptable business attire.

The day is marked with colourful Heritage parade with decorated floats. It is remarkable that the locals tend to "reserve" their place along the parade route from the night before. They use all means necessary – ropes, buckets, flip-flops, some even sleep on the pavement to make sure nobody can steal their spot. There had been occasions of visitors tripping on ropes or tapes in the night before the parade.

Two major races are held on this day – a cycle race and a marathon. Both cross half of the island. This is also the start of the season for the Fitted Dinghy boat races.

A fascinating view is the Gombeys – groups of 10 to 30 locals, dressed in brightly coloured costumes adorned with mirrors and bells, with remarkable headpieces, representing the African, Caribbean and British heritage of the island. They dance under the beat of few traditional drums and the whistle of a Captain (the leader of each Gombey group). The Gombeys derive from a slave celebration –slaves were allowed to dance once a year, so they disguised themselves, danced and sang songs about their misfortunate fate. And because of the masks they wore, they were not afraid of being recognized and punished by their masters.

The city streets are lined up with market stalls selling local merchandise and food such as the typical wahoo nuggets and fish sandwich.

Travel to: Bermuda Islands (Hamilton). The parade route starts from the Western part of the island and ends in Hamilton. The races start either from St George's (East) or Somerset (West), however the finish is in Hamilton.

Other holidays on this date: National Scavenger Hunt Day, Victoria Day, Elf Fest (USA).

25 May: Cooper's Hill Cheese Rolling Day (England)

This is an annual event, taking place on a hill with the same name, on Spring Bank holiday (the last Monday in May). The origins of the celebration are not clear, however one theory is that it has Pagan roots – in relation to the Pagan rituals of rolling objects down a hill, which symbolizes the birth of a New year and encourages richer harvest. Allegedly, the cheese rolling down this particular hill started sometime in the 1800s.

4kg wheels of cheese are rolled down the steep hill while extremely determined "cheese chasers" run behind trying to catch them (the cheese wheel can speed up to 110km/h!!). If none of the participants is lucky to catch one – the first to cross the finish line wins the race...and the cheese. To make sure that the fearless racers stop at the finish line and not further down in the bushes – there are volunteers from the local rugby club to catch the ones still travelling on their feet.

There are four downhill races and an uphill race – for those who prefer to play it safe.

The cheese-chasers start preparing for the race from early morning – they gather in the local pubs to exchange strategies.

As numerous accidents have occurred in past (including broken bones and concussions) – now the cheese wheels are made of foam.

Everyone with a valid health insurance and over 18 years of age can participate in the race.

Travel to: England (Gloucestershire). The cheese is rolled down Cooper's Hill in the town of Brockworth.

Other holidays on this date: Tap Dance Day, National Wine Day, National Brown Bag It Day, Towel Day (USA)

26 May: White Nights Festival (Russia)

This annual event was created in 1993 by the former Mayor of the city and runs from May till July. The festival gives stage to classical ballet, opera and orchestral performances. And as it takes place during a White Nights natural phenomenon – midnight sun and nights as bright as a day.

The Scarlet Sails, a tradition created after the end of World War II, with its magnificent show and fireworks display is the highlight of the celebration and marks the end of the school year.

Many smaller carnivals take place within the festival days, the most famous one including actors who dress in period costumes to represent kings and queens of the past and to perform acts of historical significance. Carriages with "royals" and "aristocrats" can be seen on the streets and in the parks.

The "Long Night of the Museums" also takes place within the festival dates – the museums are open all night and the entry is free.

Held in one of the most magnificent cities in the world, this is a festival of poetry and sophisticated music for culture-aficionados and night owls.

Travel to: Russia (St Petersburg). The festival begins at the Mariinsky Theater. Most of the events take place at the theater and Mariinsky Concert Hall. The best Carnival is held at Peterhof Park. The Palace Square hosts many open-air concerts.

Other holidays on this date: Don't Fry Day, National Heat Awareness Day (USA)

27 May: The Islay Festival of Music and Malt (Scotland)

Held annually in the last week of May, the festival has a long history. In 1984 a Gaelic Drama Festival was created to promote the Gaelic culture and language – it was so successful, that in 1985, local craftsmen joined in with workshops on traditional instruments such as flute and fiddle. The next few editions of the event went even better, and so in the 1990 – the first whisky tasting was introduced. It was in the year 2000 when the Distilleries got massively involved, making the festival a unique experience for visitors from near and far.

The festival features garden parties, whisky nosing, Ceilidh dances (accompanied by the tunes of traditional Gaelic folk music), bowling competition, whisky and cheese tastings, tours of the breweries and historic sites, distillery open days, classes and discussions on the Gaelic cultural heritage, fishing, recitals, live music, dances, poetry and much more. A true Scottish warm welcome!

Travel to: Scotland (Island of Islay). The small island, known for its smoky-flavored whisky, is the home of Lagavulin, Bowmore and 7 other distilleries.

Other holidays on this date: National Cellophane Tape Day, Sun Screen Day, Zuni Festival (USA)

28 May: Carpet Day (Turkmenistan)

A National holiday created in 1992, celebrated annually on the last Sunday in May. The aim of the celebration is to preserve a unique Turkmen cultural heritage – the carpet weaving (historians believe that the Turkmen carpet weaving is one of the most ancient, dating 2,000 years back).

Carpet manufacturing has always been an integral part of the Turkmen culture – as per the local traditions, the carpet is a symbol of social status, power and wealth of a family. The country is well-known for its magnificent handwoven carpets and rugs – even the National flag is adorned with carpet patterns. One of the secrets is the natural vegetable dyes used by carpet weavers in wool colouring since ancient times (in the past, the famous Turkmen rug was produced only by the nomadic tribes who used natural materials from the surrounding environment – wool from the herds, roots and plants for the colouring).

An International Carpet Exhibition showing rare carpets, as well as an International Conference, are held in the capital city. Many scientists and researchers in the field of carpet weaving and dyes attend the workshops and discussions.

The President holds a celebratory speech, highlighting the importance of the unique technique used by carpet masters. Concerts, contests, carpet bazaars and theatrical performances are held all around the country and the "Honorary Carpet Maker" awards are given to the most distinguished. In the capital, a special Turkmen village is built, showing how the ancient nomadic tribes had weaved carpets on portable looms in front of their yurts.

The Golden Epoch of Great Saparmurat Turkmenbashi (1,200 kg; 300sq.m.) was included in the Guinness Book of World Records as the largest handmade carpet.

Turkmen carpets are mentioned by Marco Polo, in Thousand and One Nights, and the Indian epic "Ramayana".

Travel to: Turkmenistan (Ashgabat). Concerts are organized next to the National Carpet Museum downtown.
Other holidays on this date: National Hamburger Day (USA)

29 May: Dragon Boat Festival (China)

The traditional festival with a history of over 2,000 years, commemorates the life and death of Qu Yuan (an ancient Chinese poet who had lived around 280 B.C.), who drowned himself tying a heavy rock to his chest. The Dragon boat festival represents the long search and attempts to save him, although his body was never found in the water. The event is held annually on the fifth day of the fifth month on the Chinese calendar (May or June).

Celebrations include writing spells, carrying perfumed medicine sachets, eating the famous rice dumplings wrapped in bamboo leaves, drinking realgar wine (traditional for the festival, this drink is made of cereal wine and powdered realgar which is a "ruby sulphate") and balancing raw egg on its end at noon time – all these are ancient rituals to chase away diseases and all evil. The ancients used to throw rice dumplings into the river so that the fish would eat the rice instead of Qu Yuan.

And, of course, the Dragon Boat race.

The Dragon boats, up to 30-meters long, are made of wood and accommodate from 30 to 80 paddlers. They have a unique and colourful design – the front end is shaped like a dragon head and the back end as a long tail. A sacred ritual of painting the dragon's eyes is performed before the race – this is believed to bring the boat to life. Then the paddlers set sail guided by a beat drum. The goal of each team is to grab a flag at the end of the race. It is also believed that the winner will have good fortune during the following year.

The Dragon Boat race is included in the UNESCO List of World Intangible Cultural Heritage.

Travel to: China. Many areas hold Dragon Boat races during the festival. The best to attend are: Victoria Harbor in Hong Kong; Yueyang Prefecture in the Hunan Province; Xixi National Wetland Park in Hangzhou city.
Other holidays on this date: National Paperclip Day (USA)

30 May: Lantern Floating Ceremony (USA)

The spiritual tradition is observed annually (since 1999) on the last Monday in May and is a replica of the American Memorial Day. This is a beautiful ceremony honouring the deceased loved ones and symbolizing hope for the future.

The ceremony starts with the sounding of the pū (an oversized Hawaiian shell trumpet) to sanctify the area and mark the beginning of the ritual. Traditional drumbeat calls the people to gather and pray for peace and harmony. The prayers are accompanied by ukulele music, Hula dances and lighting of the Light of Harmony by various community leaders. Six main lanterns carry the sorrows and hopes of all folks, their wishes for well-being as well as their eternal love for the victims of war, natural disasters and diseases. The scattering of flower petals showing the love and respect to the loved ones who had passed away and the ring of a bell announce that it is time to float the lanterns. Thousands of small candle-lit silk and paper lanterns with written wishes set sail in the crystal waters of the Pacific Ocean. The floating procession takes place at sunset which brings magical ambience to the ceremony, making it one of the most spectacular events in the world.

The Lantern Floating Ceremony is officiated by the Head of the Shinnyo-en Buddhist Order.

Travel to: USA - Hawaii Islands (Oahu). The ceremony is held at the Ala Moana Beach Park on Magic Island.

Other holidays on this date: National Water a Flower Day, National Hole in My Bucket Day (USA)

31 May: Harvest Festival (Malaysia)

An annual thanksgiving festival dedicated to the rice gods celebrated for ages by the indigenous Kadazan people of Malaysia in May.

Many exhibitions, cultural performances, buffalo races, cloth weaving demonstrations, beauty pageant and open markets take place during the festivities. Specially built ethnic houses showcase the culture and traditions of each tribe. Inside, performers, dressed in full regalia entertain the visitors with typical songs and dances– some even offer local food and wine. A centrepiece is the free-flowing local rice wine which is also used in Thanksgiving and blessing rituals.

This celebration is very important to the Kadazan, as they believe that each rice seed carries the spirit of Huminodun (the only daughter of the Almighty Creator), who lived during a terrible famine and was sacrificed by her father to ensure that her people will not starve. After her body was buried – rice grew out of the soil. The festival was created to honour the noble act of Huminodun.

When the last grain of the harvest is collected, locals perform Magavau ceremony to invite the Rice Spirit - without his presence, the celebrations cannot proceed. The High Priestess surrounded by her descendants, chants prayers and performs a blessing ritual. Offerings of food are given to the gods – chicken, eggs, tobacco and rice wine, but no green vegetables, as they are a symbol of disrespect in accordance with the local beliefs.

This is a happy and vibrant celebration, and one full of colours too – from the unique to each tribe traditional clothing, finished with beautiful flower headpieces and the street statues decorated with locally produced fruit and vegetables, to the dogs dressed in festive clothes.

Travel to: Malaysia (Sabah and Labuan states – home of the Kadazan people). Celebrations take place throughout the whole month of May in many villages – each, having its own distinct festival. A spectacular two-day state festival is held in Hongkod Koisaan in Penampang on the 30th and 31st of May.

Other holidays on this date: Save Your Hearing Day (USA), World No Tobacco Day

... JUNE

Culture: mix of unique characteristics and knowledge identifying a behavioral pattern of a group of people - their habits, customs, language, music, cuisine, clothes and religion. The word "culture" was allegedly first mentioned in the XVth C. and derives from the Latin "colere" which means "to cultivate".

01 June: Dano Spring Festival (South Korea)

This is an ancient shamanic ritual honouring the god of the Sky at the end of the sowing season. It also celebrates the beginning of Summer. Observed annually on the fifth day of the fifth month in the Korean lunar calendar (May or June), the festival is included in the UNESCO List as a Masterpiece of the Oral and Intangible Heritage of Humanity.

Women dress in traditional hanbok dress and sway standing up on swings, as high as they can to get the attention of men. The latter take part in traditional wrestling games to show off their strength – tied in pairs around the waist with a cloth belt, they try to knock each other down. The winner receives...a bull. These rituals are performed because the people believe that on this day the positive energy (yang) is strongest and it is easy to fall passionately in love.

Koreans give hand-made paper fans with written fortunes as gifts to their friends, wishing them to cope with the summer heat (traditional wish).

As the festival marks the beginning of the hot and rainy season which had brought diseases in the past, women wash their hair with iris infused water and men wear iris roots pinned on their trousers – this is done to chase away the evil spirits and bring health. Folks also wear red and blue coloured clothes.

The rich cultural celebration also features masked drama acts mocking the aristocrats, shamanic rituals to ward off evil spirits, traditional dances, tug-of-war, ancient wedding ceremony, ritual around a sacred tree symbolizing the deities, lantern processions welcoming the gods, festival market named "Place of chaos" and cultural exhibitions.

Traditional food is herbal rice cakes, cherry jelly and cherry punch. Sacred liquor used as an offering to the deities is brewed a month in advance (the main ingredients are rice and malt). Shamans perform ritualistic purification ceremony during the brewing process.

Travel to: South Korea (Gangneung City). The festival venue is in the Danojang quarter.

Other holidays on this date: National Olive Day, National Go Barefoot Day, National Penpal Day, Dare Day, Flip A Coin Day (USA)

02 June: Bilum Festival (Papua New Guinea)
The annual festival is held over three days in June and celebrates local women, known for their exceptional bilum weaving skills. Bilum is a string bag made by hand using fibres from different plants. The string itself is also handmade. The bag has an important role in the life of the locals, because it is used as currency, as a gift and most importantly as a carrier bag to put water, food supplies and newborn babies.

The festival features a display of bilums that follow traditional and modern designs, flower show, weaving workshops, indigenous sing-sing troupes with their traditional tribal songs and dances, cultural performances, live music, arts and crafts. Food stalls offer the traditional for the island dish made of galip nuts.

The festival was created to boost the local economy as well as to show the rich cultural heritage of the locals.

Travel to: Papua New Guinea (Kar Kar Island)
Other holidays on this date: National Leave the Office Early Day, National Doughnut Day, National Rocky Road Day (USA), Randol Fawkes Labor Day (Bahamas)

03 June: Urs Festival (India)
An annual festival held over six days in the seventh month of the Islamic lunar calendar (May/June) to honour the death of the Sufi Saint Moinuddin Chishti, known as a benefactor of the poor. The Saint established the Sufi religion about 800 years ago. The celebrations include a night-long singing of Qawwali – devotional music from over 700 years ago. Thousands of pilgrims visit shrines to pray and listen to poetry readings. This is a commemoration of the time the Saint spent in meditation before his death.

His tomb is cleaned and washed with rose water. Then it is covered by a silk cloth. The Sufi followers pray and recite poems accompanied by clapping and make offerings of flower petals, sandalwood and incense sticks. Ritual "kheer" or "blessed food" (rice pudding) is prepared in two huge XVIth C cauldrons and served to the devotees.

There is, however, another aspect of the festival as some Sufi devotees take it a step too far – they harm themselves to show how strong their faith is. People sticking sharp knives literally behind their eyeballs, piercing their cheeks with different objects and driving hooks into their backs can be seen marching on the streets.

There is a huge open market during the days of the festival where local merchants sell food, clothes, books, handmade carpets and souvenirs.

The festival ends with firing cannons.

Travel to: India (Rajasthan). The festival is held in Ajmer City at the tomb of the Sufi Saint.

Other holidays on this date: National Egg Day, National Repeat Day, Fires Rising at Four Quarters (USA)

04 June: International Horseradish Festival (USA)

The festival, created in 1987, is annually celebrated for three days in the first weekend of June. It honours the white root vegetable which is a member of the mustard family.

Many competitions and workshops take place within the onsite Craft Village which is purposely-built on the festival grounds, such as – root toss (check how far one can throw a horseradish root), root sacking contest, root golf, Horseradish Race, Little Miss Horseradish Festival Pageant, hot air balloon rides, discussions on homemade recipes, Bloody Mary contests and much more.

The typical dishes to eat on this day all include horseradish in some form – burgers, steaks etc. And the accompanying drink (icy-cold beer) is provided by the sponsors of the event.

Travel to: USA (Illinois). The event takes place at Woodland Park in Collinsville.

Other holidays on this date: National SAFE Day, National Cognac Day, Hug Your Cat Day (USA)

05 June: Devil Dancing Tradition (Venezuela)

A centuries-old Pagan-Christian tradition, the Devil Dancing which is part of an annual Feast of Corpus Christy celebrations (commemorating the presence of Christ in the

Sacrament), depicts the triumph of good over evil. The Devil Dancing is held on nine Thursdays after Holy Thursday.

Men, dressed as devils bow and kneel on all fours, making their way to the church, showing their submission to religion.

There are many theories on how and when this odd ritual had begun. Most likely it happened in the Vth C in Spain, when the Church used pagan traditions and dances to convert more people into Christianity. Another popular theory is that in the XVIIth C, a local priest didn't have the means to hold a proper celebration so he told the people that devils will come to feast. After a heavy storm hit the town, men dressed as devils presented themselves on the next day in front of the church.

The Dancing Devils of Venezuela are divided into 11 groups – the so-called "cofradias" (brotherhoods) – depending on the region they inhabit - the costumes differ in colours and style. In one area, all "devils" wear scary devil-red masks, red costumes, red shoes and hold whips and maracas shaped like devils; whilst in other areas they wear brightl costumes with amulets and images of saints drawn or sewn on them; the celebratory costumes are often adorned with blessed palm leaves, bells, crosses and other religious symbols to ward off evil.

Each cofradia makes its own masks and has a strong hierarchy. The dancers usually start learning the dance and the craft of making masks at a very young age – it is a spiritual journey overseen by the family and the whole group of dancing devils.

The size of the mask depends on how long each member has been in the cofradia – the more time had a person been a "dancing devil" – the bigger the mask and higher the place in the hierarchy.

After paying tribute to the Church, the devil dance begins.

Masked creatures move chaotically under the rhythm of spooky musical poems accompanied by drums, maracas and bells attached to their feet. They make their way along the procession route, flooded with people and handmade altars.

The dancers are known as "promeseros" (promise-keepers). As they dance, they make wishes. And if their wishes come true during the year – they make a promise to dance the ritualistic dance in the following year as well.

The culmination of the festivity comes in the evening when all devils surrender to the forces of good.

The Devil Dancing is recognized by UNESCO and is on the list of the Intangible Cultural Heritage of Humanity.

Local merchants sell all sorts of souvenirs and rosary beads, there are even workshops on how to create a Dancing Devil mask.

Travel to: Venezuela (Naiguata). In this coastal town, the costumes are colorful, and the masks represent sea creatures, whilst in the mainland – the masks depict characters from the mythology. In San Francisco de Yare the dancing devils are dressed in red and wear scary red masks – it is believed that this is the oldest fraternity not only in Venezuela, but on the American continent.

Other holidays on this date: National Gingerbread Day (USA)

06 June: Feast of the Lobster (Madagascar)

Feria Oramena. An annual feast to celebrate the history and cultural heritage of indigenous Antanosy people of Madagascar. It is held over a week at the beginning of June in a beautiful coastal town setting.

A week to promote the local culture of the people known as great fishermen ever since the IXth C – no wonder that the festival is also known as Feast of the Lobster – almost everything is focused on seafood – lobsters, in particular, accompanied by the unbeatable carnival atmosphere.

During the festival, the sun-kissed town offers to its visitors seafood open-air markets, conferences, workshops, contests, exhibitions, seafood fairs, craft schools and much more.

Traditional Malagasy music, played around every corner, embraces the streets and turns the town into a non-stop feast to all senses.

Locals and visitors alike can enjoy the traditional island delicacy – the spiny lobster – everywhere and in all forms: succulent and fresh with coconut rice, in orange or lime-butter sauce, crispy grilled, with Tapioca risotto and herbs, lobster bisque or in creamy pasta with edible flowers...

Travel to: Madagascar (Fort Dauphin). The festival takes place in the town of Taolagnaro – the capital of the region.

Other holidays on this date: D-Day, National Eyeware Day, National Gardening Exercise Day (USA)

07 June: Lunar Festival (England)

Created in 2012, this is a rather new but upcoming festival. Held over four days during Bank Holiday in the beginning of June, the event is more of a garden party with intimate acoustic music and magical ambience. The setting is a genuine working farm and the accommodation is in Gypsy Bowtop Caravans and Bell Tents.

The music is psychedelic and experimental – from Beatles impersonators to Mariachi and Andean folk music orchestras. There are two stages on which the bands perform during the day, open-air movie screenings and rave parties at nighttime. There is also a huge fire pit, around which participants and guests can mingle in the meantime.

Visitors can also join in any of the other activities such as bird spotting, wood carving, sausage making, foraging, feeding ducks, milking goats, handling baby bunnies, yoga and more.

There is a Pagan ritual involved as well, although there are no theories of why... A huge effigy made of firewood, representing a giant bird, is set ablaze.

To sum it all up - it's three days of fun in the open air!

Travel to: England (Tanworth-In-Arden, Warwickshire). The event is held on the grounds of the Umberslade Farm.

Other holidays on this date: National VCR Day, National Running Day (USA)

08 June: Wild Mint Folk Festival (Russia)

The event was created in 2008 as a one-day music festival. Today, it runs for three days annually in the beginning of June and is the largest stage for world music in Russia – featuring acts from local celebrities and independent artists drawn to folklore to world-known artists performing at a huge camping ground with teepees and rural cottages. The event is ranked as the World's Top 50 Festivals.

Variety of musical styles to be seen – traditional Russian songs, Balkan folklore songs and dances, Celtic tunes, Latin beats, ethnojazz, indie-pop, African rap and reggae.

The Wild Mint festival is a huge pot where different cultures melt. The event is of interest not only to music aficionados but to all that have a thing for world culture and traditions as well.

In the spirit of Wild Mint – the organizers considerably thought about offering a variety of food too and created the "World-on-a-plate" area. Performers and party-goers can treat themselves to Ukranian, Lebanese, South-American, Chinese, Mediterranean or any other food and spice they wish.

A dedicated Green Age area for spiritual recreation offers yoga classes, meditation and Asian healers.

Homemade, organic and eco-friendly products such as cheeses and tea can be found at the largest market of handmade gifts!

The festival grounds turn into a street theatre, outdoor movie and fire-dancers' stage.

Not only for the great music, this event is a must-do for it is a showcase of the cultural traditions of the world.

Travel to: Russia (Moscow). The event is held in the cultural and ethnographic Ethnomir Complex in Petrovo village.

Other holidays on this date: National Name Your Poison Day, National Upsy Daisy Day (USA)

09 June: Red Earth Gathering (USA – Native American)

An annual Native American festival held over three days in the beginning of June since 1987. Representatives of more than 100 Native American tribes take part and showcase their cultural heritage and rich traditions.

The event starts with a magnificent street parade featuring Native tribe members dressed in full regalia attire with beautifully decorated feather headdress. Some of them ride on horseback and wear wolf skin, others dance their way through the city, but they all highlight their tribal diversity and uniqueness.

Many stalls with tribal merchandise offer souvenirs, pottery, bead necklaces, sculptures, paintings, handwoven baskets, traditional tribal attire and more.

The festival also features educational talks, Native art markets and Gourd dances (believed to have its origins from the Cheyenne and Arapajo tribes, this is a dance honouring the victorious warrior or a defeated enemy).

This is a true Powwow as the Natives call it, meaning – a social gathering with lots of singing, dancing, socializing and honouring the tribal culture.

Travel to: USA (Oklahoma). The festival takes place in Oklahoma City at the Cox Convention Centre. The parade circles the Myriad Botanical Garden.

Other holidays on this date: National Earl Day, Donald Duck Day (USA)

10 June: Muscogee Nation Gathering (USA – Native American)

The Muscogee (Creek) People are a confederation of Native American tribes – descendants of the tribes that inhabited the region of South-eastern US around 1500 A.D., before their homelands were exchanged to new ones in the state of Oklahoma in the XIXth C. They were known for their remarkable building skills – the Muscogees constructed magnificent earthen pyramids and ceremonial grounds along river banks.

Since 1974, the festival celebrating the cultural heritage of the Native people is held over four days every year in June, gathering thousands of Muscogee families to celebrate the rich traditions of their predecessors.

The grand opening is marked by a massive stomp dance around a ceremonial fire – the word for that dance in the native Muscogee language means "drunken" or "inspirited".

The celebration features live concerts, street parade, tribal art exhibitions, marathons, All Indian Rodeo, horseshoe tournament, Muscogee gospel singing, tennis, volleyball and softball tournaments and many more. There are street food booths and souvenir kiosks too. This is the largest and longest running event in the Okmulgee County and attracts thousands of visitors for a weekend of fun and games.

Travel to: USA (Oklahoma). The venue of the festival is the Claude Cox Omniplex in the city of Okmulgee.

Other holidays on this date: National Ballpoint Pen Day, National Black Cow Day, Tinker Inter-Tribal Powwow (USA)

11 June: Pudding Boat Race (England)

In the 1990s a man watched a waitress who carried trays of roast beef and Yorkshire puddings and was entertained by the idea of sailing down the river... in a giant Yorkshire pudding. That is how the festival started. There is a theory that in the past, giant pudding boats were "baked" to be used in severe flooding.

The Yorkshire pudding "boats" are baked days in advance using huge amounts of flour, eggs and water, and are covered with few layers of yacht varnish. The contestants try to paddle the enormous pudding vessels in a pond to the finish line.

Travel to: England (Yorkshire). The race is held at Bob's Pond in Brawby.

Other holidays on this date: National Call Your Doctor Day, National Making Life Beautiful Day, National Corn on The Cob Day (USA)

12 June: Celtic Festival (Australia)

This annual festival celebrates Celtic ancestry, music and culture and is held over four days in June.

The small bay village becomes a stage for all-things-Celtic, as the whole infrastructure is utilized – churches, hotels, restaurants and halls are turned to Celtic performance stages, huge marquees are set up to house the Celtic market and the Celtic village. It is the grandest event to celebrate Celtic ancestry.

The festival program is diverse. Each year aims to show the rich cultural and historical heritage of one of the Celtic nations – Ireland, Scotland, Wales, Brittany, Cornwall and the Isle of Man.

Numerous Celtic music and pipe bands take care of the festival spirit while others immerse the visitors in the magic of Celtic dances. There are also street parades, fun run, flag raising ceremony, poet breakfasts and afternoon teas, Celtic dinners and nights, boomerang painting, workshops, storytelling, play-writing and dancing classes as well.

A highlight of the festival is the Limerick competition. Limerick is a five-line poem, usually humorous or obscene, in which the 1st, 2nd and 5th lines should rhyme. The winner is chosen according to how loud the laughter and applause are.

Traditional Celtic food is served during the festival such as venison burger, blood pudding and Haggis! Oh, yes... and tons of the world's most famous stout - Guinness!

Travel to: Australia (Portarlington). The event is hosted in this small coastal town, cuddled amidst vineyards and mussel farms.

Other holidays on this date: National Loving Day (USA)

13 June: Muju Firefly Festival (South Korea)

A magical festival dedicated to the fireflies. Created in 1997, it is held every year in June for 9 days. The event is listed as National Treasure No. 322. It is also a very important environmental factor, as fireflies inhabit only regions with crispy clean air – that is why scientists from all over the world gather to observe their population very carefully during the festival. In fact, the event was created to raise awareness about the contamination of the Earth.

The area where the festival takes place is one of the most beautiful in South Korea and the visitors do not only enjoy the lighting show performed by fireflies in the evening but the breath-taking nature as well.

The festival features traditional Chinese and Korean dance troupes, talent show, martial arts performances, weaving tutorials, dance-off's, river rafting, bare-hands trout fishing, fashion show, live music performances and street theatre. Local merchants sell firefly souvenirs, ginseng, traditional pottery and artwork, tea, food and wine.

Travel to: South Korea (Jeolla Province). The festival takes place in Hanprungnu-ro in Muju County. Worth a visit is the Bandiland Museum – it hosts an indoor firefly exhibit where a handful of the glowing insects, buzz around in a darkened room.

Other holidays on this date: National Weed Your Garden Day (USA)

14 June: Vine Jumping Ritual (Vanuatu)

This ancient ritual (predecessor of bungee jumping) is still practised on a small Vanuatuan island.

A tradition, banned in the beginning of the XXth C by European missionaries for being too dangerous, somehow managed to survive in one coastal village...

Men jump off 30-meter high wooden towers secured only by a few strings of vine, tied to their ankles.

The ritual has quite an odd origin...

According to a legend, a village woman was distressed by her husband's sexual wants and ran away in the forest. Her husband followed, so she climbed up a tall tree. But he followed once again. Desperate and scared, the woman tied nearby vines to her feet and jumped off the tree landing safely. Again, her husband followed. Unfortunately, he didn't secure himself properly – so he fell and died. The woman ran back to the village to share what had happened. To show strength and support the village wives decided to jump too. However, their husbands stole the tradition for themselves.

The story has it that from this day on, village men re-enact the jump every year in April, May or June depending on the yam harvest season (from a wooden platform and tying the vines around their feet), just to make sure that they would not be tricked by a woman ever again.

This is one of the most dangerous rituals in the world because the so-called "divers" are not secured by anything else but vines. To the locals, this is not just paying tribute to a legend – they believe that the jump is a self-purification ritual. That it will ward off the evil spirits, chase away all misfortunes and illnesses and bring good fortune.

The preparation includes building of a wooden tower and diving platforms and mind-purification of the diver who isolates himself for some time and refrains from all physical contacts with women. Women are not allowed to go anywhere near the wooden tower as it brings bad luck to the divers.

On the previous day, brave divers clear any unsettled debts in case they die.

They are blessed in the morning and anointed with oils. They paint their bodies and wear boar tusks around their necks.

The village women, who are only spectators to this ritual of manhood wear grass skirts, sing and dance for moral support.

The ritual is also a rite of passage for young boys who jump from lower platforms.

Vine Jumping dive is like experiencing the greatest g-force in the non-industrialized world.

Travel to: Vanuatu (Pentecost island). The Vine Jumping Ritual is performed in the town of Bunlap.

Other holidays on this date: National Flag Day, National Bourbon Day (USA), International Bath Day

15 June: International Viking Festival (Iceland)

The festival, created in 1995 to honour the Viking cultural heritage, is held annually over four days in June. This is the oldest and largest celebration in Iceland.

Unique as it is, it feels like travelling back in time – jesters performing on the streets and Vikings riding on horseback (and fighting every now and then).

A special Viking Village and Middle Ages market are set in the festival town, which for the duration of the festivities is inhabited by real Viking descendants from Scandinavia, England, Germany and Iceland. At daytime, one can learn how to throw an axe, shoot with bow and arrows or have his fortune told by a nomad fortune teller in a market tent. There are also wood-carving workshops, Viking school for children, Viking dances, storytelling in caves and sword fighting as well as many artists, musicians, artisans, blacksmiths and masters of the Vikings crafts. Even Viking

Christening and Viking wedding have been performed on past festivals. Many merchants sell furs, horns and delicious food like a roasted lamb shank. There is a daily Viking Lunch with traditional Icelandic folk songs and typical Viking food - shark, dried fish, braised lamb shank, fish soup, Aquavit (potato brandy), Brennivin (Black Death – it is a drink!) and yoghurt with blueberry sauce. For those who really get into the mood – Viking kidnapping is available upon request! Once kidnapped, one will find himself in a cave, sitting next to a fire with a Viking singing Icelandic folk songs. Then he will be treated with a lush Viking dinner and returned home.

The end of the festival is marked by an almost historic battle and dances around a huge fire all night long.

Travel to: Iceland (Hafnarfjordur). Book a stay in the Viking Village Hotel – it is a family operated hotel, which in fact sponsors the event.

Other holidays on this date: National Lobster Day, Smile Power Day (USA), Vidovdan (Serbia)

16 June: Fisemana Purification Ritual (Madagascar)

This centurial ritual takes place annually in June and is performed by the oracles of the indigenous Antakarana people. The name of the tribe means "people of the rocks" – in the past, Antakarana were chased away by another powerful tribe and had to live for over a year in limestone caves, where many died and were buried. The caves became a sacred place. Their King made a promise to the gods that if the tribe survives – they will embrace Islam. And so, it happened. However, today, the descendants who claim to be Muslim, still practice ancient pagan ceremonies worshipping animal gods.

For the Antakarana people, most celebrations and rituals are observed to honour the ancestors and the dead in general, because they are the ones who look after the living ones. Locals believe that the soul is immortal and should always be respected.

During Fisemana, the folks perform ancient sacred ceremonies, led and closely observed by the oracles –high priests. A ritual which takes place in most ceremonies is the "tromba" (spirit possession) – this is a way to communicate with the spirits.

Ritualistic dances and animal sacrifices are common.

Unfortunately, there is an insufficient historical trace on how and when the ceremony was initiated as well as more details on how it is observed today.

Currently, there are missionaries working on the island of the Antakarana people and their purpose is to integrate them into the religion, culture and traditions of the today world.

Dessi Nikoltchev:

Travel to: Madagascar. The Antakarana people live on the secluded island of Nosy Mitsio close to the shores of Madagascar. The island has no electricity or running water.

Other holidays on this date: National Fudge Day, National Flip Flop Day, Fresh Veggies Day, Iowa Tribal Powwow (USA)

17 June: Flower Festival (The Netherlands)

The annual festival is held over a weekend in June and turns the city into a flower kingdom from a fairy tale. The streets, the promenade, shops and houses are magnificently decorated with colourful flower installations such as giant birds amidst a flight, enormous bouquets lying on sidewalks, floating in water flower flamingos and more.

There are Ikebana contests, flower arrangement workshops, bouquet workshops, flowers trivia quizzes etc. There's lots of music, street theatre performances, afternoon tea in a rose garden, edible flowers tasting and refreshing cocktails. A beautiful place to be!

Travel to: The Netherlands (Aalsmeer). The festival is held in the historic garden of the city, Fort Kudelstaart, Boerma Institute, the Belle Époque Rose Nursery and next to an old windmill.

Other holidays on this date: Eat Your Vegetables Day (USA), National Day (Iceland)

18 June: Mermaid Parade (USA)

Created in 1983, the Mermaid Parade takes place on a day in June every year and is the largest art fest in the country. More than 3,000 participants celebrate a colourful mix of ancient mythology and modern partying. The event marks the official start of the summer season, so it is usually held on the first Saturday closest to June 21st.

The parade features decorated floats representing sea kingdoms, mythic creatures or sandy beaches. The participants in the procession wear mermaid and sea creature costumes with glittering tales, seashell bras, pearl necklaces and tiaras.

Right after the parade, King Neptune and Queen Mermaid are led to the beach by the parade founder, for the official Beach Ceremony marking the opening of the summer swimming season.

Travel to: USA (New York, Coney Island). The parade starts from West 21st Street and Surf Avenue and ends at Steeplechase Plaza.

Other holidays on this date: Father's Day, International Picnic Day, International Panic Day (USA), International Sushi Day, Five-petalled Rose Festival (Czech Republic), El Colacho (Spain)

19 June: Wyndstock Country House Party (England)

This is a true fairy tale blast! Think grand! Think Gatsby! Think shiny and spectacular! And all that is thanks to two gentlemen who despised mainstream festivals with their crowds, mud and mixed performances so much, that in 2011 decided to create Wyndstock – a new belle époque gathering for dandies held over a weekend in June.

The dress code set by the organisers is simple – your finest attire. People can wander anywhere inside of the hosting estate and on the grounds – there are tours, games like croquet and badminton, petting the deer, falconry, afternoon tea, bonfire, storytelling, drawing classes, classic novel readings, philosophy discussions, Jazz, cocktails in the secret garden bar, late night in the woods and live band performances. Lunch, dinner and breakfast are included in the ticket price – all ingredients are locally produced and the meals - freshly cooked.

The organisers offer "glamping" bell tents for accommodation – they include a mattress, an apple, an overnight bag of eyeshades and a toothpaste. Classy!

Travel to: England (Norfolk). The event is hosted at the Houghton Hall - the Palladian home of the Marquess of Cholmondeley (and former home of the first Prime Minister of Great Britain – Sir Robert Walpole).

Other holidays on this date: National Martini Day, National Kissing Day (USA)

20 June: The Bonfires of San Juan (Spain)

Las Hogueras de San Juan is one of the biggest and most popular festivals in Spain. It lasts for five days, ending on the night of the Summer Solstice. The tradition has been going on for centuries, but the official celebration was formally constituted in 1928. This fire festival was originally part of a pagan ritual marking the longest day of the year.

On the night of June 20th, huge bonfire pyres piled with cheeky cardboard figures are built across the city and the beach to protect from evil spirits. A centrepiece is a giant papier-mâché figure symbolizing an event or a person of the past year. The bonfire piles are often built of old furniture and junk items as the festival coincides with the summer cleaning.

The following couple of days are filled with festive atmosphere - there is an international folklore parade with dance troupes from around the world, every day noon-time fireworks, dance processions and much more. Thousands of locals and visitors gather for a festive dinner in the many "barracas" (tents) build especially for the festival. Typical treat is figs and "cocas" (pastry with tuna, onions and pine nuts). Unique ritual is the "waking up of the neighbours" – everyone makes as much noise as possible at nighttime.

The peak of the festival comes at midnight on June 24th (the night of San Juan) when all bonfire piles are set ablaze. As per tradition, the locals dance around and jump over them while firefighters bathe them with water. Optional cleansing ritual is jumping in the sea, or bathing in perfumed water – they both are believed to chase away the evil spirits.

During the festival days, the city comes to a complete shut down as everyone is out celebrating. In fact, even after the festival is over, celebrations continue with a few days of Medieval market and a firework show set in the historic centre of the city.

Travel to: Spain (Alicante). Make sure to be at Plaza de los Luceros square every day at noon time for the massive fireworks show.
Other holidays on this date: National Ice Cream Soda Day

21 June: Midsummer Day (Sweden)
Midsummer Day in Sweden is celebrated on the Friday following the Summer Solstice. In a land of long and dark winters, celebrating the longest day is the best party of the year. On top of that, the legend has it that the night before Midsummer Day is a magical time for love! Imagine flower wreaths, singing songs and dancing around a flower decorated Maypole. With deep Pagan roots, this is a feast celebrating sun and light, love and nature.

The dance around the maypole is quite spectacular as it resembles an ancient ritual– folks dance around it in frog-like movements and sing a song which has become part of the Swedish cultural heritage - Små Grodorna (Small Frogs). The lyrics? Here they are: The little frogs, the little frogs, they are funny to observe. They have no ears, no ears, no tails etc. According to the Nordic folklore, the maypole represents the axis connecting the world of the living with the underworld. Another theory has it that it is a symbol of fertility. Both though, highlight the importance of reviving nature.

The locals wear traditional costumes (white lace shirts, embroidered vests, ankle skirts and white hats) or put on "hippie" clothes, braid wildflowers into their hair and spend the day out in the open air. They go out in the countryside, set up huge dining tables and enjoy a feast of pickled herring, new potatoes with dill, sour cream and chives, wild berries and lots of alcohol. An ancient tradition is for unmarried girls to collect 7 different species of wildflowers and put them under their pillow overnight. The legend has it that they will dream who their future husband will be.

Travel to: Sweden (everywhere). Huge events are held in the Skansen open-air museum in Stockholm and in Slottsskogen Park in Gothenburg.

Other holidays on this date: National Selfie Day, National Daylight Appreciation Day, International Yoga Day (USA), Aymara New Year (Bolivia), National Aboriginal Day (Canada), International Go Skateboarding Day

22 June: Electric Forest Festival (USA)

This is an iconic psychedelic event held deep in the forest over eight days (divided in two weekends) every year in the end of June and beginning of July. The festival was created in 2011.

Huge art installations, coloured light bulbs hanging up in the trees, phenomenal laser shows and the best DJ's in the world turn the dark forest into a kaleidoscope of experiences. The lights blended with electronic music play with all senses to create a surreal feeling throughout. The wooden shelters and nearby lakes add mystical ambience to the venue.

All attendees camp in tents on the festival grounds. There are also hammocks to chill during the day, a pop-up restaurant, water park, horse-riding lessons, general store, showers, free water and a golf course.

Travel to: USA (Michigan). The festival takes place in Rothbury. There are official Electric Forest shuttles departing from Muskegon, Grand Rapids and Chicago.

Other holidays on this date: National Chocolate Éclair Day (USA)

23 June: Scarlet Sails Tradition (Russia)

The Scarlet Sails tradition, which is one of the biggest water shows in the world, is performed on the weekend around June 22nd – the shortest night of the year (the event is within the White Nights Festival held annually from May till July). The magnificent show, which started as a way to rebel against school and all rules, marks the end of the school year and is attended by millions of people from around the world, including many celebrities. The tradition started in the end of World War II when few schools decided to get together and celebrate the end of the term. At this very first celebration, a boat with scarlet sails sailed along the city promenade. The school leavers thought this was a sign because of a short story published in 1923 by the Russian novelist Alexander Grin – "The Scarlet Sails". It is about a poor young girl who met a wizard. He predicted she will meet a prince on a boat with red sails who will take her away to his kingdom. All her friends mocked the poor girl. Much later, one day a wealthy ship captain arrived from England and fell in love with her. He had heard about the words of the wizard and had painted the sails on his ship in scarlet. When the girl saw the ship, she knew this was her prince. They married and lived happily ever after. This story is a huge part of the Scarlet Sails celebration, as it shows the power of dreams and brings hope for a better future.

The festivities include many open-air concerts, motorboat races, a real pirate battle in the river and, of course, the highlight of the event – the appearance of a ship with fiery-red sails under a beautiful rain of colorful fireworks and pyrotechnic water show in sync with the music by symphony orchestra – a hearty wish to all graduates for a bright future. There are graduation parties everywhere and the embankments are full of visitors admiring the beauty of this romantic event.

Travel to: Russia (St Petersburg). The breath-taking views of the city, combined with the fireworks and the water show in the Neva River, and accompanied by the symphony orchestra create magical ambience in one of the lightest nights of the year in this part of the world.

Other holidays on this date: Take Your Dog to Work Day, National Pink Day (USA), Festa de São João do Porto (Portugal), Tonkawa Tribal Powwow (USA)

24 June: Incan Festival of the Sun (Peru)
This is the second largest festival in South America.

Peruvians re-enact one of four sacred ceremonies for the Inca people – the Sun ceremony, honouring the god of the Sun. This is a spectacular festival marking the winter solstice and the Inca New Year. The ritual was first held in 1412 but banned by the Spanish in 1535 due to its Pagan roots which contradicted with the Catholic beliefs. It featured nine days of celebration, dances and animal sacrifices to please the most important deities – Inti (the god of the Sun) and his wife and Goddess of fertility - Pachamama. The ceremony was held in honour of the god of the Sun and his wife as they were the very reason for the existence of everything. Another reason is that in June, the sun moved away from the Inca lands and it was necessary to ask for its return.

Nowadays, the Festival of the Sun is celebrated annually on June 24th.

Each year two participants are chosen to play the roles of the god of the Sun and his wife. At the beginning of the celebration, representatives of the four Inca regions (East, West, North and South) arrive to summon the god. Then a ceremonial reading of a sacred coca leaf foresees the upcoming year. The deity is then taken atop of a hill carried in a golden palanquin (a replica of the original 60kg one) by three men, dressed as a snake (representing the Underworld), a Puma (representing the life on Earth) and a Condor (representing Heaven). The procession starts from the ruins of Qurikancha – the sacred golden Temple of the Sun. Locals, dressed in colourful costumes with feathers, gold ornaments and typical hand-woven masks, accompany the golden palanquin with dances and Peruvian songs. They represent the warriors – descendants of the Inca Empire. Local women sweep the streets (the evil spirits) and layer them with flowers. Once the procession reaches the top of the hill, the head priest holds a speech in Quechua (the Inca language) and offers blessed corn seeds to please the Sun God. Then he sacrifices an animal and offers its blood and heart which pleases the deity and he accepts the gift, this way ensuring a good harvest in the upcoming year. In the past, a white llama was sacrificed, and the high priest, dressed in a ceremonial robe, would read the future from the bloodstains on the animals' heart. Nowadays, a faux sacrifice and a faux heart are used in the ritual.

The ceremony ends at sunset with a huge bonfire lit under a symphony of horns and panpipes. Inti and Pachamama are then returned to Cuzco, carried in their golden palanquin while priests and representatives of the four Inca regions give blessings to the crowds.

The festivities continue for a week and include open-air Peruvian music concerts, dances, street fairs and vendors selling local food, souvenirs and other merchandise.

Travel to: Peru (Cuzco). The city is the historical capital of the Inca Empire during the XIIIth and XVIth C. and a UNESCO World Heritage Site. A theory has it that it was built to represent a puma - a sacred animal to the Incas. The Festival of the Sun (Inti Raymi) starts from Qurikancha – an ancient citadel close to Cuzco and ends in Sacsayhuamán (the ruins of an ancient Inca stone complex).

Other holidays on this date: Seurasaari Midsummer Bonfires (Finland), National Pralines Day, Swim A Lap Day (USA), The Feast of St John (Italy), Day of Dew (Lithuania), Herb Festival (Bulgaria), Pa Puul Ceremony (Mexico)

25 June: Maori New Year (New Zealand)

The celebration was abandoned in the 1940s and revived in the year 2000. The Maori New Year – Matariki, celebrated on the day of a new moon in June, is named after a cluster of 7 stars (the Pleiades) which rise in mid-winter. The name Matariki, literally means "eyes of God" in Maori. According to a legend, Father Sky and Mother Earth were separated by their children. The god of the winds got so angry at his brothers for separating their parents, that tore out his eyes and threw them to the sky.

Originally, Matariki was celebrated to honour the ones who had passed away during the year, but it also coincided with the time when all crops had been harvested and there was plenty of food, so it was time for dancing and singing. The Maori people believe that the brighter the seven stars are – the richer the harvest will be in the upcoming year.

Traditional celebrations include gathering of the whole family to honour the deceased relatives and remember their genealogy. The celebrations can last up to 3 days and include planetarium events and community gatherings with songs, tree planting, sharing of myths and legends, workshops and lots of food. Some people sleep under the stars. The highlight of the event is flying kites as a symbol of being closer to the stars.

Travel to: New Zealand. The biggest celebration is the Matariki Festival in the Te Papa Museum in Wellington. Maori events are held throughout the country - in Auckland there is a Matariki Festival and an event at the Stardome Planetarium; the Monrad Park in Palmerston North hosts a Matariki by Candlelight event.

Other holidays on this date: National Strawberry Parfait Day (USA), Freezer Burn (Canada)

26 June: Blessing of the Fisheries (England)

This is a good example of a Pagan ritual being Christianized. The ceremony was first mentioned in mid-1800s, believed to be one of the oldest surviving. The divine protection of fishing boats has always been important to local folks and the ritual is considered as a thanksgiving to the sea for the food it provides.

The event takes place annually on the last Sunday in June.

Local parishers, the clergy, the Mayor and all fishermen gather in church for a short service and then parade to the town harbour to perform a ritual of blessing. Once the procession, led by a bagpiper, reaches the harbour, a Bishop holds a speech and blesses the sea, the fish, the fishing boats and the fisheries by splashing holy water and shaking incense over the harbour railings. In the past, men would decorate their vessels for the ritual, but this is no longer practised. After the blessing, town folks return to the church for refreshment drinks.

Travel to: England (Kent). The event takes place in the ancient fishing town of Folkestone which has depended on the fishing industry for centuries. The procession starts from St Peter's Church.

Other holidays on this date: National Chocolate Pudding Day, Forgiveness Day (USA), Eid-al-Fitr (Jordan), Korite (Senegal)

27 June: Turning of the bones Funerary Ritual (Madagascar)

The oddest of them all... and yet celebrated with great cheer!

Famadihana, known as "turning of the bones" is an ancient ritual still practised by indigenous Merina people. It involves digging up the mummified bodies of the dead ancestors from the family tombs, cleaning them, changing their clothes and dancing with them in front of the crypts... if it only could get more bizarre!

The ceremony derived from a pagan custom centred around the immortality of the soul. The Merina people believe that the soul doesn't die with the body but continues to live. It only joins the underworld after the body has been decomposed and after performing certain rituals to ease the transition.

The locals believe and worship the dead, as they are the ones who look after the living ones and their descendants.

The custom is observed every five to seven years (between June and September) and is a huge celebration which can even bring estranged families together.

After the body has been exhumed, it is gently cleaned, sprayed with perfume and redressed with fresh silk garments by the family members.

Then – it is all loud music, chatter, dances and fun as the family members and all invited (or not) enjoy the little time they can spend again with the dead relative. Sadness is not allowed – this is a celebration of the good moments, it is a time to show respect to the dead. The "dance with the dead" also has a purpose – to familiarize the dead with their final resting place. That is why the relatives dance in a circle around the tomb.

During the ritual animals are sacrificed and the meat – shared with the whole family.

The celebration lasts for two days (ending before dark when the evil spirits start to roam) and the exact day for opening the tomb is diligently calculated by a local astrologer.

After the ceremony and the dances, the body is returned to the crypt and placed upside down along with many gifts from the family, neighbours and everyone invited to the "happy" occasion (usually money and alcohol...).

Fun fact is that at the beginning of the XXth C, the Catholic Church (allegedly) declared the ritual as an important cultural practice.

Another fun fact: selfies with a dead relative are very common (?!).

The last Famadihana was held in 2011, which means that most likely the next one will be in 2018.

Travel to: Madagascar. The ritual is performed in the southern highlands of the island.

Other holidays on this date: National Orange Blossom Day, California Witchcamp, Iroquois Strawberry Festival (USA)

28 June: Vartavar (Armenia)

This Christian tradition, too, has deep Pagan roots. Celebrated on a Sunday, 14 weeks after the Armenian Easter, it honours the Goddess of Water, Beauty, Love and Fertility. In the Gregorian calendar, the date falls between June 28th and August 1st. The legend has it that a goddess – Astghik, which is always covered with roses, spreads love on Armenian earth by pouring rose water from the sky. The name of the holiday comes from the Armenian "vart" meaning rose and "var" meaning rise.

Another theory (after adopting Christianity) is that Noah's Ark landed on Mount Ararat and he ordered his sons to drench themselves in water to commemorate the Great Flood.

Whatever the roots, Vardavar is one of Armenian Apostolic Church's five main feasts, that commemorates the transfiguration of Jesus in front of Apostles Peter, John and Jacob.

This is a favourite holiday for locals, because for a day – everyone is allowed to drench friends, family or total strangers in water. And this happens in the peak of the summer heat. People walking in the park, waiting on a bus stop, walking under balconies – nobody is safe during Vartavar and that is what makes it especially popular among children as they can get away with any mischiefs. One can get sprayed with a water gun or be poured over a bucket of icy-cold water. The locals even pour water over the balconies onto unsuspecting walkers by. The only thing to do is...smile!

In the old times, people would start pilgrimages to the holy water sites in the mountains, picnic in the open-air and dance around bonfires at night. Young girls would pick wildflowers and throw them into their neighbour yards for which they received presents in the morning. These customs are long forgotten now, but the so-called water festival Vartivar is much anticipated and celebrated with great joy every year.

Travel to: Armenia (Yerevan). The best and biggest celebration is held at the Swan Lake. There are DJ's and water cannons too! There is a Christian celebration at the Geghard Monastery which starts with a liturgy in the church and is followed by songs, dances and releasing of doves. The Pagan celebration takes place at the Garni Pagan Temple (near Yerevan) and starts with a ritualistic theatrical performance followed by folklore songs and dances from around the world.

Other holidays on this date: Paul Bunyan Day, Great American Camp Out in The Backyard Day (USA)

29 June: Wine Battle Day (Spain)

The annual event is held on June 29th and is part of a week-long Wine Festival. The celebration coincides with the religious St Peter's Feast Day, however most people are focused on the wine battle. The Wine Festival attracts locals as well as wine aficionados from all around the world.

Created in the XIIIth C when the small wine-producing city was ordered by a judge to mark its territory with purple banners every year at St Peter's Day. If refused to do so, it would have become part of a neighbouring bigger village. So, locals started an annual procession going up to the nearby hill. Four hundred years later, the banners were substituted with red wine - peole started pouring it at each other – and that is how La Batalla del Vino started.

The day starts early in the morning with a procession led by the Mayor riding on horseback up the hill. The historic battle begins after a religious mass.

All participants wear white shirts and red scarves. All means are used to soak in wine as many people as possible – cups, buckets, pots, hoses, water guns etc. The drenched in wine pink-ish clothes of the participants look a lot like the ordered in the past banners, used to mark the city borders.

After a few hours of spraying and pouring with wine, the crowd gathers in the city centre for a feast with great local food, wine and dances. Lots of merrymakers make impromptu concerts on the cobbled streets and people just stop and sing along (with or without knowing the lyrics). The end of the day is marked at the bullring where small-size bulls run and chase people (no animals are harmed).

By the end of the day – everyone is soaked in red wine and pretty drunk (around 40,000 litres are used during the festival).

How to participate: Spain (La Rioja). The battle takes place on the Cliffs of Bilibio in the outskirts of Haro – a rather small but very important for the region wine-producing city. The festive lunch is held at Plaza de la Paz right after the end of the wine battle.

Other holidays on this date: Camera Day, Hug Holiday, International Mud Day (USA), The Feast of St Peter and St Paul (Italy)

30 June: The Chap Olympiad (England)

Posh! Posh-er! Posh-est! A Chap Olympiad!

Held in the end of June or beginning of July every year since 2006, this is a very typical English event celebrating all things gentry! Imagine a setting taking you back to 1920s-1950s and a competition for old-fashioned English chaps who appreciate the finer aspects of life. Different contests in which the participants compete for most immaculate trouser creases and cravats (both inspected by butlers), racing while smoking pipes, umbrella jousting, mixing dry martinis, human champagne pyramid, Aunt Avoidance, Tea Pursuit (trying to pour tea while riding a bicycle), riding a bicycle with a brolly, beach Volleybowler (using a bowler hat instead of a ball) and the Tug of Hair in which a rope is substituted for a lengthy handlebar moustache. The spectators who prefer not to take a turn in the competitions indulge their senses with an old-fashioned picnic with scones, jam and clotted cream, chilled champagne and lots of tea – of course, all served on starched tablecloths.

The holiday is sponsored by ... a famous Gin producer.

Travel to: London (Bloomsbury). The event takes place in the Bedford Square Gardens.

Other holidays on this date: Social Media Day (USA)

... JULY

Tradition: allegedly first mentioned in the late XIVth C, the word derives from the Latin "traditionem" which means to hand over, to give for safekeeping. A tradition evolves thousands of years and lives for as long as it is part of the culture of a group of people (society). Most recognizable attributes are traditional clothes, traditional dishes, traditional songs, greetings and more.

01 July: July Morning (Bulgaria)

The feast of the Rising Sun. A holiday unique to Bulgarians that is observed only in the country, or by more than two Bulgarians abroad. It is a fundamental reminder of the golden hippie years (1960s-1980s) with singing around bonfires and free-spirited people dancing in the moonlight till the the early hours.

Folks from around the country travel to the seaside to meet the first rays of the sun on July 1st – many of them hitchhike which is in the true spirit of the celebration. On the night of June 30th, they set up camps on sandy beaches, play the guitars and sing songs around bonfires in wait for the rising sun.

The holiday adopted its name from the famous in the 1980s song "July Morning" by Uriah Heep – this song has become an anthem of the event. On July 1st, it is played on beaches, rooftops, in mountains or abroad – everyone sings along welcoming the sun. A popular theory on the origin of the celebration and it's connection with this particular song is that in still Communist-ruled Bulgaria, this was a way for people to express their will for freedom and new beginning. There was no real hippie movement in the country unlike other countries in the world. In times of many bans by the government (including ban on all Western music to be played or sold), the people looked at the morning sun in hope for a better future.

Since no one can confirm exactly when the observation began, it can be also an inheritance from a Pagan ritual like sun worshipping ceremony.

Whatever the reason – this is one of the most celebrated and loved holidays for Bulgarians, which also coincides with the start of the school summer holidays, so – many excuses to sit on a beach and wait for the sun! The observation still keeps its "rustic" form and has not been commercialised at all.

A regular guest to the July Morning celebration is John Lawton from Uriah Heep himself (who for many years didn`t know about the observation and had no clue that the "July Morning" song was so important and had such a strong message!).

And yes, John Lawton performs "July Morning" live on the July morning, on a sandy beach in Bulgaria.

This observation is a must do for the free-willies!

Travel to: Bulgaria (Kamen Bryag). July Morning is celebrated on all beaches along the Black Sea Coast as well as on Vitosha Mountain near Sofia. There is a July Morning Seaside Resort near the coastal town of Kavarna.

Other holidays on this date: Creative Ice Cream Flavours Day, International Joke Day, Quapaw Tribal Powwow, Hopi Festival (USA), Gion Matsuri Festival (Japan), Schifferstechen (Switzerland), Walking with Spirits Ritual (Australia)

02 July: Fiesta del Fuego (Cuba)

The Fire Festival (also known as Festival del Caribe) is one of the most important celebrations in Cuba and is held annually in the first week of July. Created in 1981, its goal is to showcase the historical and religious traditions and diverse cultural identity of the people in the Caribbean region. In the beginning, the event was more of a "serious" one, hosting various discussion panels, workshops and conferences, however in time it`s scope broadened with more festive events in the program. Over 200 000 participants including the mystical Santeros (priests practicing Santería - "worship of saints". Some of their rituals include deep trance under sacred drum beat, animal sacrifice, communicating with the ancestors etc.), Rastafarians (who believe that a single God partially resides within every individual) and Indigenous Indians perform music, dances, hold literature readings, magic and religious ceremonies, art exhibitions and cultural workshops. Every year the festival is dedicated to a different Caribbean country, focusing on the native folklore.

The festival begins with The Serpent Parade – participants from all Caribbean regions in their typical attire (colourful clothes, feathers, headdresses, beads and more), parade in conga pace through the streets, dancing, singing and waving their national flag.

Then it is a week of non-stop dancing and partying. The festival occupies more than 50 venues, most of them – open spaces. A highlight is the fire dance – performers, dressed in traditional for the region attire, dance and juggle with fire under a rhythmic drumming.

Along the week-long celebrations, numerous local food markets, drink stalls, souvenir pop-up shops, theatre art and visual performances showcase different segments of the Caribbean culture.

The festival ends with Burning of the Devil under raging storm of drum beats. A huge effigy is set alight by the sea shore. The Devil symbolizes all things evil, so once it is burned to ashes – it clears the way and shows a commitment to meet again for the next Fire Festival.

Travel to: Cuba (Santiago de Cuba). The Serpent Parade starts at Plaza de Martes and ends in Parque de Cespedes.

Other holidays on this date: I Forgot Day, Build A Scarecrow Day (USA), World UFO Day, Aomori Nebuta Festival (Japan)

03 July: Calgary Stampede (Canada)

The first Calgary Stampede was held in 1912 as a successor of a cattle market and Agricultural Fair initiated by local cattle owners in 1886. During World War I it also featured a military tattoo parade and military exercises. Now it is a rodeo, exhibition and festival held every year in July, attracting more than a million people.

Also known as the Greatest Outdoor Show on Earth, the 10-day event brings the Old West to Canada – cowboys, horsemanship and rodeo competitions, bull riding and bareback riding, cattle roping, chuckwagon races, a midway carnival, live music, Stampede Queen contest, arts and culture. And all that accompanied by great food including hundreds of pancake breakfasts and barbecues, and tons of maple syrup.

The show starts with a two-and-a-half-mile parade featuring beautiful floats, live music bands, horses, celebrities and cultural performances. Then it`s time for competitions. The show is known to have the richest payout – with prizes starting from $100 000!

The hosting city is completely gets transformed completely – country music concerts are held in the open air, office buildings and storefronts are decorated and painted in cowboy themes, residents dress up in western wear.

During the fest, the five indigenous nations build an Indian Village on a river bank– they erect tipis, organize traditional pow wows (social gatherings with dances) and sell souvenirs.

Travel to: Canada (Alberta). The event is held at Stampede Park in Calgary. The Indian Village is on the banks of the Elbow River.

Other holidays on this date: Compliment Your Mirror Day, Disobedience Day (USA), Carnival (St Vincent and the Grenadines)

04 July: Obonjan Festival (Croatia)

This is a newly created (in 2016) ten-week festival taking place on a Croatian island and is held annually from the end of June till the beginning of September. It features music, dances, comedy, astronomy talks, cinema and many thematic workshops. Most music gigs take place in an ambient lit stone amphitheatre, or round open-air swimming pools and sun-kissed bars. There are Taro card readers, Yoga classes and group hypnosis sessions, underwater sculpture park, movie screenings, Eden Labs where talks on building a sustainable future are held, Zen Den café, outdoor hot tubs, Forest Bar located under beautifully lit centurial trees, Drift Bar with various options for refreshing cocktails and a market. The accommodation provided is in bell tents surrounded by pine trees, safari-tent style "lodges" overlooking the sea and secluded forest lodges. Relax during the day and party all night long at one of the most picturesque festival settings in Europe. The idea of the organizers is to turn the island into a year-round unique concept, combining huge parties with sustainable living in fun and creative accommodation.

Travel to: Croatia (Obonjan Island). The venue is a 40-minute boat trip from Šibenik. A dance music festival promoting company from Leeds, UK has leased the island for 45 years.

Other holidays on this date: Independence Day (USA), Hiragasi (Madagascar)

05 July: Chiang Ku Ceremony (Taiwan)

The festival is organised in July and is absolutely spectacular. Although being banned a couple of times – this century-old tradition dating back to the Ching Dynasty (the 1820s) continues to be celebrated annually.

The legend has it that a young man led a group of settlers who left their homes in China and moved to Yilan (in Taiwan). They enjoyed a happy life but eventually, all of them died, many having no family or children at all (they were all male). A local belief is that if someone dies far away from his home with no relatives to give him proper ancestral offerings, he becomes a ghost. And if a ghost is not happy and pleased – he will not return to the Underworld. The ceremony is performed in the so-called Ghost Month when all ghosts come to the land of the living to visit their relatives. They should, however, return before the 29th day of the seventh lunar month when the gate to the Underworld closes.

The locals build giant bamboo poles (around 30 meters high) fixed on a huge wooden platform and hang offerings on them – rice, duck, chicken, candy, seafood, dumplings, ornaments, flags and many more. The purpose of the offerings is to feed the hungry ghosts so they can go back to the underworld. After the poles are smeared with grease and blessed by the priests, teams consisting of 5 people each, try to climb up and get as many goods as possible (the participants represent the hungry ghosts). They form human pyramids and help themselves with ropes to climb further up the poles. They throw the goods they catch into the crowd down below. The end of the "contest" is marked by one of the teams seizing the flag on the very top.

Afterwards, a special Chiang Ku ceremony is performed in temples – Chiang Ku is a deity protecting the humans from evil spirits.

Travel to: Taiwan (Yilan County). The ceremony takes place in the small fishing town of Toucheng in front of the Kaicheng Temple.

Other holidays on this date: Work-A-Holics Day (USA), Shearing of the Beasts (Spain), Fisherman`s Day (Marshall Islands), Bikini Day (France), Walk on the Fire (Tahiti)

06 July: San Fermin Bull Run (Spain)

The event is held annually from July 6th till July 14th on the streets of a Spanish city. The festival honours St Fermin – a patron saint of the Navarra region (once a Basque kingdom). In the past herders would hurry their cattle from the outskirts of the city to the market (the bullring) using fear. Years later, this turned into a fierce competition between the local cattlemen - that is how the tradition of running the bulls started. The earliest evidence goes back to the early XIVth C, involving running in front of six toro bravo fighting bulls that have been let loose on the town's streets. However, once the rub joined forces with the religious celebration of St Fermin in 1591 – it led to a festival.

The bulls are let loose after a launch of two rockets. They charge behind the runners for 825 meters (the distance to the bullring). Many "bull shepherds" run behind to make sure that no bull turns around and people don`t poke the animals from behind. The so-called "dobladores" also run with the crowd – they are folks with bullfighting knowledge who help the runners escape safely from the raging bulls. Two groups of "mansos" also take part – they run in front and behind the animals, making sure they follow the direction to the bullring.

Before the start, the runners chant a prayer to St Fermin to guide and help them get the bulls into the bullring safe from harm. The prayer is repeated three times.

After the run that lasts just a few minutes, a third rocket is launched to announce that all bulls are in the bullring. The animals are the actual bulls that feature in a bullfight later in the day when they are fought and killed by toreros (bullfighters).

Running backwards towards the bulls is strictly forbidden.

Interesting is that Ernest Hemingway brought the Pamplona Bull Run to its world glory – and he did it with his book "The Sun Also Rises" in 1926.

Severe injuries are common because as people often get rammed and stepped on by the bulls.

Travel to: Spain (Pamplona). The bull run starts at 8a.m. from Santo Domingo Street. A fence made of more than 3 000 wooden planks is built along the route.

Other holidays on this date: International Kissing Day, National Fried Chicken Day (USA), NOS Alive Festival (Portugal), EXIT Festival (Serbia), Noisily Festival (England)

07 July: Ivan Kupala Day (Russia)

An annual holiday celebrated on the night of July 7th. The Slavic holiday coincides with the summer solstice when the nights are the shortest. The origins of the celebration are rooted in an ancient Pagan fertility and water purification ritual, at some point (after the Christianization in Russia) adopted by the Christian Orthodox church as the Day of St John the Baptist (in Russian "Ivan" is John and "Kupala" derives from the word from bathing, related to baptizing through full immersion in water).

The holiday is celebrated with fire, water, herbs, wildflowers and fortunetelling.

The locals spend the day in singing songs, lighting bonfires and jumping over them for good luck – the ritual once again re-directs to the Pagan origin of the holiday, as it was believed that jumping over a fire chases away the evil spirits.

The legend has it that water on Ivan Kupala day has magical and healing powers, so the people swim in rivers and lakes for good health and luck (once again a Pagan ritual - water was used in many purification ceremonies) and the children spray and pour water over random people for good fortune.

In the evening, young girls decorate herb and wildflower wreaths with burning candles and set them afloat in rivers to read their future in the floating patterns. Young unmarried boys try to catch the wreaths in hope to to receive attention and maybe meet their future wives.

It is believed that the night of Ivan Kupala is magical and is the only time of the year when a specific fern blooms deep in the forest. This flowering fern is said to direct the finder towards treasure, power and good fortune. By tradition, young girls enter the forest first, followed later by young men – as it is a magical night, many new relationships may be forged while searching for the blooming fern.

Another belief is that all witches, mermaids and werewolves celebrate on Ivan Kupala day too and do as many mischiefs as they can. Maybe that is the excuse for children to pull as many pranks as they can on this day and get away with it unharmed.

A popular belief is that those who take part in the celebration will find love and happiness. No one is supposed to sleep at Ivan Kupala night because it is a charmed and mystical night.

Travel to: Russia (Novosibirsk). Ivan Kupala is celebrated by almost all Slavs in Russia, Ukraine, Belarus, Lithuania and Poland. In Novosibirsk, the ritual of pouring water over people is broadened to spilling buckets of water on buses too, so it is a real water battle.

Other holidays on this date: Chocolate Day, National Strawberry Sundae Day (USA), Kupalle Night (Belarus), Star Festival (Japan), Saba Saba (Tanzania)

08 July: Bilbao BBK Festival (Spain)

A music festival created after an unsuccessful attempt of the city to host a Formula Renault 3.5 street circuit in 2005. Held annually in the first weekend of July, the event lasts for three days. It is the largest festival in the Basque region and one of the biggest on the Iberian Peninsula, visited by more than 100 000 people. The venue spreads on the impressive 30 000sq.m. offering camping sites, three main stages, bars and food markets, DJ tent and backstage facilities. Nearly 60 artists and bands from around the world perform during the festival days. Bilbao BBK was nominated twice for "Best Foreign Festival" at the UK Festival Awards in 2010 and 2011 and three times for "Best-Medium Sized European Festival" at the European Festivals Awards (2009-2011). A visit to Bilbao BBK can easily be combined with a visit to one of the world`s best-surfing sites - the San Sebastian coast, about 90km west from the city. And, certainly, there is no need to mention that Bilbao is worth a visit!

Travel to: Spain (Bilbao). The event is held in a specially build complex in Mount Cobeta – Recinto Kobetamendi, Calle del Monte Kobetas.

Other holidays on this date: National Blueberry Day (USA)

09 July: San Fermin Festival (USA)

This is a milder version of the traditional Bull Run festival in Pamplona. The event was initiated in 2007 by an American, who took part in the Pamplona Bull Run and decided to organize a similar event in the USA. But instead of running raging bulls, girls dressed in white with red scarves and handkerchiefs, horned helms, AND on roller skates chase the runners. If, or when, they catch up – the girls whack the poor runner with a foam ball bat. The celebration begins and ends with a huge party, so think lots of food, drinks and music!

The US version of San Fermin is organized in the first week of July every year.

Travel to: USA (Louisiana). The event takes place along the Convention Center Blvd in New Orleans.

Other holidays on this date: National Sugar Cookie Day (USA), Hunting and Baiman Festivals (Taiwan – Thao tribe)

10 July: Splash! Festival (Germany)

This is the biggest Hip Hop & Reggae party of them all! Started in 1998 at a former powerhouse in the city of Chemnitz in Germany, the festival now is held at Ferropolis – an open-air museum and a former coal mine, located on a small peninsula on the Gremminer Lake. The setting is very much industrial - old-time excavating machines and tall mining cranes are scattered all over the place. For the festival though, they are decorated with ambient lights. This is a festival suitable for street art aficionados, skate culture, beatboxers and break dancers.

Mobile homes and caravans are allowed on the camping site. There are also volunteering opportunities available such as info guides and onsite help (a fantastic way to attend the festival in case you are short on cash). Many people go for a swim in the lake after sunset and listen to the bass beats while floating in the water. A must visit event!

Travel to: Germany (Gräfenhainichen). The event is held in Ferropolis – an open-air industrial museum known as the "City of Iron" because of the many towering mining cranes, machines and excavators onsite, which are lit in different colors during the festival days.

Other holidays on this date: National Pina Colada Day, Teddy Bear Picnic Day (USA), Bohemia Jazzfest (Czech Republic)

11 July: Lower Keys Underwater Music Festival (USA)

The Underwater Music Festival has been running for about 30 years. A local radio station sponsors the event to promote responsible diving, environmental sustainability and preservation of North Americas' only living barrier coral reef.

Sea-themed music is played through underwater speakers suspended under boats situated above the reef. Participants (amateur and professional divers) are encouraged to wear quirky costumes (giant shrimps for instance) and play mock "underwater instruments", such as a "trombonefish" (created by a local artist specifically for the occasion), while listening underwater to the pre-selected playlist and competing for prizes. And since sound travels about 4 times faster in water than in air, the experience is quite surreal.

Travel to: USA (Florida). The underwater venue is the Looe Key coral reef in Key West – part of the Florida Keys National Marine Sanctuary.

Other holidays on this date: World Population Day, Riddu Riddu Festival of the Sami people (Norway)

12 July: Oyster Festival (South Africa)

The 10-day festival is held annually in July, since 1983 when it was initiated as a Winter Festival to attract more tourists during the quiet months. In general - this is a celebration of good life and one of the most popular events in the Western Cape.

Two major sports events accompany the festivities – the Pick n Pay Forest Marathon and the Pick n Pay Cycle Tour. Over two weeks more than 100 smaller competitions take place, such as Geo Oyster Geocaching Competition, Pick n Pay Fun Event for the disabled, Navigation Drift Dive Challenge, the Night of 1 000 Pictures (fundraiser for the local Hospice), Wine Festival, Oyster Mardi Gras, Whisky Bowls tournament and others.

A centrepiece is the oyster – over 30 pop up oyster shops (so-called Tabasco Hotspots) are available for visitors and serve oysters prepared to anybodys liking – raw, cooked or garnished. More than 200 000 oysters are eaten each year during the festival days.

There are also oyster tastings, oyster recipe workshops and cooking classes, oyster farm tours, oyster-themed dinners as well as oyster and champagne matching classes and tastings.

The festival town offers scuba diving, mountain hiking, paddling, football, music concerts, theatre shows, markets, wine & oyster tastings, gala evenings, whisky and jazz cruises, magicians, jugglers and of course a showcase of about 50 of South Africa's premier wine estates. The general event is free, although charges may occur for individual events like wine tastings and jazz cruises.

Travel to: South Africa (Knysna). The event takes place at Knysna Quays.
Other holidays on this date: National Different Colored Eyes Day, National Simplicity Day (USA), World Paper Bag Day, Orangemen's Day (Canada)

13 July: The Three Games of Men (Mongolia)

Held in July every year since 1206 (!), the most loved festival in the country is about three games the Mongolians absolutely adore – games of strength, wisdom and courage. The Three Games of Men or the Nadaam Festival is a major holiday in the country, with roots dating back to nomad wedding assemblies and hunting extravaganzas of the Mongol Army. The three games are in fact the three sporting passions of the Mongolians – horse racing, wrestling and archery. The Mongolian nomads, who roamed steppes and hills, have a rich history of more than 2 000 years and in the past, it was a matter of life and death for them to master these crucial surviving skills.

The Three Games (Nadaam) was recognised as an official State Ceremony in the beginning of the XIIIth C with the enthroning of Chinggis Khaan – the founder of the Mongol Empire.

The festival is celebrated over three days in most parts of the country, however the Grand Opening ceremony takes place in the capital and is...impressive. It begins with marching horsemen dressed in medieval attire, waving the banners of Chinggis Khaan up above their heads (nine horsetails, representing the nine tribes of the Mongols). They are followed by dancing performers, representing all ethnic groups in Mongolia wearing traditional clothes for their region.

The wrestling competitions are in traditional Mongol wrestling style – meaning there are no weight categories nor age limits. The contestants flap their arms imitating a falcon or tiger and try to knock their opponent down so that he touches the ground with his knee and elbow. The traditional wrestling costumes consist of knee-high boots, shoulder vest, shorts and hat.

The archery competitions use typical Mongolian bows – very heavy and difficult to bend (it can take years to make one). The archers aim at 33 leather cylinders from 75-meter distance. Every time an archer prepares to shoot, judges start singing an ancient tune.

The horse races are held in open grassland and unlike the western short course races – they cover a course up to 30km. An average of 26 000 horses compete around the country. And the jockeys are from 5 to 13 years old.

There's also a knucklebone shooting tournament, lots of traditional food such as deep-fried meat dumplings, cold meat pancakes and craft stands.

The Nadaam festival very much represents the cultural identity of the Mongolians and is a way to show their ancient traditions and rich cultural heritage.

The Three Games of Men is on the Representative List of the Intangible Cultural Heritage of Humanity of UNESCO.

Travel to: Mongolia (Ulan Bator in the Gobi Desert). One can explore the nearby historic sites on a two-humped Bactrian camel. For truly authentic experience – book a stay in a yurt (ger) in a real nomad camp where the locals will cook for you.

Other holidays on this date: National French Fry Day (USA), FIB Benicàssim (Spain)

14 July: Mud Festival (South Korea)

Initiated in 1998, the annual event held over two weeks in July brings more tourists to South Korea than any other (2 to 3mln people every year).

The festival is held on the beach of a coastal town and it certainly wasn't intended to be a huge mud fight when it was established. It was created to promote cosmetics made from the local mud which is very high in mineral ingredients.

On the weekend of the festival, different areas on the beach are set up - mudslides, mud pits, a mud prison, giant mud baths, children's area, mud fountains, mud skiing slope and a mud swimming pool. There is also coloured mud for bodypainting. The point is to get as muddy as possible.

Oh, well – why not? It's fun AND good for the skin after all!

The festival tweekend features also acupuncture and mud massage sessions, live music concerts, fireworks, competitions, street parades, dancers and a market selling cosmetic products from mud.

Travel to: South Korea (Boryeong). The event is held in the Daecheon Beach area.

Other holidays on this date: International Nude Day (USA), Nachi-no-Ogi Festival (Japan)

15 July: Northeastern Primitive Rendezvous (USA)

A holiday initiated in 1788 as local settlers' trade fair, celebrated annually for a week in July.

Travel back in time and live like the people from the 1640s-1840s. Sunglasses, modern footwear and cell phones are strictly forbidden during this celebration of the old times. All participants live as the ancestors, sleep in canvas tents, cook their own food over a fire and sell authentic meals and artisan merchandise outside the tents. There are hawk and knife throwing competitions, tribal performances, live music and lots of dancing involved! Anyone wanting to get involved in the organization can donate ice, wood, fresh water, ropes or anything suitable for a rustic camping to the National Rendezvous Living History Foundation.

Travel to: USA (Maine – Orrington). The event takes place in the Wiswell Farm – the only home in the area, still occupied by descendants of the town's first settlers.

Other holidays on this date: Cow Appreciation day, Toss Away The "Could Haves" and "Should Haves" (USA), Country Thunder Saskatchewan (Canada)

16 July: Melt! (Germany)

Melt! Is held annually over a weekend in July. The festival was created in 1997 and is one of the biggest and most distinguished open-air electronic festivals in Germany due to its renowned artists' line-up and its current location. Since 1999 the venue is a former coal mine site neighbouring a forest and a lake. Many party-goers combine the festival with a refreshing dip in the water and return to dance under the stars. This event features the best of what the rock, rave and pop scene has to offer. The music is 24/7 on the Sleepless Floor stage and until 7 am on the other stages, so all-night fun is guaranteed. Within the two camping sites in the festival complex, there are art and craft tents such as the "Creative Crazy Pony" tent where visitors cover themselves head-to-toe in glitter.

The "Forest" area offers a tree house, hammocks and another stage.

The festival complex is much like an art installation – monstrous excavators and mining cranes utilized as music stages lit by spotlights, lasers and hundreds of colourful light bulbs, and a horde of bagpipers roaming the campsite calling people to the main stage.

A quirky option to get to the festival is by The MiXery Melt! Train departing from the Netherlands (Amsterdam) and stopping in few German cities. It has a DJ Party wagon and a bar. For the duration of the festival, one can rent a bunk bed and sleep on the train. However, many call it "The Non-Sleeper", so if one plans on a good night sleep – better have earplugs!

Travel to: Germany (Gräfenhainichen). The venue is Ferropolis – an open-air industrial museum known as the "City of Iron" because of the many towering mining cranes, machines and excavators onsite, which are lit in different colors during the festival days.

Other holidays on this date: National Ice Cream Day, Fresh Spinach Day (USA), Our Lady of Mount Carmel (Chile)

17 July: Tribal Mask Festival (Papua New Guinea)

The annual four-day festival initiated in 1995 and held in July is an expression of the rich culture and traditions of indigenous people on the island. It is one of its kind and gathers folks from different tribes, all in their celebratory attire, to perform ritualistic dances and show their tribal identity.

Unique to the Papua New Guinea tribes are their masks – they are sacred and involved in every ceremony. Each tribe has a distinctive pattern – some are so big (over 10m tall) that they are not fit to wear, some of them are used as lucky charms or amulets, others are worn but as a part of a larger assemblage. It is only the men who wear masks, however not before they have been initiated in the according cult – because once they put a mask on, they become spirits. Most masks are made of bamboo and soft bark and painted in colours – they usually have enormous eyes or cone-shaped top with a huge smile, sometimes decorated with feathers, teeth, bones or leaves (depending on the region).

The celebration starts with cleansing ceremony, tribal dances and storytelling. The opening ritual to welcome the spirits is performed at dawn. It is accompanied by chants, fire dances and beating of traditional drums. The tribesmen paddle wooden canoes during the night humming ancient chants – they re-enact the arrival of their ancestors to the island and create a mystical and haunting atmosphere. They wear the ritualistic handmade masks.

A highlight of the festival is the Fire Dance – performed around a huge pyre only by men –dressed in traditional attire (skirts of plant leaves, flowers, seashells), their bodies painted and wearing the quite scary masks. They dance in and out of a fire, to monotonous drum beat and chant of elders.

The festival ground offers plenty of curiosities – tribal women baking python in an earth oven and preparing celebratory feast, warriors with tusks re-enacting an ancient tribal battle, dancers carrying statues of Virgin Mary on their heads and hopping like frogs in a ritualistic dance, the Mud Men tribe with their entire body painted in white, spiritual shows, fortunetellers and much more. There is also an arts and crafts market with handmade ancestral and spirit masks – some of them decades old.

Some people still practice black magic around here...

Travel to: Papua New Guinea (Kokopo). The festival takes place along and around the Kokopo Beach area.

Other holidays on this date: Global Hug Your Kids Day (USA), Lucca Summer Festival (Italy)

18 July: Crop Over Festival (Barbados)

The Crop Over tradition started in the 1680s during times of slavery. It featured singing, dancing and playing different musical instruments like fiddle, guitar, bottles filled with water and even bones.

The Crop Over festival was created in the 1780s, marking the successful end of the sugar cane harvest season (Barbados being the largest producer of the crop). Over the years, the event developed into the biggest and most anticipated festival in Barbados, lasting from June till the beginning of August.

The Ceremonial Delivery of the Last Canes ritual is the official opening of the festival when a King and Queen are crowned, based on their "cane cutting" performance. The ceremony is followed by a Decorated Cart Parade with people dressed in colourful costumes, riding on decorated donkey carts and any other means of transportation.

A highlight is the Calypso music and Calypso dancers performing in the purpose-built Calypso Tents. Originating from Trinidad, this music style features satirical lyrics depicting life, politics and people of the past year. There are Calypso competitions, street food markets, craft markets, street parades, masquerades, live bands and tropical drinks. During the festival, many street food stalls offer typical Bajan food – flying fish, dolphin, barracuda, black belly sheep, yams, sweet potatoes, breadfruit are some of them.

The Crop Over festival ends on the first Monday in August with a grand carnival – Kadooment Day, known as one of the best Caribbean celebrations. It is a massive street masquerade with glorious feathery costumes, colourful masks, fireworks and lots of Calypso and Soca music!

The word Kadooment itself is a Bajan word meaning "a big occasion filled with fun & merriment".

The celebration ends with a massive party in the Spring Garden and a swim at the nearby beach.

Travel to: Barbados (Bridgetown). The event is held at at Tim's On the Highway, St Michael and culminates at the Spring Garden.

Other holidays on this date: Caviar Day, National Sour Candy Day (USA)

19 July: World Eskimo Indian Olympics (USA)

Since 1961, the games are held annually over four days in July or August and are a display of the human preparedness for survival. Every part of the body and mind is tested to the limit through games of ancestral survival techniques, indigenous dances and storytelling. Must have skills are strength, agility, and endurance. The Winter Olympics were created to preserve the culture and tradition of the Alaskan Native Americans in times when the western culture was widely spreading into the north.

For an authentic experience, participants should envision themselves in a small village hut with the temperature outside at 60 degrees below zero. All attending men are celebrating the successful seal hunt. In the meantime, whaling captains are looking for the best "fit" to their whaling crew in the following season – that would be the fastest, the strongest, the one showing great endurance to pain. They are carefully observing young village boys who compete in different games to show strength in hope to be picked by the whaling captains and take part in the hunt.

The opening ceremony features The Race of The Torch –winners from the previous games run to light up a stone lamp filled with dried moss and seal oil – a symbol of fair play and sportsmanship.

Some of the games featured in the Olympics are: Muktuk Eating (frozen whale skin and blubber); greased pole walk, toe kick, seal hop, kneel jump, Eskimo tug-of-war, seal skinning, ear pull, blanket toss (dancers tossed into the air by a number of people holding a blanket) and more.

During the 4-day event many indigenous craftsmen open shops for handmade merchandise and, of course, traditional native food.

Travel to: USA (Alaska – Fairbanks or Anchorage). In Fairbanks the games are held in Carlson Center and in Anchorage – at the Sullivan Arena.

Other holidays on this date: National Raspberry Cake Day (USA)

20 July: Pavement Spectacle (Austria)

The festival was created by a former Mayor of the city in 1987, inspired by a birthday celebration for the Moroccan King, held in a marketplace in Marrakesh. Today, Pflasterspektakel is one of the biggest street performances in Europe and brings together artists, clowns, singers, mimes and acrobats from around the world. This is a 3-day festival featuring improvisation theatre, street music and concerts, dance, circus artistry, high-wire and fire acrobatics defying gravity, clowns and comedic performance art at the highest level. Participants from more than 40 countries audition months before the event to take part in transforming the city into an international art scene. Any performer interested to participate can do it – the event is sponsored by the municipality and all travel costs and meals are covered. As for the rest – artists rely on the bills and coins from the appreciative audience!

Travel to: Austria (Linz). The main events take place at Hauptplatz in the city center.
Other holidays on this date: Moon Day (USA)

21 July: World Snail Racing Championship (England)

Ready! Steady! Slow! It is the World Snail Racing Championship! Held annually in July since the 1960s, the race attracts many snail breeders and race snail trainers from around the country. The event was created by an eccentric farmer to raise funds for the local church.

The rules are simple – all participants are placed in a red circle in the middle of a round table (covered with a specially embroidered tablecloth facilitating the best sliming conditions), with the winner being the first to slime its way into the outer ring. In 2016 the defending champion George "The Storm", who almost broke the world record, unfortunately, died two days before the event. The winner takes home a lovely fresh lettuce! No need to mention – all snails should follow a strict diet just like any other athlete – the recommended meal plan is lollo rosso lettuce. And the best daily workout is sliming up on tall French windows.

BBQ and lots of beer accompany the sports thrill!

Travel to: England (Norfolk). The race is held at the cricket field in Congham.
Other holidays on this date: Junk Food Day (USA), Curious Arts Festival (England), Tramlines Festival (England)

22 July: Bula Festival (Fiji Island)

A festival showing the hybrid culture of the Fijian people – a mix of Melanesian and Polynesian tribes, European missionaries and indigenous Indians. The festival, created in the 1960s, is held annually over a week in July, in a small coastal town on the main island. The purpose is to present and preserve the cultural diversity and history of the natives. Maybe this is the reason for naming it "Bula" - "Hello/Welcome" in the local language.

The opening ceremony features a parade with floats, music and tribal dances performed by indigenous people in tribal clothes. This is one of Fiji's biggest festivals and offers entertainment galore – dancing, food stalls with local delicacies, Miss Bula beauty pageant, themed nights, rides and more.

All proceeds from the festival go to local charities.

Travel to: Fiji Island. The festival takes place in the city of Navi in the Koroivolu and Prince Charles Parks.

Other holidays on this date: National Rat Catcher's Day, Hammock Day (USA), World Championship Bathtub Race (Canada)

23 July: Secret Garden Party (England)

This is a four-day independent music & arts festival taking place annually in July in a beautiful countryside setting neighbouring a river and a lake. Starting with just one stage in 2004, now the festival has fifteen stages, gathering tens of thousands of people. Every year a group of designers create the spectacular setting and bring magic to the venue. The Great Stage, The Next Stage, The Pagoda, Lost Woods Disco, Chai Wallahs, The Spiritual Playground, Lost Horizon and more areas offer different music performances throughout the festival days. There is a Kids Area with crafts, pony rides and a circus. For accommodation, the organizers provide Yurts, Tipis, Octopads, Royal Safari Tents, Sleeping Huts and Festibarrows (quite unusual - a wheelbarrow with a sleeping bag in it!). This is the first UK event to offer people the chance to have their illegal drugs tested to establish their content (provided by an organization called The Loop). The musical line-up is a mix of current and past sonic glory. There are also Speaker's corner, poetry readings, stand-up comedy, Dress Up Day, flash mobs and many other intellectual activities to enjoy too.

Travel to: England (Cambridgeshire). The event is held in Abbots Ripton, Huntingdon - part of the grounds of a Georgian farm house with its own lake, river and landscaped gardens.

Other holidays on this date: National Parent's Day, National Hot Dog Day (USA), Love Week Festival (Croatia)

24 July: Blue Dot Festival (England)

The unusual intergalactic festival initiated in 2016, celebrates fascinating science, art and technology. It is an annual three-day event held in July, set in a deep space observatory next to the impressive Lovell telescope.

Dessi Nikoltchev:

A feast of stellar music, live science experiments, sustainability talks and workshops, it celebrates all things Earth. Some of the spots one can find on the festival grounds are The Lovell Stage – the main stage set in the shadow of the huge telescope, Nebula Stage – with top-notch multimedia that travels deep in space, Mission Control – an exhibition space where talks are held, The Space Pavilion offering mind-blowing tricks and brain illusions, Stargazing spots, Planetarium, G`Astronomy village and Luminarium – a maze of air bubbles with cool air and soothing music where one can sit and think about life and existence.

The mission of the festival is to celebrate science, to show how fragile the Earth is and to present new scientific ways to preserve it as long as possible.

Travel to: England (Cheshire). The festival is located in the Jodrell Bank Observatory near Manchester.
Other holidays on this date: Amelia Earhart Day, National Tequila Day (USA)

25 July: Cobán Folkloric Festival (Guatemala)

Held annually since 1936 over five days in the end of July, this is a festival of Guatemala`s native people –Mayans being the dominant ethnicity. Its purpose is to show and preserve the rich cultural heritage and the ancient traditions that have existed for thousands of years. The event was created as a regional fair by a group of successful businessmen - coffee exporting moguls (Cobán is Guatemala`s cardamom and coffee plantation centre and in the 1930s prospered greatly from export).

A highlight of the festival, locally known as Rabin Ajau, is the election and crowning of a new Princess Tesulutlan (Daughter of the King) to lead the opening ceremony in the following year. The election process is accompanied by indigenous dances, marimba songs and authentic Mayan rituals. The candidates are judged not on their beauty, but on leadership skills and commitment to preserve the Mayan traditions and values.

During the festival, there are street parades, indigenous dances performed by Kekchis people, folklore singing groups, finger-licking food, drinks and numerous souvenir stalls.

This is the most impressive festival of Mayan traditions in Guatemala.

Travel to: Guatemala (Cobán). The event takes place on the streets and the center square of the small town.
Other holidays on this date: National Merry-Go-Round Day (USA)

26 July: Carnival of Santiago de Cuba (Cuba)

Carnivals – feasts held in the months before Lent, brought to Cuba by Spanish settlers, became popular in the middle of the XVI C. The Carnival of Santiago de Cuba (having its origins in the XVIIth C), however, is special. Not only because it is held at the end of July, but also because it evolved from an old time Fiesta de Mamarrachos (main activities of the mammarachos or the "Mad Ones": huge masquerades, bonfires, singing mocking songs, throwing objects and liquids at other people, spontaneous parading on the streets, dancing and lots of drinking). The carnival was known as "Carnaval de las classes bajas" (the carnival of the lower class) because it was held in July when the sugar cane harvest was over and all labourers were free, so they could participate in the celebrations.

The Carnival of Santiago de Cuba is the biggest, loudest and most loved festival in the country. It has a different theme set every year – referring to a prominent event, a greeting to neighbouring country or a satire act to the government.

The streets and houses are decorated with flowers and ornaments, folks in bright costumes dance everywhere, there are street markets with food stalls, local merchants, jugglers, street conga drummers and music everywhere! A highlight is the parade of the comparsas (performers of similar ethnic groups) under the non-stopping rhythm of congas (Cuban drums), bells and chants. Groups of "diablitos" (little devils) follow the comparsas – male dancers, masked head to toe in raffia costumes.

The Carnival starts with children's parade, followed by Carrozas (decorated floats). Then comes the Conga Parade which takes place in each neighbourhood. It is led by the comparsas and its goal is to get the residents out of their houses – so... it is common to see locals parading in their slippers, or still wearing their PJ's.

The Carnival goes on for a week turning the whole city into a massive party stage.

P.S. Some people describe the event as a general disorder with noise and abuse of alcohol...

Travel to: Cuba (Santiago de Cuba). For a real taste of the Cuban culture – arrange an accommodation in a private home with a local family. After all, Santiago is considered the most exotic city in Cuba with many different ethnic groups settled there over the centuries – African, French Haitian, Chinese, Spanish and Indigenous.

Other holidays on this date: Aunt and Uncle Day (USA)

27 July: Kendall Calling (England)

The independent music and arts festival created in 2006, is held annually, in the end of July for 3 days. Awarded as 'Best Medium Festival in the UK', it has 9 stages with performances from renown international artists and bands, and tickets usually get sold out months before the event. Some areas on the festival grounds are: The Glow Tent (DJ sets), Calling Out (a stage for new and upcoming artists), Woodlands with a Silent Disco, Housparty (a purpose-built furnished house with kitchen and really loud music), Lost Eden (art installations and performances like fighting robots and flying plastic owls), Riot Jazz, Lost Disco, Cinema, Jagerhaus – featuring four stages for performers who are about to make it big. The Jagerhaus is named after the famous drink Jagermeister and its entrance, named the Entrance Tunnel sprays the audience with a mist of some of the 56 herbs and spices used to create the drink itself. As this is a family-friendly festival, there is a Kids Area with carnivals, cinema, creative workshops, games, inflatable castles and kids disco. There is also a market with handpicked merchants and more than 18 restaurants onsite – BBQ, game meat, vegan, sweet bars, pies, Thai, Creole, Mexican, British and many more. There also is a Real Ale Festival offering the special festival's brew - Kendall Ale and the Oh Deer Ale!

The accommodation options within the festival grounds are Bunkpad, Safari Suite or Tenthouse Suite.

Facts:

- in 2011 the festival-goers broke the world record for making the largest ever mint cake onsite the festival grounds!

- in 2012, the festival got its own gingerbread house.

- in 2013 the festival broke another world record – for the largest gathering of Supermen lookalikes.

This festival is a true fairground. And it is topped off with heart-shaped confetti!

Travel to: England (Cumbria). The event is held at the Lowther Deer Park in the Lake District. There is a dedicated party train departing from Manchester – the Kendalino Express, and it offers free Prosecco!

Other holidays on this date: National Scotch Day, National Crème Brulee Day (USA), Womad (England).

28 July: World Bodypainting Festival (Austria)

A unique combination of a musical event mixed with surreal body-painting, this is one of the only festivals of its kind. For body painting fans and enthusiasts, this place really is a world capital, because for three days, men and women transform their bodies into beautiful and bizarre works of art. Established in 1998 in Seeboden as a regional event to promote tourism, the festival takes place in June or July and offers weeklong festive atmosphere with participants from more than 54 countries. All artists are given a theme in each category they compete into – Brush & Sponge, Airbrush, Makeup, Photography and Special Effects. Numerous workshops and events are held during the festival days - special effects, beauty make-up, head dressing including colour theory and history, the smallest art nouveau theatre in the world, Surreal Costume Ball (Body Circus), after dark contest with UV lights and

Zombie Crawl. There are stages with live music and DJ's, and a street food market as well.

Fun to know is that a full-body paint can take up to 6 hours!

Travel to: Austria (Klagenfurt am Wörthersee). The event is held on the lake Wörthersee known as Bodypaint City for the duration of the festival.

Other holidays on this date: National Talk in An Elevator Day, System Administrator Appreciation Day, Kihekah Steh Powwow (USA), Bellybutton Festival (Japan)

29 July: Festival of Near Death experiences (Spain)

Ok... a rather odd celebration but it actually celebrates life – every year on July 29th! This festival pays tribute to the saints of death in a small Spanish town, where pagan rites have been part of the local culture forever.

During the Festival of Near Death Experiences, or Santa Marta de Ribarteme (the patron saint of resurrection), folks who have had nearly death experience during the past year climb up into coffins and play dead while being carried in a mourning procession to a church. All coffin bearers are relatives or friends, and all are dressed in black...as they would for a real funeral. If a "participant" doesn't have a family – he bears his own coffin. The procession starts from a church with a mass, heads to the cemetery and after a "burial" returns once more to the church. It is led by a huge effigy of Santa Marta – the sister of Lazarus who was brought back to life by Jesus.

The purpose of the festival is to thank the saints for bringing people back to life after almost certain death. After the lucky survivors are carried in coffins around town – they rise and tell their storiy accompanied by brass bands and fireworks. After that, the dances begin, and everyone celebrates life and being alive.

Accompanying the procession are locals and visitors eating pulpo a la gallega – Galicia's 'signature dish' prepared with octopus.

Some people claim that this is one of the most outrageous religious pilgrimages in the world.

Travel to: Spain (Las Nieves). Worth visiting are – visit Santiago de Compostela or Porto in Portugal as it's not that far!

Other holidays on this date: National Lipstick Day, National Lasagna Day, National Dance Day (USA), Beselare Witch Parade (Belgium), Moreska Sword Dance (Croatia)

30 July: Beer Floating Festival (Finland)

Now, this is a thing beer lovers wouldn't want to miss! The celebration? Well... How about floating down a river in a rubber boat or a raft while drinking beer? This annual festival known as Kaljakellunta is located near Helsinki. The authorities have tried to ban the event many times because of the mess people leave behind, but it turned out that the festival has no official organizer, so by law, it cannot be banned (in Finland there is no law against unorganized events).

The idea for a festival was born in 1997 in a rehearsal room, when around 10 music band members decided one day to float down the river in inflatable boats and drink beer in search of inspiration. Nowadays the participants are over 5000 people. Some of them get creative and bring inflatable pools instead of rubber boats.

The date is... well – floating. The attendees spread the word on the social networks, but the date is usually the last weekend in July or the first in August.

The floating event comes to an end at a beach in Helsinki.

Travel to: Finland (Helsinki – Vantaa River). For best experience – join the afterparty in Crazy Horse Western Saloon on Kirkonkyläntie 12 in Helsinki.

Other holidays on this date: National Father-In-Law Day, International Friendship Day (USA), Feast of The Throne (Morocco)

31 July: Bardentreffen Festival (Germany)

This is a huge three-day annual open-air music festival in July, first started in 1976 as a singer-songwriter competition, marking the start of the Bavarian Summer Holidays. This is Germany's biggest free outdoor festival (there are no entry fees as the event is heavily sponsored by the municipality). Performing artist and bands who must mix their own vocals and instrumentals are covered for all expenses as well (cover bands are not allowed to take part). It is one of the biggest festivals in the city and covers the whole historical centre with nine stages nestled between medieval buildings and pavilions where more than 200 000 people gather to listen to the on-stage bands and street musicians. The set style is traditional folk, trendy and experimental.

Steaming hot pretzels, sauerkraut, sausages, ice cold beer and piercing rock sound embrace the city for three days.

Travel to: Germany (Nürnberg). Good option for accommodation is Saxx Hotel which overlooks the main stage.

Other holidays on this date: National Mutt Day (USA), Heiva (Tahiti)

... AUGUST

H**oliday**: The word Holiday derives from the Old English word hāligdæg – hāli meaning "holy" and dæg meaning "day". It was first mentioned around the year 950. In the past, Holiday referred only to religious observances when people were allowed not to work and to devote the day to prayers and worshipping. Centuries later, in the 1200-1500s, the word gained a new meaning – a day for feast and amusement (besides attending religious services). In Middle Ages England, folks celebrated the holidays preparing a flatfish called butte (known as holy butte) – this fish is nowadays known as "halibut".

01 August: World of Faeries (USA)

A magical fantasy-related festival. Held over two days in August since 2004, it keeps gaining popularity and participants. Just imagine - faerie dance lessons and tea parties in a Wildflower Garden, belly dancing, bubble shows and mystical merchants, harp music, mythical animals and elves, and much, much more.

The program also features on-stage bands, street artists, henna body art and falcons flying in the sky. Local merchants sell fairy wings, wizard robes, hope stones and tutu skirts.

Travel to: USA (Illinois – South Elgin). The venue is Vasa Park.

Other holidays on this date: Respect for Parents Day, National Girlfriends Day, National Mountain Climbing Day (USA)

02 August: Carnival and J'ouvert Party (Antigua)

For various reasons, some Caribbean islands hold carnivals during the summertime. The Antigua Carnival, held for 11 days in late July till the first Tuesday in August, celebrates the emancipation of slavery and the cultural heritage of the residents. Many locals are descendants of African slaves brought to the island to harvest sugar cane.

In 1957 Antigua celebrated its first official Carnival, although feasts had been organized ever since the abolishment of the slavery in 1834.

A highlight is the Calypso singing competitions – the music invented by slaves as a way to communicate in times when they were forbidden to speak to each other in the fields. It is a secret language – a mix of sounds taken from different cultures and weaved into a melody.

The program includes as well Calypso dancers, street musicians playing on steel drums, marching bands, onstage music bands, street parades with decorated floats, magicians, a Carnival Queen pageant, masquerade parties and parades, lots of tropical fruit and local cuisine representing the ancient culture and of the locals.

Often, they spray water over the crowd to cool people off.

The Carnival ends with a massive street party - J'ouvert (daybreak, morning), with Calypso bands and dancers, wearing colourful costumes.

There is a tradition in Trinidad and Tobago, brought by French plantation owners more than 200 years ago –participants in the J'ouvert part of the carnival should cover themselves head to toe in paint, chocolate, mud, white powder or anything else that will stick to the skin to hide their identity (known as Jib Jab). In the past, J'ouvert allowed disguised wealthy men to mix with the poor in anonymity. In line with the tradition, some of the locals paint themselves in colours head-to-toe.

Travel to: Antigua (St John). The Carnival takes place on the streets of St. John's, and in Carnival City at the Antigua Recreation Ground. There is as well, a purpose-built festival village for the duration of the Carnival.

Other holidays on this date: National Coloring Book Day (USA), Royal St John's Regatta (Canada)

03 August: Minguito Festival (Nicaragua)

Celebrated every year in the beginning of August until the 10th of the month, this religious festival honours the patron saint of the capital – Santo Domingo (the faithful refer to him as Minguito, a diminutive form of Domingo).

It was first held in 1885 when a 7cm statuette of Santo Domingo de Guzman (founder of the Dominican religious order) was discovered by a peasant who was cutting a tree.

The celebration starts with a parade with the miraculous statuette of Santo Domingo carried on a wooden float. The statuette, covered with garlands of flowers and feathers, is carried to the Santo Domingo Church downtown. The procession is known as "Descending the Saint". At the end of the festival another procession brings back the statuette to its original location in Las Sierritas Parish Church, known as "Ascending the Saint".

The festival features Philharmonic bands, equestrian parades, bullfights, fireworks and "promisers" – people who had asked the saint for a miracle promising to return to the festivities the following year. They wear colorful costumes, cover their body with grease and dust or add red color to look devilish, dance and share traditional drinks and snacks with the crowd. Given promises can be inherited from one generation to another. Some promisers "walk" the last 200 meters to the church blindfolded and, on their knees, (supported and guided by relatives or friends) to show respect and obedience to their faith.

An interesting fact is that the same family has been in charge of the floral decoration of the statuette for decades (it was their promise).

During the festival, lots of street merchants sell sombreros, ribbons with the phrases like "Viva Mingo", games of chance, religious items etc.

Travel to: Nicaragua (Managua). The miraculous statuette of Santo Domingo can be found year-round at Las Sierritas Parish Church in Managua.

Other holidays on this date: National Grab Some Nuts Day (USA), Harvest Festival (Taiwan – Thao tribe)

04 August: Verbier Festival (Switzerland)

An annual two-week international festival of classical music held in the beautiful setting of the Swiss Alps. It takes place from mid July to early August when the mountain peaks are covered with blooming flowers. The Verbier Festival has its own Academy that is in constant search for new talents to join any of its three orchestras. The festival offers to the audience breathtaking performances from renown choirs, orchestras, outdoor jazz concerts and intimate recitals. More than 100 free events are held in different venues – churches, cinema, chalet and the Salle des Combins which is the main concert hall. There are also outdoor yoga and meditation classes during the day held on meadows and terraces overlooking the majestic peaks. About 40 000 people visit the spectacular event nestled in the mountain. There is a shuttle service available from the festival site to the main train station in Martigny to facilitate transportation to and from. The festival was in fact created by a Swedish expat who's idea was to establish a musical workshop and forum for young musicians.

Bonus option is a trail up in the mountain, offering views of the majestic peaks Mont Blanc, Matterhorn and Les Diablerets.

Travel to: Switzerland (Verbier Mountain resort). Good option for accommodation is Hôtel Les Chamois as it is located in the heart of the resort.

Other holidays on this date: National Chocolate Chip Cookie Day, Kaw Nation Powwow (USA), Navajo Festival of Arts and Culture (USA)

05 August: Crocodile Festival (Papua New Guinea)

The annual three-day festival takes places over the first weekend in August along the bank of the Sepik River – one of the most culturally diverse areas in the country famous for its indigenous carvings and masks, colourful costumes and weird traditions. The festival, locally known as Pukpuk show, highlights the significance of the crocodile to the people of the River symbolizing strength, power and manhood. In the local folklore, the animal is a centrepiece in all myths and legends.

The locals are known for their skin-cutting rituals - men proudly wear the scars cut deep into their skin during the festival celebrations (skin-cutting takes place in sacred spirit huts). These scars resemble the back of a crocodile and run from shoulder to hip.

This ancient initiation is a rite of passage into manhood and honours the centurial bond between man and crocodile.

During the celebrations, locals dressed in tribal costumes adorned with clams, beads, feathers and animal bones, perform ritualistic dances with live crocodiles.

Another aspect of the Crocodile Festival is to preserve the biodiversity in the region.

Travel to: Papua New Guinea. The festival takes place in the village of Ambunti along the Sepik River - one of the largest rivers in the Asia-Pacific and home to some of the world's largest crocodile populations.

Other holidays on this date: Work Like a Dog Day, National Underwear Day, National Oyster Day (USA), Akita Kanto Festival (Japan), Chocolate Fest (Canada)

06 August: Chivalric Tournament (Croatia)

This is a 300-year old tradition held annually on the first Sunday in August. The event is called Sinjska Alka - equestrian competition promoting the spirit of chivalry. The tournament was established in the early XVIIIth century to commemorate a victory over the much more powerful Turkish army which besieged the town.

Participants dressed as medieval knights ride horses at full gallop and aim their lances at an iron ring hanging on a rope. Only locals can take part in the tournament and this is considered a great honour! The winner receives numerous awards and is celebrated as a Hero.

The rules promote ethics and fair play, and involve the whole community –locals help with the costumes and weapons months in advance.

Since 2010, the tournament is on UNESCO List of the Intangible Cultural Heritage of Humanity.

Travel to: Croatia (Sinj). The town of Sinj is known as The Land of Heroes.

Other holidays on this date: Sisters Day, Wiggle Your Toes Day (USA), World Hen Racing Championship (England)

07 August: Jalan Jaksa Street Festival (Indonesia)

Since 1990, the event is held annually for a day in July or August. The festival was created to promote local tourism and revive the dying culture of the Batawi people (native Jakartans). It takes place on Jalan Jaksa - a 400-metre long street known as a low-cost traveller's haven! Food stalls, cheap drinks, hostels, dubious tattoo shops and late-night bars. This is a feast of the culinary wild side of Jakarta. During the festival, the street is closed for traffic and full of street artists, local craft workshops and lots and lots of the local Batawi food. Strange food, that is – glow-in-the-dark desserts, swamp fish stew, steaming noodles with fiery spices or crocodile bread. Life-sized puppets, combining a cuddly fairy-tale character and a grotesque mythical giant roam the streets, while local bands take care of the festive spirit. Eye-pleasing are also the chaotic demonstrations of Palang Pintu –local martial art, performed by two fighters dressed in bright costumes, doing all sorts of acrobatic tricks.

Worth visiting to catch a glimpse of the local culture.

Travel to: Indonesia (Jakarta). The festival takes place on Jalan Jaksa Street (known hot-spot for expats). Good option for accommodation is Istana Ratu Hostel which is right in the center of the venue.

Other holidays on this date: International Forgiveness Day, Purple Heart Day (USA), Viking Festival (Spain)

08 August: Culturama Festival (Saint Kitts and Nevis)

This annual 5-to-7 day festival is held in the end of July and beginning of August. It was initiated in 1974. The purpose of the event is to preserve the local culture, to honour the customs and folk art of the indigenous people and celebrate the emancipation of slaves in the 1830s. It is one of the most anticipated celebrations on the small island of Nevis and features Calypso King contest, Miss Culture Queen, Miss Swimwear, Miss Caribbean Culture pageant, Night of the Arts, street jamming, boat races, house and street parties and lots of Calypso dances. There are also colourful street parades and fairs with local merchants selling handmade souvenirs, local food and drinks. Participants in the parades, who must be residents of St Kitts and Nevis, are dressed in bright costumes, covered with sparkling beads and feathers. This is a time when people from all walks of life – locals and visitors alike – get together and party day and night!

Travel to: Saint Kitts and Nevis. The event is held on Nevis Island, usually the best festivities being in Charlestown.

Other holidays on this date: National Dollar Day, Snuck Some Zucchini into Your Neighbor's Porch day (USA), Peace Festival (Germany, Bavaria).

09 August: Amis Tribe Harvest Ceremony (Taiwan)

The Amis are one of the 12 indigenous Taiwanese tribes officially recognized by the government. The Harvest Ceremony is the most important event for them and celebrates the end of the harvest season. The festival, lasting four days, is held on a night of a full moon in July, August or September – depending on the area it takes place. The dates are announced close to the celebrations by a young boy - a messenger, who is sent to the neighbouring villages to invite the tribal leaders to join the festivities of the celebrating tribe.

This is one of the most sacred ceremonies, in which the Amis people thank the gods for the rich harvest and pray for stock breeding and blessing of the new crops. They believe that every living thing on earth possesses a spirit, therefore people should treat everything with respect. Thousands of folks dressed in tribal attire gather holding hands to sing songs in their native language accompanied by monotonous drum beat. Part of the traditional costume is a beautiful hat decorated with rooster feathers – the number of feathers symbolizing one`s place in the tribal hierarchy.

The opening ceremony includes a dance that should be performed only by male participants and the closing ceremonial dance - only by females.

Locals dance holding hands and sing all the time – their songs blessing the fishermen, the pigs that will be sacrificed for the festive dinner, the ancestors, the rich millet harvest.

During the ceremony, priests and elders sit in the centre of the dance while youngsters dance around them and propose toasts. The village Chief along with the Elders organizes different activities and assigns tasks to the young ones that highlight the unity and the respect among the tribesmen. The boy who shows most respectful behaviour and has the most potential to be the next Chief is chosen this way.

The festival includes tug-of-war, arrow shooting competition and an Adult Ceremony – every boy needs to pass certain training and a test before becoming an adult.

The last night is St Valentine`s Night – young unmarried boys and girls dance all night long around a fire and sing songs. The boys carry a bag on their backs and the girls - a single vine leaf. If a girl finds a potential partner, she drops the vine leaf into his bag. If the boy likes her too – he gives her his bag and they become a couple.

Visitors are allowed to join in some of the festivities and it is appreciated if the invited bring presents to the tribe.

Travel to: Taiwan. The Amis populate the coastal area from Hualien to Taitung and each tribe sets the ceremony on a different date so they don't overlap.
Other holidays on this date: National Rice Pudding Day (USA)

10 August: Wichita Tribe Powwow (USA)

An annual two-day Wichita tribe Powwow held since 1976 (powwow - a social and dancing event), displaying breathtaking costumes, aiming to preserve the traditional tribal dances and distinct culture of the Wichita people. Although participants in the dances can be only members of the tribe or their descendants, the event is open to public and is quite spectacular, because it is one of the few traditions to the Native Americans that are still being celebrated. The celebrations include war dances, colour guard, a Gourd Dance – believed to originate from the Cheyenne and Arapajo tribes, this dance honours the warriors or the defeated enemy. The participants, dressed in full regalia including the adorned with feathers headpieces, dance and whirl under traditional drum beats. This is a festival of colours! Local merchants sell native food and tribal souvenirs.

Travel to: USA (Oklahoma). The dance takes place in the Wichita Tribal Park in Anadarko.
Other holidays on this date: National S'mores Day (USA)

11 August: Black Pudding Throwing Championship (England)

An annual event created in the 1980s, although the tradition is said to date back to 1455 and the War of the Roses, when factions of the House of Lancaster and the House of York met for battle in Stubbins, Lancashire. Local legend has it that the troops ran out of ammunition and started throwing food at each other- black puddings from Lancashire (a northern speciality of pig's blood, onions and oats) and Yorkshire puddings from Yorkshire (made of flour, eggs and milk).

Today, the only ammunition used are bespoke black puddings about the size of a fist, tied in women's tights (transported via steam train to the venue). And the target is... a pile of Yorkshire puddings. All throws must be underarm. Each contestant is allowed 3 throws. Whoever knocks down more Yorkshire puddings is declared the winner.

The festival features a farmer's market, food stalls and music festival.

Travel to: England (Lancashire). The event is held in the town of Ramsbottom, in front of the Royal Oak pub.

Other holidays on this date: National Son's And Daughter's Day (USA), Neretva Boat Marathon (Croatia)

12 August: Baliem Valley Tribe Festival (Indonesia)

The annual indigenous festival brings together for two days in August all local tribes for a mock war and a colourful party. The people show their ancient way of life which is synchronized to perfection with the surrounding environment.

A highlight of the festival is the mock war between the different tribes (this way each tribe maintains the preparedness to defend itself and its village). About 25 groups participate – each consisting of 30 to 50 warriors. The "war dance" is accompanied by Pikon players – Pikon is a traditional musical instrument made of wood skin (very much resembles a flute).

The festival aims to preserve the centurial traditions of the Papuan indigenous people and features also pig races, rattan spear throwing competition, traditional dances, art and cultural performances.

The tribesmen wear traditional costumes – the women - Rumbai alang-alang (a skirt-like clothing made of dried palm leaves or coconut fibre), the men - Koteka - a clothing to cover the genitals (resembling a hollow bamboo stick, or a horn). Colourful feathers from Paradise Bird adorn the clothing – usually worn as accessories like necklaces, anklets and bracelets.

Local delicacies during the festival are sweet potatoes, bananas and pig cooked in an earth oven (one of the most ancient cooking techniques using a pit in the ground).

For a truly authentic experience, visitors can put on real Koteka costumes and have their skin blackened.

Travel to: Indonesia (Papua New Guinea). The festival takes place in Baliem Valley, in the town of Wamena. Baliem Valley and its indigenous population were discovered only in 1938.

Other holidays on this date: National Vynil Record Day, National Garage Sale Day, National Bowling Day, Melon Day (Turkmenistan)

13 August: The Pig Festival (France)

A festival to honour one of the most eaten animals on the planet takes place every year for a day in August. It has been celebrated since 1975 and takes place on the second Sunday of the month in a place known as one of the busiest pig-rearing areas in the country.

It is a day full of pig-related events: a piglet race, best-dressed pig, quickest sausage eater, best pork sausage, best pork recipe and many more. A highlight of the event is the Pig Imitation competition (where one should not only squeal like a pig but move and eat as one too) –contestants put on swine ears and snout, and imitate sounds made by the pig during various stages in its life – from birth to being slaughtered.

There is also a black pudding eating competition.

Of course, there is plenty of piping-hot food (all pork) – casseroles, bacon, ham, sausages, chops, salami, crackling...

Live music bands and open bars take care of the festival spirit.

Travel to: France (Trie-Sur-Baise). The event is organized by the Brotherhood of the Pig.

Other holidays on this date: National Prosecco Day (USA), Awa Odori Dance Festival (Japan), World Tango Festival (Argentina)

14 August: Scarecrow Festival (England)

Hundreds and hundreds of handmade scarecrows flood the streets of a town for a week in August. The annual festival has been around since 1994. The event was initially created as a fundraiser for a local school.

A popular game is to find hidden letter to help solve a riddle. The letters make a mystery word, however, all of them are scattered in the clothes of hidden scarecrows (the organizers sell treasure hunt maps with clues for £1).

The entire village takes part in the festival – some locals help to build and decorate the scarecrows along the streets, others offer freshly baked food and drinks to the visitors.

It reminds a lot of a Halloween celebration, but with stuffed scary and cute monsters. People get very creative on this one – some contesting scarecrows resemble the singers from ABBA, Peter Pan, Alexander Bell, George of the Jungle, Nemo, Cleopatra or even the Royal family. They all appear very interactive – as if they are about to talk, or laugh, or eat an apple, or handshake with the passers-by. The décor is also thought of – for instance a scarecrow-pilot can be seen resting on the wing of a real Spitfire airplane.

Travel to: England (North Yorkshire). The event is held in the town of Kettlewell.

Other holidays on this date: National Creamsicle Day, Carnival (Grenada), Mantoro Lantern Festival (Japan)

15 August: Festa Major de Gràcia (Spain)

The concept of the so-called best block party in the world? The streets in this neighbourhood compete to win the prize of being the best-decorated street and there are absolutely no limits to the imagination of its residents. In 2017, the festival celebrated its 200th anniversary!

Each street chooses a theme – this could be a fairy-tale, space battle, nature scene, art & lights installation or any other interactive masterpiece. Residents work all year to create the best decoration and are rewarded with tons of awe-ing people during the week-long festival which takes place every year from August 15th to August 21st.

So, envision yourself walking through narrow cobbled streets where giant playing cards fall from the sky, rabbits in hats and towering blue caterpillars loom overhead. Giant papier-mache sculptures are stretched between buildings turning the streets into cave-like passages. One might want to pinch himself and say "Toto, we're not in Kansas anymore" as this is a real Wonderland. A celebration of local creativity fitting to perfection with the famous Gaudi architecture. Different music is played in line with the decorations on every street – from rave to opera. Some locals can be seen serving Mojitos from their front windows, while others might just decide to read poetry to visitors sitting quietly on a table and enjoying a bowl of crema Catalana.

The festival starts with a massive street parade including Giants, Big Heads and Dragons and continues with a "fire run" - groups of disguised devils chase people around.

No need to mention that the party is non-stop – so think sangria and think lots of it.

Travel to: Spain (Barcelona). The fest takes place in the boho area of Gràcia Barrio and covers 20 streets. More than 1.5mln people visit the event every year.

Other holidays on this date: Bathtub Regatta (Belgium), National Relaxation Day (USA), Flooding of the Nile (Egypt)

16 August: Kadayawan Festival (Philippines)

The annual festival is held every third week of August since its initiation in 1988. Originally started as a thanksgiving ritual to the Supreme Being and the Moon Deity, now the event spreads to a Thanksgiving celebration of life, the cultural and historical heritage of the natives, the productivity of nature and most of all - the bountiful harvest season of fruits and orchids.

It is a huge street party with tons of fresh exotic fruits and beautiful local flowers.

The opening ceremony showcases the 10 indigenous tribes ("Lumads"), dressed in full regalia, performing tribal dances. The folks paint their faces in bright colours and wear headpieces adorned with grapes, bananas, mangos and other fruits. The streets are also decorated with various fruits and vegetables.

The festival features lots of dancing under the scorching sun, a Floral Float Parade, a beauty pageant, open-air concerts, horse fighting, boat races, Queen of the

Orchids competition, local street bands performing on the streets and the people of Mindanao performing their traditional dances.

In the Philippines, the event is known as "The King of Festivals".

Travel to: Philippines (Mindanao Island). The event is held in Davao City. It's best to look for accommodation near San Pedro Street, Peoples Park or Roxas Avenue as they're all within walking distance to the parade route.

Other holidays on this date: National Roller Coaster Day, National Rum Day (USA), Yamaga Toro Festival (Japan)

17 August: The Crow Fare Powwow (USA – Native American)

The Crow Fair was created in 1904 by an Indian government agent to bring the Crow Tribe of Native Americans (the Apsáalooke) into modern society. Held annually in the third week of August, this is the largest gathering of Native Americans in the state and one of the largest in the country. It has more than 1 500 teepees set for the participants and attracts over 50 000 visitors from around the world. The purpose is not only a giant family reunion, but also to show the rituals and art, and the rich cultural heritage of the Crow people.

The festivities begin each morning at 10:00h with a breathtaking parade around the campsite. A Colour Guard leading the procession is followed by Elders and then by people from the Crow tribe and their descendants – most of them on horseback using old-time saddles made of bone and leather. All are dressed in traditional clothes, adorned with colourful eagle feathers and beadwork which is one of the most proficient in the world.

The late afternoon and the evening are time for party – the Crow people host a huge powwow (dance and social gathering) – they perform traditional dances and often throw dance contests.

There are also contests for best traditional dress, homemade jam, butter, household goods and activities such as drum group contest, woodcutting and different games with prizes.

A highlight of the event is the Crow Tribe Rodeo and horse race, with professional Indian cowboys and cowgirls.

Travel to: USA (Montana). The venue is on the land surrounding the Little Big Horn River near Billings, known as the Tipi Capital of the World. The Rodeo is held Edison Real Bird Memorial Complex in Crow Agency, Montana (the headquarters of the Crow Tribe).

Other holidays on this date: National I Love My Feet Day, National Thriftshop Day (USA), The Long Way to the Cemetery (Romania)

Dessi Nikoltchev:

18 August: Paneurhythmy – The Sacred Dance of Life (Bulgaria)

A religious-philosophical doctrine, the Paneurhythmy is the art of praising Nature and becoming one with the Universe. Invented in 1932 by the spiritual leader Peter Duenov known as Master Beinsa Douno, the White Brotherhood performs the Sacred Dance of Life (paneurhythmy) every year on August 18th to celebrate the Solar New Year. The ritual is performed out in nature and starts before dawn welcoming the first rays of the morning sun and the wisdom it brings. The White Brotherhood (counting thousands of people) sets camp the day before – they welcome all tourists and visitors of this sacred ritual in their tents, offering tranquil atmosphere, amicable conversations and organic food. Then, on the next morning, the White Brotherhood gathers on the nearby hill – all dressed in crisp white clothes, they wait for the rising sun to sing, perform energizing exercises and a ritualistic sun dance accompanied by the relaxing sounds of violins and acoustic guitars. The dance itself consists of very precise counterclockwise consequence of 28 steps (mechanical, organic and mental) danced in concentric circles – it is a meditation in motion, which connects the participants with nature, the universe and each other through living geometry – aligning meridians and chakras and bringing to the dancers awareness of what is around. It is based on the frequency and correlation of tone, movement, form and colour and how each corresponds to the others. Not only a dance, but a cluster of good vibes, harmony, relaxing music and movements balancing body, mind and soul. It is believed that the Dance Of Life improves mobility and blood pressure and in general is good for the health, as well as it has positive mental results. Paneurhythmy takes 45 minutes and is suitable for all ages. It can be followed by two more dances – Sun Beams (exchange of Sun energy) and Pentagrams (exchange of power with the Universe). The afternoon is spent hiking, sitting in silence or picnicking in the beautiful surroundings.

Today, the beautiful dance of Love, Wisdom and Truth - Paneurhythmy is practised all over the world. The White Brotherhood is a recognized global religious movement characterized by practising yoga, meditation in motion, breathing exercises and prayer. It is active in Argentina, Mexico, USA, Australia, Canada, Great Britain, Costa Rica, Ireland, France and others but its home are the Seven Lakes in the majestic Rila Mountain in Bulgaria.

Travel to: Bulgaria (the town of Sapareva Banya). The event takes place near the kidney-shaped Babreka Lake in Rila Mountain where the White Brotherhood sets camp.

Other holidays on this date: Bad Poetry Day, National Lentil Festival (USA)

19 August: Big Resting Place Celebration (Ghana – Ashanti Tribe)

The festival dates to the 1690s and coincides with the yam harvest season. Europeans know it as the Yam Custom, but locals call it Adae Kese and for them – it is so much more than an end of harvest season.

It is a celebration of the indigenous Ashanti tribe to glorify their kingdom and its prosperity through the years. After many wars, in 1935, the British granted Ashanti self-rule sovereignty and the title Asantehene (Ashanti King) was revived. The tribe now inhabits Southern Ghana and parts of Côte d'Ivoire.

The date of the celebration is not set – it varies from July to October every year in accordance with the Akan calendar. Within a six-week cycle, Adae is celebrated twice – on a Saturday and on a Wednesday. This cycle is repeated 9 times in the year – the 9th time is known as the Adae Kese Festival.

The purpose of the celebration is to connect the living with the spirits of their ancestors.

In the past, the festival was a time to consecrate the dead kings whose bodies were kept in a mausoleum. Back in the days, human and animal sacrifices of huge proportions were made to the gods - to chase away evil spirits, to please the souls of the ancestors and most importantly to link the living and the dead. When the festival was announced by a monotonous drum beat, people would run and hide, fearing they may be selected for a sacrifice.

The celebration includes Odwira (purification) ceremony performed on the burial shrines of the ancestral spirits - sacrifice of a sheep and sprinkling with its blood the Golden Stool (a symbol of power to the Ashanti - it is supposed to contain the soul of the nation), which is Ashanti's royal and divine throne. The Ashanti believe that the spirits of the deceased kings are intertwined with the throne. The ceremony is accompanied by fontomfrom drums (traditional Ashanti drum) and ivory trumpets made of the elephant tusks. A royal messenger collects holy water from various parts of the kingdom prior to the beginning of the ceremony (it is used to purify the Golden Stool).

The festival is also an occasion to pledge confidence in the present king. This is a very highly regarded festival by the Ashanti's because it showcases their heritage. Folks parade in their traditional attire and sandals, the Ashanti King is carried on a gold-decorated float, amidst drumming and dancing. The main purpose of the celebration is to make the Ashanti people stronger and more prosperous while showcasing their rich cultural history for the rest of the world to come and see.

Travel to: Ghana (Kumasi). Huge celebrations are held on the main square and in the Manhyia Palace - used by the Ashanti Kings until 1974; the current King now lives close to the museum.

Other holidays on this date: National Soft Ice Cream Day (USA)

20 August: Silent Dance Festival (Japan)

The annual event created in 2009 takes place in mid-August. It was created after elderly neighbours filed complaints because of a loud party.

The festival is a silent disco - everybody dances to music wearing headphones. The music is broadcasted via a transmitter with the signal being picked up by the wireless headphone receivers. This way people without them can amuse themselves simply by observing a room full of people dancing to nothing.

There are open bars with sake, light installations, projection mapping and stalls selling merchandise.

Travel to: Japan (Aichi Prefecture). The event takes place in the town of Otomachi. Another option is to follow up for alternative dates and locations with the event planning company Ozone – the producers of the Silent Fes as they call it.

Other holidays on this date: National Radio Day, National Chocolate Pecan Pie Day (USA)

21 August: Giants of Ath (Belgium)

For five days in late August (the culmination being on the fourth Saturday), a city becomes the land of giants. The festival held annually attracts thousands of people from around the world.

People come to witness the heroic battle between David and Goliath, others - Samson walking down the street among other gigantic allegoric figures, biblical characters and heroes from the local history. During the festival, the city is called "City of Giants" - there are just so many of them and they are everywhere. All Giants perform in historical short plays and dance to cheer the public.

The festival originated in the Middle Ages (XVth C). People taking part in it, start preparing months in advance – building giant effigies, perfecting their moves for the street parade and decorating floats which will carry the giants through the town.

A highlight is the epic battle between David and Goliath which takes place after Goliath's wedding (the whole wedding is being re-enacted including the ring of the church bell and the happy couple being accompanied by the French army).

There is a legend that if David manages to puncture Goliath's effigy with his stone – then it will be a good year for the small medieval city.

After the fight is over –locals and visitors are treated to a piece of a traditional to the city cake made with almonds.

The festival is on the UNESCO List of the Masterpieces of the Oral and Intangible Heritage of Humanity.

Travel to: Belgium (Ath). The event takes place everywhere – on the streets, in the city park and inside some of the Medieval buildings.

Other holidays on this date: National Brazilian Blow Out Day (USA)

22 August: Cleaning of the Corpses Ceremony (Indonesia)
A rather gruesome ceremony...

The ritual dates back hundreds of years and is performed every three years. It was started by an animal hunter who found an abandoned, decaying body in the mountains. He dressed it and performed a proper burial. The hunter believed that the gods blessed him in return for the noble deed. This ritual was adopted by the indigenous people of the Toraja tribe who believe they will be rewarded for taking care of the dead.

The sacred ceremony called Ma`nene involves exhuming dead family members to clean and re-dress them. In the meantime, relatives repair the coffins and clean their tombs. The ceremony shows honour to the ancestors and prepares the living for the afterlife. As death is an integral part of life for the Toraja people, they spent much time thinking and talking about it. They prepare and perform every burial with great care and respect. When a member of the Toraja tribe dies, the relatives wrap him in a cloth and wait until they collect enough means for a proper burial (some people save their whole lives for a burial). They refer to the deceased one as he is sleeping. They don`t believe someone is dead until he/she is buried. When the funeral, usually lasting for a week, finally takes place, hundreds gather to honour the life of the person. The ceremony starts with slaughtering of buffaloes and pigs, so the deceased will have a peaceful afterlife. After the sacrifice, animal horns are placed outside the family home – the more horns, the higher the status of the deceased. Then he is buried in a stone cave, or put in a wooden coffin up on a mountain cliff. The Toraja people have the so-called "open tombs" in the mountains surrounding their village. They believe that the dead soul should return regularly to its village of origin, its body cleaned, dressed and walked around the village (they even take family photographs with the deceased!).

If a child dies before it has started teething, it is buried in the hollow trunk of a tree (the burial ground is known as "The Baby Trees") – the Toraja people believe the child`s soul will become part of the tree as it grows.

The ritual is a bond of life and death.

Travel to: Indonesia (Sulawesi Island). The ceremony takes place in the village of Baruppu – the home of the Toraja people.

Other holidays on this date: National Tooth Fairy Day (USA)

23 August: Orange Race (England)
The story began when in the 1580s Sir Francis Drake (known for navigating the Globe) bumped into the overloaded cart of an orange seller, sending the oranges

rolling down the hill. At that time oranges were ridiculously expensive, so many folks started running down the steep street after the spilt goods. Around the 1970s the myth was somehow revived, and the Orange Race was officially held for the first time.

The event takes place annually on the third Tuesday or Thursday in August to commemorate Sir Francis and the orange-incident-turned-to-odd-tradition.

People gather at the top of the highest street in town, each holding an orange in hand. When the town crier announces the start of the race with a giant bell – they all throw the oranges and chase them downhill. The contestants should keep their orange rolling by kicking it all the way down the street. The first person to cross the finish line with an orange that is still mostly intact wins the race.

The prize is an orange trophy!

Travel to: England (Devon). The race takes place at High Street and Fore Street in the town of Totnes.

Other holidays on this date: Ride the Wind Day, National Sponge Cake Day (USA)

24 August: Totonicapan Mayan Dances (Guatemala)

Created in 1993, this annual event is celebrated over two days in late August and commemorates ancient Mayan traditions.

The indigenous people celebrate their cultural heritage through series of rituals and dances.

Participants start preparing months in advance to practice their moves and tailor their colourful traditional Mayan costumes. More than that – a lot of time is dedicated to purification ceremonies of the dancers, blessing the masks and costumes etc.

Various folklore groups from different regions of the country perform ritualistic dances some of them are:

- The Dance of the Deer – re-enacting an ancient Mayan hunting ritual which includes 26 dancers acting as humans, tigers, lions (the hunters), deer (the pray) and monkeys. The scene represents a fight between wild animals and hunters for a piece of fresh meat. An interesting fact is that the dancers playing the role of hunters are isolated for a month to purify themselves.

- The Dance of the Monkeys – it depicts the fate of twin brothers converted into monkeys by their elder brothers because they possessed special powers. The dance includes 23 dancers, a 30-meter high wooden pole, marimba music and a traditional Ah Xul flute.

- Dance of the Conquest – a battle dance including Mayan and Spanish soldiers, a sorcerer (Mayan advisor) dressed in red and holding a red doll, and many

children. The performance re-enacts a historic battle which ended with the Christianization of the Mayan people.
- Dance of the Pascarines – the dance depicts a fight over adultery between two families. The adulterer is beaten by long whips (for real!), so he usually spends the next few months recovering...
- Dance of the Cowboy – 32 people take part in this dance which is about cattle breeding. The performance satirizes the bullfights - a privilege to the Spaniards in the past.
- Dance of the Mexicans – the dance satirizes life on the plantations and includes mariachi, pistols and bullfights.
- Dance of the Xacalcojes – one of the most popular dances, it depicts the resurrection of Jesus.

The festival town is flooded with kiosks and stalls offering Mayan textiles and ceramics, handmade masks and costumes used in the dances, mouth-watering local food and drinks.

This rare festival is a hidden gem and a breath-taking display of the ancient Mayan dances, sounds and taste.

Travel to: Guatemala (Totonicapan). The small town hosting this plethora of colors and vibes is referred by the locals just as "Toto".
Other holidays on this date: National Peach Pie Day (USA)

25 August: Janmashtami (Bangladesh)
The annual Hindu festival is celebrated according to the lunar calendar and falls on a day in August or September. This is the birthday celebration of Krishna, the eighth avatar of Vishnu, and is observed with great anticipation and enthusiasm.

The celebrations aim to show the innocent and naughty side of the little Krishna and include huge processions starting from the Krishna and Vishnu temples, dance-drama enactments of the life of Krishna, devotional singing at midnight (when Krishna is believed to have been born) and a festival. It is a colourful celebration – the locals wear bright festive costumes, elephants are adorned with shiny coins, various kinds of vehicles are decorated for the occasion and the streets are full of happiness as if the folks are celebrating their own birthday. Many people colour themselves head-to-toe in blue to represent the dark complexion of Krishna while the children, dressed as the little Krishna parade the streets on carnival floats.

At midnight, small statues of baby Krishna are washed, clothed and placed in a cradle - this ritual representing the birth of the god. After the ritual, locals break the fast and share food, sweets and exchange small presents. Women draw tiny footsteps in front of their houses (as if little Krishna had visited their home).

Travel to: Bangladesh (Dhaka). The President of Bangladesh hosts a festive reception at Bangabhaban - his official residence and principal workplace. Celebrations are held in the Dhakeshwari National Temple (the temple of the Goddess of Dhaka) and everywhere in the Old City of Dhaka. The holiday is also observed in India, Nepal, Pakistan, Fiji, USA and the Caribbean.

Other holidays on this date: National Whisky Sour Day, National Secondhand Wardrobe Day (USA)

26 August: Ganesh Chaturthi (Bangladesh)

This is an annual festival (since 1892), celebrating the birthday of the Hindu God Ganesha - god of good beginnings, prosperity and obstacle remover, he is also a patron of the arts, intellect and wisdom. Ganesha is one of the most worshipped gods in Hinduism and his elephant head makes him easy to be identified.

In preparation for the festival which falls in August or September, artisans create clay models of Ganesha which locals put in their homes, folks decorate the homemade shrine with garlands of flowers, scented sticks and candles. The idols are worshipped every morning and evening by the whole family for the duration of the festivities which is 10 days. On the tenth day, the day of the birth, a huge street procession takes place –people, dressed in bright celebratory costumes, cheer and chant mantras to honour Ganesha. On this day, a huge Ganesha clay idol is carried by devotees to the nearest lake, sea or ocean and bathed in the water. When the idol dissolves, he returns to his home on Mount Kailash to join the other deities. Some people immerse their own small idols – hoping Ganesha will remove any obstacles from their lives and bring a new beginning and good fortune.

On the streets, Ganesha idols are installed in temporary shelters, known as mandaps or pandals. The celebration features different worshipping activities, singing and theatre performances.

The festival is also a time for charity –locals donate food and clothes to the poor. They also do free medical check-ups and donate blood.

Typical dishes during the festival are modak - a steamed or fried dumpling made from rice or wheat flour, stuffed with grated coconut, jiggery and dried fruits (Ganesha's favourite according to a legend), and karanji - similar to modak but in a semicircular shape.

Travel to: Bangladesh (Dhaka). The festival is also celebrated in India, Nepal, Trinidad, Suriname, Fiji, Mauritius.

Other holidays on this date: National Web Mistress Day, National Dog Day (USA)

27 August: Notting Hill Carnival (England)

The English capital city turns Caribbean! About 50 years old, this vibrant annual carnival held over two days in August (including Bank Holiday Monday) attracts more than 1 000 000 people every year! The event was created in 1966 when the first ever Notting Hill Carnival combined two other festivals – the "Caribbean Carnival" - with main purpose to respond to racist attacks at that time, and the "Hippie Festival" held in Notting Hill, with its main purpose to promote cultural unity and peace. This way, the "new" Notting Hill Carnival managed to build a bridge between the two cultures and create a unique venue for people from all walks of life to express their diversity.

The festivity is one of the biggest street gatherings in the world and is voted to be an English Icon. The event highlights the rich historical heritage of African-Caribbeans and the great mix of different cultures co-existing in harmony.

Processions with decorated floats and colourfully dressed performers adorned with beads and feathers, street bands, Calypso music, samba, reggae jam sessions and dances praise the Caribbean culture and turn the celebration into one of Europe's largest street parades with more than 50 000 performers.

An important feature of the Carnival is the pop-up sound system installed in the small streets surrounding the main parading route – blasting out salsa, reggae, soca, house and other music beats.

Delicious food and drinks are available from the many food stalls in the area – all Caribbean style, so expect lots of BBQ, jerk chicken and rice as well as goat curry and salted fish.

However, there are incidents reported every year, hence the massive presence of police during the carnival days.

Travel to: England (London). The carnival takes place in Notting Hill at the Royal Borough of Kennsington and Chelsea. The hot-spot is Portobello Road – home to the world's largest antiques market.

Other holidays on this date: Just Because Day (USA), Global Forgiveness Day

28 August: QiXi Festival (China)

One of the oldest festivals in the world with earliest-known reference dating back to more than 2000 years ago. Known also as the "Double Seventh", the annual Qixi Festival falls on the 7th day of the 7th month in the Chinese calendar (in August). Celebrating the annual meeting of a weaver girl and an oxherd in the Chinese mythology, the romantic holiday is celebrated in the country as Valentine's Day.

The legend has it that the girl who was the seventh daughter of a Goddess and the oxherd fell in love and got married in secret. When she found out that her daughter had married a mortal, the Goddess got angry and summoned the girl to

Heaven, separating her forever from the oxherd by a river of stars (the Milky Way). However, a flock of magpies would take pity on the two lovers, fly to Heaven and form a bridge for them to meet once a year – on the 7th day of the 7th month.

Young girls visit temples to pray for wisdom and to find a loving husband. They make rice paper figurines which are burnt as offerings to the celestial couple.

In the past (some rural areas still honour the custom) the festival featured different dexterity games to show strength and skills, such as: to speedily thread a needle under moonlight, or to carve exotic flowers, animals, and unusual birds on a melon skin. In the evenings, young girls gathered to sing songs about finding a suitable husband and living a happy life, children hung wildflowers on the horns of the oxen.

Because this is the Chinese Valentine`s Day, celebrations involve giving gifts and flowers to romantic partners. It is important never to give an umbrella as a gift – the Chinese word for umbrella sounds the same as the word for "break up".

In the evening, locals gaze up to the sky in search for two stars (the weaving girl and the oxherd) and a third star that appears between them – symbolizing the bridge of magpies. The people believe that if it rains on the day – it is the tears of the separated couple.

Qixi Festival is an essential part of the Chinese spiritual culture but unfortunately is less and less known by the new generation who prefer to celebrate the day just as Valentine`s Day.

Travel to: China (Shanghai, Beijing, Hong Kong, Guangzhou). One of the top romantic sites to celebrate the festival is the West Lake in the marvelous city of Hangzhou. Another option is Xitang Water Town – one of the six ancient cities south of Yangtze River.

Other holidays on this date: Race Your Mouse Day (USA)

29 August: Raksha Bandhan (Bangladesh)

This Hindu festival dating back thousands of years honours the relationship between a brother and a sister – the name Raksha Bandhan literally means "bond of protection" in Hindu.

It is observed annually on a day of full moon in the Hindu month of Shravana, which falls on a different date in August.

Girls and women who have brothers buy traditional rakhi (a ceremonial thread made of cotton or silk and tied as a bracelet) and perform aarti - ritual of worship in which light from wicks soaked in purified oils is offered to the Gods (Aarti in Sanskrit means something that removes darkness). The brothers too, buy gifts for their sisters – usually small tokens of appreciation.

In the morning, the whole family gathers in the house to light candles and oil lamps in honour of the God of Fire. The siblings face each other, and the sister ties a rakhi onto her brother's wrist while saying a prayer for long and happy life. After she puts a tika (red mark) on his forehead, he makes a promise to take care of her no matter what. The ritual ends with the sister feeding her brother with sweets.

It is not unusual for random people to tie rakhi around the wrists of soldiers, police officers or border troops – as a token of appreciation for their service.

Relatives abroad often choose to send by post the ceremonial threads to remind that they have not forgotten their loved ones.

This is a day of spreading love and joy and enjoying delicious traditional dishes.

Travel to: Bangladesh (Dhaka). The holiday is celebrated in India and Nepal as well.

Other holidays on this date: National Chop Suey Day (USA)

30 August: La Tomatina (Spain)

One of the messiest festivals ever! Since its creation in 1945, this has been the biggest food fight in the world. The event is celebrated annually on the last Wednesday in August.

The legend behind the odd event has it that a group of young boys had a quarrel during a town parade featuring enormous figures with big heads. The quarrel turned into a vegetable fight because a nearby market stall fell a victim of the furious crowd and a man wearing one of the big carnival heads. The local police intervened, but the boys had made history already without even knowing it. The next year, another group brough along tomatoes and picked a random fight during the same festivity. The police intervened again but the tomato fight was already turning into a local tradition. In the 1950s La Tomatina was banned by the local authorities, however this didn't stop the people from gathering at the same place and throwing tomatoes at each other. They didn't mind being arrested too. Seven years later, in 1957, townfolks held a formal tomato burial – they carried a coffin with a huge tomato inside, accompanied by the tunes of funeral marches. They wanted to show that they want their festival back. So, the municipality just decided to go with the flow and officially recognized La Tomatina as a local festival. More than that – now, La Tomatina is an official trademark and a true icon for the region, generating great income.

La Tomatina attracts more than 50 000 people who are more than happy to take part in a 90-minutes free-for-all tomato-throwing frenzy.

The ammunition? More than a hundred metric tons (about 150 000kg) of squishy over-ripe tomatoes are dumped on the city streets by loads.

The purpose? Just for fun!

In preparation for the massive battle, local shop owners use huge plastic covers on their storefronts to protect them. Residents cover their windows – especially the ones residing on a lower floor.

The actual event begins after a lucky winner grabs a piece of ham tied up on a greased pole while being hosed with water. This marks the start of the tomato fight and the chaos begins.

After an hour and a half, a gun is fired to signal the end. The people, the streets, the houses are all covered in squashed tomatoes and tomato peel.

It is then when the fire brigade comes to help – the firemen hose down the tomatoes which makes the streets sparkling clean due to the acidity they contain.

Some thoughtful locals bring hoses out on the streets for the people to clean themselves.

There is, however, a very important rule to be followed: tomatoes should be squashed before being thrown to avoid hurting others.

The weeklong festival features also a paella making contest, street parades, lots of concerts, dancing and fireworks.

Interesting fact: the tomatoes cost about 36 000 Euro to the local authorities.

Travel to: Spain (Buñol). The event takes place in the center of the small town – Plaza del Pueblo. The tomato fight starts at 11am.

Many visitors prefer to set base in the nearby city of Valencia (38km) as the small city of Buñol with population of just 9 000 people has limited options for accommodation.

Other holidays on this date: National Toasted Marshmallow Day (USA), Santa Rosa de Lima (Peru)

31 August: Balls of Fire (El Salvador)

The tradition of celebrating this rather odd custom dates to more than 100 years ago. Las Bolas de Fuego (Balls of Fire) is celebrated annually on August 31st due to two main reasons – a historical one and a religious one:

A volcano eruption (El Playon volcano) destroyed the small town in El Salvador in 1658. The locals describe that during the eruption, balls of fire were thrown into the air. The people were forced to evacuate, leaving their houses and belongings behind. They built a new church and named it after their patron saint – San Jeronimo. However, the holy image of the saint faces the wall because he failed to protect their city. This is the historical background.

On the other hand, the religious background of the festival is based on that same volcano eruption. The local churches have embraced an urban legend that the hot lava that flowed from the volcano, was, in fact, the patron saint - San Jeronimo fighting the Devil with balls of fire. By celebrating the day, townfolks re-enact the apocalyptic battle between the Saint and the Devil and thank the saint that nobody was hurt during the eruption.

The bizarre celebration looks more like a war scene from a movie.

The participants (divided into two groups) paint their faces in war colours, dress in black Halloween-ish scary costumes and throw fuel-soaked flaming rags at each other, which is ... a little on the strange side. The "warriors" positioned on the two ends of the street, wear gloves and water-soaked clothes to protect them from getting seriously burnt. Just the sound of that would delight any pyromaniac. Of course, there have been occasions when participants caught fire, but they are rather rare.

The festival starts with a music festival and lots of street merchants selling coffee, tamales and pupusas (fried dough stuffed with cheese). Visitors should also try the local delicacy during the festival – Crazy Hot Milky Shot – a mix of milk and alcohol.

Some people comment that with all the violence and gangs in El Salvador – being hit in the face with a fireball is the least dangerous thing that can happen.

Anywhere else in the world, one would get locked up for doing that, but since this is an age-old tradition, the local authorities turn a blind eye (allegedly).

Travel to: El Salvador (San Salvador). The fiery battle takes place on the streets in the small town of Nejapa.

Other holidays on this date: Language Day (Moldova)

Dessi Nikoltchev:

... SEPTEMBER

C**ult:** allegedly first mentioned in the late 1600s, the word derives from the Latin "cultus" which means to cultivate and worship. Cult is usually associated with ancient rituals and practices, and black magic. Some existing cults aim to take 144 000 chosen people away in flying saucers or to restrict from dancing and laughing. Others believe that they are descended from Atlantis.

01 September: Day of the Geese (Spain)

The 350-year old tradition is locally known as Antzar Eguna and is celebrated in a small fishing town in the Basque region of the country. It is one of the most important days in the week-long celebrations honouring the city patron saint - San Antolin. The annual festival takes place in the first week of September.

The event is quite an odd one, as it involves a group of men trying to decapitate a dead goose hanging from a rope, hung over a harbour from one dock to the other, pulled tug-of-war style by two groups of men. The goose-grabbers approach the hanging dead goose by a boat and are then lifted into the air and plunged into the water repeatedly until they pull the head off the poor animal or fall into the water. Oh, there is a catch too – to make it even more challenging, the organizers cover the goose in grease. The big prize – the winner gets to keep the headless goose!

For the whole duration of the festival, the town turns blue - all residents and visitors dress up in blue cotton shirts and wear gingham style neckerchiefs. The ones to stand out are the dressed in white wool pullovers (to prevent from sliding) goose-grabbers.

Other attractive features of the festival are a water gun fight which takes place all over the town, greasy pole games, carnival rides, lots of local food stalls with sandwiches and tortillas, BBQ`s with sizzling chorizo sausages, merchants selling wine, beer and the specialty – kalimotxo (equal parts red wine and cola drink). Lots of street musicians with portable speakers take care of the festive atmosphere.

In the past, this event took place in the town square with horses instead of boats and a perfectly alive goose!

The celebration can be traced back to its Pagan roots –the Basques were very much agriculture orientated, many of their gods (it was believed) could take the form of different animals. The actual trace of why the odd tradition was initiated fades with the Christianization of the Basque people.

Travel to: Spain (Lekeitio). The small Basque fishing town is the only place to keep the Dead Goose tradition. It used to be celebrated throughout the country before it was banned.

Other holidays on this date: National No Rhyme Day (USA), Tabaski (Benin)

02 September: International Highline Meeting Festival (Italy)
The annual festival dedicated to highlining thrill seekers was created in 2012.

The participants in this cool and at the same time terrifying event sleep in hammocks strung up on tightropes, hundreds of meters above the Italian Alps. The gathering of daredevils is a huge party in the clouds – there is a kitchen, bars, yoga classes, paragliding courses and great jam sessions to keep the good mood. The festival-goers spend most of their time hanging in hammocks playing the guitar or having a beer, enjoying the great company of like-minded people and the majestic view. They call themselves "slackers" because of the slacklines they balance themselves on (they use a flat slacked rope that lets them swing and chill in the hammock).

In fact, this is considered an extreme sport, because participants not only lounge in hanging hammocks, but also walk across the tightropes with extreme skill and bravery.

The exact dates of this festival depend on weather conditions, however, the festival takes place in early September.

The idea behind the event is to commemorate in a fun and pleasant way 15 000 young soldiers who gave their lives in that exact place during WWI.

Travel to: Italy (Monte Piana). The participants set camp high in the sky in the Misurina Lake area.

Other holidays on this date: International Bacon Day (USA), Feast of the Sacrifice (Egypt), Eid-al-Adha (Jordan)

03 September: Cherokee National Holiday (USA – Native American)
The annual holiday held over two days in the beginning of September (Labour weekend) aims to reunite Cherokees and their descendants and to raise awareness about the cultural heritage of this nation. The festival was initiated in 1953 to

commemorate the signing of the 1839 Cherokee Constitution and the Act of Union reuniting Cherokees both East and West after the Trail of Tears - series of forced relocations of Native Americans from their ancestral territories to designated Indian reservations along the Mississippi River. During the trips about 4 000 people, from which many Cherokees, lost their lives. The last relocation of Cherokees was in 1838 when gold was discovered in their homeland in the state of Georgia (which caused the Big Gold Rush).

Considered to be one of the largest events in Oklahoma, the Cherokee National Holiday attracts more than 100 000 visitors every year.

The celebration features a Cherokee Parade as well as many games throughout the festival days – from traditional Cherokee marbles, horseshoes, drum contests and cornstalk shoot games to golf and softball. A highlight of the event is the Inter-Tribal Powwow – traditional Native American social gathering with singing and dances performed by the different tribes. All participants wear tribal costumes and adorned with feathers and bones headpieces.

Local merchants set up stalls, selling authentic Native American-made products and foods. There are gospel and bluegrass music, a toe-tapping fiddler's contest and a concert from the award-winning Cherokee National Youth Choir.

The festival is very important to the Cherokees also because the Principal Chief of the Cherokee Nation delivers his annual State of the Nation Address.

Travel to: USA (Oklahoma). The powwow takes place in Tahlequah – the historic Cherokee Nation capital. One might want to remember the word "Osyio" - the Cherokee word for "Hello"!

Other holidays on this date: US Bowling League Day, International Birdman Festival (England)

04 September: Harvest Festival (India)

One of the biggest harvest festivals in Southern India. It is annually celebrated over 10 days in the months of August or September (the locals follow the Malayalam calendar – a solar and sidereal calendar created in 825 A.D. and used only in Kerala). This is the New Year for the Malayali Hindus.

The locals are well known for their ability to present in a most fascinating way the heritage and rich culture of the region during the days of the event.

The importance of this Harvest Festival, or Onam as it is locally known, lies in a legend:

In the past, King Mahabali ruled over Kerala – his subjects worshipped him, the region was very rich, and the people were prosperous and happy. They loved their King and cherished his virtues. However, Mahabali was very selfish, which disappointed the Gods, so they decided to end his rule. But because his people loved him so much, he was allowed by the celestials to visit his subjects once a year. This visit takes place on the Harvest Festival, so the people put their best efforts to make the celebration majestic and impress their King.

It is a time of thanksgiving, singing, dances - including the Women dance (performed in a circlular motion around a lamp), a Tiger dance (performers disguised as tigers, dancing to drum beats) and a Mask dance. Women wear new sarees and dress the children in colourful clothes.

The opening ceremony features a colourful street procession with dancers wearing masks, adorned with gems elephants and decorated parade floats.

Everybody puts a traditional "Pookalam" in front of the front door (a beautifully arranged by hand fresh flower carpet). The size of the Pookalam grows with each day of the festival. More and more blossoms are added to the pattern. Such flower carpets are made in front of temples as well.

Typical to the celebration is the Snake Boat race or Vallam Kali. It uses war canoes in the shape of a snake, with 650 years of history.

The traditional dish for the holiday is served on a plantain leaf and consist of 9 courses - banana chips, curries, sweet pickles, tamarind soup, various vegetables with coconut milk, dahl, black-eyed peas with ginger and coconut milk etc.

The festival ends on the tenth day when the much-loved King returns to the celestials.

Travel to: India (Kerala state). The holiday is celebrated within the entire state, but for authentic experience visit the capital city of Thiruvanathapuram on the Indian's tropical coast.

Other holidays on this date: Labor Day, National Newspaper Carrier Day, National Wildlife Day (USA), Monster Praying Festival (Japan)

05 September: Hungry Ghost Festival (China)

This is a traditional Buddhist and Taoist festival held on the 15th day in the 7th month of the Chinese calendar (the end of August/beginning of September). The earliest proof that such festival was held dates to the 700 A.D. The celebration comes from ancient Asian folklore and there are similar beliefs in India, Cambodia and Japan as well.

The date is not chosen at random – in Asian culture, the 15th day is Ghost Day and the 7th month is regarded as Ghost Month. During that month, all spirits and ghosts, including the ones of deceased ancestors, come out from the Underworld to visit the living in search of food and entertainment.

On the 15th day, Buddhists and Taoists believe that Heaven, Hell and the world of the living open their gates, so they perform ancient rituals to please the spirits. They believe all ghosts leave the realms of the Underworld on the first day of the seventh month and for thousands of years, this has been the scariest month. Some folks even avoid being alone at night or swimming after sunset in fear that a lost ghost might spook them.

The festival celebrates the souls of deceased relatives – people burn incense sticks and figurines made of joss paper (in the shape of clothes, jewellery, houses, money and everything that the deceased could possibly need in the Underworld), make food offerings, have dinner keeping an empty seat for each of the deceased, release paper boats and lanterns on water to lead the way for the lost souls etc. The "lost souls" are the ancestors of those who had forgotten to pay tribute to them after they had died. These ghosts have long needle-thin necks because they have not been fed by their family.

The first day of the Ghost Month is very important – on this day people burn money made of joss paper to make sure the ghosts will have enough means for their long stay in the realm of the living.

On the fifteenth day (Ghost Day), locals make food offerings. They believe the ghosts are hungry after having fun for two weeks. Besides, if they are fed – they won't do any mischiefs.

On the last day of the festival, the gates close and all ghosts must return to the Underworld. In temples, the monks chant to make them leave – it is believed that the ghosts hate the sound of the chanting so much, that they return willingly. Many people float lotus lanterns to make sure that any lost souls will find the way to the Underworld.

Open-air celebrations, opera shows and concerts are held everywhere throughout the whole month. The front row seats at all performances are always empty as they are reserved for the ghosts. The monks perform different rituals to ease the suffering and often throw rice in the air to distribute it to the hungry souls.

The families have meals three times a day – always keeping an empty chair for a ghost to sit.

There are a few taboos during Ghost Month too, such as:
- Don't move into a new house
- Don't marry
- Don't pick up money found on the street and bring it home
- Don't wear red (ghosts like red)
- If one accidentally steps on a food offering on the street – should apologize aloud
- Don't sing or lean on walls (ghosts like songs and they often stick on walls)

The legend has it that if one is born during the Ghost month, should avoid celebrating his/her birthday at night.

Travel to: South China, Taiwan, Hong Kong, Malaysia, Singapore.

Other holidays on this date: Be Late for Something Day, Cheese Pizza Day (USA)

06 September: Umhlanga Ceremony (Swaziland)

The annual Umhlanga or the Reed Dance Ceremony celebrated since the 1940s, takes place over eight days in late August/early September and is observed by the Swazis (and the Zulus in South Africa). The date is not fixed as it derives from ancestral astrology. The custom was developed from an ancient ceremony of preserving women's chastity which is no longer observed in its original form.

The Umhlanga Ceremony was created to preserve and improve the ancient custom, but also to provide tribute labour to the Royal Family and show that by working together, women are stronger. At least, these are the official perks of the strange ceremony.

Anyway, this is the biggest party in Swaziland and one of the best in whole Africa!

However, a strict ritual is followed every year:

Young, unmarried girls (from 8 to 22 years old) from around the country gather at the Royal Village to cut reeds for the Queen Mother.

On the night of their arrival, the girls scatter around the village and cut tall reeds all night. On the following night, they bring the bundled reeds to the Queen Mother. They are for repairing a tall fence surrounding the Royal Village.

After a day of rest (the maidens sleep in huts or in classrooms of nearby schools), the girls get ready for the ceremony – they prepare the traditional costumes, which consist only of a brightly-coloured skirt, a sash, beaded necklace and rattling anklets. Some of them carry a bush knife used for cutting the reed – as a symbol of their virginity.

On the day of the ceremonial dance, the girls (split into groups of around 200 each) parade the streets wearing the costumes which leave them bare-chested, guarded by Swazi warriors decorated with cow tails and shields. They sing songs and perform a special dance (depending on the region they come from) in front of the King while the spectators and visitors cheer the half-naked maidens. Some warriors and spectators even throw money at their feet to show appreciation of their skill. The King's many daughters also take part in the dance – they can easily be identified by the crowns of red feathers tucked in their hair.

On the last day of the fiesta, the King orders for 20-25 cows to be slaughtered. The meat is then cooked and distributed to each participating girl and her family.

Every year the King chooses a new wife among the bare-chested dancing girls. Families who refuse to send their daughters to the dance are fined a goat or a cow. Each girl is paid money to participate in the ceremony. The rumour has it that about 40 000 take part in the ritual every year.

Travel to: Swaziland. The ceremony takes place at <u>Ludzidzini Royal Village</u> which is the home of the Royal Family of Swaziland. The Zulus in South Africa observe the ceremony in Nongoma.

Other holidays on this date: Fight Procrastination Day (USA)

07 September: Yam Festival (Ghana – Ashanti Tribe)

This is an annual harvest festival which takes place over 5 days (starting on a Tuesday) in the months between September and December and is celebrated by the indigenous Ashanti people. It is observed at the end of the autumn yam harvest, just after the monsoon season. The observance of the Yam Harvest can be traced back to 1817 or maybe even earlier.

Having its roots in Pagan times – today, the festival is a mix of religious ceremony and a huge farming event - much anticipated one.

The Ashanti Tribe women, dressed in colourful costumes, stroll down the city balancing yams on their heads (yams being a traditional food source for the tribe and in the most of West Africa). These yams are sacrificed at an altar dedicated to the Ashanti tribe ancestral gods.

The first offerings of harvested yams are carried in a procession led by the chief priest of the tribe to the ancestral grounds.

The celebrations include lots of music and dancing throughout the five days and start with sweeping the path to the burial grounds and a purification (cleansing) ceremony of the ancestral Royal throne which was descended from the sky to the first King. The Royal throne is sacred, has never touched ground nor has anyone sat in it. It is a divine object and is stored in a secret place.

Before the purification ceremony – the King orders his royal subjects to remain in their huts. This is to prevent them from seeing the sacred throne being carried to the river to be cleaned.

The festival is a time when ancient royal gold ornaments are melted and fashioned into new designs (with the approval of the King).

During the celebrations, the King does not allow the death drum to be beaten (a death drum was beaten during human sacrifices associated with the festival in the past).

This is an important festival for the Tribe – in general Ashanti's are not religious people, but they believe that trees, animals and plants have souls. They also believe in monsters, witches and fairies.

Travel to: Ghana (Kumasi). More than 1.5million (of total 7 million) Ashanti people live in the capital of the Ashanti region. The throne is washed in the ancient Draa River.

Other holidays on this date: National Beer Lover's Day (USA), Rificolona Festival (Italy)

08 September: Rakizio (Greece)

The festival takes place on Greece's greenest island with a population of only 500 people. The 64sq.km island offers to the visitors around 200 Byzantine chapels, Crusader castles, abandoned villages and an ancient cave-museum full of dwarf elephants – the last of their kind in Europe.

Every year on September 8th, a lovely festival takes place in one of the island villages – Rakizio.

Raki is the traditional drink of Tinos Island and is used anywhere and anytime – as a drink, in food recipes, at social events etc. So – it is logical to have its own festival day.

The name of the event – Rakizio is:
- The name of the space where Raki drink is produced
- The name of the distillation process
- The name of the festival that follows

The locals keep an old tradition and produce the drink the same way it has been produced centuries ago, so for them, it is a sacred ritual. The owner of a Rakizio cauldron (the Maker of the drink) must buy a 48-hour license to produce the drink. The license is sold only once a year and is valid only during the Rakizio festival.

The Raki is usually flavoured with fennel, sage or thyme.

On the day of the festival, the locals gather to celebrate and drink Raki straight from the cauldrons...this is from production to consumption straightforward!

P.S. The first glass of Raki from the cauldron is so strong that it is good only for chest rubbing against the flu. However, the locals do enjoy that first glass immensely!

Travel to: Greece (Tinos Island). Visit the village of Falatados where the Raki drink is produced and celebrated on this day.

Other holidays on this date: Pardon Day, Stand Up to Cancer Day (USA), Our Lady of Meritxell (Andorra)

09 September: Knabenschiessen (Switzerland)

This is a traditional regional shooting competition in the Canton of Zurich. It is held every year on the afternoon of the Monday following the second weekend in September (easy to remember, huh?).

The contest was created by a Marksmen club in 1899 with the main purpose to attract more young boys to join the Swiss Army. Initially, it was intended for boys only, but since 1991 girls can also take part. The participants (around 5 000 boys and girls) should be in the age limit 13-17 years and be residents of the city or the Canton of Zurich.

However, the custom can be traced back to the XVIIth C, when all young boys had to practice their shooting during the summer holidays.

Although not an official holiday, many businesses close for the afternoon of the shooting.

The contest has evolved over the years and now it resembles a folklore festival – with merry-go-rounds, Ferris wheel, adventurous rides, funfairs, food stalls with delicious local fresh food and drinks. And, of course, the highlight – the shooting contest.

An interesting fact is that the children use standard rifles – just like the ones used in the Swiss Army! The winner is crowned as The King/Queen of Marksmen.

Travel to: Switzerland (Canton Zurich). The holiday is observed in the city of Zurich in Albisgütli in the foot of Üetliberg mountain.

Other holidays on this date: Teddy Bear Day, National Hug Your Boss Day (USA)

10 September: Abbots Bromley Horn Dance (England)

It is believed that this is one of the oldest customs in Europe dating back hundreds of years. In fact, no one can pinpoint how it was started, although some folklorists claim it is a surviving Druidic custom.

According to historical sources – it is a Medieval English folk dance from the XVI-XVIIth C. However, a thorough analysis of some of the antlers used in the dance, clearly show that they are from the XIth C. But apparently at that time, there were no deer in England and Wales, so they must have been imported from Scandinavia.

Another theory connects the dance to a magical Pagan ritual for affirming hunting rights. This one dates even before the Xth C.

The most bizarre guess, however, leads to the nearby Lascaux cave. The cave paintings found on the walls look a lot like the horn dancers. The bizarre part? Well, the paintings are 20 000 years old... Go figure!

The official year of the first festival is 1221 – the year when local authorities granted the city a permission to host it. The celebrations are held on the first Sunday after September 4th.

The Horn Dance features 4 characters:
- Reindeer with antlers
- Hobby Horse
- Maid Marian (a man in a dress)
- Dancing Fool holding something inflated tied on a stick

The festivities start with a blessing service in a church where the antlers are stored. The Deer-men wearing Tudor-style costumes, collect their antlers to dance outside the church. They dance in the village and around it but never leaving the borders of the parish. The deer are followed by the Hobby Horse, a boy with a triangle and a boy carrying a bow and arrow. The horse and the boy with the arrows engage in a unique dance accompanied by a man in a dress – Maid Marian, and street musicians playing the accordions.

The merry men dance from the morning till late afternoon when they return to the village – hungry and thirsty, so they make their way around pubs and houses, making stops for refreshments.

In the evening, the antlers are returned to the church which marks the end of the celebration.

Everyone can volunteer to join the dance!

Travel to: England (Staffordshire). The venue is the village of Abbots Bromley. The dances take place in Yeatsall, Admaston over the reservoir and in front of Blithfield Hall. The antlers are kept 364 days a year at the St Nicholas Church.

Interesting fact is that until the XIXth C all dancers were members of the local Bentley Family.

Other holidays on this date: Swap Ideas Day, Grandparent's Day, National TV Dinner Day (USA)

11 September: Shrimp Fishing on Horseback Custom (Belgium)

This is an ancient way of fishing for the famous Belgian grey shrimp which has turned into a custom, unique to the country.

Shrimp fishing on horseback – a tradition from the XVth C, is still performed on the northwest Belgian coast and takes place annually during the months of June to September.

A small group of well trained in the odd craft fishermen mount their horses and gallop to the seashore. They plough shrimps in nets dragged behind the horses (chains tied to the nets cause vibrations which make the shrimp jump directly inside the net). Each horse has a willow basket attached to the side and that is where "the catch" is stored.

The tools and the clothing have evolved through time to make the fisherman feel more comfortable and enable them to perform their custom with ease.

The men are dressed in yellow raincoats and wear rubber boots and rain-proof yellow hats. This is the traditional outfit.

The fishing takes place only during low tides. After an hour in the shallow waters, the fishermen check the nets and throw back in the water all small fish, crabs and jellyfish caught in them.

The grey shrimp fishing brotherhood consists of just above a dozen men, representing 12 local households, who are well trained and had all passed a two-year course and an exam at the local fisheries museum. More than that – each one has gone through the long process of finding the right horse – they say that the horse and the fisherman match for life!

Each member of the private society has a speciality – weaving baskets, training draft horses and even seafood cooking.

The Medieval tradition is included in the UNESCO List of Intangible Cultural Heritage of Humanity.

As the custom is open to the public and anyone can attend, the organizers often do shrimp cooking masterclasses and tastings directly on the beach.

Travel to: Belgium (Oostduinkerke). There are statues of fishermen on horseback placed on the beach.

Other holidays on this date: No News is Good News Day, Make Your Bed Day, National Boss/Employee Exchange Day (USA), Geez New Year (Eritrea), World Puppet Theater Festival (France)

12 September: Day of Conception (Russia)

Skip work, have sex!
Make a baby. Win a prize!

This pretty much explains the purpose of the celebration. The annual "holiday" held on September 12th was initiated in 2007 by the local government because of declining birth rates, rising death rates and unequal proportion of women to men in Russia. Considering this a serious issue and trying to keep the Russian bloodline, the local government granted 1 day off from work for the people to stay home with their loved ones and...have sex.

The only thing participants need to do is to register for the contest. Parents whose babies are born exactly nine months after that day receive government grants, electronics, cash, cars and are welcomed by the Russian National anthem.

The statistics are phenomenal!

You might guess that the holiday is massively celebrated!

During the day many retailers and restaurants offer discounts for families with children.

Travel to: Russia (Ulyanovsk). It was the Governor of Ulyanovsk who introduced September 12th as a half day off work.

Other holidays on this date: National Encouragement Day (USA)

13 September: Feast of Sacrifice (Kazakhstan)

This three-day holiday commemorates Ibrahim's willingness to sacrifice his son as an act of submission to Allah`s command and is one of the most significant

Muslim celebrations. Just before the sacrifice, a voice from Heaven stopped Ibrahim and told him to sacrifice something else instead so he sacrificed a ram.

In Arabic, the holiday is known as Eid al-Adha.

In the Islamic lunar calendar, the celebrations are held on the 12th day of the 10th lunar month (which falls in September or October in the Gregorian calendar, but the date drifts about 11 days earlier with each year).

People wake up early, put on celebratory clothes, gather their whole family and pray for their deceased relatives in mosques.

They also spend a great part of the day donating to the poor – food, clothes, money etc. as charity is one of the Five Pillars of Islam.

Two places are overcrowded on this holiday – the mosques and the livestock market.

On this day, everyone should slaughter an animal (as a sacrifice), distribute 1/3 of it to the poor, 1/3 to the relatives and the rest toward the holiday meal when the family gathers. It is believed that this will bring happiness and prosperity to the family.

At a designated time, the animal is turned to face Mecca and its throat is cut with the words "In the name of Allah".

Only camels, cows, bulls, buffalos, and sheep can be sacrificed and during the holiday the markup of a single live animal could reach up to 200%! Another important aspect is that the animal cannot be ill, blind or disabled in any way.

People are not allowed to sell the skin but they can use it as a rug for praying.

An interesting fact is that around 100 million animals are sacrificed every year on Eid al-Adha around the world.

Travel to: Kazakhstan (Astana, Almaty and Karaganda). The whole country celebrates, but the best live stock markets are usually around the big cities.

Other holidays on this date: National Kids Take Over the Kitchen Day, Fortune Cookie Day, Defy Superstition Day (USA)

14 September: The Living Chess Game (Italy)

This game of live chess is held in a small town of Medieval castles close to Venice. It is held every two years – on every second Friday, Saturday and Sunday.

There is a romantic theory that the first occurrence was in 1454 when the city was part of the Venetian Republic. The story behind the initiation of such a game was...love. Two noblemen fell in love with the daughter of the Lord of the Castle and challenged each other to a traditional duel (win the duel – win the girl's heart). However, the Lord forbade it and commanded the two young men to play a game of chess instead. The game took place on the square in front of the castle with living persons carrying the Blacks and Whites across the chess board drawn on the ground.

It didn't matter who the winner was, because the Lord had promised that one of the noblemen will marry his daughter and the other one will marry her younger sister. The game was honoured by all subjects and noble families. The Lord insisted that fireworks, dances and songs should also take place after the game to mark the happy occasion of his daughters' marriages. He also insisted on an exhibition with live soldiers, infantry, archers, pikemen, knights, pages, bridesmaids, falconers, dames and gentlemen, jugglers, fire-eaters and musicians.

However, the historical facts lead to another theory – after World War I, the local chess club members decided to play a game of live chess on the city square – this was in 1923.

Today, the event re-enacts the game from 1454 – with knights and noblemen and brightly dressed cheering crowds. The orders to the characters are still given today in the old Venetian language. Many players are actors trained in stage combat.

An impressive Medieval ceremony is held when the Lord's daughter is handed to the winner!

A true recreation of the Renaissance!

Travel to: Italy (Marostica). The game takes place on the square in the center of Marostica – on a pink and white marble giant chessboard.

Other holidays on this date: National Cream Filled Doughnut Day, National Live Creative Day (USA), Krastovden or Holy Cross Day (Bulgaria)

15 September: Moon Festival (China)
This is the second biggest festival after the Chinese New Year and its first celebrations go back 3000 years. In a scale for preparation and celebration - it is equivalent to Christmas or Thanksgiving Day.

The Moon Festival is held on the 15th day of the 8th month in accordance with the Chinese lunar calendar (in September or early October). It is celebrated on a day when the moon is fullest and brightest.

The festival has deep Pagan roots as it deviated from an ancient moon sacrificial ceremony. In the past, Chinese observed that the moon phases have a direct connection with the change of seasons and the agricultural production. That is why after the harvest season (in the autumn), they made offerings to the moon. At the beginning (1000 B.C.) this was a privilege only to the royals, but centuries later – the custom became so popular that the common people started celebrating it as well.

Another theory is that Chang'e – the Chinese Moon Goddess, levitated all the way to the Moon after overdosing on her husbands' elixir of life. She lives on the Moon with the Jade Rabbit and a man condemned to an eternity of tree-cutting...

A figurine of the Jade Rabbit – it is one of the first decorations to be bought in preparations for the festival.

The Moon Festival is a time for family reunion and peace, and a time to remember the relatives who live afar.

Usually, the family gets together for a traditional dinner and to admire the full moon, which is a symbol of happiness and prosperity. The traditional food on the festival are mooncakes – they are presented as offerings to the Moon and shared with the family and friends. They are round-shaped wheat-flour pastries (a symbol of harmony and unity, and family reunion) and come in many flavours. A true magic experience is eating a mooncake while admiring the full moon. Other common foods are pomelo, duck and pumpkin.

Typical activities to celebrate are lighting paper lanterns, writing riddles for the others to guess and drinking wine flavoured with flowers. Many Chinese spend the evening up in the mountains worshipping the bright moon in the night sky.

Of course, making and sharing mooncakes is a highlight and the most important part of the festival.

In some places, locals celebrate with Dragon and Lion dances. The dragon, as a symbol of China, is believed to bring luck to people. The Dragon dance features a paper-made brightly coloured gigantic dragon figure held on poles, manipulated in serpentine movements by a group of dancers.

The Lion dance features a lion figure manipulated by two dancers. The fundamental movement of the lion are movements from Chinese martial arts.

In some parts of China, food offerings are placed on tables set on the village square or outfront homes. In other parts of China and Asia in general, people perform different ceremonies like "beating the Moon" (the Oroqen people beat the moon's reflection in a basin of water), "stealing Moon vegetables" (the Dong people believe that the Moon Goddess sprays all vegetables with sweet dew and they are to be shared among all the people – therefore stealing a veggie from your neighbor's garden is not considered an offense); "chasing the Moon" (the Mongols ride towards the Moon all night until the Sun rises and the Moon disappears) and others.

Travel to: China. The whole country celebrates the festival, but these are truly special places to be: Shanghai - Tongli Water Town (49 bridges joining 7 islands created by 15 rivers and 5 lakes) or Zhangjiajie – Grand Canyon of Hunan Province (the world's longest and highest glass-bottom bridge with wonderful views of the numerous waterfalls).

Other holidays on this date: Greenpeace Day, National Online Learning Day, National Double Cheeseburger Day (USA), Hiri Moale Festival (Papua New Guinea)

16 September: Octoberfest (Germany)

One of the best known and most loved events in the world – the famous German Beer Festival!

Dessi Nikoltchev:

Oktoberfest is the world's largest annual beer folk gathering - a 16-day festival with more than 6 million people from around the world attending the event every year. It is all about beer, beer and only beer. Traditional huge glasses of beer are brought to the table by servers wearing traditional folklore costumes – dirndl for the ladies and lederhosen for the gents. Its a party well endowed!

It all started in 1810 with the Royal Wedding of Crown Prince Ludwig (later King Ludwig I) and Princess Therese of Saxony-Hildburghausen. Horse races and a five-day feast were held on the fields in front of the city gates to mark the happy occasion and everyone was invited to join in the celebration. It was a festival for the entire region, so the locals decided to host an annual festival. And... as the wedding was in October – the name which stuck with the event was... Octoberfest.

On the following year, an Agricultural show became part of the program.

With time, horse races were dropped but the Agricultural show still features every three years. In the first few decades, the amusement rides were a carousel and two swings. Small beer kiosks were gradually introduced, only to become the major part of the event in 1896 when the first beer tents were set on the festival grounds. Later on, Octoberfest received the backing of the local breweries.

The festival was eventually prolonged to the impressive 16 days and moved to September to allow better weather conditions. The last day of the event is the first Sunday in October.

Today, the Mayor of the city opens the festival at noontime by driving a wooden tap into a beer barrel and announcing: "It is tapped!" (O, zapft is!).

On the first Sunday, The Costume and Riflemen's Procession takes place on the streets of the city. The participants in the parade are groups in traditional and historic uniforms, marching bands, livestock, agricultural workers, old-fashioned carriages with horses and many others showcasing the diversity of the city and the region.

On the second Sunday, a huge open-air concert takes place.

For its 200+ years of history, the festival has been cancelled 24 times due to war or epidemics.

And some numbers:
- Over 5 million litres of beer are consumed during the 16 days of the festival;
- 400 000 pork sausages and 480 000 roasted chicken are eaten;
- 6 breweries are permitted to serve beer on the festival: Augustiner, Hacker-Pschorr, Hofbräu, Löwenbräu, Paulaner, and Spaten;
- Octoberfest brings over 450 million Euros to the city every year.

Oktoberfest beer is of a variety called Märzen which is darker and stronger. This type of beer used to be brewed in March and was ready to drink by late summer or early fall. Like all German beer, the Oktoberfest beer is brewed according to the strict

German standards from 1516 (Reinheitsgebot) that precisely define the four ingredients allowed in the brewing: barley, hops, malt, and yeast.

Travel to: Germany (Munich). The festival grounds and tents are along Wirtsbudenstrasse.
Other holidays on this date: Collect Rocks Day, Step Family Day (USA)

17 September: Floriade (Australia)

One of the largest and most beautiful spring festivals in Australia, created in 1988 by two landscape designers to celebrate the city's 75th birthday. The event was so successful that the locals created an annual festival. The flower show is held over 30 days – mid-September to mid-October.

It is a display of more than a million exotic bulbs and flower gardens planted across 8,000 square meters of parkland.

The festival also features concerts (including a twilight concert of the Symphony Orchestra), pop up performances, late night light shows and installations, art displays, sculptures, horticultural workshops, an amusement park with giant slides, bouncy castles, Ferris wheel and other recreational activities.

Visitors can take part in morning walks around the park, photography workshops, flower arrangement workshops, edible flower tastings, painting a garden gnome and many other activities.

There is also a marketplace within the festival grounds, with stalls offering handmade soap bars, clothes, flowers and plants, food and much more.

Once the gates close on Floriade, the event's volunteers are offered to take home some of the plants. The rest is distributed to local nursing homes and hospitals.

Many people refer to the flower extravaganza as "a true feast for the senses!".

Travel to: Australia (Canberra). The event takes place in the Commonwealth Park alongside Lake Burley Griffin.
Other holidays on this date: Citizenship Day, Constitution Day, Wife Appreciation Day (USA)

18 September: Egremont's Crab Fair & World Gurning Championship (England)

This annual festival held on the third Saturday in September is celebrating its 750th anniversary. The Egremont Crab Fair, established in 1267 is one of the oldest fairs in the world and got its name from a tradition of giving away crab apples, started by the Lord of Egremont.

It features a pipe smoking event, ferret racing, wheelbarrow races, pig's bladder football game, horse and pony leaping, greasy pole climbing (participants climb up a lard-covered pole trying to secure as a prize a lamb leg tied to the top), Apple Cart

Parade (participants ride in apple carts and throw apples to the cheering crowd), amusement rides, live bands and lots of entertainment, local food and beer tents.

However, a highlight is the World Gurning Championship taking place within the festival. A gurn is simply a distorted facial expression. The participants put their head through a horse collar and try to pull the ugliest face possible. The winner in each of the three categories (men, women and junior) is voted by the public. There are some basic rules – no make-up is allowed, but manipulation of false teeth is allowed for those who have them.

Travel to: England (Cumbria). The fair takes place at the Market Hall in the town of Egremont.

Other holidays on this date: National Cheeseburger Day (USA), Respect for the Aged Day (Japan)

19 September: Goroka Tribal Gathering (Papua New Guinea)

This is an annual gathering of more than 100 indigenous tribes, taking place over three days in the week around September 16th, which is the National Holiday of Papua New Guinea. It is celebrated since 1957 and is one of the largest cultural festivals in the world. The event was originally organized by Australian patrol officers as a competition on the most organized district, but it turned out to be one of the cultural wonders of the world.

Each tribe member is dressed in traditional dress representing his/her tribe. The typical festive attire includes colourful costume, headdress adorned with as many feathers as possible and brightly painted face. Huge necklaces covered with seashells and bones, as well as leaves from different plants, complement the festive look (even grass skirts are quite common). Some tribes have woven wings strapped to their backs, others are covered in mud and wear white clay masks.

Forty to fifty "sing-sing" groups represent different tribes in various competitions – singing, dancing, playing traditional instruments and performing tribal rituals. The winning tribe gets a contract to perform concerts in many hotels all year round.

The festival aims to preserve the truly unique cultural heritage of the indigenous people of Papua New Guinea and to showcase their way of life by presenting their rich traditions and ancient rituals. And the ticket costs...$2!

Travel to: Papua New Guinea (Goroka). The small town has only 25,000 residents, so the accommodation places fill up quickly as the festival attracts tens of thousands.

Other holidays on this date: National Cheeseburger Day (USA)

20 September: Kishiwada Danjiri Festival (Japan)

Teams of up to 500 men pulling a portable shrine through the town streets at break-neck speed?!

This is one of the largest and best-known festivals in the country. It was created in the XVIIIth C as a harvest festival, but in time it evolved into a showcase of the rich cultural heritage of the region. It is held over two days, every year in September/October, and attracts many visitors from around the country and the world.

The floats (danjiri) are 4 meters tall, 4 meters long, 2.5 meters wide and weigh about 4 tons. Every part of the massive wooden construction is adorned with sculptures representing ancient myths and heroic battles which make it look like a shrine or a temple. A rope that can accommodate more than 500 people (to pull the cart) is attached to the front. More people hold another rope that goes behind the vehicle for steering (the wheels don't turn, so they have to skid the whole construction). A band of 4-5 drum and gong players is positioned on the platform. Dancers perform on the roof.

Each float has its specific rallying cry, chanted by the pullers. This way the participants honour the gods.

Around 35 hand-made and carved danjiri take part in the festival. Each one represents a neighbourhood and a carpentry guild of the port city where the event takes place. The master craftsmen have the best spot on the float – they perform acrobatics on the roof, sometimes with a great risk to their life. The most famous dance which they perform is the "Airplane Dance".

All participants in the cart-pulling procession are dressed in white shirts and Happi Coats (a traditional Japanese coat worn during festivals – made of cotton, with wide sleeves and tied with a sash around the waist).

This dangerous pull-through town at crazy high speed is considered a show of strength, endurance and community bonding. The crowd cheers on every "pull" and "stop" command yelled by the team leader and applauds when the float turns successfully over a tight corner.

In the evening, all participants hang paper lanterns on their floats and have snacks and drinks in the ambient light.

The festival is considered as dangerous as the bull runs in Spain and takes casualties every year.

Lots of local food and souvenir stalls are positioned along the route of the float procession.

Travel to: Japan (Kishiwada). The best place to observe the procession is west of Kishiwada Station.

Other holidays on this date: National Punch Day (USA), World Children's Day

21 September: Cat-eating Festival (Peru)
The scary annual festival held on September 21st honours Santa Efigenia – the Black Virgin from Ethiopia, celebrated in a town on the southern coastal part of Peru. The commemoration recognises an ancient connection between the African and Peruvian cultures. Santa Efigenia is a Patroness of the National Black Art and is celebrated by all writers, painters, musicians and artists. Since the mid-1700s, a statue and a wall-sized Baroque painting are stored in a private chapel in La Quebrada.

Part of the festivities, honouring the saint, include La Festival Gastronomico del Gato (Gastronomic Festival of the Cat) which is... a cat-eating feast. The legend has it that the event was created to commemorate a time when the first settlers - African slaves, had no choice but to survive on cat meat. On this day, the natives commemorate their ancestors.

The controversial cat-eating ritual has led to many lawsuits by upset cat lovers and animal rights associations through the years, but this hasn't ceased the celebrations (yet).

About 100 cats are bred specially for the occasion every year. The animals are held in cages for a year just to be tied in bags and drowned on the day of the festival.

The meat is then cooked and distributed to the locals. Featured dishes include spicy cat stew and grilled cat with native huacatay herbs, and the meat reportedly tastes much like rabbit. Some locals say cat meat can cure bronchitis and boost fertility. They also believe that it is an aphrodisiac.

The festivities include lots of Afro-Peruvian music, songs and dances, and a cat race (the loser ends up on a plate, unfortunately).

According to sources, animal rights activists have accused the organizers of cruelty and have insisted the festival to be banned, reasoning that cat meat can as well be dangerous to human health. The Peruvian Health Ministry, however, backed the celebration by regulating the amount of cat meat consumption and the methods of breeding the animals. The locals argued that the cat-eating custom through years of repetition has become part of their identity.

In 2013, a provincial judge ruled that cat-eating should be banned. She succeeded to ban La Festival Gastronomico del Gato. However, there was no ruling against cat-eating under a domestic animal protection law (the magistrates took no further action) – therefore the festival became a place to exchange cat-eating recipes and cooking techniques.

Off the record – the festival is allegedly still around despite the ban.

Travel to: Peru (Lima). The festival is held in the town of La Quebrada in San Luis District.

Other holidays on this date: International Peace Day, World Gratitude Day (USA)

22 September: Blessed Rainy Day (Bhutan)

This is a day marking the end of the monsoon season and beginning of harvest, and has been observed for centuries.

Celebrated annually on September 22nd, the water from all natural water sources on this day is believed to have magical powers - it is blessed by Buddha himself. The people are encouraged to take an outdoor bath to cleanse bad karma and from evil spirits. The most favourable hour for the outdoor ritual to be performed is precisely calculated by astrologers who refer to the Tibetan lunar calendar. Allegedly, this time is 4 p.m. on September 22nd.

The locals wake up at dawn, go outside their houses, pour water over their heads and bathe while saying prayers. They believe that Buddha is also taking a bath in the sky and is blessing them from above. The "blessed water" purifies and clears the sins. This soul cleansing ritual takes place a few times during the day.

The locals spend the day bathing in the open air and playing Khuru – a traditional Bhutanese game – similar to darts. The game is played only by men dressed in Gho – a national dress in Bhutan introduced in the XVIIth C.

Each participant makes his own two darts (called khurus) out of a wood plank and a nail. The players divide into teams of 10 people, every one of them trying to hit a target standing about 20 meters afar. After throwing the two khurus, each player stands next to the target (a small wooden plate). They gather as close as possible so that each can try to navigate its teammate`s khuru to hit the target. This is done by running, jumping and shouting around the target and it is a lot of fun for everyone. And when a player hits the bullseye – the entire team starts dancing and cheering very loudly.

Other typical games are dancing around a bonfire and shooting arrows. The Bhutanese use feathers for arrow decoration, however only the ones collected from the ground, as they consider it wrong killing a bird for its feathers.

Traditional food on Blessed Rainy Day is Thukpa soup (a variation of porridge), sweetened saffron rice and buttered tea.

Travel to: Bhutan (Pema Gatshel). The town is known for its intense ceremonies on Blessed Rainy Day.

Other holidays on this date: Car Free Day (USA)

23 September: Grape Throwing Festival (Spain)

Yet another food fight in Spain...

The annual festival held in a small wine-producing town over the last weekend in September is one of the messiest in the world. On the other hand – it is one of a kind!

The event has its roots in ancient Roman times. In the past, local wine-makers celebrated a good harvest by removing "the bad grapes" before the winter season. They just didn't know what to do with the grapes that were not good enough for wine.

As this turned out to be such a fun event, the tradition stuck and the people decided to create a festival to have a good time and get the job done. Unfortunately, no one can pinpoint the exact year of the first official festival although it can be traced back to as early as the 1930s.

The event takes place around the central square of the town after the Mayor fires a rocket to mark the start of the festivities. A traditional piper then leads the crowd out of the city and into the surrounding fields. They all gather around a huge pile of grapes (about 90 tons).

Then, after a whistle blow, all participants take part in a grape-stomping competition, grape-treading and the grape-throwing fight.

After the battle, everyone is invited for wine-tasting at the central square! A special treat is wine from Manto Negro - a variety of grape used to produce local wines in Mallorca (Manto Negro is only cultivated in the small town and nowhere else in the world!).

Another perk – the grape fight kicks off a festival that lasts 2 weeks!

Travel to: Spain (Majorca). The festival is held in the town of Binissalem.
Other holidays on this date: International Rabbit Day

24 September: Rosh Hashanah (Israel)

This is the Jewish New Year and is celebrated in every Jewish community around the world. According to historical facts, it started as an autumn harvest festival sometime between 516 B.C. and 70 A.D., evolving to a New year celebration only years or maybe centuries later. It began with the early Egyptians and was preserved by the Hebrew nation.

The festivities last for two days and are held in the Jewish month of Tishrei (an ancient Babylonian word meaning "beginning") - exactly 163 days after the first day of Passover (which places the holiday in late September, rarely - the beginning of October). Rosh Hashanah - "the head of the year", starts at sunset on the first day and ends at sunset on the next.

Allegedly, the holiday is celebrated over two days because of a miscommunication in the past! Every new month started with a new moon. The rise of the new moon was determined by a council of Rabbis in Jerusalem. A messenger was then sent to all parts of the land to announce the beginning of the new month. However, some parts were too remote and by the time the messenger got there...the day was already over. So... because of the communication problem, the holiday was celebrated over two days. Even when the new months were no longer announced this way – the authorities decided to stick with the two-day feast.

Rosh Hashanah commemorates the end of the seven days of creation of the universe. A Jewish tradition has it that over these two days, God judges people's deeds in the past year and decides their fate in the year ahead – punishment for the sinners, reward for the righteous. The ones whose fate is undecided are given a period of repentance until another big Jewish holiday – Yom Kippur which follows 10 days later (The Day of Atonement when the fate of mankind is sealed). The period between Rosh Hashanah and Yom Kippur is known as "The Days of Repentance".

The Jewish people visit synagogues for lengthy services and liturgical songs. Through quiet observance and prayers requesting forgiveness for their sins, they allow God to decide their fate for the following year.

A centurial tradition is the blowing of a Shofar (ram's horn) at synagogues early in the morning – it symbolizes the divine supremacy of God and reminds to the people of the ten commandments and Judgement Day. After all, this is also a very introspective holiday – the Jewish folks believe that people bear personal responsibility for their behavior. Therefore, the holiday is a time to seek forgiveness and be a better person.

Another typical ritual is the Tashlikh (started in the XVth C) –people walk down to a river, lake or the sea and shake their pockets to cast away their sins. Sometimes they throw breadcrumbs in the water as a symbol of committed sins.

A symbol of Rosh Hashanah is a honey-dipped apple – a traditional treat on the festive table. The sweetness signifies positivity and the welcoming of a better year ahead. Pomegranate is also important as it represents a plentiful year. Other dishes are fish (symbolizing the will to keep ahead), leek, black-eyed peas, wine and lots of sweets. Each meal signifies a wish.

Folks exchange small gifts, like pomegranate pendants, honey dippers, Shofars and Shofar-holders etc.

"Leshana tova, tikateivu vetihamtemnu!" – this is the greeting on Rosh Hashanah and means "may you be inscribed and sealed in the Book of Life for a good year".

But the people simply say "Shana Tova", meaning "have a good year".

By the way, the Jewish people celebrate the year 5779 – that corresponds to 2018 in the rest of the world!! The Hebrew yearcount starts with the Creation.

Travel to: Israel. The holiday is celebrated throughout the country with synagogue services taking place in every city and small town. Best places to be – Tel Aviv, Jerusalem and Haifa.

Other holidays on this date: National Custodial Worker Day (USA), Gerewol Festival (Chad)

25 September: Nine Nights – Navratri (India)

One of the biggest annual Hindu festivals, marking the harvest season, celebrated over nine nights/ten days in the end of September/beginning of October (in accordance with the lunar calendar). Navratri means "nine nights" in Sanskrit.

The holiday honours the Goddess Mother and motherhood, and the epic triumph of good over evil. Dedicated to Durga (goddess of power, energy and strength), this is one of the few festivals in any religion to celebrate motherhood, as well as the victory of life and happiness over destruction and misery.

As India has a vast territory, the ways Navratri is observed differ. But in all parts of the country – it is a happy and festive occasion.

In some states, Navratri is celebrated with nine nights of dancing –performers dance in a circle, wearing colourful and festive clothes. Small sticks adorned with ribbons and small gems are used in the dance.

In other states, women make displays of dolls, which symbolize the feminine power. The dolls are positioned on an uneven number of steps – 3,5, 7, 9 or 11. Friends visit each other's homes to admire the different displays and exchange sweets.

Every evening, scenes from the Ramayana are performed in most cities around the country.

In some areas, women buy a a small clay pot which they decorate. On the first day of the celebrations, they put a candle inside and dance around it.

It is common for people to make flower arrangements and immerse them in water on the last day of Navratri.

It is a tradition to wear a different colour dress on every day of the holiday – each day corresponds to the life cycles of the Goddess Mother:

Day 1: Different rituals are performed to invoke the Goddess. On this day she is worshipped as "The Daughter of the Mountain" – the unmarried Goddess Parvati. The colour to be worn is royal blue.

Day 2: The Goddess is worshipped as the married Goddess Parvati, riding on a tigress/lioness – a symbol of bravery. The colour to be worn is yellow.

Day 3: The Goddess is worshipped for creating the Universe and giving light and energy to everything living. The colour for this day is green.

Day 4: The Goddess is worshipped as a Mother. The colour is grey.

Day 5: The Goddess is worshipped as a great warrior. The colour to wear – orange.

Day 6: The Goddess is worshipped as the deity of wisdom and knowledge. The colour on this day is white.

Day 7: The Goddess is worshipped as a protector of all evil. The colour to wear is red.

Day 8: The Goddess is worshipped as graceful and righteous. The colour is sky blue.

Day 9: The Goddess is worshipped as possessing all eight supernatural powers which she grants to her son – God Shiva. The colour on the last day is pink.

On the 10th day, Goddess Mother effigies are carried in huge processions through the streets, for her victory to be celebrated by everyone.

Relatives who live afar, get together for the entire duration of the holiday and celebrate their unity with dances and feasts. This is a time of prayers for health and prosperity and a time for reunion with the community.

Animal sacrifices of goat, chicken or water buffalo are performed at Shakti temples, to honour the Goddess as a great warrior.

Travel to: India (Gujarat). The whole country celebrates, but the biggest festivities are held in the state of Gujarat and in Mumbai. The festival is also celebrated in Bangladesh and Nepal.

Other holidays on this date: National One-Hit Wonder Day, National Tune-Up Day (USA)

26 September: Phoo Festival (Pakistan)

This annual two-day festival is held in the end of September and celebrates grape and walnut harvest.

It is observed only by the indigenous Kalash people which are great winemakers and the only minority still practising pagan rituals – a very ancient form of Hinduism.

The festival is a time for joy, time to celebrate the strong family bonds and party with friends and neighbours. As much as a religious festival, the event is also one marking the seasonal cycle.

The event is a true kaleidoscope of colours. Kalashi women dress up in full festive regalia – the predominant colours are orange, yellow and red. Their traditional robes are embroidered with symbols, flowers and folkloric motifs. Around the neck, they wear a plethora of beaded necklaces. The finishing touch is a majestic crown-looking headpiece – encrusted with shiny beads, feathers and pompons.

The Kalashi perform traditional dances, sing songs and celebrate the day of the grape harvest – thanking the gods and praying for good fortune.

The observance is held only in one small part of the country where the Kalash people live.

Unfortunately, due to lack of ethnographical research, not many things are clear around when and how the festival originated, but in line with a theory - it derived from a pagan autumn harvest celebration.

Photos are allowed only after a granted permission from the locals (the Kalashi are a very private society).

Travel to: Pakistan (Birir Valley). The Kalashi inhabit three valleys, however the Birir Valley is the most traditional one and the only one celebrating this pagan tradition.

Other holidays on this date: National Dumpling Day (USA)

27 September: Meskel (Ethiopia)

The annual feast celebrates the recovery of the True Cross (parts from the actual cross upon which Jesus was crucified) by the Roman Empress Saint Helena in the IV C. The holiday is observed in accordance with the Ethiopian calendar (which derives from the Egyptian calendar), falling on September 27th or 28th in leap years. This is one of the largest and most important holidays in the country. The day has been observed for more than 1600 years (as a Pagan celebration in the past).

According to a legend, Queen Helena had a dream in which was ordered to make a huge bonfire. She was told the smoke from the fire will show her the way to the long-lost True Cross. And so, she did. The smoke did show her where the relic had been buried. It is believed that Queen Helena gave parts of the cross to all Orthodox churches and parts of it were transported to Ethiopia.

The day is celebrated with lots of liturgical services, singing and dancing. The locals visit churches and burn incense sticks. On the street - crowds cheer to parading floats decorated as biblical themes, and processions of boys and girls carrying huge crosses and torches adorned with olive leaves.

In the evening, a huge bonfire of firewood decorated with a cross made of daisies is lit by the Patriarch of the Ethiopian Church. The smoke from the daisies can be seen for miles. It is very important in which direction the burning woods collapse – north, east, south or west – it is significant for the harvest season if it will be plentiful or not. Locals, dressed in traditional white robes, use charcoals from the remains of the fire to draw crosses on their foreheads.

Many people gather with their families for a festive meal which includes the traditional flatbread called injera.

The Gurage people which are an ethnic group in Ethiopia celebrate Meskel a bit different - they add another custom – the grown up children who had moved away should bring to their parents a bull or a goat to be slaughtered. Those who fail to do that are considered to have failed the family. The animal is killed by the Head of the household. What is important is that the bull/goat must fall on its right side after being slaughtered (or at least turned to its right side afterwards). The meat is distributed to each member of the family and is cooked in a variety of ways.

The Pagan background of the holiday is that it coincides with the end of the heavy rain season when all food supplies fall short. In the past, Meskel may have been celebrated as the end of the winter and beginning of the plentiful Spring season. Also, a particular bird appears only during this holiday – the "Yemeskel Wof".

Religious belief, spiritual and non-spiritual chants, lots of delicious local food and drinks – this is Meskel in Ethiopia.

Meskel is on the UNESCO List of Intangible Cultural Human Heritage.

Travel to: Ethiopia (Amba-Geshen Mountains). It is believed that part of the True Cross was brought to Ethiopia from Egypt and is held in the Geshen Mariam Monastery.

Huge celebrations are held in the capital city of Addis Ababa – around Meskel Square.

Other holidays on this date: National Chocolate Milk Day (USA)

28 September: Manit Day (Marshall Islands)

Manit is a word which locals use to describe their cultural heritage and customs. The festival held on the last Friday in September every year, aims to preserve the history and craftsmanship of the indigenous people, known to have been skilled boat builders and navigators prior to the arrival of the Europeans in the late XIXth C. With their arrival, the Marshallese adopted many Western habits – including the one to cover their bare bodies with more than hand-made skirts woven of native materials, usually hibiscus leaves.

During the festival, huge displays show original Marshallese artefacts. Many food stalls and booths sell handcrafted merchandise, traditional food and drinks, coconut oil products, hand soaps and laundry detergents. The Marshallese are known for their handmade woven baskets, fans, hats, wall hangings, purses, mats and more - all made using natural products like coconut, pandana leaves and likajir shells.

The festivities include colourful parades, canoe races, craft fairs and workshops, storytelling, songs, singing and dancing, as well as traditional contests – coconut husking and basket weaving.

The most important word in Marshallese is "yokwe" - it means "hello", "bye" and..." love".

Travel to: Marshall Islands (Majuro Atoll). The festivities are held near the Alele Museum.
Other holidays on this date: National Drink Beer Day (USA)

29 September: Roadkill Cook Off Festival (USA)
One of the quirkiest celebrations ever!

The rather odd festival is held annually over two days in the end of September. It was created in 1991 as a way to celebrate good food, provide entertainment and have fun.

The participants and visitors alike, are free to bring their own roadkill to cook and taste. This strange cuisine includes squirrel gravy, marinated bear, deer sausage, iguana nachos, baked rattlesnake, boar chips, porcupine skewers, BBQ racoon and more.

As a rule – the participants can bring and cook animals found dead on the side of the road...or at least that is how the festival was created... Years later, the rule was amended to: "animals must be of the sort that gets hit by a car".

Before the actual cook-off, all meat is inspected. The "chefs" are not allowed to precook any products in advance and the animals cannot be gutted on site.

The winner goes home $1 200 better off.

The fest offers stalls selling local crafts, live entertainment, Roadkill Cook-off Pageant and wine.

Many shops sell locally produced fresh vegetables and all kinds of meat.

The event attracts tens of thousands of people from around the country.

Travel to: USA (West Virginia). The festival is held in the city of Marlinton.
Other holidays on this date: National Coffee Day, Confucius day (USA), Whitebait Festival (UK, Essex)

30 September: Namsadang Dancers Festival (South Korea)
An annual festival of the performing arts, taking place over a week in late September/early October. The event was created in 2001 to maintain the local cultural heritage.

The village where the event takes place is a birthplace of the "namsadang" – groups of male dancers who represent the Korean folklore, sing, rope-dance and perform acrobatics and puppet shows. In the past, these artists travelled around the country to entertain – mainly using the open-air markets as a stage. The Namsadang is the country's oldest performing troupe (allegedly spontaneously formed in the 1900s).

In the past, they were considered "low class" and often had hard time making a living. That is probably the reason why they incorporated in their acts social remarks and pleads for a heavy reform, turning them into the voice of the public.

Today, they perform six different acts – "nori", featuring hat spinning, rope dancing, mask play and puppeteering.

The festival starts with a grand opening ceremony and drum bands, followed by a colourful street parade. It also features a traditional wedding ceremony, forest imagination playground, street performers, art and craft workshops, puppet shows, open-air evening concerts, fashion shows, folk games, soap bubble experience, agricultural experience, comedy routines, street theater actors performing historical scenes that can last for hours, beautiful parade with traditional folklore dances (with colorful handmade fans) and more.

The festival ends with a spectacular closing ceremony.

Travel to: South Korea (Anseong). The event takes place at Leports Park. Don't miss the chance to visit the traditional market (including live animal market) in the city – the very first performing stage of the Namsadang troupe.

Other holidays on this date: National Ghost Hunting Day, Save Your Photos Day (USA), Vijayadasami (India)

... OCTOBER

Lunar Calendar: A calendar based on the phases of the Moon – unlike the Gregorian calendar which is based on the movement of the Earth around the Sun. The most well-known lunar calendar is the Chinese.

01 October: MassKara Festival (Philippines)

The name of the festival comes not only from "Masquerade" but also is a combination of words – "Mass" in the meaning of "a large group of people" and "cara" - the Spanish word for "face" – hence MassKara.

This is a heartwarming and beautiful event, known as "The Festival of Smiles" because it was created in times of crisis.

In 1980, the price of sugar cane which was the main source of income to the island (the area is known as the "sugar bowl" of the region), dropped very low due to the introduction of sugar substitutes like the corn syrup from the USA. The year was catastrophic for the local economy, but this was not the only reason for local artists and government officials to create a festival to boost the spirit of the people. In the same year, an inter-island ferry carrying many locals collided with a tanker and sank. 700 people died in the accident.

Ever since that year, locals celebrate this 20-day extravaganza to share their culture, customs and creativity. They celebrate a festival to remind them that no matter what – they will stay strong and prevail all mishaps.

It is a very vibrant event with street dancing, dance group contests, sports events, concerts, food tastings, agricultural and garden shows, pig catching and pole climbing competitions, coconut-milk drinking and mask-making contests, MassKara Queen beauty pageant and Giant Puppets Parade. All participants are dressed in colourful costumes, wear huge wigs and exotic glittering masks, adorned with beads and feathers. Each mask weighs between 1 and 5kg and is made of durable fibreglass. The masked groups represent different guilds as well as all regions on the island. It is like the locals have combined the best from the Venice and Rio carnivals. Important to note is that all masks should be "smiling" – this is a general rule.

There is a market too, with many locals selling orchids and handcrafted items. Pop-up beer gardens can be found everywhere in the city. A must taste is the local delicacy – Chicken Inasal (charcoaled chicken).

Since 1980, the festival city is known as "The City of Smiles" and the smiling mask has become a symbol.

Travel to: Philippines (Negros Island). The masquerade is held in Bacolod City. Suitable accommodation is Sea Breeze Hotel on St Juan Str – it is the oldest in town and a great vantage point. Don't miss to visit The Ruins near Talisay City – once a sugar baron mansion, now the ruins of the former palace are turned into an open-air restaurant.

Other holidays on this date: World Vegetarian Day

02 October: Old Man's Day (England)

This is not a festival, nor a commemoration. Every year since the XVIth C, on this day the locals celebrate... a funeral gone terribly wrong!

The year was 1571. A local farmer - Matthew Wall, was thought to have died unexpectedly. A mourning service was organized and his body was put in a coffin. On the way to his funeral down Fleece Lane, the bearers slipped on wet leaves and dropped the coffin apparently jolting Mathew's body. Everyone froze in horror. However, more terrifying was a knock everyone heard from inside the coffin. It turned out that Mathew had woken up from a coma – very much alive and thumping the lid for dear life! Fellow villagers helped him out of the coffin and he lived happily for 24 more years! He married his fiancé who was at the "funeral".

When he did die years later, he left his money to the village and asked for the day of his non-burial to be remembered – hence the tradition.

According to his will, every year on October 2nd, the leaves on Fleet Street should be swept. The sweeper should be paid £1.

Today, however, it is the children from a local school who arrive armed with brooms. As they are not paid any money – they receive sweets as compensation for their labour. Which... doesn't make any sense as the slippery leaf was the very reason Matthew got to live for another 24 years?!

As per Matthews' will – the person who resides in his cottage should pay the amount of £1 to the vicar every year (maybe he included that just as an insurance that someone will sweep the leaves!)

Once the children sweep the street, locals gather in the churchyard round Mathew's grave to say prayers. The church bells are tolled as if for a funeral. Minutes later, the children sing songs and eat sweets, the church bells ringing as if for a wedding to celebrate Matthew's marriage (another stipulation in Matthew's will).

The odd celebration begins outside the Golden Fleece pub, where the vicar tells the story of the dramatic event.

Travel to: England (Hertfordshire). The non-burial celebration is held in the town of Braughing. Look out for Matthew Wall's simple gravestone in the churchyard, towards the East End.

Other holidays on this date: National Custodial Worker Day (USA)

03 October: Autumn Eve (South Korea)

Autumn Eve is a harvest festival celebrated in South and North Korea. For South Korea, it is one of the largest events in the year.

It is observed annually, on the 15th day of the 8th lunar month (on a day of a full moon). According to the Gregorian calendar, the 3-day feast falls in mid-late September or the beginning of October.

Allegedly, the custom dates to the 57 B.C. (or 935 A.D.) and was a shamanic ritual with priests acting as intermediaries between the spirits of ancestors and humans.

Today, Koreans celebrate by visiting their ancestral hometowns and reuniting with their families. They perform worship rituals early in the morning. In the afternoon, they visit the tombs of their ancestors to trim and clean the graves. They make offerings of food and drinks.

The Koreans don't believe that their deceased relatives are really "dead" – they think that the spirits roam freely and protect their descendants. That is why they make offerings of special food, willing to please and honour the spirits. The meals are arranged in strict order on the table: rice and soup are placed on the north while fruits and vegetables are on the south, meat is on the west and rice cakes and drinks are on the east side.

Traditional food during the days of the festival is small rice cakes called songpyeon (colourful dumplings stuffed with sesame seeds, beans, cinnamon, nuts and honey arranged upon piles of pine needles and steamed) and rice wines which are believed to enhance men's stamina. The shape of the rice cakes is significant to the Koreans and is tied to the local mythology. The dumplings are round-shaped, but after the stuffing is put – they resemble half-moon. The two forms are important to the locals and that is why they gather with their families to eat half-moon rice cakes (symbol of good fortune) under the full moon (symbol of unity) in the sky.

The Koreans exchange small gifts – usually associated with food as Autumn Eve is a harvest festival. Typical gifts are a jar of honey, red ginseng root, dried salted fish, rare wild mushrooms, dried fruit and other.

Traditional games are played during the days of the festival, such as archery, ssireum (a wrestling game with over 5000 years of history), cards, tug-of-war; chicken fight - two teams of participants who bend their left knees, the goal being to knock off the opponent using only that knee.

In some areas, women wear traditional costumes and perform a celebratory circle dance while men dress as cows or turtles and visit random houses accompanied by a band of musicians. In other areas, the locals enjoy playing swinging games and catapulting off a see-saw.

Travel to: South Korea. Although the whole country celebrates, some of the most significant places to be are: Changdeokgung Palace and Huwan, and Jongmyo Shrine in Seoul, Korean Folk Village near the city of Yongin.

Other holidays on this date: Techies Day, Virus Appreciation Day, Day of German Unity (Germany)

04 October: Blak Markets (Australia)

The Blak Markets are held every first Sunday of the month throughout the year. Their purpose is to popularize the arts and crafts of Aboriginal and Torres Strait Islander people.

The markets feature not only handmade goods for sale but also authentic entertainment in the form of traditional dances, plays and songs.

The locals set numerous stalls offering indigenous arts and crafts, such as jewellery, clothes, woven baskets, amulets, skin care with all-natural ingredients, outstanding bracelets and necklaces made of beads and shells.

The visitors have the chance to participate in many of the workshops offering knowledge and hands-on experience on boomerang and spear making, shell carving, weaving and traditional Aboriginal cooking.

Blak Market day also features smoking ceremonies, whale ceremonies and healing ceremonies.

Keeping the festive spirit are traditional bands performing acoustic music intertwined with ritualistic chants.

A huge part of the local cultural heritage is also the food – many food stalls line along the market and offer mouth-watering traditional Aboriginal delicacies like Emu sausage rolls with freshly picked thyme, kangaroo BBQ and red wine pie, shellfish with lime sauce, crocodile on a stick and grilled fish with herbs. A special Catch`n`Cook event teaches the participants how to catch and cook their own lunch.

The Blak Market event is held in many cities in Australia with the sole purpose to preserve the ancient culture of the Aboriginal people.

Travel to: Australia (Sydney). One of the best Blak Markets is held on Bare Island – the tiny island spotted by Captain Cook and described as "small bare island" in his journal is also used as a setting in Mission Impossible 2.

Other holidays on this date: National Frappe Day (USA), Grape Harvest Festival (France)

05 October: Golden Eagle Festival (Mongolia)

The art (or sport) of falconry is first mentioned in the Bronze Age (2500 B.C.).

The Golden Eagle Festival is a unique event, held only in this very western part of Mongolia. A place, where locals still use eagles for hunting their prey. It is held annually, since 1999, in the first week of October and is a competition of agility, speed and accuracy – both for the birds and for their trainers (the Kazakh hunters). This is the biggest gathering of eagles and eagle hunters in the world.

The festival is a fantastic way to show the hunters` traditional culture (the nomadic tribe had depended mainly on eagle hunting in the past). The Mongolian nomads are one of the world`s last enduring horse-based nomadic cultures. Passed from generation to generation, the skill of eagle-hunting (falconry) is only preserved among this community in Mongolia. The event is also a wonderful opportunity for visitors to join in the celebration of a unique cultural heritage.

The festival is recognized as a UNESCO World Heritage Cultural Event.

It starts with an opening ceremony and a parade of the hunters riding on beautifully groomed horses. They are all dressed in full regalia. The traditional Kazakh dress is made of cloth, animal skin and fur and is decorated with birds` beaks, animal horns and hooves, horsehair and jewellery. The cloth used is leather, cotton, wool, silk and velvet dyed in distinct colours using natural dyes (for example pomegranate for orange).

Golden Eagles compete in various categories such as: catching a fox`s skin dragged behind a horse and returning it to the trainer, catching a running hare, a camel race, archery contest, typical Kazakh games like picking up a coin on the ground and carrying a dead goat while riding a horse. A highlight is the goatskin tug-of-war – performed while the two contestants gallop their horses.

The event is accompanied by traditional Kazakh crafts, music and food and the end is marked by a live fox hunt with the winning eagle. For a better understanding of this custom, visitors can ride on a horse alongside the nomad hunters while they hunt.

Travel to: Mongolia (Bayan-Ölgii Province in the skirts of the Altai Mountain). There is big celebration in the capital of the region – Ölgii with a beautiful parade down the city center.

Other holidays on this date: National Do Something Good Day (USA)

06 October: The Candle Festival (Malta)

The annual three-day festival takes place in the beginning of October, in one of the oldest cities in Malta. The event was created to celebrate Citta Vittoriosa – the former name of the city. The aim – to highlight the historic and architectural charm of the former Maltese capital.

The Candle Festival is part of Birgufest and takes place on a Saturday night. The winding cobblestone streets and hidden staircases are lit with the soft glow of thousands and thousands of candles, turning the coastal town into the most romantic spot on the island.

Thousands of people roam the streets of this waterfront gem, admiring the boats decked out in string lights, the songs of a saddened woman and the small Mediterranean balconies overhanging the streets and sprinkled with candles.

The festival features historical re-enactments, street parades and processions, free entrance to many of the landmarks including historical buildings and ancient churches, art exhibitions, modern and classical concerts.

Local merchants sell handmade ceramics painted in honeycomb yellow and Mediterranean blue.

The aroma of sweet pastry-wrapped dates, candyfloss, burgers and sweets fills the air...

This is a festival to all senses!

Travel to: Malta (Birgu). The tiny Medieval town is a former capital of Malta and one of the oldest settlements on the island.

Other holidays on this date: World Smile Day, Come and Take It Day, Mad-Hatter Day (USA), Boat Racing Festival (Laos).

07 October: Albuquerque International Balloon Fiesta (USA)

An event to inflate the imagination! This colourful panorama, created in 1972 to celebrate a birthday of a local radio station, takes place annually in the beginning of October.

Colourful hot air balloons of various shapes and sizes sprinkle the sky for whole nine days.

More than 1 000 balloons fly up before the morning sun, illuminated by the blue-green flame of propane burners. It is like an awakening of nature and its fantastic colour palette. Red, green, blue, yellow, dotted, spotted, striped and plain balloons lift up before the eyes of the aweing spectators.

All balloons are launched at once which makes it a breath-taking and unforgettable moment for participants and visitors alike. Some balloons are hand painted by artists, others come in unique shapes such as Yoda or Darth Vader.

Once the balloons reach their height – they stand static and the view from the ground is absolutely stunning.

A few events accompany the magnificent view of ascending hot air balloons:

- Dawn Patrol – a few hot air balloons with lighting systems fly before dawn. This is beautiful to watch but also helps the other contestants to calculate the wind speed.

- "Glowdeo" – balloons standing static on the ground and glowing in various colours. This category is for the unusual-shaped balloons.

- Mass Ascensions – the balloons launch to the sky in two waves. And yes, there are traffic officers to coordinate each ascending.

- The Gas Balloon Race – contestants with special long-distance balloons race to see who will go farthest. A participant reportedly landed in Canada.

- A pilot competition – pilots have to reach a tall pole (without colliding with other balloons) and get an envelope containing a key. The winner gets a brand-new car!

And not only that, but all visitors are allowed to walk among the balloons as they inflate on the festival grounds every morning before lift-off!

No wonder this festival is the largest and most beautiful hot air balloon event in the world and broke a record in the Guinness book!

Million visitors come here every year to share that experience.

Travel to: USA (New Mexico). The event takes place in Albuquerque (in fact... over it).

Other holidays on this date: International Frugal Fun Day, World Card Making Day (USA), National Wine Day (Moldova)

08 October: Renaissance Fair (USA)

This annual festival is held for nine weeks in October and November and claims to be the nations' largest Renaissance fair, attracting over half a million visitors. The event was created in 1974 with small theatre performances and locals selling their merchandise on blankets.

Today, the festival features 25 stages and 400 shops with artisan crafts, tarot card reading, local food and drink delicacies, Renaissance clothing and weapons, and more. Singers and dance groups perform and entertain the visitors with Medieval sounds and moves. Music bands play on bagpipes, fiddles and harps.

Numerous performers dressed as noble gents and corseted ladies roam the festival grounds to entertain the public with tricks and wit. For those who really want to travel back in time and feel "Medieval" – there are many workshops where one can try glassblowing, armour forging, pottery making and coin minting. There are even a few wedding chapels!

For the little ones, there are face painting events, costume parties, fun rides, a zoo where one can ride an elephant or a camel, hair braiding and more.

Typical food to be found on the festival grounds is roasted turkey leg, cheesecake on a stick, kettle corn, sausage on a stick, bacon on a stick, beef stew, blood sausage, soup in a bread bowl and other delicacies.

Each of the nine weeks of the event has a different theme – that means that everything in terms of appearance has to shift – the decorations, the performers and their costumes, the food and the music. Some of the themes are:

- Octoberfest – with focus on the draft beers, polka music and dances, and of course, the traditional Octoberfest clothing for ladies and gents!
- 1001 Dreams – flying fairies, magic dust falling from the trees, wizards with big hats and elves hiding pots of gold. This theme is a colorful kaleidoscope of the imagination.
- All Hallows Eve – a Halloween, celebrated Medieval style.
- Pirate Adventure – Ahoy! Captains with hooks and sailors conquer the fairground.
- Roman Bacchanal – everything Roman is permitted. Even a spaghetti competition!
- Barbarian Invasion – inviting all brave warriors to join forces in one of the many battle competitions available during that week.
- Heroes and Villains – re-enactment of stories from the past involving mighty heroes and the darkest villains.
- Highland Fling – Scottish theme. Imagine kilts, bagpipes and lots of singing and dancing.
- Celtic Christmas – an alternative way to celebrate Christmas – involves many carolers, Christmas lights and decorations, Candy Cane hunt and more.

The highlight of the festival is the re-enactment of a Medieval Joust which is performed with great attention to detail – the knights and the horses are dressed in matching armour and the weapons used are authentic.

Another show of interest is the Birds of Prey – eagles, vultures, hawks and owls perform tricks as instructed by their trainers.

The Grand Royal Finale includes lots of fireworks.

Note: The dress code for all visitors is: XVIth C!

Travel to: USA (Texas). The event is held in a dedicated park – New Market Village, near Todd Mission. The place is a recreated Medieval English township. The fairground features a camping site.

Other holidays on this date: Clergy Appreciation Day (USA)

09 October: Yom Kippur (Israel)

Yom Kippur is widely celebrated in Israel and within all Jewish communities around the world. Known as "The Day of Atonement", it is one of the most anticipated and holiest holidays for the Israelis. The day is observed ten days after the Jewish New Year (Rosh Hashanah) and falls on a day in late September or early October. It begins at sundown and ends at sundown on the next day.

The holiday is the culmination of the "Ten Days of Repentance", meaning that the people whose fate has not been decided on the Jewish New Year (the righteous receive a reward and the sinners get a punishment), had ten days to confess their sins for the previous year and ask for forgiveness. According to Judaism, on Yom Kippur judgement is passed on each person for the coming year.

This is the day when Moses came down from Mount Sinai giving the tablet with the Ten Commandments to the Israeli, forgiving them for their sins.

In the past, Yom Kippur was the only day when a High Priest would enter the inner premises of the Temple, in which the Ark of the Torah was kept.

The people visit services in synagogues five times on this day, some choose to fast all day abstaining from both food and drink (usually having a light breakfast before the first service). Others, have Sabbath meals with cream cheese and salmon bagel, stews, braided sweet bread called "challah"; noodle and raisin pudding.

As Yom Kippur is treated like a Sabbath (a strict day of rest), all businesses close, meaning no open restaurants nor any transportation (including taxis). TV and radio stations` programs are also suspended for the day.

A few things observed on this day by the religious people which are worth mentioning:

- Wearing leather shoes, perfume or accessories are not allowed as they are associated with wealth, nor is the washing of any part of the body (including teeth). The colour for this day is white as it symbolizes purity.
- A Kaparot ritual is performed in some Ashkenazi communities – live chicken is swung over a member of the family in a belief that it will take away his/her sins. Then, after a special prayer, the chicken is slaughtered and sold or given to the poor.
- The people ask forgiveness from friends and family, or from anyone they have might have offended in the past year.
- There is a special prayer cancelling all vows made during the past year (Kol Nidre). This way, people are excused for not being able to keep a given vow.

The end of Yom Kippur is marked by the sound of a Shofar (ram`s horn) from the synagogues.

Travel to: Israel. The whole country literally shuts down for the holiday, but the best places to be is Jerusalem and Tel Aviv.

Other holidays on this date: National Chess Day, Curious Events Day (USA), Mbantua Festival (Australia)

10 October: Maroon Day (Suriname)

Although being celebrated for decades, this holiday became official only in 2011 and is observed on October 10th.

Maroon Day celebrates the historic and cultural heritage of the Maroon people (from Latin American Spanish "cimarrón" meaning "fugitive") – African slaves who escaped from working on the plantations. They joined with indigenous tribes and formed independent settlements in Central and South America.

One of the tribes which settled in Suriname – Ndyuka, signed a treaty with the Dutch in 1760 declaring them "free people". The treaty also defined the territorial rights of the Maroon people in the country (Suriname received its independence from the Netherlands only in 1975).

Today, the Maroon people live in isolated villages deep in the Suriname rain forest, surrounded only by flocks of parrots, Capuchin monkeys and camps of Brazilian gold-diggers.

The most important men in the tribe are the Chief and the Shaman who treats all medicinal problems with chanting and potions brewed from leaves, vines and tree barks.

The day is observed with wreath-laying ceremonies and a traditional 'prodowaka' procession. Members of all Maroon tribes parade along the street wearing their celebratory colourful clothes, playing the drums, singing and dancing.

The streets are adorned with exotic flowers, there are many food stalls offering local delicacies and tropical fruits, local women sell handmade clothes in typical for their tribe colourful patterns.

The Maroon officials hold speeches and share the story of the tribes and the how they fought for their independence and their lands.

Traditional food on this day is the homemade cassava bread (made from yuca root) and kasiri (a root beer).

Travel to: Suriname (Santigron – a multi-tribe city). Large festivities are held in the capital city of Paramaribo where local politicians hold speeches.

Other holidays on this date: National Cake Decorating Day (USA), Party Foundation Day (North Korea)

11 October: Signal Festival (Czech Republic)

Since 2013, the city celebrates a four-day long festival of video mapping and light installations in its historic centre. The event is considered as one of the best light art festivals in Europe, attracting more than half a million visitors every year. The show is held in mid-October.

The participants/light designers, illuminate the night sky over the majestic buildings in the Old quarter and display the latest and upcoming light technologies.

Audio-visual art and complex installations stimulate every human sense and take the visitors on an unforgettable journey through a kaleidoscope of colourful lights. Some of the shows even require 3-D glasses.

Fluffy clouds descending over narrowed streets, all-seeing eyes mounted on top of historical buildings, optical illusions, natural phenomena and an enchanted forest in the middle of the city square are just a few of the magical performances taking place. Historical landmarks are turned into canvases of modern artists who paint with lights.

The festival blends innovative technologies with modern art.

The organizers aim to turn the event into a fun techno-art hub for new talents, that is why there are many workshops on audio-visual techniques, multimedia, animation and more.

There is a daytime program for kids projecting topics from the Czech history.

Travel to: Czech Republic (Prague) - Old Town Square, Hybernia Palace, The Fruit Market, Kampa.

Other holidays on this date: It`s My Party Day (USA), Ryusei Matsuri (Japan)

12 October: Día de las Culturas (Costa Rica)

The holiday, known as Día de la Raza in many Latin countries and Columbus Day in the USA, commemorates Christopher Columbus`s journeys to the Americas and the merging of European with American culture. In 1502, on his fourth journey to the newly discovered continent, Columbus arrived in Costa Rica.

The celebrations are held annually on October 12th.

The locals celebrate not only the great explorer but also the blending of European and American language, people and culture which have shaped the Costa Rican society the way it is today.

The day was celebrated as Columbus Day but changed its name to Dia de las Culturas in 1994. That is because some locals felt like they celebrated the colonization of their country and not the cultural diversity of the nation.

An interesting fact is that after the discovery of the landlocked between Nicaragua and Panama country, the Spaniards, were given so much gold by the natives, that they called the land Costa Rica – the "rich coast".

The day is much anticipated and celebrated with great pride.

The indigenous people put on their traditional costumes, recite the national anthem, dance and sing songs, while the communities of European, African or Asian descent, dress up in their own traditional costumes, highlighting and celebrating their difference. Natives share their national food with everyone.

The holiday is about promoting respect and tolerance among people of various cultural background and sharing customs, food and history.

As Columbus Day is observed throughout the Americas - the holiday unites all Spanish-speaking cultures in celebration with music, dances, parades, piñatas, games and more. It is a huge party – with "beauty queens" on richly decorated floats, marching bands in bright costumes, steel drum performances, very colourfully dressed and extremely coordinated dancers and lots of fireworks.

Travel to: Costa Rica (Limon province). Visit Café Milagro in Manuel Antonio Park – coastal area with rainforest, white-sand beaches and coral reefs (the owners grow and brew their own coffee). Porto Limon is known to throw the best parties marking Dia de las Culturas (lasting whole 12 days!).

The holiday is celebrated in Argentina, Mexico, Uruguay, Chile, Honduras, Ecuador, Guatemala and Venezuela.

Other holidays on this date: National Freethought Day, Columbus Day (USA)

13 October: Expo Tequila (Mexico)

Started in the year 2000, this is the biggest and grandest exhibition of the traditional Mexican drink – the tequila. The world-famous drink made from blue agave plant was called mezcal brandy and agave wine before it got its final name – Tequila (named after a small town near Guadalajara). It was used as a spiritual drink (booster) in ancient rituals more than 2000 years ago.

Expo Tequila is held annually over three days in October.

The event showcases over 300 different versions of the fiery drink produced by 40 of the local distilleries, plethora of tastings, talks and workshops, as well as live Mariachi, folklore ballet, dances and mouth-watering Mexican food.

The many tasting classes urge participants to distinguish the taste, colour and aroma of a good tequila.

A drink bearing the name "tequila" has to be up to very high standards and has to be produced in a certain way, with certain ingredients and in certain areas of Mexico.

The best tequila contains 100% agave and that is clearly marked on the label. If the drink contains less percentage of the blue plant – it is called mixto.

There are five types of tequila:
- White Tequila (Bianco, Silver) – aged less than 60 days with pure agave taste;
- Gold Tequila (Joven, Oro) – the best for shots (and a headache), this type is often mixed with caramel and sugars;

- Reposado Tequila (Rested) – 3 to 9 months aged in wooden casks adding a distinct oak flavour;
- Añejo Tequila (Old) – aged minimum 1 year in oak or used bourbon barrels – that is where they get the dark colour. They are some of the most expensive on the market.
- Extra Añejo Tequila – aged 4 years and more.

Fun fact: Jose Cuervo was the first to commercialize tequila.

Travel to: Mexico (Tijuana). The event takes place at Avenida Revolucion.
Other holidays on this date: World Egg Day

14 October: Galungan and Kuningan (Indonesia)

This is a holiday celebrated twice a year, because the Balinese calendar has 210 days. It is a celebration of the battle of good against evil and takes place in early Spring and in October (or early November). The festivities start on Galungan day and end on Kuningan day which is 10 days later.

For the whole duration of the religious festival, the entire island is decorated with giant bamboo poles (curved at the top) adorned with plenty of fruit, flowers and fresh coconut leaves. These poles, representing all harvest fruits on the island, are erected on the right side in front of each Balinese home. Small bamboo altars for offerings are placed next to the poles.

The communal feast starts with slaughtering of pigs and cooking them into a ritualistic spicy dish. Traditional food prepared for the celebration are colourful rice cakes and cooked bananas. The locals, dressed in traditional costumes, visit family shrines and temples, bringing overflowing baskets of food offerings to share after the prayers (some make offerings of food and flowers, others – of live chickens).

Typical for the holiday is the Ngelawang ceremony – a dancing beast known as "barong" visits homes to chase away everything evil. The residents perform rituals and dance before the disguised dancing beast. After the ritual, he gives them a piece of his fur as a keepsake.

The celebrations end on the 10th day when locals return to their hometowns and spend the day with family and relatives. Again, they visit family temples and shrines, but this time they make special offerings of yellow turmeric rice (yellow is the colour of Vishnu). Sacred dances and rituals are performed in all Hindu temples.

The historical background of the celebration: The Hindu God of thunder (Indra) fought the Balinese King, who denied his subjects to practice Hinduism and destroyed all their temples bringing plaque to the land. The King was so mighty, that Indra had to descend from the sky to overcome him. While under siege, he tried to escape turning into a stone, a wild boar and a statue. The King managed to escape covering his footsteps, but Indra killed him with a magic arrow. The site where he died allegedly turned into a water spring.

After the victory of good over evil, the Balinese were free to worship Hinduism. The bamboo poles erected on the holiday represent the fight for Hinduism and wisdom.

The day of the victory is known as Gulingan.

However, the locals were not convinced that The King was dead – they thought he had tricked the God, turning himself into a tree or something else. That is why, the news that he was defeated, and dead were announced 10 days later – on Kuningan (literally meaning "to announce").

The Balinese people believe that during this festive period, the Gods and the spirits of the ancestors return to earth to be entertained. During the festival days, locals run up and down the streets pushing overflowing carts of offerings to the Gods.

One can also encounter the odd ritual of a village elder seemingly "stabbing" himself with a ceremonial dagger while in a trance-like state.

Travel to: Indonesia (Bali Island). The village of Kuta is a great place to take part in the celebration.

Other holidays on this date: Midwest Witches Ball (USA)

15 October: Celtic Colors (Canada)

This festival is held over nine days in October every year since 1997 and is a deep dive in the living traditional culture of the area. The setting is in the backdrop of beautiful yellow, red and brown trees and a magnificent lake – the largest saltwater reservoir in the country.

A music event at its core, Celtic Colors is a showcase of all things Celtic. It was inspired by the XIXth C settlers from Scotland and Ireland and influenced by the local Aboriginal people.

The fest features a load of musical acts – from folkloric troupes to world-known artists, Gaelic singing, fiddlers, accordion and bagpipe groups, Celtic dances, story-telling and more.

Visitors can enjoy a visit to a Farmers Market offering homegrown herbs and golden honey or take part in the various workshops and open-air art performances, including a square dance.

The festival also features visual art and light installation exhibitions and evening ceilidhs – social gatherings with Celtic music and dances.

Travel to: Canada (Cape Breton Island). The festival moves around the island and is held at a different community every year.

Other holidays on this date: Teacher`s Day (Brazil), Global Handwashing Day

16 October: Niihama Taiko Ritual (Japan)

Taking place on October 16th -18th every year, the sacred ritual with a history of more than 300 years, derives from a harvest festival and is full of energy and good vibes. It is also a competition of power and strength.

The event is dedicated to the traditional and ancient instrument - the Taiko – a drum, which comes in a variety of sizes, used in the past by samurai in battles. Taiko is used in ceremonies and rituals in shrines, as well as in traditional plays and dances.

The Taiko festival features representatives from 47 neighbourhoods (each group consists of around 150 men), carrying heavy floats shaped as gigantic drums (each neighbourhood sponsors one float). The colourful and quite noisy parade slithers through the streets while crowds cheer for the men bouncing the sometimes weighing up to 2 tons floats.

The parading floats are mounted on platforms supported by huge wooden poles which rest on the shoulders of the carriers. On top of the platforms, groups of men dance and perform different acts sometimes jumping so lightly from one pole to another as if they are dancing in the air. The actual floats are decorated with gold thread embroidery in the shape of dragons, wild birds or historical characters and can reach up to 5 meters in height. They are beautiful in the daytime, but magnificent at night when they are illuminated by the lights of numerous paper lanterns.

A highlight of the event for sure is the "kakikurabe" – a battle between the floats by lifting and throwing them in the air – showing the strength and dexterity of the bearers. The "fighting" is accompanied by the monotonous beat of thousands of taiko drums.

On this event, the police show up in riot gear due to the amount of sake enjoyed by the participants beforehand.

Tip: While enjoying the magic of the traditional taiko – don`t miss to taste the typical dish to Niihama – Fuguzaku – puffer-fish with green onions and fish liver, seasoned with local spices.

Travel to: Japan (Shikoku Island). The festival takes place in the small seaside town of Niihama.

Other holidays on this date: World Egg Day, World Food Day

17 October: International Festival of Mayan Culture (Mexico)

This is one of the largest cultural events in the country inspired by the rituals and traditions of the pre-Hispanic civilization.

The festival, held annually over a week in October showcases the rich heritage of the Mayan whose main belief is that the universe and our planet co-exist in the same energy field and are in constant dialogue.

Each edition of the festival has a different theme/concept. Every year there is a guest state and a guest country to highlight the cultural interaction. However, the main purpose of the event is to preserve and show to the world the unique history of the ancient Mayan people and their descendants who inhabit the Yucatan Peninsula.

The festival was created on December 21st, 2012 – a date, not chosen at random but coinciding with the beginning of a new cycle in accordance with the ancient Mayan solar calendar.

The breath-taking opening ceremony takes place in the backdrop of some of the magnificent monuments of Mayan culture such as Chichen Itza.

The event features conferences, exhibitions, artistic performances, talks and workshops with main focus – deciphering the message left by the Mayan.

Must see are the authentic ceremonies, ritualistic dances, flamenco performances, magic and circus acts, theatre plays, cooking demonstrations, encounters with Mayan shamans, traditional ball games (Pok`Ta Pok), discussions about Mayan medicinal plants, Yucatan folk art and costumes workshops, literature readings and more.

Throughout the festival, visitors enjoy encounters with Mayan descendants dressed up in traditional attire, adorned with flowers, beads, feathers and symbols from the Mayan mythology.

The festival takes place in and around the town in various historical areas such as archeological sites, monuments, parks, museums and haciendas.

And the best part of the event are the food stalls selling magnificent Mexican food like hot chocolate (the Maya were the first to roast and use cacao seeds to make a drink), guacamole, Poc Chuc (slow roasted salty pork meat with orange sauce, coriander and sautéed onions), corn tortillas and tamales with variety of cooked meats and freshly chopped veggies, fiery salsa dishes, scrambled eggs, beans and more. Of course, the juicy dishes are accompanied by a glass of traditional Margarita or ice-cold water infused with hibiscus flower. Horchata is another traditional drink which is ideal to enjoy the scorching summer temperatures – rice milk with almonds and cinnamon.

Travel to: Mexico (Mérida). The city is in the middle of the ancient Mayan Empire. Merida is also the gateway to Uxmal and the Puuc Zone - area known for its rich indigenous history and fantastic haciendas.

Other holidays on this date: Finno-Ugrian Days (Estonia), Edge Day, Sweetest Day (UK)

18 October: Tarnanthi Aboriginal Festival (Australia)

Tarnanthi, meaning "to rise" in the local indigenous language, is a contemporary art festival showcasing the rich cultural and historical heritage of the Kaurna people (part of the Aborigines and Torres Strait Islanders) – the oldest living ancient culture on the continent. Started in 2015, it is held annually over ten days in October.

The etymology of the name refers to "light, appearing light", which is related to a new beginning. The event aims to preserve the arts and crafts of indigenous people and to share them with the rest of the world.

The festival welcomes and provides a stage to all Aboriginal and Torres Strait Islander artists and performers willing to present their work.

The event starts at the local Sea Port with traditional smoking ceremony. Afterwards, the city is revealed to the visitors as an ancient home to the indigenous Australians by sound, light and visual effect shows.

Parks, streets, museums, city halls, factories, botanical gardens, art galleries and universities turn into exhibition venues.

Some of the works exhibited include beautifully handcrafted and painted ceramics, clay figurines and totems, ancient spears and warrior shields made of wood and leather, handwoven textile works and grass vessels, indigenous paintings, Aboriginal storytelling about ancient totem sites, ancestry, plants and hunting, Barangaroo Ngangamay ceremony, indigenous string games, motorcar and bush mechanics exhibition, beads embroidery and much more.

The festival presents the unique craftsmanship and culture of the indigenous people as a legacy, to be shared and cherished by all people.

A rare privilege is that some of the works are for sale.

Travel to: Australia (South Australia). The festival takes place in and around the city of Adelaide on the lands of the former Kaurna territory.

Other holidays on this date: Mother`s Day (Argentina), Persons Day (UK)

19 October: Diwali Festival of Light (India & world)

The Festival of Light is celebrated annually over five days in October/November and is one of the most important and loved festivals in the Hindu year. It is an event to celebrate prosperity as well as the victory of good over evil, light over darkness.

Allegedly, Diwali derived from an ancient Harvest Festival – it coincides with the end of the cropping season and the time to hold bountiful celebrations, offering praises to the gods for granting good harvest.

The name Diwali or Deepawali comes from the row of clay lamps the people light ("deepa" = clay lamp, "avali" = row) to symbolize the inner light that protects from spiritual darkness.

Preparations for the holiday include cleaning and decorating houses with flowers, shopping for new clothes and preparing lots of sweets and traditional meals to share.

On the first day, the Goddess of Wealth and Prosperity – Laxmi, is worshipped. The people clean their houses and shop for gold.

On the second day, the women make beautiful flower patterns (Rangoli) in front of their homes to welcome the deity. They use coloured rice, flower petals and flour for the design.

On the third day, which is the most important one –locals visit temples for prayers and then share mouth-watering feasts and enjoy fireworks displays. Oil lamps are lit inside the houses and on the streets to welcome Lakshmi and her blessings for health and good fortune.

The fourth day is the first day of the New year. Families and friends exchange gifts for good luck.

On the last day, brothers visit their married sisters, who welcome them in their homes with festive meals.

Playing cards is a traditional activity during Diwali. The legend has it that on this day, the Goddess Parvati played dice with her husband Shiva and decreed that whoever gambled on Diwali night would prosper in the upcoming year.

Traditional food for the festival are various sweet pastries – it is common to share them with family and neighbours for good fortune.

People exchange small gifts and eat sweets – dried fruits, cakes and diyas (cookies in the shape of an oil lamp). They gather at the temples to pray and enjoy the many street parades with colourfully decorated floats on which artists perform different scenes representing gods and goddesses from the Hindu tradition.

On Diwali, the Indian border patrols offer traditional sweets to their counterparts on the Pakistani border – as a gesture of good will and in the tradition of the festival spirit.

Diwali is a festival of emotions and a celebration of flavours!

Travel to: The holiday is celebrated in India, Guyana, Suriname, Trinidad and Tobago, Malaysia, Singapore, Fiji, Sri Lanka, Mauritius or Myanmar.

In India, Diwali is widely celebrated in the state of Kerala.

Other holidays on this date: Tihar Festival (Nepal)

20 October: Limon Festival (Costa Rica)

The annual two-week Carnaval de Limon was initiated in 1949 by a social activist who supported many initiatives including a Black Universal Improvement Association. Today, the event is considered as one of the most important cultural gatherings in the country. It starts in mid-October after Columbus Day (usually on the 12th).

The festival was created to unite the people of Costa Rica – from one side the Spaniards, from the other – the indigenous tribes and descendants to the African, Caribbean and Chinese settlers.

The Carnaval aims to show the best of the local culture mix as well as traditional music and dances.

This is an explosive display of energy and colours! Cheering crowds line the streets and welcome the parading dance troupes moving in the rhythm of Brazilian Samba and Latin Salsa. Followed by loud marching bands, the Beauty Queens wave to the visitors standing on huge floats decorated with effigies, flags, sparkling gems, feathers and painted tropical motifs. Men wearing gigantic dresses and huge handcrafted masks run around and interact with the public – they are known as "Mascaradas". The game they play is called "Rass`em" – the one with the biggest mask chases the other guys and whoever he catches, must put on the big mask and chase the others from the group. Sounds quite silly, but it is a lot of fun, having in mind the chase takes place amidst a colourful kaleidoscope of parade-goers.

Many "Chinamos" (small booths) offer local food delicacies like eschabeche de pesado (marinated fish), cola de chancho frita (fried pigtail), pan bon (sweet bread), rice and beans with coconut beans and chillies, Patacones (double fried plantains), cajeta (coconut fudge) and ale (a lemony drink).

In between the parades and the piping hot food, and refreshing drinks, the locals and visitors alike dance everywhere – on the streets, on stages, on platforms, in pubs and on the beach. There are parties on every corner of the coastal town and Reggae music sounds from almost every open house window.

So... forget all troubles and jump in the party!

Travel to: Costa Rica (Limón). The festival literally takes full control of the coastal city.

Other holidays on this date: 294th day of the year!

21 October: Fantasy Fest (USA)

Fantasy Fest was created in 1979 by a group of businessmen who wanted to attract more tourists during the winter months when most of the shops were closed with a hanging sign on the door "Gone fishing!". And so, they came up with the idea of a huge masquerade party as a warm-up to Halloween. It turned out to be huge success!

Over the years, the ten-day festival evolved to featuring more than 60 parties, street fairs, themed balls and the highlight – The Fantasy Fair Parade.

The visitors can immerse themselves in a fantasy world full of speaking trees, a marching lollipop guild, burlesque show, body painters, foggy evenings with re-enactments of heroic battles, glow show, circus, tiki party, zombie bike ride, heroes and villains marathon, jungle costume competitions, kinky carnival, tutu parade, pet masquerade, the smallest parade in the universe, drag queen contest, gay parade, headdress ball, toga party, bowties and birthday suits party, concerts, ukulele band parade, Festival King and Queen and much more.

The festival takes guests on a high-speed trip from the past, to the present and future, embracing them with a colourful mix of fairy and scary creatures.

It all starts with a Masquerade March from the local cemetery and finishes at the Fantasy Zone. The parading creatures stop at various pubs for refreshments.

The main event – the Fantasy Fest Parade, is on the next day. Over 50 richly decorated floats carry thousands of people wearing bright costumes and headdresses adorned with sparkling gems and feathers, dancing to the beat of Caribbean steel drums.

During the days of the event, more than 100 000 people visit the tiny island with only 25 000 residents.

How to participate: USA (Florida). The event takes place in Key West. The Fantasy Parade is on Duval Street.

Other holidays on this date: Dramathon (Scotland)

22 October: Ashura (Bahrain)

Ashura is observed annually on the tenth day of the month of Muharram (the first month on the Islamic calendar). Muharram itself means "forbidden", this is one of the holiest months of the year.

The first recorded outdoor procession on this day dates to 1891. A few other countries also mark the holiday, however, Bahrain is unique as it is the only Arab country in the Persian Gulf with Shia Muslim majority.

Ashura or the Day of Remembrance is a festival of mourning and commemorates the death of Imam Hussein in the battle of Karbala in 680 A.D. Imam Hussein was a grandson of the Prophet Mohammed.

During the whole month of Muharram, locals visit mosques and listen to various reading about the life and example of the Imam. It is a month for charity, so food and clothes are given to the poor, blood is also donated.

The National flag changes colours during the holy month and is transformed into a white-and-black flag. The so-called mourning flags are hung up over public buildings and along the streets. The right to change the colours and hang up these flags is included in the country`s constitution.

There are large processions down the streets with musical bands, breath-taking white horses and camels, re-enactments of the Battle of Karbala and chanting devotees.

However, there is another side to the festival and it is the ultra-religious one - many male devotees whip and cut themselves with razor blades, swords, chains and knives (called "Haidar") and some drive knives into their scalps – re-enacting the blood-shedding of Imam Hussein and washing away their sins. Women in the procession beat their chests. Children as little as babies are cut by their fathers too. The procession of people winds along the streets in a mourning march.

The way the event is marked divides the Shia and Sunni Muslims and shows the two sides of the story: Sunny Muslims believe it is a day of joy and gratitude as it is the day when Allah saved the Israelis from their enemy in Egypt, while the Shia Muslims believe it is a day of sorrow and mourning because of the death of Imam Hussain.

Travel to: Bahrain (Manama). The locals set stalls and offer food and tea to the mourners every day.

Other countries celebrating Ashura include: Lebanon, Bangladesh, Iraq, Pakistan, Myanmar and India.

Other holidays on this date: Kurama Fire Festival (Japan)

23 October: Jodhpur Riff (India)

This is the Rajasthan International Folk Festival which runs for 4 days in October every year. Created in 2007, it is held during the brightest full moon of the year.

The venue is a magnificent XV C. fort situated 125m above the city, voted Asia's Best Fortress by Times Magazine. The aim of the festival is to celebrate and popularize the local folklore music, arts and culture.

The event has been endorsed by UNESCO as a "People's Platform for Creativity and Sustainable Development" with Sir Mick Jagger of The Rolling Stones being its international patron.

During the festival, the best artists, Sufi singers, fire and ethnic dancers, bands, "tandura" (a string instrument) and "jhanjh" (a cymbal-like instrument) players, storytellers and DJ's from India and around the world perform on stage. A unique experience is listening to the traditional aero-phonic instrument players of Rajasthan in the Desert Lounge located just outside the Fort – a true acoustic, moon-lit experience under the night sky. The rarely heard wind instruments are part of the fast-disappearing rural culture of the desert people in the region.

The accommodation is arranged in tents set up within the fort. Many food stalls with local delicacies take care of the hungry visitors.

Gathering more than 250 participants from around the world, the Rajasthan Folklore Festival celebrates the cultural diversity by creating innovative collaborations between artists and ethnic instruments. Traditional Rajasthani folk, jazz, early morning ragas and gipsy dance music also feature on the program.

Travel to: North India (Rajasthan). The event is held at Jodhpur's Mehrangarh Fort. The organizers set up huge tents within the fort which can be used for accommodation.

Other holidays on this date: Sourest Day, Punk for A Day (USA)

24 October: Nine Emperor Gods Festival (Thailand)

This is an annual nine-day Taoist holiday, observed in the 9th month on the Chinese calendar (late October) since the 1860s.

It is believed that the roots of this celebration are in the XIXth C. when a wandering Chinese opera group fell ill of malaria. According to a Chinese belief, abstaining from eating meat products during the ninth month, purifies the body and clears the mind. And so, they decided to stick to a vegetarian diet and pray to the Nine Emperor Gods in hope to get better before the upcoming performance. And so... in nine days they were cured.

The festival is known for the acts of self-mutilation performed by religious devotees to invoke the gods. Acting as messangers of the deities and believing that this way the gods will keep them from harm - they pierce their cheeks with sharpened poles, knives and skewers, walk barefoot over burning coals or climb a ladder made of sharp objects. They believe the gods use their bodies as vehicles when blessing the crowds.

The festival begins with the raising of the Lantern Pole – representing the descent of God Shiva to the event. The pole invokes the spirits of around 36 000 gods...

People visit 40 of the participating shrines and temples with offerings of food and flowers and bring their personal home shrines to take some of the spiritual power to their homes.

The festivities proceed with huge street processions with many people walking as if in trance.

For the whole duration of the festival, participants should observe the following commitments:
- To shower every day
- To keep all kitchen utensils clean and not to let them be used by others who do not participate in the festival
- To wear only white clothes
- To behave correctly

- Not to eat meat
- To avoid sex
- To avoid alcohol
- Pregnant women and people in mourning should not participate

Wonderful local food can be found in the many food stalls set around the procession route and next to temples. All, of course, is vegetarian!

Travel to: Thailand (Phuket Island). One of the main ceremonies is in Phuket Town in the Jui Tui Shrine.

Other holidays on this date: National Food Day (USA)

25 October: Celebraciones de la Gente (USA)

Since its initiation in 2003, this event is celebrated annually over a week at the end of October.

A festival to mark the unique cultural heritage of the Aztecs and to honour the Mexican traditions.

Celebraciones de la Gente includes Mariachi music, sugar skull decorating, cockfighting, ritualistic Aztec dances, lots of cultural workshops and art presentations.

The celebration features the Day of the Dead event (celebrated on November 1st in Mexico, commemorating the souls of the dead which cross over from the underworld to the world of the living) when all participants dress up in scary costumes, skeletons and ghouls and paint their faces.

There is a special After Dark evening showcasing authentic Aztec altars on candlelight and Mariachi performers, while the visitors enjoy a cup of hot chocolate and pan dulce (sweet bread).

Travel to: USA (Arizona). The festival takes place at the Museum of North Arizona.

Other holidays on this date: Sourest Day, Punk for A Day Day (USA)

26 October: Market Day with A Difference (Dominica)

This day is part of the independence celebrations of Dominica which gained its independence from Great Britain in 1978 (remaining a part of the Commonwealth).

Market Day with a Difference is celebrated annually during the Creole Week on the last Saturday in October every year.

The event aims to honour the contribution of local farmers and vendors to the national development effort.

The markets across the country turn into art masterpieces with their many and carefully set on shelves vegetables, citrus fruits, coconuts, root crops, meat, coffee, cocoa, spices and more.

The whole island is full of excitement and beautiful colours, celebrating the local produce. Many local farmers are dressed in their national Creole clothes (Madras or Jip, or Jupe) and their stalls are decorated with the national flag. Creole-African drummers entertain the visitors while they browse through the adorned with fruits, veggies and exotic flowers stalls.

There are various speeches held by government officials focusing on the importance of every individual and his/her contribution to the society. A highlight are the awards given to the youngest and oldest vendors on the market, best crop, youngest shopper and best-dressed vendor etc. and a plantain display with a variety of plantain recipes.

Performing artists and art workshops accompany the festival.

Travel to: Dominica (Roseau). The day is celebrated across the country, but the best experience is at the Old Market of Roseau.

Other holidays on this date: Angam Day (Nauru)

27 October: Sea Turtle Festival (Mexico)

Since 2003, this annual eco-friendly festival is held over three days in October along one of the most breath-taking sand strips in the world – Riviera Maya.

The sea turtles swim out of the sea at night, dig a nest on the beach with their flippers and lay between 85 and 120 eggs. Then, they bury them in sand and return to the water.

The celebration dedicated to the endangered gracious reptile coincides with the hatching season and includes many talks on preserving the turtles' natural habitat, environmental workshops, fishing competitions, kite making competition, bazaar and the highlight – releasing baby turtles into the turquoise waters of the Caribbean Sea.

The festival begins at the Marine Turtle Sanctuary with a sand sculpture contest and continues with a carnival, games and art performances. Lots of small booths lined along the route of the festival offer visitors turtle souvenirs, refreshing drinks and Mexican street food.

A traditional Mayan ceremony with Mayan dancers arriving on canoes to pay respect to the sea creatures marks the end of the festivities.

Travel to: Mexico (Tulum beach). The festival is held in Tulum, Xcacel and Akumal. The species that inhabit the beautiful sand strip of the Riviera are Loggerhead and Green Turtle.

Other holidays on this date: National Architect Day (Colombia)

28 October: Tihar Festival of Lights (Nepal)

This is an annual five-day Hindu festival taking place in the end of October (or beginning of November, depending on the Nepalese Lunar calendar). It is celebrated in Nepal and in some parts of India.

There is a theory on why the festival was created – a dying King was told that a serpent will come to take his life. He was so eager to live, that decided to ask the Goddess Laxmi for help and forgiveness. To please her, he lit thousands of oil lamps and candles inside his palace. Laxmi was indeed very pleased, and the king lived happily for another 70 years. The festival has been celebrated ever since – to please Laxmi.

Another theory is that the God of Death was always busy and didn't have time for his twin sister. She sent a crow, a dog, a cow and finally herself to summon him. She drew a circle of oil from an oil lamp around him and told him he cannot move until the oil dries. As this wasn't happening any time soon, they had hours and hours to talk and laugh which strengthened their relationship.

Tihar is celebrated as the festival of lights, but it is also a time to honour the gods, the humans and the animals. That is why – every day during the festival is different:

On the first day, locals make flower patterns outside their homes – they use coloured rice, flower petals, flour and sand to create beautiful natural mats. These stunning masterpieces are to welcome the gods.

On this day, crows and ravens are honoured and offerings of sweets are placed on rooftops. As these birds are associated with mishap and sorrow and are also "the messengers of death", the sweets are to please and keep them busy, so they won't have time to bring bad news. This way the families hope to avoid grief in their homes.

On the second day, locals celebrate the dogs and put calendula garlands over their necks (to symbolize the wearer is important), treat them with delicious food and put tika on their forehead (red mark). According to the Hindu mythology, dogs are the gatekeepers of death. The locals believe that dogs can guarantee that the souls of the deceased ones go to Heaven.

On the most important day of the festival – the third day, worshippers treat cows to the best grass and adorn their necks with colourful garlands. The animal is a symbol of wealth and prosperity. It is believed that on this day Goddess Laxmi descends to earth to bring good fortune to the devotees. To get her attention, locals make their homes as luminous as possible – they turn on every single light bulb and light candles. Oil lamps made from cotton wick and a small clay bowl are lit in front of every home to welcome the Goddess and her divine gifts. In the evening, children visit random houses to sing and dance. In return, they are given money, fruits and sweets.

The fourth day worships the ox as an indispensable helper to the farmer.

On the fifth day, sisters put a multi-coloured tika on the foreheads of their brothers to protect and thank them for the care. They also give them a special flower garland and a Tantric thread to tie on their wrist. Then brothers follow the same ritual and put tika on their sisters' forehead. The ceremony aims to strengthen the bond between the siblings.

The festival is celebrated as New Year by the Newar community in Kathmandu. The Newaries gather to worship, sing and dance.

Tihar is a time for the families to clean and redecorate their houses (to show respect to the gods), wear new celebratory clothes and make promises to be better people.

All Nepalese towns and villages, every street and shop turn into a kaleidoscope of glittering colourful festive lights. It is a time to celebrate light over darkness and good over evil!

Travel to: Nepal (Kathmandu). This is the only chance to visit the Rani Pokhari Temple as it is open to public only during the festival. One can also feed the crows on the historic Durbar Square in Kathmandu.

Other holidays on this date: Ochi Day (Greece, Cyprus)

29 October: Le Salon du Chocolate (France)

Since 1994, the city of love celebrates the sweetest annual trade fair – Paris Chocolate Show where world-known chocolatiers, pastry chefs and cocoa aficionados join to taste and exchange the hottest trends in the industry.

The delicious event takes place at the end of October and lasts... only 5 days. More than 500 participants represent around 60 countries.

Numerous gourmet workshops, cook-offs, chocolate fountains and displays set foot in the city attracting thousands of visitors. Cocoa producing countries show off their best beans and introduce new techniques of making the mouth-watering blocks of white and dark chocolate, all competing for the winners' spot at the International Cocoa Awards.

Wine-chocolate pairing masterclasses and fusion cooking stir the appetite of the participants.

Some accompanying events feature fashion shows, talks with nutritionists on the positive effect of the cocoa, chocolate sculpturing classes, cocoa clinic, culinary contests and exhibitions on the history of chocolate-making.

Salon du Chocolate even hosts the World Chocolate Masters Final where artisans from around the world compete to bring the grand prize to their home country.

Travel to: France (Paris). The event is held at the Paris Expo Porte de Versailles.
Other holidays on this date: Mawlid Un Nabi (UK)

30 October: Mischief Night (England)

This is a century-old tradition observed in the end of October or beginning of November in Northern England. Usually takes place on the day before Halloween night and is combined with trick-or-treating.

According to historical facts, the day was first mentioned in the late 1700s/early 1800s when there was a custom of Lawless Hours in Britain. In the past, Mischief Night and Halloween were part of the same festival.

Mischief Nights is also known as Tick-Tack Night, Tricky Night, Mizzy Night, Devil's Night and Hell Night (depending on the region) and is a time for trouble-makers to cause some chaos which most of the times involves petty acts of vandalism. It is much loved by children and especially teenagers who pull pranks on everyone and try to get away with it.

Some of the "mild" pranks include: Swapping shop's signs; throwing cabbage at someone; putting peanut butter on door handles, knock on doors and run away (this game is known as Ding Dong Ditch and Knock, Knock, Ginger), tying the doorknobs of two front gates together so the people can't get out, covering trees with toilet paper, attaching strings of tinned cans to cars, throwing flour and eggs at houses and people (supermarkets ban the sale of flour and eggs to those under the age of 16) and more.

There have been many disputes if Mischief Night is just harmless fun or it should be banned. This is because some people cross the line and commit serious acts of vandalism such as throwing bricks at windows and launching fireworks at oncoming traffic.

So far, the police take extra precautions during the holiday.

Travel to: United Kingdom (Yorkshire and Merseyside). In Leeds and Liverpool, Mischief Night is celebrated on November 4th (before Guy Fawkes Night).
Other holidays on this date: National Candy Corn Day (USA)

31 October: All Hallows' Eve - Halloween (world)

All Hallows Eve goes back to 2000 years ago.

One of the best known and much-anticipated observances of the year, Halloween is celebrated annually around the world on the night of October 31st (the last day on the Celtic calendar). Some believe that Halloween began as a holiday of its own, but others speculate.

The holiday with deep Pagan roots, deriving from a Druidic tradition called Samhain (Summer's End), today is more about costumes and fun rather than ghosts and ghouls as it was in the past.

For the ancient Druids, this day marked the end of the autumn harvest season and the beginning of the winter. They believed that every change of seasons opened the gates between the world of the living and the underworld for the souls of the dead to cross over and reunite with their families. However, they believed that demons in the form of spirits, fairies and witches stealing children and destroying crops also tagged along. The Druids called them Aos Si (ees-Shee) – divine creatures with lots of energy that could be good or evil. To please them, the community left offerings of food.

Later in the years, the masses started to disguise like Aos Si, believing that this way they will scare away the evil spirits and protect themselves.

There is a theory that the early Church adopted some of the Samhain rituals to ease the Celts into Christianity.

In the Christian calendar, Halloween is the first of three days when the deceased should be remembered – relatives, martyrs and Saints. The days are All Saints Eve (Halloween or Hallows' Eve on October 31st), All Saints Day (November 1st) and All Souls Day (November 2nd).

The Church adopted the ritual of disguising, however, the rumour has it that at that time, it didn't have enough means to display relics of martyrs, so the parishioners began dressing up as Saints. They would carry hollowed-out turnips with candles inside – symbolizing the souls of the dead.

The custom of trick-or-treating began in the XVIth C. when people masked as scary creatures (evil spirits) started knocking on neighbours' doors, threatening to do mischief if not given a treat.

Carving pumpkins became popular in the USA in 1837, replacing the turnip which was not as soft and much difficult to carve.

The usual activities on Halloween are: trick-or-treating, carving jack-o-lanterns (representing the ever-roaming Jack with his hollowed lantern who tricked Satan and was denied entry to both Heaven and Hell), costumed parties, visiting haunted places, lighting bonfires, watching horror movies (or at least The Nightmare Before Christmas – a classic!), decorating houses and streets with spiderwebs, scarecrows, pumpkins and skulls.

There are a few games associated with Halloween – all of them considered to be deadly serious practices or even dark magic in the Middle Ages. One of them, which is still played in some parts of Scotland is "Apple bobbing" – apples float in a basin of water and the participants try to catch them using only their teeth. The apples were associated with the underworld and immortality by the Celts.

Dessi Nikoltchev:

Traditional colours on Halloween are black and orange and typical food during the holiday are candies shaped like skulls, spiders or bloody fingers, toffee apples, corn and nuts.

Travel to: UK and the USA (anywhere) have a centurial tradition of celebrating the holiday. However, nowadays, Halloween is observed in most parts of the world.
Other holidays on this date: Carve A Pumpkin Day (USA)

... NOVEMBER

Getting ready for the Christmas Carolers: They go door-to-door and cheer up the hosts singing merry songs. But where did they come from in the first place? There is a theory that the practice, dating back to the Middle Ages, was a tradition in Great Britain, observed by peasants and their Lords at Christmastime. Because the latter were presumably wealthy – they would give Christmas treats to the peasants who, in return, would sing songs and spread happiness in the spirit of Christmas.

01 November: El Día de los Muertos (Mexico)

Annually celebrated on November 1st, the Day of the Dead has been around for 3 000 years and is probably the most famous of the bizarre festivals in the world. In the past, the observation was held to honour the goddess known as The Lady of the Dead and lasted for a month in August (the ninth month in the Aztec calendar), but with Christianization, it shortened and moved to November.

It is a day to remember the deceased relatives and to celebrate their life with a smile and an enormous fiesta.

For the indigenous people of Mexico, death was just a passage to a new life. They believed that above the earth, there were thirteen layers of heavens and below it – nine layers of the underworld. In the past, many were buried with their favourite objects, clothes, jewellery and even their pets were sacrificed to join them in the journey. To be as close as possible to their deceased relatives, the ancient Aztecs buried them in tombs within close proximity to their homes, some – even underneath them.

With Christianization and the introduction of All Souls and All Saints day, the Mexicans started celebrating the pagan holiday the way it is celebrated today – pre-colonial customs intertwined with the Roman Catholic ones.

Dessi Nikoltchev:

They believe that the souls of the departed visit the earth for one day to rejoin with their families – this day is between October 31st and November 2nd. It is said that the spirits of babies and young children ("los angelitos") visit earth on the night of October 31st and the adults visit the day after.

The locals dress up in traditional costumes and paint their faces as colourful skeletons (most commonly as bride and groom skeletons). Some incorporate flower petals, glittery crowns and jewels too. They decorate homes and streets with skulls, coffins, skeletons and crosses. As it is a festive occasion that celebrates Life, vibrant parades with music bands and processions are a major part of this day. Some visit cemeteries to light candles and lay a path of flowers from the grave of the deceased relative so that his soul can find its way home. Statues sculpted out of wood, stone or sugar – all in different sizes situated on city squares or hanging from street lamp or balcony, adorn towns and villages. The Mexicans also make elaborately decorated altars in their homes (ofrendas) and put the favourite food of the deceased as an offering, as well as favourite objects, religious items, incense sticks, candles, flowers and paper decorations (cutouts) in different colours.

Traditional foods on this holiday (including the ones prepared for the altars) are:
- Pan de Muertos – round-shaped, sweet bread with bones and skulls on top.
- Calaveraz de Azucar (Sugar Skulls) – the skull was a symbol of life and death and a very important part of the culture of both Mayan and the Aztec. The colourfully painted sugar (or chocolate) skulls are of small size and are usually not eaten, but placed on altars.
- Tamales – "tamalli" means "wrapped" in the ancient language of the Aztecs. Tamales are corn dough pastries with a filling, wrapped in corn or banana leaves and steamed.
- Calabaza en Dulce – Sweet Pumpkin cooked with brown sugar and cinnamon.

The yellow marigold (the flower of the dead), white amaryllis and wild purple orchids (the flowers of the souls) are used for decorating graves, houses, streets and even costumes.

The Day of the Dead aims to spread a sense of love and respect for the deceased relatives, to celebrate the continuance of life and the importance of family relationships. It is the most visually striking way to let people find humour in death and accept it as a stage of life.

The Día de los Muertos is on the UNESCO List of Intangible Cultural Heritage of Humanity since 2008.

Travel to: Mexico. Some of the best celebrations are held in the state of Oaxaca – in Pátzcuaro, Michoacán, and in the town of Mixquic, near Mexico City. The holiday is celebrated in many countries in Latin America, but nowhere to the extend it is in Mexico.

Other holidays on this date: All Saints Day (USA), Voodoo Day of the Dead (Haiti), Day of the Dead Kite Festival (Guatemala)

02 November: Camel Fair (India)

One of the most attractive and one of the last traditional livestock fairs in the world is organized annually on a full moon in November and lasts for five days.

This is one of India's most epic tribal experiences when Rajasthani farmers gather to buy and sell their camels, cattle, horses, goats and sheep.

The festival starts with a camel race and is followed by music, songs and exhibitions. The event attracts over 400 000 visitors every year.

Once the livestock tenders are over and bargains are sealed – the animals are decked up with beautiful clothe, adorned with gems and glittering ornaments for public displays in the backdrop of the endless sand dunes.

A highlight of the fair are the camels. Tens of thousands of them - shaved, dressed in bright fabrics and adorned with shiny ornaments, beads and pom-poms "participate" in camel market, beauty competitions and camel dances. Their owners proudly stroll along the festival grounds, catching the eye of every visitor.

Besides the livestock market, there is a fairground with Ferris wheel, camps with tents where one can hire a camel-pulled cart to explore the grounds, magicians, turban tying contests, tug-of-war, longest moustache competition, snake charmers and gipsy women.

As the small desert town is a sacred place, many visitors take the opportunity to purify their souls and bodies in the holy waters of the Pushkar Lake nearby with more than 52 bathing spots (each one healing a different disease and cleansing a different sin). Those who bathe on the day of the full moon are said to receive special blessings.

The Fair features also cultural and spiritual walks, folk concerts, temple dancing and crafts bazaar. There are many stalls selling local merchandise – ornaments, footwear, artefacts, bracelets, clothes, textiles and fabrics. One can even get the famous Rajasthani tattoo by one of the nomad tattoo artists.

Plenty of traditional local food accompanies the days of the festival – mouth-watering dishes cooked with love, rich Indian spices and homemade yoghurt!

Travel to: Northern India (Rajasthan). The event takes place in the city of Pushkar – a sacred Hindu site bordering the Thar Desert. Look for accommodation in Camp Bliss.

Other holidays on this date: Saxophone Day (USA)

03 November: Mombasa Carnival (Kenya)

The Carnival is as spectacular as the hosting city itself – a mélange of Persian, Chinese, Arabian, Portuguese, Indian, European and African cultures. The largest coastal port in East Africa and a popular hot spot for wandering traders since the XIIth C becomes a home of sassy Afropop music and Swahili cuisine every year in the month of November.

The so-called multicultural street party involves two parades with richly decorated floats, representing the cultural diversity of the various indigenous ethnic groups, flowing into one massive street parade.

There are Maasai warriors, belly dances, fire dancers, local Taarab bands playing traditional music, merchants selling hand-made souvenirs and artefacts on the streets, arts and crafts market, fashion shows, local food stalls and lots of free coconut milk for the crowds.

The participants in the processions are dressed in traditional clothes (kikoy and kanga) with Swahili sayings printed on them.

The Carnival ends on the Indian Ocean shore with a spectacular sailing regatta and night-long dances.

Travel to: Kenya (Mombasa). The two parades converge on Moi Avenue. The event ends at Fort Jesus.

Other holidays on this date: Sandwich Day (Germany)

04 November: Bridgwater Illuminated Carnival (England)

The carnival, held annually in November, was created in the 1600s in Somerset by a group of locals who burnt an effigy of Guy Fawkes (the person who plotted to blow up the Houses of Parliament and kill King James I to end Protestant rule). Over the years, the not so significant bonfire party evolved to be one of the best-illuminated festivals in the world. Starting on the first Wednesday of the month, today the spectacular four-day event is visited by more than 150 000 people.

The Carnival features a procession of around 100 illuminated floats and colourful performers parading down the streets. The floats – some up to 30m long are lit by 22 000 lightbulbs and resemble houses, trains, historical moments, movie scenes, places, animals etc.

Dwarfing the streets, these magnificent edifices draw awe and wonder from the crowds and are the results of months of work in secret by the local Carnival Clubs.

The procession ends with 'squibbing' (and this is the only festival that still practices that ancient custom) - an explosive tradition where hundreds of people hold stout poles in the shape of brooms and shoot fireworks, giving the effect of glittering lights raining down.

Travel to: England (Somerset). The event takes place in the town of Bridgwater. The procession starts from Bath Road in the evening, continues through Rest Road, St Mary's Street, Cornhill, High Street, Mount Street and ends at the Northgate later in the evening.

Other holidays on this date: Sandwich Day (USA)

05 November: Guy Fawkes Night (England)

"Remember, remember, the fifth of November..." – the familiar rhyme recorded in 1742 depicts this very celebration.

The so-called "Bonfire Night" commemorates the unsuccessful attempt of Guy Fawkes and a group of firm Catholics (13 to be exact) to blow up the Houses of Parliament in London on November 5th, 1605. The Gunpowder plot aimed to kill King James I of England and to end the Protestant rule in the kingdom.

The history begins a few decades earlier when King Henry VIII created the Anglican Church to get rid of all the Catholics and the Roman Catholic influence (preventing him from divorcing his wife).

Trained in the military, Guy Fawkes decided to use explosives and blow the House of Lords in which King James I attended the State Opening of Parliament. His plan was to put a Catholic king on the throne and this way – change the world.

But... this didn't happen as someone ratted him out.

Guy Fawkes and his supporters were sentenced very harsh:

"...put to death halfway between Heaven and Earth as unworthy of both" – certain parts of the plotter's bodies would be cut off and burnt before their eyes, and their hearts removed. They would then be decapitated, and the dismembered parts of their bodies displayed so that they might become Prey for the Fowls of the Air" (from Antonia Fraser's Faith and Treason; pp. 266–269).

Thereafter, all royal subjects were encouraged to celebrate the kings' survival with bonfires on the night of November 5th every year – on Guy Fawkes Night.

The public holiday is still celebrated today – with bonfires and lots of fireworks - may be to remind what would have happened if the attempt had been successful. In some villages, people burn effigies of Guy Fawkes, or of any other public figures they disregard in that matter. Others just use the day to burn old rubbish from their garages.

Traditional food on Guy Fawkes Night are baked potatoes wrapped in foil, sausages and marshmallows cooked over the bonfire flames.

Guy Fawkes's distinctive moustache face was adopted as a mask which became quite famous with anti-capitalist groups of people.

That same mask is worn by V. in the movie "V for Vendetta", a script inspired by and representing Guy Fawkes and his plot.

That same mask is now the symbol of the "Anonymous" hacker collective.

The unsuccessful attempt though, led to one thing still being observed today - The Houses of Parliament are still searched once a year before the State Opening, to make sure there are no conspirators hiding with explosives!

Travel to: England (London). The skyline of one of the busiest cities in the world turns into a rainbow of fireworks. The best fireworks display is in front of Alexandra Palace, surrounded by Alexandra Park. The event coincides with a German beer fest, ice-skating rink, street food village and a fire-eater's parade at the same spot.

Other holidays on this date: Gunpowder Day (USA), Ottery St Mary Tar Barrels Carnival (England)

06 November: Rakfisk Festival (Norway)

This festival is dedicated to ... fermented fish – one of the oldest food traditions in Norway.

Trout, whitefish, perch and salmon are marinated in salt water for 2-3 months to become the national delicacy which is the rakfisk. This method of conservation has been in use since the XIVth C.

Initiated in 1990, the event held annually on the first Saturday of November, started as a small town gathering. Today, the Rakfisk Festival attracts more than 25 000 visitors from around the world.

Local rakfisk producers and fish merchants from around the country set more than 100 shops offering the traditional fish treat.

A small town turns into a huge open-air market where visitors can sample the rakfisk before buying it. Huge trays with semi-fermented fish literally flood the streets. The small bites are accompanied by a ring of red onion, butter, sour cream, crispy flatbread, potatoes and parsley.

Although the event focuses on the rakfisk – other traditional food delicacies such as moose meat, cured reindeer meat, shrimps, a variety of cheeses and homemade cranberry jams.

The festival features late-night concerts with dancing and lots of stalls selling all sorts of local handicrafts and souvenirs made of wood, wool and leather.

Fact: the Rakfisk is a protected geographical product which can be produced only in the Valdres region of Norway.

Travel to: Norway (Fagernes). The birthplace of the Rakfisk delicacy is the Valdres region and the festival is held in the small coastal town of Fagernes (which is in fact the largest settlement in the area with population of around 2000 people).

Other holidays on this date: Saxophone Day (USA), Obama Day (Kenya)

07 November: Paantu Ritual (Japan)

The highlight of this centuries-old folkloric ritual is mud-covered deities visiting the island to cleanse it from evil spirits and to bring good luck. These supernatural beings are known as "paantu" – indigenous god/demon figure.

Local men wearing scary-looking dark masks, cover themselves in mud from a sacred well and dwarf sugar palm leaves, and roam the island chasing away all things evil. The men are followed by priestesses covered in leaves, waving camphor twigs – they are entrusted to guard the town's sacred sites such as shrines and oracles.

The procession visits new built houses and families with newborn babies to spread mud on them – this is a sacred gesture and a blessing for good fortune in the coming year.

The fun part of the ritual is that the mud men try to catch every child on their way and splash it with some of the thick mud dripping off the disguise.

Parked cars, dogs and random people walking down the street are just a collateral damage.

By nighttime, the whole town is one big muddy puddle.

Travel to: Japan (Miyako island). The ritual is observed in the Nobaru Village in Shimajiri district. The island is one of the last surviving places in the world where matriarchy in the form of forest and village female guardians and animist religion still exist.

Other holidays on this date: Helping a Friend Day (USA)

08 November: Corroboree (Australia)

Corroboree celebrates the rich cultural heritage of the indigenous people of Australia – the Aborigines and the Torres Strait Islanders.

Since 2013, the annual festival is held over 11 days and nights at the beginning of November.

Artists, writers, singers and dancers show the magical world and rich history of the native people.

The indigenous celebration features Gurund Parade (a procession of schoolchildren who carry handmade "waratah" – crimson red flower from a local shrub) and a Firelight ceremony. This is the opening ceremony when Elders light up a firelight that burns for the duration of the festival. The very flame is brought ashore by fishermen. In the past, a flame burning from a canoe was the only signal the fishermen could make to announce their location to other boats. A small replica of the wooden canoe brings the flame to the firelight torch ashore.

The ritual is accompanied by a group of chanting indigenous people with white painted faces and arms.

The festival features also Blak Arts open-air market (showcasing indigenous arts and crafts), theatre plays and concerts, Fijian dances, educational and art workshops, traditional dances and songs, film screenings, paper canoe and bark boat making, painting, weaving and more.

Travel to: Australia (Sydney). The event is held around the Sydney Harbor.
Other holidays on this date: Journalist`s Day (China)

09 November: Torch Festival (Taiwan)
This is a local festival of the indigenous people who want to preserve the legacy of their ancestors and pass it on to future generations.

A unique cultural event taking place every year in the beginning of November in a farm, known as "The Paradise in the clouds" and "Shangri-la above the mist". The beautiful spot features recreational centre, Swiss garden with lit-up fountains, beautiful plants and LED sunflowers, ecological area, park, green grasslands, animal centre and a guesthouse.

The festival was established by the ethnical minorities of Burma and Southwest China – small in size indigenous tribes, each of them having its own customs and rituals.

The event aims to integrate newcomers and make them feel at home by adopting the local traditions and beliefs.

The folks gather holding lit torches and raise them high to light up the sky. They chant prayers for a better year and good fortune. Then they all participate in a torch procession to chase away the evil spirits and bad luck. The locals perform this custom together – as a symbol of unity.

The event features a barbecue party, water pipe competition, tribal dances and folklore songs and plays. All activities represent a mix of the unique cultural heritage brought by each of the ethnic minorities to Taiwan.

Travel to: Taiwan (Dingyuan New Village). The event takes place at the Cingjing Farm. Specialty for the area are the locally grown peaches, pears, plums, kiwis and alpine vegetables.
Other holidays on this date: Night of Broken Glass Remembrance Day (Germany)

10 November: Turnip Lanterns Parade (Switzerland)
A Halloween made... Swiss style!

This event is included in the Guinness Book of World Records and is the biggest turnip parade in the world!

The first known parade was recorded in 1884, but since 1905, it is held annually in November - on the second Saturday after Halloween.

When the night falls (around 6:30h at this time of the year), the electric lights in a small coastal town are turned off and everything goes completely dark. Then...from a narrow-cobbled street, a winding candle procession lights the facades and balconies of Medieval houses.

About 50 000 candles put inside 30 tons of hollowed-out turnips adorn 40 massive float constructions (3-5 meters high), carried by the people. These constructions represent animals, houses and palaces. Sparkling candles also shine from every balcony, shop display, church and even from a funicular train! The parade-goers sing carols and make their way through the small streets. It is a festive and yet humble and magical atmosphere.

The parade lasts for an hour and then the electric lights are turned on again.

The legend has it that in the late XIXth C, the farmers' wives, living outside of the city walls, used to hollow-out turnips to light their way back from the church. Today, the procession is led by church-going women dressed in dark clothes to commemorate how it all began.

As the turnip is the highlight of the day, visitors can taste different local specialities made of turnips, or try their carving skills. Local merchandise, food stalls with heart-warming turnip soup, sausages, mulled wine and carving workshops are placed around the procession route.

The Räbeliechtli Fest, as it is locally known, celebrates the end of the autumn harvest season and the warmth of home and family during the cold winter months.

An interesting fact is that in the past, turnips were carved for all autumn harvest holidays (before North America introduced the pumpkins which stuck as they are softer and easier to carve). According to a theory, at a time when the Church didn't have enough means to display relics of martyrs for the holiday of All Hallows' (in modern times – Halloween), the parishioners would dress up as Saints and carry hollowed-out turnips with candles inside – the turnip lanterns representing the souls of the dead.

Räbeliechtli Fest is a beautiful and special tradition everyone should experience at least once!

Travel to: Switzerland (Canton of Zurich). The event takes place in the small town of Richterswil along the coast of Lake Zurich. The main events are held at Wisshutsplatz and Poststrasse.

Other holidays on this date: Goose Piñata (Switzerland), Veteran's Day (USA), Shout in Villa de los Santos (Panama)

11 November: Martinmas (Estonia)

In many Northern countries the period between the end of harvest season in late Autumn, and the Christmas holidays is associated with souls coming to visit and reunite with their families in the world of the living. This period coincides with the darkest days of the year and the beginning of winter.

People celebrate by not working on certain days and please the visiting souls by making offerings of food.

Annually observed on November 11th, Martinmas has its pagan roots which today are incorporated into a Christian custom, inheriting a ceremony that worshipped the dead and another one that marked the end of the crop harvest.

In the past, the children, led by "Mardi-father" (representing St Martin) dressed in dark clothes and covered by a dark cloak, visited neighbouring houses to sing songs and collect sweets in return. They made as much noise as possible using all kinds of musical instruments to announce their arrival and chase away the evil spirits. Their merry visit to a house was a promise of a rich harvest.

The adults had another ritual – they dressed as mummers - in furs, smear their faces in dark colours and play tricks on their fellow neighbours. The hosts presented their handcrafted items to the mummers who brang good luck in return.

Today, in most rural areas of the country, part of this ritual is still observed – with young children dressed in dark clothes, knocking on doors.

The ritual was followed by a huge village feast featuring meals with a goose for good fortune.

And as for the goose and why it is that important – there are a few theories:

- The legend has it that at this time the contractors were let off and given a goose as a compensation, to last them through the winter until they find another job;

- There is also a story that St Martin was once annoyed by a goose and had it served for dinner.

- The legend has it that while being a soldier, on a cold winter day Martin met a man who was barely clothed. He cut his cloak with the sword and gave one half to the poor man. The following night, Martin had a dream of Jesus wearing half of his cloak. When he woke up - his cloak was in one piece again. Martin wasn't baptized until that very moment. Once he got baptized, he became a monk. It's said St Martin's parishioners loved him so much that insisted on him becoming a bishop of Tours, which honour he felt unworthy of. That is why he hid in a barn, however the geese gave him away – hence the feast with the goose.

Martinmas is marked with the biggest handicraft and folklore fair in the country which runs for 3 days. Demonstrations and workshops are organized for children and adults. Locals and visitors can enjoy numerous folklore concerts and taste the delicious local food delicacies such as homebrewed beer, wholegrain bread slices with melting butter and smoked meat.

Travel to: Estonia (Tallinn). The fair takes place at the Saku Suurhal Convention center. Worth a visit on this day is the The Estonian Open-Air Museum (Vabaõhumuuseumi 12).

The holiday is also celebrated in Germany, Belgium, Netherlands, Austria, France, Poland and Latvia.

Other holidays on this date: Goose piñata (Switzerland), Glasgow Whisky Festival (Scotland)

12 November: Slaughter of the Pig (Greece)

The ancient custom "Slaughter of the Pig" or Chirosfagia takes place annually on different dates between November and December and is a huge celebration to the locals.

It is more of a family feast rather than a public celebration although it requires the attendance of many people and helping hands.

Every member of the family has certain duties – for example, the head of the household is responsible for killing the pig, while the women process the butchered meat and collect different herbs (after cleaning the whole house and getting it ready for the feast).

The pig is slaughtered early in the morning. The family then gathers to wash the animal with Raki (the local drink). The meat and the guts are separated from the skin, leaving no part of the animal unused.

Different meals and dried meat delicacies are then prepared to last for the whole winter – sausages, bacon, pork rind, ham to be cured with herbs and spices.

Every farmhouse has a massive hook for hanging the meat, cemented between the slates that cover the porch. The butchering of the pig finishes on the same day, however the processing work (done by the women) lasts over the next couple of days.

The event is celebrated as a huge festival on the island – accompanied by piping-hot pork dishes and homemade wine.

Throughout the winter the local butchers often hang pig`s head outside their shops – this is to prove that the meat they sell is fresh and from locally bred pigs.

In the past, kids played with the pig`s bladder, while the skin was used for making shoes.

The festive dinner begins with a prayer and should include traditional braised liver with rice, and bones & meat soup.

Friends and locals are all invited to join the festivity – sometimes folks bring along a violin to play traditional music.

Travel to: Greece (Tinos Island). The best place is in Dio Choria. Each village celebrates this "holiday" on a different date, so check before you travel.

Other holidays on this date: Independence of Cartagena (Colombia), Heir to the Throne`s Birthday (Tuvalu)

13 November: White Truffle Fair (Italy)
This is the most famous festival dedicated to the unmistakable taste of the little gem - that is the white truffle.

The three-week-long gourmet fiesta takes place annually in November. The search for truffles in this area had begun more than a century ago. The Truffle Fair has been around since 1969.

Food aficionados from around the world can smell, taste, buy and hunt for white truffles on the backdrop of the breath-taking views of the Tuscany hills – a region that gives 25% of the white truffles in Italy. More than that – they are branded "White truffles of the San Miniato Hills" and are used by some of the most renown chefs in the world.

Taking part in a truffle hunt is a great way to experience the century-old tradition. Participants split in groups led by professional hunters and their irreplaceable helpers – the dogs.

Small white stalls are scattered at the Piazza del Duomo – the main square of the small Medieval town where local merchants sell, cook and exchange ancient recipes with the tourists. All that accompanied by cheer, loud talks and a glass or two of a ruby-red local wine.

Naturally, the white truffle is the highlight and centrepiece of the festival, but visitors can also enjoy tremendously rich displays of local food produce – wine, olive oil, artichokes, pastries, cheese, sausages and various mouth-watering cold cuts.

The event features workshops and different competitions such as "the largest white truffle" and "the oldest truffle hunter" – each category winner receives a prize.

For an unforgettable experience of all that Tuscany offers – book accommodation in one of the many farmhouses surrounding the town.

And, of course, one must taste the flagman of the event – the white truffle risotto!

Travel to: Italy (Tuscany). The event is held in the medieval town of San Miniato, where the world`s largest white truffle was found – weighing whole 2,52 kilograms! Also, a local hunter sold the most expensive truffle in the world for $330 000!!!

Other holidays on this date: National Indian Pudding Day (USA), World Kindness Day

14 November: That Luang Festival (Laos)
This is an annual three-day festival, held on a day of a full moon in November.

That Luang or The Grand Stupa (built in 1566) is the most important religious monument in Laos. It is a huge gold-covered stupa allegedly containing Buddha relics – hair and bosom bone.

Stupas can be found in many monasteries especially in Laos. They are composed of base, body and spire and represent the Cosmos. The most important ones are home to Buddha relics.

The religious festival is held in and around the sacred monument. Beginning at dawn with thousands and thousands of devotees gathered at the foot of That Luang to listen to prayers chanted by monks, the celebration end with majestic fireworks display, representing offerings of "colourful flowers" to Buddha, three days later.

Large candlelight procession with colourful wax castle statues starts from the city centre and goes to That Luang where people make offerings of food to the monks and pray to have a better life when they are reborn.

As well as the wax castles adorned with fruits, flower petals and gold paper, they carry candles, incense sticks and flowers, beat drums and cymbals and sing as they walk.

There is a parade of men and women dressed in Lao ethnic costumes who dance and play traditional music and songs as they approach the stupa. Led byu monks, they walk around it three times to honour the city`s founding pillar which is located inside, chanting the ancient words of Buddha.

The celebration features traditional folk music and drama performances, prayers and sermons and the traditional Tee Khee (polo) game.

Many street food stalls offer the typical for the holiday rice noodle and chicken soup.

The festival is followed by a traditional picnic – people gather with their friends and relatives over a boiled chicken and rice.

Travel to: Laos (Vientiane). The procession starts from Lat Si Muang Temple and ends at the That Luang.

Other holidays on this date: World Diabetes Day

15 November: 7-5-3 Festival (Japan)

The festival Shichi-go-san (7-5-3) is a Japanese rite of passage, observed every year on November 15th.

This is a day to celebrate the happy childhood and well-being of the 3 and 5-year-old boys, and the 3 and 7-year-old girls.

The holiday was created sometime between the VIIIth and XIIth centuries when noble women celebrated the passage of their children into middle childhood.

Over the years, the tradition was adopted by the samurai class who added their own rituals, allowing:

- 3 year-olds to grow their hair (in the past they were required to have their hair shaved up until this age, as this would encourage even more luxuriant growth)
- 5-year-old boys to wear hakama (traditional Japanese trousers)
- 7-year-old girls to use the traditional Japanese "obi" (a broad sash) to tie their kimono, instead of a basic cord they had used in the past

By the XXth C, the tradition was adopted and practised by all commoners. They, too, added their own ritual: all kids aged 3,5 and 7 to visit a shrine to chase away the evil spirits.

The children wear their fanciest clothes, as this is a day for family portraits.

However, there is a catch – the children are in fact 2,4 and 6 year-olds!! This comes from the past when the Japanese used to "add" a year to a person to account for the time they spent growing before they are born.

In modern days though, age is calculated as everywhere else in the world, BUT these alternate birthdays are still used for traditional ceremonies or fortune telling.

Chitose ame – meaning "thousand-year candy" are given as gifts - the long red and white sweets symbolize good fortune. The gifts are wrapped in bags decorated with turtles and cranes which represent long life.

This is a day to pray for the children and wish them to do well in life.

The Japanese pay attention to the numbers and their symbolism – that is why the day 15th November isn't chosen randomly – it is the sum of 3, 5 and 7 and is a lucky number. November 15th is also considered the luckiest day of the year in accordance with yin and yang.

The legend has it that this celebration was created in times of high infant mortality rate, so children were only recognized in their family register after the age of three. Although the festival is not that much celebrated today – a visit to a neighborhood shrine will reward one with a peek to the ceremony - families often mark the day dressing up their children in brightly colored kimonos and adorn their up-dos with flowers and sparkling hair clips.

In the evening, the families gather for a huge feast to celebrate and honour their children.

Travel to: Japan (Kyoto). Visit Fushimi Inari Shrine or any of the bigger Shinto shrines. Meiji Jingu in Tokyo is one of the most popular shrines to visit.
Other holidays on this date: World Philosophy Day

16 November: Winter Lights Festival (Japan)

The annual winter festival runs for 5 months, starting in mid-November. It is the biggest illumination party in the country, visited by millions of tourists every year.

The event takes place in a majestic botanical park with giant greenhouses, meticulously planted flower gardens and beautiful lakes. The cold air and delicate flower scent embrace the 7 million LED lights used in light installations, shows and the famous Tunnel of Lights – a 200m walk-through tunnel wrapped in different colours to make one feel as if walking through a magical portal. The 1.2 million lights used to decorate it are flower shaped.

There are various attractions including animated light show above a huge field transformed into a sea of lights and an observation deck that lifts visitors high above the park where they can get a full panorama of the breathtaking lights.

The lakes are also adorned and illuminated with thousands of sparkling colourful bulbs, making the water surface appear as a magic mirror.

This is Japan's most stunning display of lights – recreating scenes from the cherry-blossom season and rainbows in the sky, mythical creatures amidst flower patches and fairy tales on the water surface.

The winter wonderland offers also a free foot-SPA for visitors to warm up their feet after the long stroll! The ashiyu (Japanese public foot bath) runs with natural spring water and is a real perk in the cold weather.

The park features also a hot spring, many restaurants and a beer garden.

Travel to: Japan (Kuwana City). The event is held in the Nabano No Sato botanical park.

Other holidays on this date: International Day of Tolerance

17 November: Big Smoke (USA)

Held in November every year since 1995, this is a three-day event for cigar aficionados featuring seminars, workshops with world-leading cigar manufacturers, smoke evenings, tastings, cigar market and more.

The entry ticket includes free premium cigars handed directly by the manufacturers, spirits and delicious food from local restaurants, as well as a chance to meet some of the biggest names in the cigar industry. Great event for people who appreciate the lush life and those who simply want to join fellow cigar lovers in an atmosphere of good cigars, good drinks, good food and great companionship.

Travel to: USA (Las Vegas). The event is held at a different hotel every year, often - The Venetian and The Mirage.

Other holidays on this date: Fight for Freedom and Democracy Day (Slovakia)

18 November: Beaujolais Nouveau Celebration (France)

A lovely holiday created to celebrate the release of the new vintage of a fruity red wine that is the young Beaujolais produced in the area with the same name.

Held annually on the third Thursday in November, the day has become a true celebration not only in France but among wine aficionados all over the world.

On that day, about 65 million bottles of the two-month-old wine are released to the public.

The first bottle is opened exactly at 12:01h local time and not a minute earlier. The time is not randomly selected – this is the very moment when it is legal to release new wine!

Lacking in taste and boldness, the pink-reddish wine produced only from Gamay grape, was initially purposed as a cheap house wine to accompany a meal.

And as for the history of the celebration:

In the 1950s, French wine producers competed each year who will deliver the first bottles of wine to Paris. The city was a huge market, so everybody did their best to deliver as early as possible.

The major turnover for the Beaujolais wine happened in the 1970s when a local winemaker decided to beat the crowds and be the first to announce the arrival of his wine. The famous quote: "Le Beaujolais Nouveau est arrivé!" which continues to announce the arrival of the new vintage today, belongs to that very winemaker. He distributed posters and banners announcing the young wine and that attracted lots of media coverage and turned the so-called "winemakers race" into a festive celebration.

Today, the race doesn't exist – just because not only France but the world awaits this day for a whole year. Rumour has it that some innovative wine merchants even deliver the new bottles by elephants, rickshaws and motorcycles to emphasize the spirit of the celebration.

Note: Since 1951 the day has been celebrated always on November 15th, but this changed in 1985 when the Beaujolais regional government decided to change that. They thought that people are more prone to start the weekend early if given a good excuse to do so... and that is how a decision has been made that Beaujolais Nouveau will be celebrated always on Thursday.

This story shows the power of marketing and innovative thinking!

Where to travel: France. More than 120 different celebrations are held in the Beaujolais region alone – mainly in the city of Beaujeu. The biggest festival honoring the young wine is held on the streets of Lyon where barrels of the new Beaujolais are rolled by wine-growers through the town before being opened.

Other holidays on this date: Mickey Mouse Birthday

19 November: Festival of Masks (Côte d'Ivoire)

The most popular event in the country takes place annually in November and pays homage to the forest spirits, represented by locals wearing elaborate masks (around 60% of the population adhere to indigenous beliefs).

The Festival is held at the end of the harvest season to chase away evil spirits and illness, bring good fortune to the tribe and guarantee rich harvest in the year to come.

Numerous tribes from small villages in the Northern part of the country, hold contests to determine the best dancer and the best mask.

The villagers believe the spirits are embodied in the handmade masks which are sometimes passed from generation to generation.

The beautiful headpiece is integrated into every aspect of the local culture and depending on the tribe – it varies in colours and shapes.

Only men can take part in the sacred mask dance – they dress to cover their body, so no one would recognize the dancer, and put on a mask. As they dance to the drum music, they tell a story with the dance alone.

Each tribe serves a different purpose or ritual; hence the masks differ:
- Bedu Plank Mask – the men wear male (with horns) or female (masks). The Mask keeps the tribe safe and chases away illness and infertility.
- We Mask – used for magic and religious rituals. The person wearing the mask embodies the god or the soul which is summoned by the tribe.
- Mblo Mask – used to represent an actual member of the tribe, but adorned with colourful feathers and beautiful hand carvings.
- Guru Mask – represents animals and spirits.
- Goli Mask – used at the beginning of the harvest season and at funerals. Its features aim to entertain.

Travel to: Côte d'Ivoire. The festival is held in the city of Man and the small villages around it.

Other holidays on this date: Garifuna Settlement Day (Belize)

20 November: Natchitoches Christmas Festival (USA)

The Festival, celebrated annually since its initiation in 1927, begins towards the end of November (on Saturday before Thanksgiving Day) and lasts until January 6th.

The opening ceremony is called "Turn on the Holidays" and features live music, lots of food, official lighting celebration, fireworks display and tons of Christmas cheer.

The small-town transforms into a real winter wonderland as over 300 000 lightbulbs cast their ambient light along the riverbank. And not only that but the river twinkles with around 100 decorated platforms floating in the water.

Each night, visitors can enjoy dances, live concerts, random encounters with Santa Claus and Mrs Claus followed by a group of carolers, carriage tours, Christmas street parades and mouth-watering local delicacies such as gator-on-a-stick, hot gumbo and the famous Natchitoches meat pies (not to mention the dazzling lights and the fireworks).

The highlight of the celebration is on the first Saturday in December with a spectacular firework show choreographed over holiday music.

This event is ranked as the 3rd best Christmas Lights festival in the USA after Rockefeller Center and Disney Land.

Travel to: USA (Louisiana). The Christmas Festival takes place along Cane River in the small city of Natchitoches, named after the indigenous people in the region.

Other holidays on this date: Universal Children's Day

21 November: International Hot Air Balloon Festival (India)

Created in 2009, this beautiful festival based on the lunar calendar takes place every year in the end of November.

The festival features thousands of hot air balloons – all in different shapes and colours, lots of local food and traditional dances.

As the event is located within proximity of temples and holy sites, as well as a holy lake (its waters are believed to cure most diseases).

The Sunrise balloon flight with thousands of balloons ascending at the same time gives an unforgettable memory of the rising sun over the desert. The Night Glow Concert is magical as the hot air balloons glow with different lights and create a fairyland atmosphere.

The festival also features a hare and hound race and coincides with the annual camel fair (the biggest live-stock market).

Travel to: Northern India (Rajasthan). The event takes place in the city of Pushkar – a sacred Hindu site bordering the Thar Desert. Look for accommodation in Adventure Desert Camp and spend the night in a tent surrounded by sand dunes.

Other holidays on this date: World Television Day

22 November: Black Rice Ceremony (Taiwan)

Black Rice is an annual harvest ceremony, held over two days in the end of November by the indigenous Rukai people who believe that the black rice crop which was their main source of food in the past, was brought by gods from the depth of the pond. They are one of the 13 indigenous people of Taiwan and are known as "the people from the mountain". They believe that their ancestors reborn into a clouded leopard and a hundred pacer (a venomous viper).

The Rukai pay tribute to their deities, ask them for blessings and to chase away the evil spirits, birds from eating the seeds, bad weather, flood etc.

In the past, the Rukai people would present to the Elders their crops and the latter would distribute them to families who were not lucky and had a poor harvest. The hunters would do the same with their prey. The ritual was very special, so everyone would put on their best ceremonial dress.

However, what has been the main crop and main diet for the Rukai – namely, the black rice, is rarely seen today. That is why pagan in its origin, the ceremony today is more a time to relax and re-join with family and friends. This is also a chance for the tribe to keep its traditional rites and customs alive – for example, by playing the Black Rice Adventure Game for the visitors to learn about the ancient ceremony.

Travel to: Taiwan (Kaohsiung). The ceremony is observed in Kungdavane neighborhood at the Maolin District.

Other holidays on this date: Teacher's Day (Costa Rica), Saisiat Festival (Taiwan)

23 November: Loi Krathong and Yi Peng Festivals (Thailand)

The annual Loi Krathong festival is held on the evening of a full moon on the 12th month from the traditional Thai lunar calendar (usually in November). Its name comes from the ancient ritual of weaving baskets, decorating them with flower petals and setting them afloat, and literally means "to float a basket".

This is one of the most beautiful celebrations in Thailand, believed to have originated from an ancient ritual of worshipping the Goddess of Water after a plentiful rice harvest.

Traditional small containers (baskets) are made of banana tree leaves or spider lily. They are big enough to hold an offering to the water spirits, incense sticks and a candle. The floating art-pieces symbolize letting go of one's negative feelings and emotions.

The locals gather by a river, canal or lake to make a wish and launch their beautifully assembled miniatures, while big businesses launch gigantic floats adorned with flowers, ribbons and banners.

The water-sparkling Loi Krathong Festival coincides with another spectacular event – the Yi Peng Festival of lights. During Yi Peng, thousands of rice paper sky lanterns glow in the night sky. The lanterns, made of the thinnest paper wrapped around bamboo poles create a magical ambience as they mirror the floating baskets in the river.

The locals decorate their houses with flower garlands and put lanterns outside of their homes, on the streets and in temples.

Travel to: Thailand (Chiang Mai). This is the place where the two festivals of lights - Loi Krathong and Yi Peng are celebrated at the same time.

Other holidays on this date: St George's Day (Georgia), Black Friday (USA)

24 November: Bird Festival (Chile)

The annual two-day festival held in the end of November celebrates the migratory shorebirds that spend the winter in the area (30% of all migratory birds in the world). The species (pink flamingoes, black swans and more) travel more than 15 000 miles every year to get to the island. Thousands of people from around the world gather to enjoy the beautiful nature and to appreciate the conservation of the habitat.

There are many attractions accompanying the celebration – boat trips around the lakes, dolphin-watching, bird-themed theatre, dances and music, local food tastings, crafts workshops, bird talks and guided walks in the wetlands – the area where the birds nest.

Visitors have the chance to experience the local culture first hand, including a local seafood festival – "la mariscada", during which villagers set food stalls directly on the sandy beach. The event takes place when the sea recedes almost one kilometer and the beach is literally adorned with seafood which the villagers pick to produce their typical dishes, such as the curanto – seafood, veggies, potatoes and meat stewed in a hole dug in the ground and covered with hot stones (this dish dates to XIth C.B.C.).

Travel to: Chile (Chiloé Island - known for its wooden churches, built by Jesuit missionaries in the XVIIth and XVIIIth centuries). The event is held in the towns of Putemún and Caulin.

Other holidays on this date: Small Business Saturday (USA)

25 November: Monkey Buffet Festival (Thailand)

The world`s biggest primate banquet!

The event is held annually on the last Sunday of November since 1989. It is one of the most hilarious and bizarre celebrations.

Based on Thai legends, the mighty hero Rama gave the province of Lopburi to the Monkey King Hanuman (Hanuman`s army of monkeys saved Rama`s wife from a demon), hence all residents are his direct descendants.

For the locals, the monkeys are a symbol of luck and good fortune. They can live, travel (yes, even in buses) and enter in public buildings freely in the province and somehow, they have turned into an equal part of the society as all humans.

The Monkey Buffet Feast was created because the monkeys were harassing the tourists - stealing food and objects from them. The villagers decided that the best way to deal with the cheeky animals was to embrace them.

So, the authorities decided to take this opportunity, turn it into a local attraction and make it an unforgettable experience to the visitors.

The preparations start days before – 4 000kg of food is cooked by local chefs – fruit salads and carved fruits, rice cakes, sticky rice, peanuts, cucumbers, traditional Thai desserts with egg yolk and even refreshment drinks. The treats are all arranged on huge buffet-style tables covered in red cloth in front of the Monkey Temple where the banquet takes place.

Around 2 000 – 3 000 wild macaque monkeys join in the feast.

The event is open to public, however all visitors are strongly advised to keep their belongings in sight, as the furry fellows tend to snatch everything they believe is edible – including glasses, cell phones and necklaces.

The monkey-style holiday is accompanied by concerts and musical performances showing the local cultural heritage, market stalls offering traditional Thai food, souvenirs and all sorts of local produce.

A must-do during the festival is to taste the famous Khai Khem Dim So Phong (lime-mud salted egg) – it is a local delicacy, preserved using an ancient method of coating a raw egg in lime-mud, water, sugar and salt. The egg can be eaten raw or cooked.

Coconut Jelly is another local delicacy, produced by fermented coconut juice during which a jelly-like foam of white fungi grows. Flavoured syrups are added to the fungi and the sweet drink is then bottled and ready to use.

The monkey feast is entangled with the desire of the locals to show their heritage in a fun and exciting way.

Travel to: Thailand (Lopburi). The city is known as "Monkey City". The buffet is set outside the Pra Prang Sam Yot (the Monkey Temple).

Other holidays on this date: St Catherine's Day (France, Estonia)

26 November: San Miguel Carnival (El Salvador)

The Carnival is celebrated on the last Saturday in November and is part of the festivities honouring Our Lady of Peace (the city's Patron saint) that take place from the 13th till the 31st November every year. Created in 1959, the weeklong carnival is now one of the largest in Central America and the most popular one.

On the day of Our Lady of Peace – November 21st, locals start a street procession from the church, carrying a statue of Virgin Mary, dressed in a different dress every year. The people hold twinkling candles and throw flowers and flower petals at the statue, making a wish and a promise to the Saint at the same time. The legend has it that if one's wish comes true - the promise must be kept too.

Over the other days of the carnival, huge parades with colourfully decorated floats fill the streets from early afternoon to early morning. Each float has a candidate to be crowned a Carnival Queen.

Brightly dressed performers throw candy at the cheering crowds while dance troupes make their way through the marching bands.

Exquisite performances and lots of music accompany the festivities - onstage bands, street musicians, orchestras; samba, reggae and merengue dancers showing off their meticulous moves and many more.

The festive atmosphere is complemented by local chefs offering a variety of traditional dishes while piping hot pots attract visitors to many of the street food stalls.

The souvenir shops are a real display of the local cultural heritage with their variety of traditional bits and bots piled on the window displays.

The Carnival is a perfect starting point to get to know this beautiful country and its people – the famous for their hospitality, Salvadorians. As the festival's anthem goes:

"Ni pobre, ni rico, ni joven, ni viejo, ni bello, ni feo, ni chele, ni prieto, ni hembra, ni macho, ni alto, ni bajo, todo es igual en San Miguel, en Carnaval", or... an absolute invitation that every single person is welcome to join in the festivities!

P.S. The song "San Miguel Carnival" is created by Francisco Palaviccini and played by Gil Medina.

Travel to: El Salvador (San Miguel). Make sure to taste the delicious totopostes (local corn snack with cheese baked in clay oven) and tostacas (corn snack sweetened with brown sugar) on Roosevelt Avenue. One can also try the Mondongo soup (tripe soup with squash and lemon).

Other holidays on this date: Cyber Monday (USA), National Sovereignty Day (Argentina)

27 November: Winter Wonderland (England)

Winter Wonderland opens doors for a real Christmas extravaganza!

The event takes place annually from November till the first days in January in the beautiful setting of one of the most well-known parks in the world – Hyde Park.

For more than a decade, the small open-air Christmas market has turned into a crown jewel of the winter celebrations.

The Winter Wonderland fairground features more than 100 rides including classic carousel and a Helter Skelter, rollercoaster, the largest outdoor ice-skating rink in the UK, Ice Bar carved out of real ice blocks, shows and theater plays, Ice Kingdom, Santa's Grotto, circus, Ferris wheel, Christmas market, Bavarian village offering authentic Oktoberfest experience, karaoke cabins, live concerts and many more.

Festively decorated bars lure visitors with the cinnamon-ish scent of mulled wine and thick hot chocolate, while Santa Claus and Snow White greet everyone and spread the Christmassy spirit.

The irresistible piping-hot sausages, churros, caramel apples and homemade sweets attract thousands to the many street food stalls scattered around the fairground.

Beautifully decorated chalets glowing with sparkling lights offer handmade Christmas tree ornaments, art and craft souvenirs, trinkets, jewellery and decoration.

Winter Wonderland is visited by millions of people every year including members of the Royal family, celebrity musicians, actors and artists. The event is busiest during the weekends when the crowds cause a real "people traffic jam" in the tunnels of the London tube.

Travel to: England (London). The event takes place in Hyde Park – one of the 8 Royal Parks in London.

Other holidays on this date: Aviation Day (Venezuela), International Giving Tuesday

28 November: The Night Watchman (Switzerland)

Ever since the Middle Ages, the Night Watchman roams the narrow-cobbled alleys and guards the city from crime and fires after dark falls.

He patrols the streets for centuries – his skin pale white, dressed in black with a black tricorn hat, wrapped in a black-hooded cape and holding a twinkling lantern in one of his hands and a long spear with an axe in the other. The spear is an exact copy of the spears used by the Swiss Guards at the Vatican.

The guard guides visitors through the narrow alleys of the Old Town and tells horrific stories of executions, witches, hangmen and plagues which took place in the city many years ago.

In the past, Night Watchmen were the ones locking the gates to the city every night. Their duties also included lighting the 5 600 lanterns on the city streets.

Unfortunately, today there are only 2 remaining Night Watchmen in the city, but they still get the job done! Plus, they are a part of the European Guild of Night Watchmen including 180 members from different countries.

Travel to: Switzerland (Zurich). The Night Watchman departs from Lindenhoff every first and last Tuesday of the month, all year round, however the best time to accompany him is in the winter months.

Other holidays on this date: Proclamation of the Republic (Chad), Day of Albanians (Kosovo)

29 November: The Christmas Tree Lighting Ceremony (USA)

Dessi Nikoltchev:

Ever since its creation in 1933, this wonderful Christmas custom takes place annually in the end of November. The majestic tree, adorned with thousands of lights and topped with a sparkling Swarovski star with 25 000 crystals, stays until January 7th. Today, the Christmas centrepiece is gazed at by 125 million locals and visitors a year.

It all started in the years after the Great Depression of 1929 when the economy was at its lowest point. President Roosevelt came up with a plan involving the Rockefeller family who were working on a project to build a "city within the city" – a.k.a. Rockefeller Center employing around 40 000 people.

The tradition of placing a Christmas tree at the Rockefeller Center began by accident in 1931 when demolition workers on the site collected some money to decorate a fir tree with cranberry garlands, tin cans and paper figurines on Christmas Eve. They stood by the tree to receive their paychecks, being enormously grateful that they had jobs. The tree brought cheer to many people in those difficult years of instability.

The first official lighting ceremony began two years later when the Center was completed – in 1933, the tree was decorated with 700 light bulbs. And ever since 1951, the lighting ceremony has been broadcasted live.

Today, the Norway Spruce weighs 12 tons without any ornaments and is decorated with 50 000 LED lights. Since 1969 it is "guarded" by twelve angel figures made of metal wires and light bulbs.

On its way to the Rockefeller Center, the Norway Spruce is tied with giant red bows and mounted on a truck.

As per tradition, the tree is lit by the current Mayor of New York and celebrity guests. The ceremony is accompanied by live concerts, ice skating and lots of fun.

For many years, after the end of the holidays - the tree is donated for use in house construction.

How to participate: USA (New York). The ceremony takes place at the Rockefeller Center.
Other holidays on this date: Unity Day (Vanuatu)

30 November: Mawlid (Algeria)

The day is celebrated to commemorate the birth of the Prophet Muhammad in 569 A.D. and is a major holiday taking place in the Islamic month of Rabi' al-awwal (in the end of November).

The day was first honoured in Egypt in the XIth C but became an official holiday in 1588 when a celebration was held by the Ottoman Sultan Murad III. Today, the day is celebrated in around 47 Muslim countries.

The event is marked by street processions and parades, charity, reading poetry related to the prophet, fasting, family gatherings and singing of religious songs.

All homes, streets, cars, public transport and mosques are richly decorated. Sermons, preaching the life of the Prophet and how to live a meaningful life are held in all cities.

The legend has it that this holiday is "a chaotic, incoherent spectacle, where numerous events happen simultaneously, all held together only by the common festive time and space".

Many Sufi people believe that this was the state of the world before the existence of Muhammad.

The festivities attract tons of foreigners who can freely observe the traditions and cultural heritage of the local people and, of course, join in the celebration.

Travel to: Algeria (Béni-Abbès). The city hosts a beautiful open-air celebration on the main square featuring Karkabou music and traditional dances.

Other holidays on this date: International Computer Security Day

... DECEMBER

Banning of Christmas in Scotland: Under the leadership of Oliver Cromwell, the British Parliament banned the Christmas celebrations in 1647 (the ban was lifted in 1660), however the Scottish Presbyterian Church (The Church of Scotland) was highly discouraging all Christmas celebrations ever since 1583 as having no basis in the Bible. In fact, until 1958 Christmas was a regular working day in Scotland. This is the main reason for the spectacular festivities during Hogmanay – the Scottish New Year. Without Christmas, the Scots craved for a holiday to relax, unwind and chase away the winter cold – hence Hogmanay was created with its bonfires and fire rituals, songs of friendship and glasses filled with the world-famous scotch!

01 December: Sunday Papal Blessing Tradition (Vatican)

One of the possibilities to see the Pope is during a traditional Sunday Blessing. A beautiful and humble ritual which takes place every Sunday at 12 o`clock when the Pope is in Rome.

Exactly at noontime, he appears from the window of his apartment to give a speech and greet in several languages the large crowd gathered at the Vatican Square.

The brief speech (usually on current affairs) is followed by The Angelus Prayer which can be dated back to XIth C. Italy.

The Pope imparts the Apostolic Blessing to the people after the prayer.

The whole event lasts for about 15-20min and is broadcasted live.

Interesting is the gesture which every Pope makes with his hand while giving a blessing - the partially outstretched hand with fourth and fifth fingers curled inward – a gesture, which goes back to the first Pope – St. Peter.

According to a research conducted by a Professor of anatomy, this specific position of the fingers is because St Peter had a nerve injury preventing him to stretch his fingers in full. Every Pope after Peter followed suit out of respect to their predecessor and so – the blessing gesture became a Papal tradition.

Where to travel: Vatican City (St Peter's Square). To get the best experience – visit the Sistine Chapel and the Vatican Museums.
Other holidays on this date: Chichibu Night Festival (Japan), World AIDS Day

02 December: Sacrifice to the Short Spirit (Taiwan)

The ceremony, held every other year over four days and three nights, celebrates one of the most ancient people on the planet – a.k.a. the indigenous people of the Short Tribe believed to possess magical powers. Held for over 400 years, the festival takes place on the 15th day of the 10th lunar month (late November/early December).

The legend has it that in the past, the Short People lived next to the Saisiyat Tribe - gave them seeds, taught them how to plant and harvest, and passed on the knowledge of worship and folklore. The two tribes lived in peace and harmony. The Saisiyat invited the Short People to join in their festivals and ceremonies (with lots of dancing, singing and drinking rice wine), treating them as guests of honour.

Until... at one point, the men from the Short People tribe started to harass the Saisiyat women. This enraged the Saisiyat men and they massacred the whole Short People tribe. However, there were two survivors – they cursed the Saisiyat that their ungratefulness would bring famine and bad fortune.

The Saisiyat begged for mercy and were forgiven on one condition – that they sing songs appraising the killed ancestors. So, the Saisiyat started a ceremony to calm and please the angry spirits of the Short People, to pray for fruitful harvest and to right the injustice of their ancestors.

The ceremony, attended by all members of the tribe dressed in traditional white and red costumes with lots of beads and small mirrors, includes sacred rituals and non-stop singing and dancing. The performance of the dances is observed by a Shaman. The ceremony is divided into three main acts:

1. Welcoming the spirits – at sunrise on the first day, the Saisiyat people sing facing the East, this way calling the spirits of the Short tribe ancestors. At dawn, the tribe members face each other standing in a circle, praying in hope that the spirits will accept their offerings. Then they link their arms with each other and start dancing in a perfect circle.

2. Pleasing the spirits – the Saisiyat commemorate the day by dancing and singing trancelike, haunting chants.

3. Farewell to the spirits – farewell songs and dances continue until the dawn of the next day.

This ceremony is one of the most solemn and sacred for the Taiwan aboriginal tribes. Those with "unclean thoughts" and the ones who are drunk are chased away by the Shaman. All participants and attendees must wear or tie pieces of Japanese silver grass to their clothes – it is believed to be sacred and to chase away evil spirits.

Travel to: Taiwan (Nanzhuang). The home of the Saisiat people is the Xiangtian Lake located at Donghe Village. Nearby is the Triangle Lake where visitors can pick fruits, camp and barbecue.

Other holidays on this date: International Day for the Abolition of Slavery

03 December: Good Neighborliness Day (Turkmenistan)

This is a public holiday, celebrated on the first Sunday in December. The celebration was created based on an ancient Turkmen custom called "Goñşy Okara". According to this custom, each person should share bread and salt with the neighbours.

The government established the holiday to remind the people of their ancient customs and values of living in harmony, mutual respect, kindness and material support.

The main festive events include open-air concerts and folk festivals. The residents gather in the festively decorated areas to exchange bread and salt with total strangers. The locals spend the day cooking traditional dishes such as pilaf, sourdough pies and patties, to offer as a treat to their neighbours. They also exchange small presents, sweets and fruits.

This is a cherished holiday which shows the brighter side of human relations, highlighting peaceful co-existence and hospitality.

Travel to: Turkmenistan (Ashgabat). The main festivities are held at the East Gate of the city and at the Concert Center "Ashgabat", located in the National Park of Independence.

Other holidays on this date: Anniversary of the Coronation of King Tupou I (Tonga), International Day of Persons with Disabilities

04 December: Mass Street Tango (Argentina)

Since the creation of the "Gran Milonga Nacional" (Tango Festival), locals celebrate the passionate and daring dance in its very home – Buenos Aires.

The popular beat and moves which became a world sensation originated in the 1800s in the working-class port areas of the city.

The locals and visitors alike, fill the streets in the traditional neighbourhoods and dance passionately to the haunting sounds of the bandoneon, the rhythm of the tango – the dance of love and betrayal, nostalgia and hope.

The main avenue of the city turns into an outdoor street tango dance salon – known as "milonga".

The event celebrates the birth date of Carlos Gardel and Julio De Caro (Dec 11th)– two of the greatest tango dancers ever lived. The actual "Gran Milonga Nacional" is held on December 4th or the nearest Saturday.

Many stages are built to house the numerous orchestras and singers that will make the people dance all night long.

The unique celebration attracts thousands of couples from around the world – professional and amateur dancers, tango aficionados or just people passing by.

Many streets, even whole blocks are closed for traffic to allow the dancers to enjoy their open-air stage for the night.

Travel to: Argentina (Buenos Aires). The event takes place along Avenida de Mayo from Plaza de Mayo to 9 de Julio Avenue.
Other holidays on this date: National Cookie Day (USA)

05 December: Krampusnacht (Germany)

This pre-Christmas ritual is celebrated annually on the night of December 5th and includes not the jolly old man with white beard and red coat but... demons with horns and masks.

The folklore of Krampus – the mythical scary creature with fangs and horns goes back to at least a thousand years. For long, the Krampusnacht celebrations were forbidden by the Catholic Church, but in the end, pop culture prevailed and revived the ancient custom in the 1950s C pairing the beast with St Nicholas (Santa Claus).

Although the exact origin of the so-called Christmas Devil is unknown, its roots can be traced back to pagan times. Anthropologists have different theories including that Krampus derived from the Horned God of Witches or simply represented the Christian Devil. Some believe that he was created as a counterpart to Santa Clause. The half-goat, half-demon literally "beats" children with birch branches into being nice and not naughty. The naughty ones – he drags to the underworld.

Unfortunately, there are no historical clues as to when the horned god appeared for the first time, mostly because the druids didn't leave any written evidence of their symbols nor figures that appear in their rites of passage before the Christianization of Europe. However, horned-god characters started to appear in Medieval plays around the XIth C.

In modern era and adopted into the narrative of Christianity, Krampus appears with St Nicholas on the eve of December 5th. The creature is a sort of anti-Santa – a mischievous, child-terrorizing ghoul who gives coals to the misbehaving kids.

On this day, men dress up as Krampus (the costume is made of sheepskin and evil-looking hand-carved wooden mask with huge horns) - drink lots of alcohol, run through the streets making as much noise as possible with the cowbells and chains attached to the costume, and scare children.

Women are not too far behind – they dress up as Frau Perchta, a figure from the Nordic mythology representing the Goddess of Fertility.

During the night of the celebrations, Krampus roams the streets and visits homes in search of naughty kids. It is a custom to offer him a glass of schnapps!

Travel to: Germany (Munich). One of the best places to attend a Krampus Run is the Christmas Market in the city. Nuremberg has too, a tradition of celebrating Krampusnacht.
Other holidays on this date: St Nichola`s Eve (Czech Republic)

06 December: Black Pete (the Netherlands)
Celebrated annually in the night of December 5th (December 6th in Belgium) this is one of the most controversial celebrations in the world due to its "hidden" racist background.

Black Pete is the companion of St Nicholas (Santa Claus). The character depicted as a dark-skinned male from Spain first appeared in a book published in 1850.

The exact origin cannot be traced, although there are many theories linking Black Pete to the Germanic mythology. One of them depicts an enslaved by St Nicholas devil who returns to earth to serve him as a dark-skinned man. Another theory is that Pete is dark-skinned because he stands by the chimney and listens to the children – deciding who has been naughty and nice. The legend has it that if a child had been naughty, Black Pete and St Nicholas would take him to Spain.

Another one is that St Nicholas freed a boy from slavery and the latter became his lifelong companion.

The people who dress up as Black Pete paint their face in black colour, wear Renaissance attire, curly wig, red lipstick and earrings.

Black Pete takes part in the pre-Christmas celebrations which start in late November and continue in early December. He visits schools and houses and marches in street parades alongside Santa Claus.

The actual "job" of the controversial character is to welcome St Nicholas who arrives usually by boat from Spain, to amuse the children and give them traditional treats such as spice nuts, peppernuts and small sweets.

Some businesses have altered the traditional appearance of Black Pete due to accusations of racism – on the window displays in the department stores, for example, Black Pete is gold.

On the other hand, there is an "Action group for preserving Black Pete" established in the country, which defends the character as a fun and harmless tradition.

Even the UN Committee on the Elimination of Racial Discrimination printed a statement on the topic: "the character of Black Pete is sometimes portrayed in a manner that reflects negative stereotypes of people of African descent and is experienced by many people of African descent as a vestige of slavery".

The debate on the faith of this Christmas character is ongoing.

Travel to: Netherlands (Amsterdam). At the Amsterdam Christmas parade, Black Pete is named "Chimney Pete" and his attire represents a Spanish nobleman.

Other holidays on this date: St Nicholas Day (Bulgaria, Hungary)

07 December: Burning the Devil (Guatemala)

La Quema del Diablo.

Created in the XVIIIth C, but celebrated annually since 1990, the custom takes place on December 7th at 6 pm sharp.

According to historians, the celebration began when people used to light lanterns in front of their homes or make bonfires from their garbage (if they were poor and couldn't afford to buy lanterns) to celebrate special occasions.

Another theory puts the priests in the spotlight and how they wanted to emphasize the Virgin's triumph over evil.

Today, families make huge bonfires outside their homes and burn an effigy of the Devil in a form of piñata, to chase away the evil from their houses – that is the devilish creatures lurking under the bed and behind the furniture.

The ritual can be traced back to pagan times when fire was used in cleansing ceremonies. The idea behind it? – to burn all things evil from the past year and clear the way to the upcoming bright Christmas celebrations.

The locals get really creative with the effigies – they represent the Devil with human-height figures painted in red with huge horns, scary demons with black boots and paper goats often holding a pitchfork. As the celebration has a different satirical theme every year – sometimes the devil figure can be seen wearing a blond wig and grotesque clothes. After the effigy is burnt on the main square of the city – the Devil's will is read aloud.

Most of the "burning devils" have a belt of firecrackers attached to their body for dramatic effect.

Local merchants sell devilish costumes, light-up horns and sizzling meat!

Reportedly, around 500,000 bonfires are lit in the city alone on that day.

Travel to: Guatemala (Guatemala City). Many merchants sell piñata devils and firecrackers. The historical center of the city is the best place to celebrate as Burning the Devil comes right before the Feast of the Immaculate Conception which celebrates the patron saint of Guatemala City.

Other holidays on this date: Día de las Velitas (Colombia), The Feast of St Ambrose (Italy)

08 December: Pooping Log (Spain)

This is a rather hilarious name for a holiday, but it is a much loved Christmas tradition celebrated annually in Catalonia. It has its roots in pagan times when people celebrated the Winter Solstice by cutting a huge tree and burning it to keep warm during the cold months. Somehow that evolved into painting the trunk of the tree and filling it with treats...

Every year on December 8th locals put outside their houses a 30cm hollow log. It usually stands up on four legs (sticks), has a smiley face, red nose and a hat. From that day on, the family "feeds" the log with chocolate and sweets every night and keeps him warm and comfortable with a thick blanket. On Christmas Day it will "poop" presents for the children. The presents are sweets, dried figs, nuts and the traditional turrón – a nougat made of egg white, honey and almonds. This traditional Christmas sweet is typical across all of Spain – the earliest evidence coming from the XVIth C. when the sweet was mentioned to have been consumed around Christmas since "time immemorial". It was reserved for special occasions and given as part of the salary as well (due to its high price at the time).

To make the log poop, kids beat it with sticks while singing Christmas carols. One of the variations of the Christmas Log song goes like this:

"(Poop) Log,
(poop) nougats, hazelnuts and mató cheese.
If you don't (poop) well,
I'll hit you with a stick,
(Poop) log!"

When the beating ritual is over, the kids get their presents from under the blanket and share them with each other.

In the end, the poor log gets burnt in the fireplace.

Travel to: Spain (Catalunya). One can make or buy a Pooping Log (Caga Tio) from any store in Barcelona.

Other holidays on this date: Student holiday (Bulgaria)

09 December: Szopka (Poland)

This beautiful tradition in the Polish capital, dates back to the XIXth C. Unique feature to the festivity is the use of historical buildings of Krakow as a background of Nativity scene.

In December, hundreds of street performers recreate one of the most significant biblical scenes using wood toys and movable puppets – some of them up to two meters high and three meters wide. They bring a magical street theatre alive before the spectators.

What is interesting, is that this art-nouveau involves figurines resembling current politicians, satirical scenes and renown artists together with historical features and people. They are communicated to the audience in the form of puppet shows, pageant plays and shimmering fairy tale scenes celebrating the birth of Jesus Christ. This, of course, has led to many controversial opinions on should the street plays be banned or not. And so, it happened in the XVIIIth C – such performances were banned from the Church, which led to creating a whole new "folk art" as a way for people to express themselves.

It all started with the masons and woodworkers of XIXth C Krakow – they started to carve and sell small avant-garde nativity-scene figurines and soon flooded the local markets. They gained popularity very fast, although their initial intention was to make some extra income before the Christmas holidays. People were lining in a queue to sneak a peek at the masterfully crafted figurines. At the same time, Christmas carolers were selling the items door-to-door.

In 1937, the government decided to support the newly-created business and recognize the "szopka" (nativity scene) figurines as official souvenirs representing Krakow and its artists and craftsmen. The authorities even created a competition for the best nativity scene set up.

There is, however, one condition – all nativity scenes should portray Krakow`s landmarks – St. Mary`s Basilica, Wawel Castle, Sukkienice trade hall and the Krakow Barbican.

The competition takes place annually on the first Thursday in December (building and painting a szopka could easily take up to one year). The materials used are steel, wood, glass, foil in various colours, wool, electrical cables for the moving figurines, plastics etc.

The winner takes home a lump sum + strudels and cakes provided by local pastry shops.

All visitors can treat themselves to any of the food stalls offering oszypek (local smoked cheese delicacy made of salted sheep milk) and wine.

Travel to: Poland (Krakow). The best figurines are displayed until February the following year in the Historical Museum of Krakow. A display of all works is set at the steps of the Adam Mickiewicz statue on the Krakow Main Square (one of the 10 Most Beautiful Main Squares in the World).

Other holidays on this date: National Heroes Day (Antigua and Barbuda)International Anti-corruption Day

10 December: Chitramas (Pakistan)

This is a winter festival celebrated by the indigenous Kalash people – the smallest ethnoreligious community in Pakistan, practising a religion of animism and ancient Hinduism.

Chitramas is one of their longest festivals, observed between December 10th – 22nd every year and including around 50 different rituals and ceremonies. It is held to mark the end of the harvest and the field work, and its last day coincides with the Kalasha New year.

Kalasha men and women gather to dance and sing for the duration of the festivities – most events require obligatory participation from everyone.

They observe the rituals with great precision and joy, thanking the gods for the successful year and praying for a better one to come. The Kalasha believe that their main deity – god Balimain, joins them for the duration of the festival and perform folk dances and religious songs in his honour.

Some customs include animal sacrifices of goat, lamb and cow – a goat is beheaded per each adult member in the family. In others, the local women make statues out of dough in the form of different animals which are used for house decoration.

Preparation for Chitramas includes a dive in the ice-cold waters of a nearby stream – a purification ceremony.

The start is announced by a religious leader – he sends teams of boys and girls into the forest. Each group competes to make the largest bonfire and highest flames, all while they dance and sing around the fire. After that, the youngsters carrying burning branches, are warmly welcomed back into the village.

The most important ritual is "autic" - a young boy volunteers to spend 7 days in seclusion, living in the cattle houses, consuming meat from the slaughtered animals.

The rituals are so sacred to the Kalasha, that if a member of the tribe dies during Chitramas – his/her death is kept a secret until the end of the festival.

At the concluding ceremony, marking the end of the festival, the religious leader of the Kalasha makes a prediction for the year to come and frees a fox (a sign of good omen), waves his hand in the air and everyone starts dancing the last dance for the years` Chitramas accompanied by the monotonous beat of drums.

After the celebrations are over, it is time for the Kalasha to hibernate – that is how they spend the following 3 months of extremely harsh weather.

Travel to: Pakistan (Chitral). The Kalash people reside in three valleys – Bamboret, Birir and Rambur. They are known for their hospitality, however, they don`t let non-tribal members to attend ceremonies between December 18th – 21st.

Other holidays on this date: International Human Rights Day

11 December: Baroque Christmas Market (Germany)

Running from late November until Christmas, this is one of the most beautiful yule markets in the world.

Cuddled amidst a small medieval town in Germany, the market is set between two magnificent Baroque churches. Arches and angels made of thousands of tiny light bulbs glitter in the background, turning the town in a real winter dream come true.

The local merchants spread in around 170 old-fashioned Baroque booths and stalls, arranged in the same way they had been in ancient times, decorated with gold lights and green wreaths. They offer artisan goods such as handmade Christmas tree ornaments, fluffy knitted clothing, traditional arts and crafts as well as sizzling sausages, roasted chestnuts, mulled wine and gingerbread cookies. The air is buzzing with glitter and holiday cheer while merrymakers and carollers take care of the festive spirit for the whole duration of the event.

The market is especially mesmerizing at night-time as it glows with warm golden light illuminated by numerous lamps and lanterns.

A festive program featuring magicians, clowns, puppet show and concerts offers entertainment on a daily basis.

Travel to: Germany (Ludwigsburg). The small medieval town in Baden-Württemberg province is known for its "Blooming Baroque" landscaped gardens and the ceramics and fashion museums in the Residential Palace.

Other holidays on this date: Republic Day (Madagascar), International Mountain Day

12 December: Yule Lads 13 Days of Christmas (Iceland)

Most countries have only one Santa Claus (Father Christmas, St Nicholas etc.) while Iceland has a horde of hair-raising Christmas trolls!

This is the annual Icelandic interpretation of Santa Claus – featuring thirteen mischievous trolls (sons of the Mountain Trolls), instead of a white-bearded man.

The Yule Lads are believed to pull pranks and misbehave, however, they are the ones who put presents in the shoes of children and decide who has been naughty or nice during the past year.

The local kids tie their best shoe to their bedroom window and wait for the thirteen Yule Lads to start appearing exactly thirteen days before Christmas. Every night, one Yule Lad visits each child and leaves either a present or a rotten potato in the shoe depending on the child`s behaviour.

The Christmas pranksters derive from the Icelandic mythology and have often been depicted as creepy and horrific monsters who eat children. The parents would use the troll stories to frighten their children and treat them into behaving well. However, they were officially banned to torment the children with these particular stories in 1746. The way the Yule Lads behave and look in modern times was described in a book in 1932.

They are the sons of a Mountain Troll mother who wants to cook naughty children into a stew, and a lazy Mountain Troll father who doesn't go out of his cave because he is cold. The merry family lives with a blood-thirsty black cat known as the Christmas Cat. The legend has it that this lovely pet eats those children who don't receive a new piece of clothing for Christmas...

The 13 "baby" trolls have different names, each associated with their character:
1. Stekkjarstaur harasses sheep;
2. Giljagaur hides in the forest and steals milk foam on every given occasion;
3. Stúfur is very short and tends to steal pans;
4. Þvörusleikir steals and licks spoons;
5. Pottaskefill steals the leftovers from the pots;
6. Askasleikir is very ugly. He hides under the bed and steals bowls;
7. Hurðaskellir is very loud and enjoys slamming doors and waking people up;
8. Skyrgámur is very stupid and adores Icelandic yoghurt;
9. Bjúgnakrækir loves to steal smoked sausages;
10. Gluggagægir peeps through the windows to locate anything worth stealing;
11. Gáttaþefur has an extremely large nose which he uses to sniff bread;
12. Ketkrókur steals all things meat using a hook;
13. Kertasníkir spends his time stealing candles from children.

As to why does Iceland celebrates not one, but 13 days of Christmas – most likely this happened with the change from Julian to Gregorian calendar. Mid-winter was taking place on December 13th and to bring it back to where it should be – December 21st – 13 days had to be taken off the calendar. As the people were uncomfortable and unclear about the change – they decided (just in case) to go on and celebrate all of the days between the old and new Christmases.

After Christmas, the Yule Lads return to their cave – one by one and in the exact order, they had arrived. The last one to leave is Kertasníkir who heads home on January 6th (Epiphany).

Travel to: Iceland (Reykjavik). Every year, the Yule Lads come to visit children in the National Museum in the city.

Reportedly the cave of the lovely Troll family and their cat is located in the labyrinth of Dimmuborgir in Northern Iceland – they meet and greet people every day from 1pm to 3pm (except during December 12-25th).

Other holidays on this date: Day of the Virgin of Guadalupe (Mexico), Jamhuri Day (Kenya)

13 December: Mummering and Mummer Parade (Canada)

Mummering takes place annually in the days preceding Christmas.

Thought to have originated in Rome, this custom was brought to Canada by English and Irish sailors in the beginning of the XIXth C. and is celebrated ever since.

The "mummers" are a group of friends, who disguise themselves in flamboyant clothes and masks, and distort their voice to avoid being recognized. They usually visit homes within their neighbourhood during the twelve days of Christmas. Anything in hand can be used for a successful costume – curtains, lampshades, rubber boots, inside-out worn dresses, towels to cover the face, ribbons, pots as hats etc. The characters can also change their walk, weight (using pillows stuffed in their costumes) and posture.

The act of mummering comes in three forms: street parades, a dramatical play involving a hero and a villain, and house visits. Most common are the house visits.

When the mummers visit a house – they play games, pull pranks, tell jokes, sing and dance. The hosts must guess the identity of each masked mummer. Once he has been recognized, he takes off his mask. The merry group is treated to slices of Christmas cake and blueberry wine before it takes off to the next house.

The biggest event is the Mummers Parade taking place within the duration of a Mummers Festival held every year in the beginning of December. The event was created by the Heritage Foundation of Newfoundland and Labrador in 2009.

Many workshops offer to visitors the opportunity to make their own mummer's costume, participate in dress-up party, make a hobby horse with spooky eyes and crooked teeth and more. A must-have for any mummer is the so-called "ugly stick" – a self-made musical instrument with bells, pots, pans, cans and anything else that could make noise tied to it. There are also workshops on "Ugly Stick 101" for those interested.

The Mummers are much loved in this part of Canada, and as locals say: They are a symbol of the fun-loving spirit and are deeply tied into the local folklore.

An interesting part of the festival is the Screech-in ceremony – a person can become an honorary Newfoundlander by reciting a phrase, kissing a dead codfish and taking a shot of rum!

Travel to: Canada (Newfoundland). The Mummers Festival takes place in the coastal town of Colliers.

Other holidays on this date: Republic Day (Malta), National Day (St Lucia)

14 December: Hot Spring Fine Cuisine Carnival (Taiwan)

Initiated in 2007 by the government, the carnival running annually from October till January, combines in a single event two of the best things in Taiwan – the famous natural springs and the mouth-watering local food.

The event showcases the essence of Taiwan and welcomes all visitors to have a taste of the gourmet cuisine while soaking in their chosen spring (hot, cold, mud or submarine). Bars, restaurants, shopping and entertainment areas are scattered all around the outdoor spas, offering lots of discounts on food, drinks, health and beauty products made using only natural ingredients.

Each part of the country offers a different combination for one to indulge all senses. In one part, the "beauty springs", known for their rejuvenating effect on the skin are combined with the local indigenous cuisine, other part mixes mud baths with juicy pork dishes; another taints with clearwater hot springs, fresh trout and plum cuisine, and the traditional lotus meal.

More than 200 restaurants, hotels and SPA resorts take part in the carnival, offering to their guests special fine-and-dine packages and themed menus around the outdoor baths. A perk of staying with any of the participating businesses are numerous prize draws taking place for the duration of the carnival.

Where to travel: Taiwan. The event takes place all around the country with one of the 17 spring areas chosen as a kick off site.

Other holidays on this date: Roast Chestnuts Day (USA), International Monkey Day

15 December: Wonderfruit (Thailand)

This is one of the most sustainable festivals on the planet. Created in 2014, the four-day mid-December event aims to develop creative solutions for eco-friendly living and to bring the whole world together to celebrate.

The line-up includes live music, all things art, food and more. The festival grounds have their own rules: zero tolerance to plastic cups, cutlery or plates; the organizers have arranged to filter water from the nearby lake and have introduced FARMacy – green fields surrounding the site, on which various plants and herbs are grown. The performing stages look like art installations made of recyclable materials, trash, bamboo sticks and even rice.

Chairs of hay, bars converted from an old bus, hippie beach weddings, yoga classes, DIY dreamcatcher classes, plant medicine talks, meditation, hammock weaving classes, merging your soul with a tree classes, bike trailing, martial arts lessons, squirt gun championships, bodypainting, flame-spinning and galactic puppet show – just a hint of what the visitors can expect.

The festival has seen many local and international stars to perform music, plays and theatre acts alongside workshops set by environmentalists whose sole purpose is to educate more people on sustainable living and its benefits.

The food is a big part of the festival activities as award-winning chefs and mixologists design signature meals and cocktails using organic food and typical Thai ingredients. Most of the festival food is grown on the on-site farm fields. Some of the served delicacies include Wagyu Tomahawk (huge meat skewers), Lobster Rolls, various noodles, sashimi, Lamb Tacos, Reggae brunch and oysters.

This is a family-friendly festival and it has a dedicated Kids area named Camp Wonder, offering puppet shows, kite making courses, kids circus and more.

The fest, combining Thai, Asian and Western cultures runs non-stop - 24 hours a day and works with a cryptocurrency called TREE (the cryptocurrency supports the mangrove forests in Myanmar).

Fully equipped campsites are available to rent.

Travel to: Thailand (Pattaya). The festival takes place at The Fields at Siam Country Club – one of the best beaches in Thailand.

Other holidays on this date: National Cupcake Day (USA)

16 December: Tribute to Santo Tomas (Guatemala)

This is an annual 1-week festival that mixes Christian and Mayan customs and takes place in mid-December.

The fest features tons of music, dancing and abundance of wine and local food delicacies such as fried chicken and variety of corn tortillas. The whole celebration takes place in the centre of a lively marketplace which gets packed with vendors selling absolutely everything during the week of the festivities.

There are also street parades with live music bands, dancers, art performances, masquerades and more.

The people dress in colourful costumes and wear beautiful handcrafted masks or sombreros adorned with flowers, ribbons, beads and feathers. Many locals keep the Mayan heritage alive and wear traditional Mayan attire.

The days are full of firework shows, firecrackers and "small random explosions of things" outside the St Tomas` church as the locals celebrate. Each night there is a huge display of fireworks.

The culmination comes on December 21st – St Thomas` Day, the patron saint of the city when a traditional Mayan dance is performed to honour the Catholic Saint. Huge wooden poles are erected on platforms on the city square – some up to 30 meters in height. The locals perform the "palo volador" (flying pole) dance to the sound of marimba music, using two ropes tied to the top of each pole. They swing and descend in pairs – some of them tying the rope end to their ankles, other to their bodies and some just holding it with their bare hands. They fly-dance around the pole in high speed until the rope unravels and levels them to the ground. It is quite a frightening thing to watch.

This interesting mixture of Mayan traditions and Catholic saints started when the Spanish ruled Guatemala. In the small village where St Tomas is honoured, missionary priests created in the past 14 cofradías – guilds, each representing a different saint. On the celebration of its respective saint – each cofradía wears ceremonial dress and marches ahead in a street procession. A custom on the day is the transfer of power from the elders of the cofradía to a new representative who has a 1-year mandate and is responsible to organize the celebration on the following year. This ritual includes passing of a silver-decorated wooden baton onto the newly elected.

Travel to: Guatemala (Chichicastenango). The small mountainous town of Chichicastenango, called Chichi by the locals is home to the K'iche' Mayans.

The wooden poles are erected on the square near the church of St Tomas dating back to the XVIth C. The church is built atop a former temple and incorporates the temple's 18 steps, each representing a month on the Mayan calendar.

Other holidays on this date: National Day (Bahrain), Independence Day (Kazakhstan)

17 December: Pet Fed (India)

Attended by 25 000 people and more than 3 000 pets, this is the biggest pet festival spread across 12 000sq.m. and about 1 000sq.m. off-leash zone.

Created in 2014, the two-day festival gained much attention and is now held in three cities in India. The event takes place after mid-December every year.

This is a truly unique experience for all pet owners who get to pamper their furry friends in a most luxurious way possible.

The festival grounds offer anything to make the pets feel relaxed, fed and entertained – there is a huge outside green play area with pet trampolines and ball pools, dog picnic area, kids and dogs play zone; pet friendly restaurants; pet bakeries; pet care clinics; dog cafes, swings and rides, pet coiffeurs, dedicated cat zone, pet fashion shops and grooming zone. There is also a Discover Dogs zone which shows the latest breeding trends.

Some of the activities on the schedule include, but are not limited to: pet workshops, pet fashion show, Pet's Got Talent competition (jumping through a loop, dog dances, playing dead or sit pretty commands), security dogs show, Good dog citizen program workshops, dog training workshops, live music, art galleries, art performances and comedy gigs, kids zone and much more.

In 2016 the festival tried to enter the Guinness Book of World Records for most number of dogs wearing bandanas (the record is held by Australia).

A VIP Lounge and over 100 stalls with local merchandise including pet souvenirs, local food and drinks are available on the festival grounds.

Travel to: India (Delhi). The venue is NCIS Grounds Okhla.

Other holidays on this date: Day of Reconciliation (South Africa)

18 December: Kasuga Wakamiya Festival (Japan)

A stunning annual festival of traditional Japanese performing arts, tracing its origin back to the XIIth C. Its first edition was held right after the end of a plague epidemy - to offer prayers to the gods and thanks for a plentiful harvest. It has been celebrated ever since – over 4 days in December (15th – 18th).

The event is held in and around a shrine which has been the very home of the Wakamiya deity since 1136. The festival celebrates the sacred spirit after a long year of work. The locals make offerings in the form of coloured rice and folkloric performances to commemorate the god and show their gratitude.

The participating artists awe the public with pristine performances of "kagura" –music dedicated to the gods, and "bugaku" – a traditional court dance accompanied by music.

The highlight of the festival for sure is the amazing Procession of the Eras, in which more than 500 people represent the essence of each Japanese era – from the clothing and manners to the music and dances, as well as theatrical plays and acts. A statue of Wakamiya is paraded and returned to the shrine to rest. It is thoroughly covered with branches as the mortal visitors are not allowed to see it.

The festival takes place in a beautiful mountainous park where deer roam freely. The gracious animals are believed to be messengers of the gods and are treated as sacred. Magnificent and yet mystique stone and bronze lanterns embrace the paths to the shrine with dim light, turning the whole experience magical.

Visitors witness the elegance behind the masked Noh theatre performances, the beautiful moves of the swaying traditional dancers dressed in colourful kimonos and the solemn touch of the music notes played on flutes. It is a humbling and yet truly rewarding experience to be part of this centurial custom marking the noble moments of the rich Japanese history.

Travel to: Japan (Nara). The festival is held at the Wakamiya-jinja Shrine situated on the grounds of Kasuga Taisha Grand Shrine – the most cherished Shinto shrine built in 768.

Other holidays on this date: National Day (Qatar), Nigerian Republic Day (Niger)

19 December: Cave Christmas Market (the Netherlands)

This is probably the oldest in the world underground Christmas market. It is also one of the most impressive!

Organized by the Valkenburg Castle Foundation, this event takes place in the many caves scattered around a town, some of them dating back to XIth and XIIth centuries.

It runs from mid-November until Christmas and attracts thousands of people from around the world.

The visitors can roam freely the corridors inside the caves and enjoy the festive atmosphere on the backdrop of ancient mural paintings, centurial sculptures and a romantic underground chapel from the XVIIIth C.

Each gallery, illuminated by hundreds of sparkling lights and adorned with green Christmas wreaths, is a setting for numerous merchant stalls selling Christmas ornaments, decorations, antique jewellery and souvenirs. Some parts of the caves are turned into cosy candlelit bars, offering sizzling sausages, gingerbread, roasted wallnuts complimented by a glass of hot chocolate or mulled wine.

The underground market is part of a beautiful Christmas Village set above the caves. Some of the attractions include Christmas street parades with dancers, floats and singers performing Christmas songs (the processions take place twice a week!), nativity scene, Christmas carolers, Fairytale Forest and Santa's Grotto.

In fact, for a whole month, the small town of Valkenburg is known as "Christmas Town".

Travel to: the Netherlands (Valkenburg aan de Geul). The Christmas market takes place in the caves under the Valkenburg Castle. They form a labyrinth of underground passages – in the past allowing knights to safely escape the castle in case of an enemy attack. The Velvet Cave – the most famous one, has a temperature of exactly 12C all year round.

Other holidays on this date: International Horse Show (England)

20 December: Ignazhden (Bulgaria)

The day has its roots back in pagan times. It is believed that before the Christianization of the Bulgarians, Ignazhden and Christmas Eve coincided with a winter solstice ritual, both celebrating God Kolada on December 20th. The two holidays were separated only after the Christianization. Until the XIXth C, many locals used homemade candles to light in churches as a way to chase away all things evil.

Ignazhden celebrates The Feast of St Ignatius of Antioch who in the beginning of the IInd C., was sentenced to death and thrown to lions because of his Christian faith. On this day, Virgin Mary's labour pains began and continued until Christmas.

The Christmas and New year celebrations begin from Ignazhden. In some areas, the holiday is known as the beginning of the New year and is called "New Day".

In the morning, women sweep the dirt from the fireplace and dust it outside around the house. This keeps away evil magic from the household.

The most important ritual on that day is "polazvane" (crawling). It is very important who sets foot first into a home – the following years' fortune depends on this person and his character. If the person is good and fortunate – the year would be fruitful and successful, and the family will invite him again on Ignazhden the following year. However, if the person is of bad nature – the family would send him away as he would bring misfortune. If a family member goes out of the house – he must bring along something back with him.

In the past, the first person to step in would take a small stick or branch from the yard, bring it along inside the house and put it in the fireplace – a ritual symbolizing wishes for good luck and fertility – for the cattle and the household. The hosts would treat the honourable guest to dried fruit and nuts.

The legend also has it that the 12 days following Ignazhden predict the weather for the upcoming 12 months (Dec 20th shows what the weather will be in January, Dec 21st respectively in February etc.). It is believed that if Ignazhden is rainy and cloudy – the year to come will be good with a plentiful harvest.

A few ancient traditions are associated with the holiday: one mustn't borrow any money on this day, one should not sew or knit as it is considered it will bring bad luck; nothing should be taken out of the house during the day to keep the good fortune inside the home.

Only Lenten dishes are served at the festive dinner, such as "sarmi" (sauerkraut leaves stuffed with rice), sweet boiled wheat, corn and a ritual round bread.

Ignazhden is associated with another pagan ritual still performed in some parts of the country – "Vardene". The ritual lasts for 12 days and starts on the night of Ignazhden. Close friends and relatives (women only) gather at one's house in the evening to roll dough. The elder women add special herbs believed to have magical powers in it. Then the rolled dough is set aside overnight while the women dance all night long. The ritual is repeated every night for 12 nights. On the last night, the women share the rolled dough between themselves – it is used for medicinal and magical purposes.

Travel to: Bulgaria. The "Vardene" ritual is still observed in Rousse and Razgrad. Ignazhden is celebrated across the country – especially since it is also a Name Day and everyone bearing the name Ignat, Iskra, Plamen and others celebrate!

Other holidays on this date: International Human Solidarity Day

21 December: Burning the Clocks (England)

This is a town gathering to celebrate the shortest day of the year and is observed annually on December 21st since its creation in 1993. The idea behind it was to create an urban festival that brings people from all walks of life together and to clash with the too much commercialized Christmas.

The locals prepare well in advance and make their own paper and willow lanterns. Although a different theme is set every year, the image of a clock is always a centrepiece in every lantern.

After a beautiful candlelit parade through the city streets, the lanterns are lit and passed into a blazing bonfire on the beach.

The celebration reminds of a carnival, with the parading people dressed in colourful clothes carrying white paper lanterns in various shapes and sizes, and the marching bands taking care of the festive atmosphere covering the streets as a blanket.

The parade-goers put all their thoughts, hopes and wishes into the lanterns before burning them, making a promise for a better year to come.

The event is much loved and anticipated and relies solely on crowdfunding.

After the bonfire on the beach, there is a spectacular display of fireworks.

Travel to: England (Brighton). Burning the Clocks takes place in the city center and on the beach. The parade starts at 5pm from the Corn Exchange.

Other holidays on this date: Ice and Snow Festival (China)

22 December: Dongzhi Festival (Taiwan)

This is the Winter Solstice festival, celebrated in China and East Asia around the 22nd December every year. It is associated with the Yin and Yang philosophy of harmony and balance between two opposites, as it marks the shortest day and the beginning of longer days, more daylight and more positive energy flowing in.

It is a holly and very important holiday for the Taiwanese. It is also a time to reunite with the whole family and spend time together.

Taiwanese prepare the traditional for this day tangyuan (brightly coloured balls of glutinous rice which represent reunion), which is a favourite dish served with sweet broth but also used as an offering to ancestor shrines and temples. Often the tangyuan is coloured in pink or green to look more festive and can be stuffed with sesame, meat or fruit puree. There is a story that in the Khan Dynasty, a young Doctor was horrified at how malnourished and weak the poor villagers were, so he decided to make dumplings stuffed with meat.

The locals keep an odd custom rooted in an ancient legend - according to it, the sticky rice balls used as offerings should be stuck behind doors and windows to serve as amulets to protect the children and keep away the evil spirits.

A unique ritual to the Taiwanese is to make a "sacrifice" to the ancestors – but instead of sacrificing a real animal, they steam nine-layer rice cakes and shape them as different animals (which are offered to the gods).

The celebration is accompanied by many nourishing dishes. The Taiwanese philosophy is that the winter is a time when the body hibernates and has a slower metabolism, therefore fat foods should be eaten to fight the cold weather. Some delicacies that can be found at this time of the year are mutton or duck hot pots infused with lots of ginger and ginseng.

Travel to: Taiwan (Taipei). An ancient custom to make the special "chicken puppies" tangyuan is still observed only on the Penghu Island. The chicken puppies are shaped as the 12 animals on the Chinese zodiac and are used as offerings in shrines before being eaten.
Other holidays on this date: Unity Day (Zimbabwe)

23 December: Night of the Radishes (Mexico)

This odd Christmas tradition has been celebrated in Mexico for over a century. Started in 1897 by the Mayor of the city, the time for carving the ruby skin of the radishes and shaping them like animals and people is one of the most anticipated times of the year for locals.

The Night of the Radishes is an official holiday and takes place annually on December 23rd.

The radishes used for carving are grown for that purpose only and are not meant to be eaten. They can be up to 3kg in weight and 50cm in length.

The local artists have only a few days to spin their imagination because the veggies are harvested on December 18th. They carve nativity scenes, creatures and objects from the Mayan history, animals representing the local wildlife, grotesques, real-life people etc.

It is believed that the celebration was inspired by local merchants, who inspired by the priests, carved intricate religious figurines out of vegetables to attract more shoppers before the Christmas holidays. With time, the people started buying radishes not only to eat but to carve for the Christmas dinner as well.

Thousands of people gather and queue for hours to sneak a peek at the masterpieces. Everyone competes for prizes in different categories, the grand prize being 12,000 pesos.

The quirky celebration ends with a display of fireworks and a great open-air concert.

Local merchants set food stalls with hot chocolate, champurrado (thick chocolatey drink) and buñuelos (fried dough).

Travel to: Mexico (Oaxaca). The city has a long-history growing radishes which were introduced to the region by the Spaniards in the XVIth C.
Other holidays on this date: Emperor`s Birthday (Japan)

24 December: KFC Christmas Spree (Japan)

This is a holiday worth mentioning!

It's Christmas Eve in Japan – the families are getting ready to have a festive dinner... in KFC!

This, let's just call it an odd custom, was created after a 4-year marketing campaign wherein the fast-food chain successfully convinced the Japanese that fried chicken is the ultimate American Christmas dish.

In 1970, a group of foreigners struggled to find a turkey for Christmas and substituted it with chicken from the first KFC restaurant in Japan (opened in a joint venture with Mitsubishi Corporation). In general, it is extremely unlikely to buy a turkey in Japan (it does not breed naturally there) unless one orders it online, but this became available only in the recent years. On top of that – it is quite a challenge for one to find an oven big enough to roast the whole bird...

The KFC Manager overheard the conversation between the foreigners struggling to find a turkey and acted accordingly. Few years of savvy marketing brainstorming followed...

Four years later, KFC started a campaign with the catchphrase "Christmas=Kentucky" and a horde of superstar local actors and singers featuring in commercials, finally caught the eye of the Japanese public. The company started selling Christmas chicken buckets filled with holiday cheer with unprecedented success. More than that –nowadays, no means are spared in decorating the Japanese KFC window displays and even put a countdown clock to Christmas!

Reportedly around 3.6million Japanese willingly line in queues for up to 2 hours to get their hands on the "finger-licking good" chicken strips (some even preorder their Christmas bucket in October!!).

The signature treat is the "KFC Christmas Barrel" – invented by the first CEO of KFC in Japan, it comes in various sizes and includes layers of party plates, ribbons, chicken, salad, cake and even a bottle of sparkling wine.

The bottom line – the company just filled a void – since there are no Christmas celebrations in Japan (only 1% of the population is Christian), KFC just said: You should do this!

And it worked.

The Christmas campaign from the 70s is studied abroad as one of the most successful business decisions.

Travel to: Japan (Tokyo). The festive KFC dinner is an adopted tradition now and it even requires pre-booking your order.

Other holidays on this date: Yap Constitution Day (Micronesia), Independence Day (Lybia)

25 December: Race Around the World (Antarctica)

This is celebrating Christmas Day – South Pole style!

Every year since 1979, the researchers and the whole crew of the South Pole research facility observe a "Race Around the World" tradition as a way to celebrate Christmas.

The distance to be covered is 3 laps passing through every line of longitude (it only takes a few minutes because the contestants run in a circle). This way, they celebrate Christmas in every time zone on Earth. All means of transportation are allowed – feet, ski, sleighs, snowmobiles etc.

The participants in the race enjoy the weather as it coincides with the Antarctic summertime – so, the temperatures are high... that is only -27C!

And... to keep the spirit festive – funny costumes are more than welcome.

After the race – everyone gathers inside the station to celebrate with a festive brunch. However, the brunch comes in turns. As there are more than 200 people stationed in the facility, every "seating" has about 1 hour to finish the meal... then comes the next group of starving people.

The lucky winner in the race gets a great prize – a 5-minute hot shower, which is a treat (the residents are allotted only 2 min)!

Travel to: Antarctica (Amundsen-Scott South Pole scientific station). The Christmas Tree in Antarctica is welded and decorated with wires, old respirators, spark plugs tied with silver duct tape and rocks because of the strong wind and low temperatures.

Other holidays on this date: Christmas Day

26 December: Junkanoo (Bahamas)

Junkanoo is colours galore! The festival of West African origin is the most anticipated event on the Bahamas.

There are few theories on how the celebration was created: by a West African Prince or the French 500 years ago? Or in the XIX C by European traders, who celebrated Christmas in the local bars wearing masks and colourful costumes? Or in the XVIIIth C in the years of slavery, when Europeans brought their slaves with them? The legend has it that the slaves were given 3 days off around Christmas and they celebrated, sang and danced disguised in colourful masks, thus turning the holiday into a social gathering and quality family time event.

Nowadays, this is a huge street festival with art, music, culture, masquerade and a street parade, to bring in the new year. It is celebrated annually over Christmas and New Year.

Large street processions of the traditional local dance troupes (groups of up to 1 000 dancers), drummers with goatskin drums, cowbells and whistles attract tourists from all over the world.

The members of each dance group (Colors, Music Makers, One Family, Roots, Saxons and Valley Boys) appear on huge floating platforms made of styrofoam. The musicians play an exotic mixture of West African drum beats, American Blues and Caribbean rhythms.

For the breath-taking handmade costumes, the performers use feathers, beads, mirrors, jewels and richly decorated headpieces made of cardboard. As the festival has a different theme each year - both dancers and musicians, spend about 6 months to prepare for the grand show, perfecting their moves, sound and rhythm.

At the end of the festivities, judges award cash prizes for best dance, costume and overall group presentation.

No need to mention the food stalls with delicious local food such as conch fritters, chicken wings, baked mac & cheese and lots of daiquiris!

Travel to: Bahamas. The biggest party is in Nassau, but the festival is celebrated on Grand Bahama Island, Eleuthera/Harbour Island, Bimini, The Exumas and The Abacos too! The street parade taking place downtown Nassau starts at 2am!

Other holidays on this date: Boxing Day, St. Stephen`s Day, Wren Day (USA), Day of Goodwill (Namibia), Wren Day (Ireland)

27 December: Festival of Winter Traditions (Romania)

The best festivals in Romania take place between Christmas and New Years and this one is no exception - a grand winter festival held on December 27th every year since 1968. This is the oldest and most renown festival in the country showcasing the rich winter traditions of the Maramureș ethnocultural region. The event was created to preserve the ancient wintertime rituals of the inhabitants of the northern part of the country and share them with the world.

The atmosphere is festive and the whole town where the event occurs turns into a real winter wonderland.

There is a huge street procession with carolers and merrymakers, people with masks or dressed as peasants from Medieval times, horses and carriages - each group representing a different part of the country with its own and unique wintertime traditions, songs, dances, games, costumes and cheer. They parade through the town accompanied by the melodic rhythm of violins and drums. Some costumes are handmade of fur, cowbells, red tassels, embroidered and adorned with traditional symbols, and resemble various mythology creatures, scary beasts or Santa Claus.

A centrepiece in the parade is the "Dracul" - a huge effigy (or a giant mask), made of sheepskin and horns which represents the devil. It is carried around the streets by young men dressed as little devils.

After a whole day of parading, the night is time for fun. Each group including lots of folklore musicians and dancers, perform on a huge stage set up at the city square to entertain the cheering crowd. Highlights are the artists performing on old musical instruments such as the "trambita" – a ridiculous longhorn, and the "buhai" – a small barrel through which horsehairs are pulled.

Travel to: Romania (Sighetu Marmatiei). This festival is so popular that other countries often visit and participate with their own wintertime customs and traditions.
Other holidays on this date: Constitution Day (North Korea)

28 December: Fancy Dress Festival (Ghana)
The festival humouring the lifestyle of the European colonizers, locally known as Kaakaamotobi is held annually from Christmas Day to January 1st.

The celebration started in the XIXth C with the Dutch and British sailors and seaport merchants who celebrated Christmas in Ghana. They dressed up in colourful and festive costumes, wore handmade masks, drunk and sang in the local bars.

It wasn't until the 1920s when a business-minded bartender saw an opportunity and decided to turn the local custom into an annual festival. He partnered up with a fellow pharmacist and created the first festival troop – the Nobles.

In the following years, more troops were founded – each representing a different area of the town, each with its own unique theme for the masquerade, own choreographer for the street parade dances and own brass band. These groups are known as Nobles (the original group), Egyaa (formed by the fishermen society), Tumus (founded by the Royals) and Red Cross (represented by the town's elite) and they are still the ones to perform in the street parade. Each group has around 100 members who need to pass various exams to be accepted full-time members or to receive a membership as a family inheritance.

Each group has a Father (taking care of the group's business), a Mother (taking care of the food and drinks, and general wellbeing) and scouts who solicit for money during the parades.

They dress up as doctors, nurses, policemen, teachers, pastors, farmers, fishermen, prostitutes, cowboys, sailors, movie characters, Santa Claus, Christmas trees, angels and even Presidents - as a tool for addressing social-political issues. The idea behind the disguise is to satirically misrepresent the life and humour the dressing style of the Europeans.

Brass bands were added to the performance only in the 30s. The first one – a local orchestra knew only one song which was repeated through the whole day, so the public got quite annoyed.

Dessi Nikoltchev:

One of the pharmacist's brothers arranged a musical training for them (he was trading with brass instruments) – an idea, which was warmly welcomed by everyone!

Travel to: Ghana (Winneba). The event is held at the Winneba Advanced Park.
Other holidays on this date: Day of the Holy Innocents (Mexico)

29 December: Bear Dance Ritual (Romania)

The strange tradition dating back to the 1930s occurs in the winter days between Christmas and New Year in a handful of small villages along a river valley in Romania.

People of all ages – men and women, dress head-to-toe in real bear skins with the heads attached (including the large grinning teeth) and visit the homes of their neighbours. As they do, they dance to chase away the evil spirits of the past year and bring good fortune into the new one. They also carry hollowed tubes filled with gunpowder (in case of the evil needs persuasion to leave).

It is believed that the ritual began from local gipsies living in the mountains. In the past, they would visit the villages holding their tamed bears on a leash and go from house to house in search for someone with back pains (apparently a bear cub walking on the back was the best cure for the pain). An aged animal, however, would be used with different and rather cruel purpose – to walk on hot metal sheets which make the poor thing "dance" for entertainment.

With time, bear dancing and bear hunting were banned, which transformed the ritual.

Today, the locals wear bear skins adorned with huge red tassels pinned on the back of the head. They are accompanied by "bear tamers" who paint their faces in dark colours to resemble the gipsies from the past. Their costumes include long pleated skirts, colourful scarves, wigs with long and thick braided pigtails.

The group makes its way to the homes in a strange procession lead by a flutist, drummers and a singing "tamer", all dressed in traditional celebratory dress. The bears and the gipsies are warmly welcomed and cheered by crowds of people on the streets.

Before they start with the rounds, they perform on the city square. Their arrival is announced by few boys with whistles.

Fact 1: The bear costume can weigh up to 40kg and cost about EUR 2000.

Fact 2: The traditional treat for the visiting bears is cubes of pig fat and homemade palinka liquor.

Fact 3: The ritual most likely derived from an ancient pagan tradition of the Geto-Dacians who considered the bear a sacred animal with healing powers.

Travel to: Romania (Trotus River valley). The ritual is observed in the villages surrounding the town of Bacau. In Moinesti there is even an annual Bear Parade.

Other holidays on this date: Independence Day (Mongolia)

30 December: San Benito el Moro (Venezuela)

As are all Venezuelan feasts, this is no different – a true mix of Spanish, Caribbean and Indigenous traditions showcasing the rich culture and traditions that had built up the Venezuelan people of today.

Over a week in the end of December (between Christmas and New Year), the Feast of San Benito takes place. Born in a family of African slaves, he became a Franciscan friar in Sicily, later travelling the world and known for his immense charity.

San Benito is the patron saint of the Maracaibo Lake and the surrounding villages and is also known as "the Moor" and "the black Saint of Venezuela".

Every year, he is celebrated with street parades and people dressed in costumes dancing till the small hours of the night. Special music is performed by groups of chimbagueles (traditional drums).

San Benito is a centrepiece of all celebrations and is portrayed as a dark-skinned man with Creole characteristics.

Different pageants, contests and processions are held to honour the much-loved saint, who allegedly was associated with an affection for rum and beautiful women.

Sure, there is no need to mention that the event involves vast quantities of rum... it is all in good faith though, right!

Travel to: Venezuela (Maracaibo). The feast is held in an area around the Maracaibo Lake.

Other holidays on this date: St. Stephen's Day

31 December: Hogmanay (Scotland)

Hogmanay – the Scottish New year!

Rooted in the Nordic and Gaelic mythology, the feast originating from an ancient Winter Solstice ritual starts on the last day of the year and continues until January 2nd. It is believed that most of the rituals were brought by Vikings in the VIIIth and IXth C.

Much loved and celebrated with great cheer, the holiday involves gift-giving, family gatherings, songs, dances and of course, lots of scotch!

One of the most important traditions observed on Hogmanay is First-Footing.

Once midnight strikes and the calendar flips to January 1st, all eyes await the arrival of the year's first visitor. The person who steps foot in the family home first is said to be a predictor of the following year's fortune.

Top of the lucky list: a male, dark-haired visitor (?!). Women or blonde men are believed to bring bad fortune, so they are not preferred guests to the NY party.

The first-foot is also supposed to bring to the household an array of gifts including coins (symbolizing fortune), bread (symbolizing the abundance of food) and whisky (for good cheer).

As do most of the Scottish festivals, this one includes setting things on fire as well...

In some areas, the locals throw balls blazing in flames at each other. The balls are made of rags and old newspapers tied with a wire and can reach up to 50cm in diameter. Each ball is attached to an inflammable rope and tied to the hand of its owner. At midnight, they set the balls alight and start swinging them around their heads as they march the streets in a festive procession. This represents an ancient purifying ritual. Casualties have been reported...

In other parts, the locals split wooden barrels in two and fill them with flammable objects and tar. The barrels are then set ablaze. The "burning" procession ends with placing all barrels into an ancient altar which creates an enormous bonfire. The people collect the burning ambers and use them to light the fireplaces in their homes. Leaving a piece of a burned barrel in the house chases away the evil spirits and witches.

In one village, Hogmanay is celebrated on the main square where free whiskey and shortbread cookies are distributed to the cheering crowds (yes, this is the hometown of the Glenfiddich distillery and the Walkers biscuit factory).

As Hogmanay is the most important celebration in Scotland, all cities and villages have their own and unique ways to honour the New year – street processions including people dressed up as Vikings and holding lit torches, live concerts, open-air parties, beautiful and huge displays of fireworks and tons of songs and dances.

However different the celebrations may be in the different parts of the country – two customs are observed by all – when the clock strikes 12, everyone sings the famous poem-made-to-song Auld Lang Syne by Robert Burnes; and the second one – everyone welcomes old and new friends (incl. total strangers) in his/her home.

Traditional food on Hogmanay are various meat pies and stews.

Travel to: Scotland (Aberdeenshire). The burning balls custom takes place in the town of Stonehaven.

Edinburgh holds the Guinness World record for most people attending a New Year`s party – 400 000!

Other holidays on this date: Polka Dots and Coins (Philippines), New Year's Dive (Russia)

REFERENCES:

www.list25.com
www.readersdigest.ca
www.hostelworld.com
www.gooverseas.com
www.listverse.com
www.holidayinsights.com
www.nationaldaycalendar.com
www.holidayscalendar.com
www.buzzfeed.com
www.sbs.com.au
www.cherokee.org
www.festivalsherpa.com
www.islandbreath.com
www.theculturetrip.com
www.caribya.com
www.expatica.com
www.festivals.iloveindia.com
www.chinahighlights.com
www.holidayasia.com
www.tinosecret.gr
www.discover-bayanolgii.com
www.odditycentral.com
www.donquijote.org
www.wikipedia.org
www.twograces.blogspot.ch
www.largeup.com
www.caribbeanbluebook.com
www.larutamaya.com
www.adventure-life.com
www.thespruce.com
www.japan-talk.com
www.pilotguides.com
www.lonelyplanet.com
Friends and colleagues who I cannot THANK enough!

www.ingramcontent.com/pod-product-compliance
Lightning Source LLC
Chambersburg PA
CBHW020630220526
45464CB00001B/90